WRITING PROGRAM ARCHITECTURE

WRITING PROGRAM ARCHITECTURE

Thirty Cases for Reference and Research

EDITED BY
BRYNA SIEGEL FINER
JAMIE WHITE-FARNHAM

UTAH STATE UNIVERSITY PRESS
Logan

© 2017 the University Press of Colorado

Published by Utah State University Press
An imprint of University Press of Colorado
5589 Arapahoe Avenue, Suite 206C
Boulder, Colorado 80303

 The University Press of Colorado is a proud member of
The Association of American University Presses.

The University Press of Colorado is a cooperative publishing enterprise supported,
in part, by Adams State University, Colorado State University, Fort Lewis College,
Metropolitan State University of Denver, Regis University, University of Colorado,
University of Northern Colorado, Utah State University, and Western State Colorado
University.

∞ This paper meets the requirements of the ANSI/NISO Z39.48-1992 (Permanence of
Paper)

ISBN: 978-1-60732-626-7 (paperback)
ISBN: 978-1-60732-627-4 (ebook)

Library of Congress Cataloging-in-Publication Data
Names: Siegel Finer, Bryna, editor. I White-Farnham, Jamie, editor.
Title: Writing program architecture : thirty cases for reference and research / edited by
    Bryna Siegel Finer, Jamie White-Farnham.
Description: Logan : Utah State University Press, [2017] I Includes bibliographical refer-
    ences and index.
Identifiers: LCCN 2016049462I ISBN 9781607326267 (pbk.) I ISBN 9781607326274
    (ebook)
Subjects: LCSH: Writing centers—United States—Administration—Case studies. I
    English language—Rhetoric—Study and teaching (Higher)—United States.
Classification: LCC PE1405.U6 W763 2017 I DDC 808/.042071173—dc23
LC record available at https://lccn.loc.gov/2016049462

Cover illustration © Morgunova Tetiana / Shutterstock

CONTENTS

ACKNOWLEDGMENTS

This book, as a collection devoted to Writing Program Administration (WPA), reflects the generosity and collaborative spirit of the many writers, writing teachers, scholars, researchers, and directors of writing programs who have taught us and with whom we have worked. First and foremost, we thank the contributors—forty-six people who shared so much of their experience, knowledge, and time with us throughout this project. Aaron Beasley, our graduate research assistant, was reliable, astute, and organized, and we are grateful for the many hours of tedium he put into this project as well as his thoughtful questions and feedback. Thank you.

Our colleagues at each of our universities were happy to listen, offer their input, and make our days at work enjoyable. At Indiana University of Pennsylvania, Bryna is grateful to Ben Rafoth, not only for his unwavering support of her WPA work and this project specifically, but for being one of our chapter guinea pigs, and to Emily Wender, Oriana Gatta, and Curt Porter for consistently making 110 miles of Western Pennsylvania backroad more than endurable, but something to look forward to. At the University of Wisconsin-Superior, Jamie thanks Julie Gard and Jayson Iwen for always providing their serene Aquarian perspectives, as well as Heather McGrew and John McCormick for their creativity and their dedication to our basic writing students.

We are thankful to the editorial and marketing teams at Utah State University Press, especially Michael Spooner, who is as supportive as is he is kind, not to mention good-humored. We also thank the two anonymous reviewers who provided us with direct and honest feedback that shaped this book into its final form.

We thank our mentors and friends with whom we worked at the University of Rhode Island, including Libby Miles, Nedra Reynolds, Jeremiah Dyehouse, Cathryn Molloy, and Matthew Ortoleva.

While our WPA work and teaching are important to us, we are both proudest and happiest in our job as moms. And we are lucky ones. We each have incredible support systems at home. Bryna thanks David and Theo Finer for their silliness, laughter, and love, and for all of the "special daddy days" that allowed her to work even on weekends. Jamie thanks Steve, Ruby, and Claire Farnham for their love, encouragement, and laundry folding.

As women in the academy, we wish to thank publicly our children's caregivers, extremely important people in our professional lives. In academic contexts in which necessities like daycare and leave time are seen as personal problems that individuals sort out alone, we highlight and indeed celebrate the people who keep us afloat as working moms. Thank you to Alison Bergstrom, the teachers and staff at the Beth Shalom Early Learning Center, and the Douglas County YMCA afterschool program.

Finally, we each want to express our gratitude to the other for the difficult yet awesome collaboration across the 923 miles that separates Pittsburgh, Pennsylvania, and Superior, Wisconsin: four years, over a thousand emails, countless hours of video chatting, Google Doc-ing, Skyping, Dropbox-ing, texting, meeting up at conferences and in hotel rooms. We took turns being the leader, the slacker, the idealist, the organizer, the worrier, the listener, the teacher, the student. Is it a rare thing for two people to work under these conditions and remain friends? Perhaps not. But we are grateful for this project that strengthened our friendship and our shared resolve to contribute to the field that brought us together in the first place.

WRITING PROGRAM ARCHITECTURE

WRITING PROGRAM ARCHITECTURE
An Introduction with Alternative Tables of Contents

Jamie White-Farnham and Bryna Siegel Finer

Dear Jamie and Bryna,
I have to say that I submit this [chapter revision] with a vexed conscience. I was able to achieve a great deal in the first-year writing program here, and I wanted to share that with other WPAs in our field. But now with the draconian cuts to the [University of Wisconsin] system in the governor's budget, the Blugold Seminar will inevitably be undone. Enrollment caps will increase back to their old levels, the new staffing model (longer term contracts, etc.) will be reversed, our tenure track search has been cancelled and the line probably revoked, even the curriculum will roll back because it is "too hard." Plus, I will no longer be associated with this program. I have accepted a new WPA position at a different university. So revising this has entailed a very heavy heart. I think there is valuable information in what I was able to accomplish here, but it was fleeting and will go out as quickly as it came in. Surely, that cannot be the "lesson" here, which is why I don't know if I want this included in the final publication.
All best, Shevaun Watson

Toward the end of this book's editing process, we received the above email from Shevaun Watson (2015), a dedicated writing program administrator who developed the Blugold Seminar at the University of Wisconsin–Eau Claire. The governor of Wisconsin had recently proposed a shocking $125 million cut to all public higher education institutions, as was reported nationally, and every campus in the system began to shed untenured faculty and cut programs. Our initial impulse was simply to assure Shevaun that we thought her work was outstanding and wish her good luck. Upon further reflection, the situation in which Shevaun (and Jamie, the co-editor of this collection, and the WPA at the University of Wisconsin–Superior) found herself merited greater attention—there was a connection between the dismantling of her program and the purpose of this book.

DOI: 10.7330/9781607326274.c000

Though it is disheartening, the situation Shevaun describes is in fact the type of situation in which the guiding metaphor of writing programs this book offers—writing program architecture—is most useful. Writing program architecture highlights the material, logistical, and rhetorical elements of a writing program, be it a first-year curriculum, a writing center, a WAC program, a writing major, or something else. Such elements include funding sources, reporting lines, WPA jurisdiction, and other practical pieces. The metaphor of architecture allows us to imagine these constituent parts of a writing program as its foundation, beams, posts, scaffolding—the institutional structures that, alongside its people, anchor a program to the ground and keep it standing. Articulating these elements allows a WPA to disentangle their role from the program itself, something that, we know, is quite difficult to do. Many programs, as the reader will see in this collection, are literally supported by a single person's line—on a teaching release or some other contractual arrangement. That person *is* the Writing Program.

While people are of course very important to the ecology of writing programs, as explained by Reiff et al. (2015) in their recent book, *Ecologies of Writing*, we contend that additional consideration of the material, logistical, and rhetorical elements that make up a program allows WPAs to strengthen their positions in times of turmoil or in the face of dismantling. As Shevaun's email suggests, any decision made within a program is built on a structure of such elements as contracts, funding lines, and curriculum. It is these elements teased out and explained in and of themselves that constitute the architecture of writing programs in this book. We believe these explanations of writing programs are necessary because of the situations in which Shevaun and other WPAs are finding themselves. Drastic budget cuts, legislators with little regard for public higher education, and decreasing enrollment: this is the context of Writing Studies at present in the United States.

Therefore, what readers will find in this collection are case studies written by WPAs from thirty institutions across the United States. These cases detail the architecture—the underlying structures—of their writing programs. Such programs include writing centers, first-year writing curricula, WAC programs, writing majors, and others—the largest print collection of program information to date. These thirty cases are meant to inform, inspire, and otherwise help new and experienced WPAs build new programs and sustain existing ones. The cases are presented within the guiding metaphor of architecture, which we rely on both as a way to understand writing programs and as an organizational feature of the book.

We suggest that exposing the architecture of writing programs has three purposes: first, it foregrounds elements of a program that are oftentimes treated as mundane background information. In accounts of writing programs, the institutional contexts are typically (and perfunctorily) discussed ahead of the "real" project or argument. Yet, we suggest that this information deserves some attention of its own. Ask any WPA about their current project and inevitably, they will most likely begin the answer with some explanation of the structure of the unit or program in order to situate the work. For instance, a director of a WAC program might have to describe his current professional development program by first explaining that he reports partly to the dean and partly to the English Department, which puts him in a difficult position when he must convince his own colleagues in English to consider some institutional mandate from the administration. Since explanations of structure often precede argument, method, and solution, structure itself is important to highlight.

Second, we see this book as serving a research function. As a collection of case studies, the volume provides jumping off points to address and inspire myriad research questions. For instance, one might notice and believe that writing centers, so important to the support of writing education and culture on a campus, are often precarious in structure, wedged between departments and comprising fractions of a person's job. For the benefit of a project seeking to improve such conditions, this book provides evidence and documentation for support and corroboration. Each chapter is a site of research, a place where WPAs and other scholars in writing studies can look to invent, support, and challenge their assumptions and arguments.

Finally, the third purpose of this book is to model a method for WPAs to consider and articulate their own programs' architecture. For one thing, they might consider their program in a material, logistical way outside of their own performance within it. As we noted above, writing programs are often conflated with the WPA themself. Often this is because the only funding source or institutional support that exists is that person's salary. For another, WPAs might improve their own ability at focusing others' attention on the parts of the program they wish to expand, improve, or promote. Rather than rattling off what a program isn't—distinguishing the first-year writing from WAC from writing fellows, say—program architecture within the writing programs featured here exemplifies the many elements within these structures *and* models how to articulate one's own.

INSPIRATION FOR THE PROJECT

Writing programs are, as Reiff et al. (2015) describe them in *Ecologies of Writing*, interconnected, fluid, complex, and emergent (4). In some ways, this means a writing program can be unstable and even untenable without a clear sense of its underpinnings. For instance, writing programs can be multiply-funded or exist on paper only. They can rely on a person to have dual and split roles across units in the institution; for instance, a WPA might have one foot in English as a tenure-line faculty member or full-time lecturer, one foot in the writing center (under the dean), and might be expected to give faculty workshops as part (or not) of both of those. The work of Dara Regaignon, a contributor to this volume, and Jill Gladstein in *Writing Program Administration at Small Liberal Arts Colleges* (Gladstein and Regaignon 2012), highlights in particular the complexity of structure and overlapping of entities in writing program administration in their titular context.

The complexity, cultures, and "baggage" of writing programs in various institutions often obscure and even preclude accurate descriptions of what a WPA does. Although the Council of Writing Program Administrators has developed statements to help us with these challenges such as the white paper, "Evaluating the Intellectual Work of Writing Administration" (Council of Writing Program Administrators 1998), confusing situations had us, as new WPAs, asking questions that didn't have to do with our roles as WPAs. That is an aspect of the work that has been well-defined for us in our graduate education and in WPA council statements.

Instead, the questions centered on the workings of the programs themselves: how to get a program off the ground, fund it, market it, staff it, how to develop a research agenda, how to know if the program is working and develop an assessment plan, how to use technology in productive ways, the planning and sustaining of day-to-day operations, and how to innovate pedagogically and administratively. In addition, we were in need of models of primary documents, such as budget proposals, teacher evaluations, and annual reports, all hard to find or non-existent publically. Of course, the reason why they are not publically shared is because they are rote, bureaucratic necessities not meant for a wide audience. Still, we suspected such documents would afford us insights and ideas as we approached new hurdles in our institutions.

At our institutions, we each found ourselves in situations in which there were structural oddities that limited or precluded momentum: Bryna was hired to begin a WAC program and serve as the director of that "program," which only existed as a description that she wrote and then posted to the university website. Now, as director, Bryna holds faculty workshops and promotes WAC through grassroots efforts to build individual relationships with faculty who already have interest in the teaching of writing in their disciplinary courses. Meanwhile, a system of writing-intensive courses exists and is overseen by an entirely other program.

At her public liberal arts college, Jamie is the coordinator of the Writing Program, which offers first-year and basic writing courses, a business writing course that serves two other departments, creative writing gen eds, and a writing major/minor. In essence, this writing program offers several curricula with different (yet overlapping) staff, each of which could be called "writing programs" themselves (the basic writing program is described in a chapter in this collection). This is distinct yet from a WAC program, which houses the Writing Center and faculty development efforts, overseen by another faculty in the Writing Program.

Our various projects and problems (for Bryna, how to grow and establish credibility; for Jamie, how to explain that the Writing Program is not the same thing as Writing across the Curriculum) led us to ask questions of our mentors and senior colleagues, read and re-read relevant scholarship in our field, and ask questions on the WPA listserv, which is almost always a fast, helpful resource. We were trained in WPA work as graduate students together at the University of Rhode Island, each serving time as an assistant director of the Writing Center (Bryna) and of the Writing and Rhetoric Department (Jamie). Jamie attended the Council of Writing Program Administrators (CWPA) workshop in 2011, and Bryna attended its boot camp and conference in 2014. These are all excellent learning opportunities in terms of the theoretical, historical, and political aspects of our field. CWPA in particular affords new WPAs the chance to engage in some practical problem-solving at its events. Yet, the contexts and constructions of the programs in which we landed in had us looking and asking for other types of information.

One resource in particular, the CompPile writing programs document archive, inspired the type of nuts-and-bolts explanation of programs-as-architecture we sought to make public. The archive houses the types of documents programs use to get work done. According to its home page, the archive is "a (prototype) site for an archive of writing program documents. The archive will be used by WPAs to help graduate students learn to read / interpret the various documents that shape the environments in which they will teach" (Home Page 2007, par. 2).

Having not been updated since its inception in 2006, the database is somewhat sparse. Glen Blalock, one of the database curators, explained to us that this project stalled before it got off the ground because of "what has been/continues to be an ongoing issue in our discipline (writing studies and particularly WPA): we don't respond well to calls for sharing, for contributing, for participating in these kinds of long-term projects" (Blalock 2014). He noted the WPA census data collection as one recent success, but overall, he feels that many attempts to collect shared documents and information have petered out before getting off the ground. Of course, a lot of that has to do with the time and effort it takes to maintain such a project. As Blalock (2014) notes, "the diverse array of 'writing programs' and the diverse definitions of a program 'administrator' probably makes these kinds of efforts especially challenging." He asks, "how many institutions have formal programs, with designated WPAs? How many WPAs serve more than a rotation in and out of the position? How many programs have administrative infrastructure that would enable the regular updating of 'our' documents in the WPA document archive?"

To begin to address such questions about administrative infrastructure, we consulted the extant scholarship and other WPAs. Common elements that underpin the curriculum, pedagogy, rhetorical constructs, and practices in programs across the country began to emerge. What was most important to us were the sometimes-invisible structures of writing programs that we were unable to easily learn about through reading or in conversations. These elements seem to us to address our questions about writing programs outside of the purview of most WPA scholarship, focused as it has been on defining the position of the WPA less often than the variety of contexts in which s/he works.

For instance, while it might be easy to locate a list of courses or a program's mission statement, it is ostensibly more difficult to find information on a program's budget and how it uses its funding to operate. Information like this is invaluable to a WPA on the ground, for instance, who has no predecessors. Contributor Christy Wenger writes in this collection about the Shepherd University Writing Center; she, like many WPAs, is learning to work within very limited means, both materially and in terms of writing studies colleagues with whom to collaborate. Elements such as budget and operations, unavailable on a program's website or in their public documents, are arguably some of the most important parts of the program structure.

The common elements that emerged, listed below, began to shape our metaphor of writing program architecture. We liked the idea of compiling elements common to writing programs—whether large or small, whether a tight slate of first-year writing courses or a rangy WAC program—that would offer WPA/scholars models to consider, a template to inspire, and case studies to refer to when undertaking their own projects. The elements that comprise writing program architecture, then, include:

WPA's Profile
Program Conception
Population Served
Funding
Operations
Assessment
Marketing/PR
Technology
Role of Research
Pedagogical and/or Administration Highlights
WPA's Voice
Primary Document(s)

Of course, every program has its unique features and innovations. And, we want to be clear that we don't believe there is a formula or simple list of duties that substitute for the well-theorized and scholarly discipline that WPA work has become. A fuller scholarly definition of our work and field exists and continues to evolve. We do not wish to diminish its importance, nor would we make a case that the purpose of this volume is similar to those that offer theorized arguments about program-building and other concerns of our discipline.

Still, across the many specialties in the discipline of writing studies, scholars' definitions and descriptions of writing programs reflect an urge to tame the sheer diversity of approaches devoted to the unified goals of literacy education. A Writing Program can be first-year writing, writing centers, WAC/WID, basic writing, and more recently, writing majors. It is often a combination of these curricula and pedagogies. This diversity, of course, exemplifies the growth and richness of a decades-old global discipline. While we teachers of critical thinking, reason, and style appreciate the flexibility, changes, and revisions that are hallmarks of writing studies, we also tease out similarities and compare differences. We anthologize, taxonomize, categorize, define, and create metaphors. We do this to make sense of work that takes so many shapes. It must give the range of contexts in which teachers of writing, rhetoric, and literacy find themselves: the urban, the rural, the huge, the tiny, the underfunded, the unstable, the contingent-labor reliant.

The urge to tame is especially apparent in this type of book: compendia of writing programs. Such work includes *Ecologies of Writing Programs*

(Reiff et al. 2015), *Writing Majors: Eighteen Program Profiles* (Giberson, Nugent, and Ostergaard 2015), *Writing Programs Worldwide* (Thais et al. 2012), the program profiles section of *Composition Forum*, and an originator of these taxonomic efforts regarding the growth of WAC, Fulwiler and Young's (1990) book *Programs That Work*. These compendia have been mainly organized by curricula or pedagogy. For example, Fulwiler and Young (1990) report on early Writing across the Curriculum pedagogical efforts. Most recently, *Writing Majors: Eighteen Program Profiles* (Giberson, Nugent, and Ostergaard 2015) describes hard-won curricular growth in our field. We have gained greatly in our understanding of the types of writing programs operating in the United States from this scholarship.

By focusing attention to the structure of a program, we are also not trying to dismiss attention to the personal, ethical, and political dimensions of WPA work. In particular, as female untenured, junior WPAs, or jWPAs, each of us mothers of young children, we have benefited from the many accounts of identity politics in *WPA: Writing Program Administration* and in volumes such as *Kitchen Cooks, Plate Twirlers, and Troubadors* (George 1999) and *GenAdmin* (Charlton et al. 2011). Jonikka Charlton and Shirley Rose (2009) describe the role as "not just a job title, but a way of being. A WPA's work is not defined only by the official or formal responsibilities of the role but also by how those responsibilities are carried out" (115). The profession, as are we, is concerned not only with the work itself but with the ethical way it is performed.

In particular, the conversation about writing program administration and identity politics often goes hand in hand with arguments about the importance of narrative in this work. Jeanne Marie Rose (2005) has written: "the storytelling that Stephen North has termed lore has become a viable mode of knowledge production for writing program administrators, whose scholarship frequently explores WPA work in light of personal experiences. As Diana George explains, storytelling "is necessary if we are to pass on more than theory and pedagogical or administrative tactics to those who have come after us" (George 1999, xii; quoted in Rose 2005, 73).

Narrative plays a similar role in accounts of program-building. For instance, in the forward of *Writing Majors*, Sandra Jamieson (2015) describes the book's profiles as, "narratives that provide a historical archive of sorts and in the descriptions of programs, courses, and institutional politics" (vii). And, in terms of WPA training, Sura et al. (2009), in their description of "Praxis and Allies: The WPA Board Game," focus their attention on the role that narrative plays in learning to be a WPA: "it is through narrative that WPAs are best able to share with a larger audience what they do and why, how their work is intellectual" (80). Storytelling is a valuable mode of accounting for, theorizing, passing on, and—maybe most important—changing WPA work.

Therefore, narrative plays a role in the case studies within this volume. Because practitioners and scholars in our field are attuned to and respect the contextual nature of writing program administration, even a large data set such as this—rife with demographics, statistics, and quantitative information—must necessarily reflect the perspectives and even biases of its contributors. For instance, New Mexico Tech's (NMT) changing demographics of its student enrollment are factual: collaboration with Yangtze University has resulted in a sharp increase in international undergraduates in the past few years. However, the perspective of Maggie Griffin Taylor, Julianne Newmark, and Steve Simpson will influence how the WPA audience will synthesize their report of the situation at NMT with their own writing program architecture, problem to solve, or research questions.

To that end, each chapter is mixed rhetorically—that is, rhetorical modes such as narration and description contextualize and explain content that Aristotle might have labeled the "inartistic proofs": the laws, facts, and contracts that precede argument (Aristotle 2007, 103). While our contributors don't necessarily present arguments here (though they do highlight and focus the audience's attention on certain challenges and achievements), they share with us narrative and descriptive explanations of "laws, facts, and contracts" in twenty-first century academia—the foundational agreements, processes, and arrangements within programs that concern WPAs.

EXPLANATION OF THE ELEMENTS

Similar to an encyclopedia, each chapter offers information in a guided way. This configuration is similarly used in *Writing Majors: Eighteen Program Profiles*, the afterword of which describes the book as a "heuristic offering" (Giberson et al. 2015, 242). Greg Giberson explains that such a format is an "effort to help those interested in developing programs or in the process of doing so to be more intentional and prospective in their program building" (242). In this case, the heuristic refers to the constituent elements of program architecture.

For each element, we provided a few questions or prompts to help guide contributors as they wrote each section, listed below. Then, we tested the template by asking two contributors (one writing center director and one chair of a department with a writing major) to complete the template. Their responses allowed us to fine-tune the prompts that we then provided to all of the contributors. In the end, each of the thirty chapters/institutions explain their programs within the following template:

WPA's Profile

We asked contributors to tell us how they came to be WPAs, including their education, teaching experience, and other work experience. As we know, many WPAs do not come to the job of WPA via a traditional path. In this section, readers will learn about WPAs like Bridget Draxler, the director of the Communication across the Curriculum Program at Monmouth College, who like many WPAs before her began her career as a graduate student in literature and found that her experience as a student in the liberal arts trained her for a career in writing studies that she hadn't expected. While some WPAs in this collection have taken a traditional path through a PhD program in rhetoric and composition with training in WPA work, others began in an unusual or unexpected way. Stories like these uncover the often-invisible history of WPAs' knowledge bases and also their often-conflicting biases and allegiances. Despite the professionalization of the WPA role, almost all tell their story of coming to a WPA position as if they didn't expect to be there.

Program Conception

Contributors were asked to write about how they started a program or to discuss what they knew about a program's beginnings from its documented history. We asked them to describe conflicts, challenges, and the overall reception of their program in their department and university. Conception prompted contributors to tell origin stories. Often, they stretch back to the institution's year of founding, such as Arizona State Writing Programs in 1887. Others' beginnings reflect the growth of the field in the mid- to late-twentieth century, such as Colby College's Farnham Writers' Center's founding in 1984. A handful have existed for only a few years, begun with grant funding or shaped out of suggestions by an accrediting body. While in many cases, writers were not present at the founding of their programs, documentation of the past exists in their archived materials and in some cases, publications, such as the University of Rhode Island major in writing and rhetoric. Had a WPA not conceived of the usefulness of knowing the facts of a program's origins, this element suggests that ethos is gained in doing so.

Population Served

Maybe more than any other element, population served varies across institutions in the most material ways: geography, material means, race and ethnicity, religion, educational attainment and goals. On first glance, one might assume that institution size and type is the best bet for gleaning useful information from this element; yet, readers should consider geography and program type when researching this element. Of interest to readers at any open access institution is the number of students who are placed in remedial courses whom our colleagues serve.

Funding

As we've mentioned, funding information is difficult to find (as is funding). Contributors tell us about their funding sources, which are often complicated and split across units. Some literally have no money; the entire "program" is their salary or what is represented by their release time. Even those who have a large budget, such as those few endowed programs, have little or no real connection or control of the funding line. One realization readers might share with us is that few WPAs have much authority over their budgets; they have a lot of responsibility to see that the program runs effectively yet little power over the purse strings.

Operations

In this section, WPAs describe their roles and responsibilities, their staff, and how their programs run on a day-to-day basis. Originally, this section began as two: "Staff," which asked contributors to discuss their own role and the people who work with and for them; and "Operations," which asked writers to explain their daily duties and responsibilities. Contributors had trouble distinguishing between these two, helping us to realize that there is often no staff besides the WPA or that daily operations and the people who "operate" are inseparable; thus, the sections are now combined. What is notable about "Operations" is the debunking of a fear or perception that WPAs often do their jobs in a vacuum. While of course WPAs' job descriptions (and actual jobs) are comprised of an overwhelming number of sometimes thankless tasks, not a single WPA in this volume goes it alone. There is a chair, a student worker, a department support staff person, a supportive dean, a graduate assistant—someone who helps, makes suggestions, make the copies, or just listens. We found this section to be very empowering, not only by providing the type of staffing information helpful when proposing a new hire, for instance, but also by reminding us who *does* support us, even when we feel, as many WPAs honestly describe, beleaguered.

Marketing/PR

Contributors were asked "How do you get the word out about your program? How do you make sure your targeted population uses your program? What challenges arise in making sure your program is taken advantage of?" Some WPAs, in particular those that serve first-year writers, admit that they never thought they'd have to worry about marketing, but they do, even if their course is required, such as Patrick Clauss at University of Notre Dame. He admits having asked before becoming a WPA, "What is there to market? Don't students just sign up for required classes, and that's about it?," although now he spends considerable effort marketing the mission of the University Writing Program to faculty and administrators across the institution. Some contributors discuss more familiar marketing efforts such as promotional videos, websites, and brochures, while others discuss efforts that are more tactical in nature. For instance, in this section, Tim McCormack and Mark McBeth from John Jay College describe marketing English to faculty outside of the department so that those faculty understand how writing is taught and what they can expect from students as writers when they get to their classrooms.

Role of Research

WPAs see their obligation to scholarship in different ways, depending on the type of institution. We asked contributors to tell readers about the sorts of research that has been published on their program and how important it is that the program engages in research or has a research agenda. Because we are trained in traditional scholarship ourselves, we had a narrow definition of scholarship in our minds when we first proposed this section. Reading the contributions to this section caused us to learn about the different types of and approaches to research that WPAs are carrying out, such as teacher action-research, data collection for internal uses, collaborations with students on their projects, and capital R research for publication, mostly for the purpose of tenure and promotion, although the results of that research can often benefit the program.

Assessment

This element may be among the most telling of difference among institution and program types in this book. From "no formal assessments" to highly elaborate portfolio processes on a multi-site campus, WPAs report various ways they document that their programs are effective. We found that the specific assessment protocol shared among this element were of use in reflecting on our own practices and inspiring us to think about changes we could make to our own programs. For large-scale direct assessments that include student portfolio sampling, readers might turn to contributions from many of the large and mid-sized research universities represented in the collection, such as Miami University or University of Rhode Island. For other types of assessment such as surveys and self-assessment, readers might find of interest those described by contributors from Purdue University, University of Wisconsin–Eau Claire, Westminster College, and Pomona College. Readers looking to learn about new assessments and pilots might turn to this section from the University of Missouri, University of Notre Dame, Wallace Community College, and Arizona State University.

Technology

Technology responses surprised us somewhat, perhaps because our experiences with technologies that aid writing programs are what we would consider typical and not that adventurous. We find that most contributors mentioned program websites and learning management systems, technology uses that one might expect. In fact, this caused us to question whether we should include the technology section at all. We considered, though, that a "common" or "typical" way of using technology might be helpful to readers; it signaled to us that we are perhaps doing as well as we can with technology or that a limit exists in regards to the technological needs of a writing program (as opposed to classroom teaching). For instance, knowing that Colby College, Duquesne University, University of Connecticut, and Westminster College, are all using WCOnline to book writing center appointments and collect data indicated to us that this may be more than a trend but rather a best practice. Similarly, while they all use different software, Monmouth College, Old Dominion, Arizona State Online, Drew University, Westminster College, and Arizona State Writing Programs all collect ePortfolios, again signaling not repetitive information, but an important practice that is perhaps worth observing across different institutions in considering taking up at one's own.

Pedagogical and/or Administrative Highlights

We understand that programs do not want to report their similarities as much as they want to report their unique differences. We therefore asked, What makes your program special, unique, or interesting? About what aspects of your program would you like to "spread the word"? What new ideas does your program have in store? What will you be unveiling, or what are you currently working toward? This section also reveals that what is new to one program may be old hat or completely aspirational to another program.

Only a few of the I-want-to-steal-those highlights readers will find include:

- the University of Rhode Island production lab dedicated for writing majors, complete with high-end computers and multimedia software, scanners, laminator and comb binder, as well as iPads and video and voice recorders available for check-out
- the Louisiana State University Distinguished Communicators certificate, which provides students with support to build digital portfolios as well as faculty advisors and mentoring
- the Old Dominion University Faculty Writing Studio, a space for faculty to research, write, and collaborate, as well as receive feedback on their own writing
- the University of Missouri Win Horner Award, which awards $1,000 to a faculty member who has demonstrated exemplary commitment to the teaching writing-intensive courses across disciplines
- the John Jay College of Criminal Justice's EARLYstart and JUMPstart programs, two different models of first-year transition programs, both evidencing remarkable success with students whose test scores indicate they may struggle in first-year writing

Primary Document(s)

Lastly, we asked contributors to include a primary document(s) that has been of major importance to the development or sustainability of the program, something that readers wouldn't typically find available on the program's website. These documents are organized by document type and include self-studies, curriculum proposals, professional development booklets, promotional materials, and more. They are included in an online companion to this collection, which can be accessed at https://writingprogramarchitecture.com, and through the Utah State UP website. There readers will find invaluable resources unavailable anywhere else, including Arizona State Writing Programs' fifty-one-page self-study, the full proposal for the Oakland University major and minor in writing and rhetoric, and a grant proposal for Drew University's Writing Fellows program that resulted in $25,000 of funding. All of these materials, some on which these programs built their foundations, and some on which they are depending for their sustainability, were generously made available by the WPAs in this collection to serve readers as they build their own programs.

Your Voice

This is a more of a social element of a program that we know is important to WPAs and that elicited the broadest responses from contributors. We asked, What should new WPAs know about your program or WPA work in general that might help them develop new programs, improve existing ones, and create sustainable programs and relationships with university administration, students, and faculty? As the reader will see, WPAs offer less advice about practicalities and more advice about relationship-building, time management, and managing expectations. We believe these are useful "soft skills" that balance well the emphasis on "hard" structures in this volume.

WAYS INTO THE BOOK

The breadth of this reference book affords the reader several ways in. Besides linear progress, we suggest three ways of reading this large volume: (1) by program type, (2) by institution type and size, and (3) by element.

The first way into the book is to read by program type. The main Table of Contents has been organized by program types including writing majors, writing minors, graduate writing programs, Writing and Communication across the Curriculum, first-year writing (including ESL and basic writing), writing centers and support centers, and integrated programs (those programs that include more than one entity, such as a joint writing center and WAC venture). The merit of this organization is the ease with which the reader can distinguish among such a diversity of program types. A writing center director will easily find a section containing studies that detail the structure of six writing centers at various types and sizes of universities. In particular, "Part 5: Integrated Programs" might be helpful to a WPA who is charged with starting a program that encompasses a curriculum for students and faculty outreach.

A second way into the collection is to read by institution type and size, which offers the reader a group of case studies with common resources and challenges. For example, WPAs at independent institutions will read about the architecture of writing programs at five other independent schools. In doing so, they will learn what they might have in common with the structures of the programs, even if they are not building the same type of program as those represented here. In particular, for instance, both Notre Dame and Our Lady of the Lake focus their first-year writing curricula on institutional values: "virtue ethics" and "*comunidad*" respectively. Were this a priority for another independent school, these cases serve aptly as models.

Lastly, and we argue, most compellingly, readers can also make their way into *Writing Program Architecture* by element. As explained, each chapter in this book is arranged by a template of the eleven elements serving as headings. In this way, readers faced with an opportunity or challenge can focus their attention on that particular element, say, funding or technology, across thirty institutions. These elements *qua* chapter headings serve as *topoi*, or places for invention. They cut across the large number and wide variety of programs, supporting and mirroring the structural thinking required of WPAs for progress, decision-making, and action. Here, we provide an alternative Table of Contents by element:

SOME NOTES ON INCLUSION

In collecting chapter contributions, we began by considering the types of programs that a new or struggling or stuck WPA might want to read about. First, we sought to balance attention to the traditionally understood types of writing programs: first-year writing, writing majors and/or minors, WAC programs, writing centers, and, finally, what we call "integrated" programs. Integrated programs are the type, for instance, where a single stream of funding or person's line is devoted to, say, a Writing across the Curriculum program that, in addition to other projects, houses the writing center. We contribute this term to the WPA lexicon to denote multi-element programs such as the five examples in this volume: Arizona State University Writing Programs in the Department of English, Colby College Writing Program and Farnham Writers' Center, Drew University Vertical Writing Program, New Mexico Tech Writing Program and Writing Center, and Pomona College WAC-Based First-Year Writing Seminar and Writing Center. In our argument that an exposed program architecture can help WPAs articulate and argue on behalf of their programs, an integrated program stands in contrast to those more easily defined by one specific role, such as the Duquesne Writing Center or the University of Wyoming Professional Writing major.

Second, we allowed the CCCC Certificate of Excellence award to guide our initial invitations. As a peer-reviewed honor in our discipline, the award suggests a level of vetting that we imagine readers appreciate (we do). Many of these excellent programs responded warmly. They include:

John Jay College of Criminal Justice First-Year Writing Program
Louisiana State University Communication across the Curriculum
Oakland University Writing and Rhetoric Major
Rowan University Major in Writing Arts
St. Louis Community College ESL Program

University of Connecticut Writing Center
University of Missouri Campus Writing Program
University of Wisconsin–Eau Claire University Writing Program

Yet, "excellence" is decidedly not the basis for inclusion in this volume. Our invitations and choices for the remaining contributions sought to achieve a balance of types of institutions whose purposes and missions vary, including large research universities, teaching-focused regional public institutions, small liberal arts colleges, and two-year colleges, institution types sometimes missing from accounts of writing programs. We were excited by submissions from programs representing basic writers, ESL students, STEM, and fully online environments. In rounding out the collection, we strove for equitableness, choosing not necessarily to include the most ideal or famous programs, but rather those programs that provide the reader with case studies demonstrating the nitty-gritty reality of writing on the ground across the country.

Lastly, while we aimed for balance and diversity, we also sought comparability. For that reason, readers will find here two independent writing programs out of Arizona State University—one completely online and one fully on the ground. Reading these profiles together provides an interesting picture of two vastly different approaches to the way writing programs can be administered even at the same university. Readers might find it compelling to compare the Basic Writing program at the University of Wisconsin–Superior and the First-Year Writing Program at the University of Wisconsin–Eau Claire. As independent regional campuses under one public flagship system, both programs have felt the effects of the state's politics. Shevaun Watson's chapter on UW–Eau Claire profiles a program before drastic budget cuts are made (to which we refer in the epigraph of this introduction), while Jamie's chapter on UW–Superior describes how, over a period of only a few years, she and her colleagues pre-emptively revised their program in order to continue to meet the needs of under-prepared writers if and when developmental education in the state changes as it has in other states. Readers might also want to compare five profiled land grant universities: University of Connecticut, University of Rhode Island, Louisiana State University, Purdue University, and University of Missouri. Or, of similar interest might be a regional comparison, such as looking side-by-side at the four included profiles of programs at institutions in Pennsylvania: Indiana University of Pennsylvania, Duquesne University, Shepherd University, and Old Dominion University.

The full list of contributors, by institution type, includes:

COMMUNITY COLLEGES:
Onondaga Community College, page 202
St. Louis Community College, page 225
Wallace Community College, page 359

SMALL LIBERAL ARTS COLLEGES:
Colby College, page 402
Drew University, page 416
Monmouth College, page 132
Pomona College, page 451
Shepherd University, Page 348
University of Wisconsin–Superior, page 254

MID-SIZE PUBLIC UNIVERSITIES (ENROLLMENT UNDER 30,000):
Arizona State University Online, page 173
Indiana University of Pennsylvania, page 319
John Jay College of Criminal Justice, page 184
Louisiana State University, page 121
Miami University, page 27
New Mexico Tech, page 434
Oakland University, page 42
Old Dominion University, page 144
Rowan University, page 72
University of Connecticut, page 334
University of Rhode Island, page 89
University of Wisconsin–Eau Claire, page 254
University of Wyoming, page 101

LARGE PUBLIC UNIVERSITIES (ENROLLMENT OVER 30,000):
Arizona State University, page 173
Purdue University, page 58
University of Missouri, page 155
Utah Valley University, page 281

INDEPENDENT INSTITUTIONS:
Duquesne University, page 303
Our Lady of the Lake University, page 216
University of Notre Dame, page 239
Westminster College, page 373

The reader will also note that the case studies here are built on the reports of a single or small collaborative group of informants per each program. Of course, their roles in their institutions provide them a limited and biased point of view. We acknowledge that reported perspectives do not constitute the type of triangulated data on which a researcher would solely rely. The chapters also contain dynamic information such as budget figures and enrollment numbers, which might appear to be only relevant at a particular point in time. Yet, it is these details on which our teaching, writing, and administration are contingent. Further, projects of reporting to provide an array of usable and comparable information have become a priority in WPA scholarship, especially with the recent completion and publication of the WPA census.

As credible information goes, we have no reason to suspect that WPAs are intentionally misreporting the details of their programs. Our contributors conceive of their participation in this project as important to the advancement of their own scholarly and administrative work. Therefore, they report in good faith information that may change because of structural changes to their department or unit, but which nevertheless existed and which resulted in productive work in the local, contingent way that is well-documented in the collections of Writing Program scholarship that inspired this book.

OUR AUDIENCE, OURSELVES

In their article, "Twenty More Years in the WPA's Progress," Jonikka Charlton and Shirley Rose bust a common WPA myth when they write:

> The question of whether or not assistant professors should take WPA positions is an ethical question our field has contended with since Carol Hartzog addressed it in 1986 in *Composition and the Academy* and longer. Not the least of the issues is whether junior faculty are sabotaging their efforts to attain tenure with the added workload and responsibilities of administrative life. But the data we've collected suggests that even though we may have legitimate concerns about a given jWPA's ability to be tenured, our jWPAs *are* being tenured. (Charlton and Rose 2009, 132; emphasis in original)

This piece of evidence is important to bear in mind because it remains a (tired) adage that a person should not take a WPA role pre-tenure. Yet, as Christy Wenger of Shepherd University notes in this collection, many of the jobs in writing studies posted in the last several years specifically included some kind of WPA work in the title or asked for WPA-type work in the job description (e.g., assessment experience, assisting in running first-year writing). Wenger writes:

> While the early professionalization of graduate students is a contentious subject in our field, and many warn against the political and personal

> dangers of assuming administrative positions prior to being tenured, I found that most jobs on the market asked for WPA responsibilities in conjunction with assistant professor positions. Even if we are ideologically opposed to the idea of a "genAdmin," or the rise of a generation of writing studies professionals who identify as administrators early in their careers (Charlton et al. 2011), graduate training and hiring trends currently reward this identification. (Wenger, this volume, 348)

Although experienced faculty will fill some of these positions, newly minted PhDs with some coursework but little hands-on experience in administration will fill the remainder. And, while some programs will be established and running smoothly, in more cases than one might expect, new WPAs are being hired to revise and even begin new programs with few or no resources (save their own time). These new hires, like us two authors when we began our jobs as WPAs, will be seeking out examples of how programs work. They will want models and case studies of how writing programs of all types are structured and sustained.

For this audience, our colleagues, mentees, and friends, we add this collection to our WPA resources. It serves as a complement to the white papers, theory, scholarship, and valuable lore in our field. With its templated chapters and focus on architecture, readers might use it as a collection of institutional data, a reference of program types and elements, or a way to simply confirm, "Yes, I do that, too." The program elements explained here offer readers the support they might need to join, build, revise, and maybe, given the current state of higher education as Shevaun's experience in spring 2015 exemplifies, dismantle programs in careful and strategic ways, rather than risk losing them completely. If WPAs are going to perform the many roles, responsibilities, and rhetorical maneuvers expected of them, they need to take stock of what structures exist alongside others' stories and perspectives. Writing program architecture will allow WPAs to more fully articulate to crucial audiences at institutions of all stripes how their writing programs work.

References

Aristotle. 2007. *On Rhetoric: A Theory of Civic Discourse.* Trans. George Kennedy. New York: Oxford University Press.

Blalock, Glen. 2014. Personal Communication with Bryna Siegel Finer. July 2. Email.

Charlton, Colin, Jonikka Charlton, Tarez Samra Graban, Kathleen J. Ryan, and Amy Ferdinandt Stolley, eds. 2011. *GenAdmin: Theorizing WPA Identities in the 21ˢᵗ Century.* Anderson, SC: Parlor Press.

Charlton, Jonikka, and Shirley K. Rose. 2009. "Twenty More Years in the WPA's Progress." *WPA* 33 (1–2): 114–145.

Council of Writing Program Administrators. 1998. Evaluating the Intellectual Work of Writing Administration.

Fulwiler, Toby, and Art Young, eds. 1990. *Programs That Work.* Portsmouth, NH: Heinemann.

George, Diana. 1999. *Kitchen Cooks, Plate Twirlers & Troubadours: WPAs Tell Their Stories.* Portsmouth, NH: Boynton-Cook.

Giberson, Greg A., Jim Nugent, and Lori Ostergaard, eds. 2015. *Writing Majors: Eighteen Program Profiles.* Logan: Utah State University Press.

Gladstein, Jill M., and Dara Rossman Regaignon. 2012. *Writing Program Administration at Small Liberal Arts Colleges.* Anderson, SC: Parlor Press.

"Home Page." 2007. Compfaqs.org. CompPile. July 6. Accessed January 2016.

Jamieson, Sandra. 2015. "Foreword." In *Writing Majors: Eighteen Program Profiles,* ed. Greg A. Giberson, Jim Nugent, and Lori Ostergaard, vii–ix. Boulder: University Press of Colorado.

Reiff, Mary Jo, Anis Bawarshi, Michelle Ballif, and Christian Weisser, eds. 2015. *Ecologies of Writing Programs: Program Profiles in Context.* Anderson, SC: Parlor Press.

Rose, Jeanne Marie. 2005. "Coming of Age as a WPA: From Personal to Personnel." *WPA* 28 (3): 73–87.

Sura, Tom, Jaclyn M. Wells, Megan Schoen, Cristyn Elder, and Dana Lynn Driscoll. 2009. "Praxis and Allies: The WPA Board Game." *WPA* 32 (3): 75–88.

Thais, Chris, Gerd Brauer, Paula Carlino, Lisa Ganobcsik-Williams, and Aparna Sinha, eds. 2012. *Writing Programs Worldwide: Profiles of Academic Writing in Many Places.* Anderson, SC: Parlor Press.

Watson, Shevaun. 2015. Personal Communication with Jamie White-Farnham. February 2. Email.

PART 1

Majors and Minors, Undergraduate and Graduate Writing Curriculums

1

MIAMI UNIVERSITY MAJOR IN PROFESSIONAL WRITING

Heidi A. McKee

"I've always loved Miami, but one of the main reasons that I came here was because it offered a professional writing major; it was exactly what I'd been looking for in other colleges but couldn't find anywhere else."
—Kaitlyn Foye, 2015, professional writing major

"I am very happy to have found a first job doing what I want to do—writing."
—Amanda Harr, 2013, professional writing major and writer for Licking Memorial Health Systems in Ohio

Institution Type: Public Research University
Location: Oxford, Ohio
Enrollment: 15,400 undergraduates
Year program was founded: August 2011 (revision of degree in Technical and Scientific Communication founded originally in the 1980s)
Writing Program Administrator (WPA) reports to: English Department Chair
Program funded by: English Department General Budget
Description of undergraduate students: At Miami in general: 40.1 percent in-state, 49.5 percent out-of-state, 6.6 percent international students (Miami University 2009)

PROGRAM SNAPSHOT

The professional writing major is a BA in professional writing (not English) housed within the Department of English in the College of Arts and Science on the Oxford campus. Starting with five majors in August 2011, the degree has grown (as of January 2016) to over 180 majors and is now the second largest major in the department.

DOI: 10.7330/9781607326274.c001

WPA'S PROFILE

I came to WPA work eagerly—seeking to do good work in the world and wanting to create better teaching, learning, and research opportunities for writing, writers, and writing instructors. My WPA career began in graduate school. While earning an MA in 2000 from the University of Wyoming, I co-wrote an instructor's guide for first-year composition (FYC). I loved the experience of working closely with graduate student and faculty colleagues to develop resources for mentoring new instructors. During my doctoral studies at the University of Massachusetts in 2003, I served for a year as the assistant director of the Writing Center. In that position, I taught two semester courses for undergraduate peer consultants, supervised day-to-day operations of the center, and collaborated with consultants to build student workshop programming. Co-creating the workshop series was my first experience in program building, and it was exciting to see how the consultants and the students with whom they worked flourished. From both of these graduate school experiences, I came away with a clear and passionate understanding of how much WPAs matter, not just for shaping the day-to-day administration of a program but also for providing opportunities for others.

I took this passion with me to my tenure-track position at Miami University in 2005. At this time, no sections of first-year writing were taught in a computer classroom (desktop or laptop), thus limiting class activities and students' opportunities for exploring, engaging, and composing with a wide-range of genres and modalities. So working with teams of faculty and graduate student colleagues, I set out to change that. In 2006, I became the founding coordinator of the Digital Writing Collaborative, working to integrate digital writing technologies into first-year composition. As a pre-tenured faculty member, this was a WPA position I eagerly *chose* to create—with the support of the director of composition, the English Department chair, the senior director of information technology, the dean, and the provost. Thanks to the tremendous work of many people in those early years, including Jason Palmeri and James Porter, Miami's Oxford campus went from having no sections of FYC in digital classrooms (desktop or laptop) in 2005 to 100 percent by 2011. (For more information about this process of program transformation, please see Adsanatham et al. 2013 and Ninacs 2009). I served as coordinator for the Digital Writing Collaborative for many years, but then in the fall of 2010 I moved to another area of administration: administering a writing major, for reasons I'll explain in the "Program Conception" section below.

From 2011 to 2014, I served as founding director of Miami's professional writing major. At the same time that I was directing the major, I was also serving for two years as the interim director of the Howe Writing Initiative in the Farmer School of Business, which is the writing center and WAC program for the division. In 2014, I was appointed to be the Roger and Joyce Howe Professor of Written Communication and the director of the Howe Writing Initiative, so I stepped down from directing professional writing, but I am still actively involved in helping to build the major.

PROGRAM CONCEPTION

The professional writing major (sometimes referred to as PW) was a revision of an existing degree. Since the mid-1980s, Miami has had a writing major—a BA in Technical and Scientific Communication (BATSC). Students in this degree took core courses such as "Editing for Technical and Scientific Communicators" and "Designing and Testing User Documents for Technical and Scientific Communicators," and they took eighteen hours of specialization courses in environmental science, biological science, or computer science. For two decades, BATSC had about forty to fifty majors per year. But since 2000 enrollments began to decline, perhaps because of changing demographics at Miami (fewer students interested in technical fields) and perhaps because the courses in BATSC, while individually strong, collectively did not seem to keep pace with a changing workplace. By fall 2010, BATSC had just sixteen majors.

Fall 2010 was right in the middle of the financial crisis, and Miami was in the midst of major belt-tightening and program cutting. The new provost was hired specifically with a charge to cut underperforming programs. Given BATSC's low enrollments, it was certainly heading for the chopping block. (Already the year before, the MA in Scientific and Technical Communication at Miami had been suspended.) Clearly something needed to be done to keep a rhetoric and writing major at Miami.

So in fall 2010, I collaborated with Jean Lutz, the director of BATSC, to revise the program. Our goal was to create a new major that would meet the needs of Miami students more fully and that would bring all rhetoric and writing faculty in the department together to teach in one major. To understand the significance of this joining of forces, it's necessary to have a bit more background.

At Miami, while faculty in writing were certainly collegial and worked together closely at the graduate level in the MA and PhD in composition and rhetoric, at the undergraduate level there was a clear division and separation of programs. BATSC faculty (as they were so designated) taught in BATSC. Composition and rhetoric faculty (and they were so designated) taught in the graduate program and first-year composition. There were no undergraduate programs for composition and rhetoric faculty to teach in until 2009 when we launched a new rhetoric and writing minor. But the minor was small at first and often we had to cancel classes, such as "Rhetorical Strategies for Writers," because of low enrollments.

What we had then was a new minor that was still seeking enrollments and a major that was going to be cut. What we needed was a major that all writing faculty could be part of and contribute to, one that reflected a rich range of options for students. In short, we needed to broaden BATSC's focus from solely scientific and technical communication, and we had to build from the minor to create a more robust curriculum to meet students' needs and interests.

Naming this new major, as I have mentioned elsewhere (see Johnson, Zemliansky, and McKee 2014), was tricky. Some colleagues felt strongly that *professional* had to be in the title while others just as vigorously opposed it. Some colleagues felt they were not in professional writing and worried that such a title might commercialize/corporatize writing too much. Some people rallied around the idea of rhetoric and writing as the title, but others were opposed to that because it didn't bring in the professional as explicitly. Given how misunderstood rhetoric is, many of us also feared that rhetoric in the title would steer students away. We settled on professional writing because *writing* was a focus shared by us all and because *professional* encompassed technical and scientific communication as well as a broader range of writing. We also settled on professional writing because we thought, as has been proven, that it would resonate well with students and their potential employers.

In proposing the major, we revised the titles and, in many cases, the focus of BATSC classes. "Editing for Technical and Scientific Communicators" became "Print and Digital Editing"; "Writing Reports and Proposals" became "Grant Writing." Initially when we proposed the major, we tried, as much as possible, to work with the courses we already had on the books, recognizing that if the major called for a significant number of new courses, that could be a problem getting it approved in the department and the college. We purposefully designed the major to be flexible and adaptable so we would be able to continually change it to keep abreast of developments in the field and in the academic and professional needs of our students. (For further discussion of curriculum, see "Highlights" below).

Before closing this section, I want to address one more point about institutional location. Unlike the other writing majors profiled in this collection, Miami University's professional writing major is housed in the English Department. This creates some interesting circumstances. Initially when we proposed the revised major, colleagues in literature and creative writing were hesitant to approve it because they were concerned about BATSC courses having such low enrollments (often as few as five students in a class) and they did not want to be saddled with another low-enrollment major. It was an uphill struggle to convince them that professional writing could be successful. As described in "Populations Served" below, professional writing has proved successful and, in just four years, has become the second largest major in the department, just after creative writing.

In spite of this success—or perhaps because of it—there was a move afoot in the department for a while, but it has subsided now, to have the department merge its distinct majors (linguistics, literature, creative writing, professional writing) into one English major. This move to "one major" would be problematic for a number of reasons. First, our professional writing major is an independent degree. It is a BA in professional writing, not in English. Second, in our survey of majors, we asked them, as neutrally as we possibly could, if they would favor "one English major" where professional writing was a concentration; 100 percent of respondents said they were against the idea because they felt it would limit their options to tailor their studies and because they did not want to lose the rich interdisciplinary potential of the professional writing degree. If we had "one major" and had to require a certain number of literature and creative writing courses, students would not have as many options for taking rhetoric and writing courses and electives of their choosing within English Department programs and in other programs such as interactive media studies, marketing, and journalism. Given the rich diversity that is writing studies, students, in consultation with advisors and peers, should be able to craft their course of study to fit their academic and career aspirations. Because of the flexibility of Miami's professional writing major, we are able to provide those opportunities. And the most important aspect of the professional writing major is the opportunities it provides for students.

POPULATION SERVED

The professional writing major attracts a broad array of students. Some declare professional writing from their first days at Miami while others switch from another major. Students who have switched to professional writing or who have added it as a double major come from all areas of the university, including the College of Creative Arts, the College of Education, and the Farmer School of Business as well as from other arts and science majors such as journalism and strategic communications.

Because of the diverse opportunities professional writing provides and because of its explicit professional focus, the major is proving popular with students. In a recent survey of majors, some of their responses for why they chose the major included:

- I chose the Professional Writing major because I have always wanted to be an editor. This was an opportunity to do so, while also discovering other interests that I have within the program, such as the track of digital and technical communications.

- I want to go into non-profits and this major teaches a lot about grant writing and other types of writing that will be used in that setting so it seemed like a good fit.

- Professional Writing is a program that allows for me to learn useful skills and explore important topics while making it all apply to my own life and passions. I am trying to find a way to enjoy life while still living meaningfully. With a flexible and creative program like Professional Writing, I can do that.

- Writing is my life! I think this program will provide a great background in communicative skills that will be beneficial now and in years to come.

- I like that it allows me to take all sorts of writing courses and provides a better array of job opportunities than a degree in creative writing, literature, or poetry might.

- I enjoy the writing and editing, and the major really seemed to focus on the career path that I wanted to pursue. Plus "Professional Writing" is awesome to say as a major.

- I am trying to become a lawyer and wanted to expand my knowledge of writing.

- I always have loved English, but I definitely wanted to study business in college. When I found out that I had enough time to double major in business and another subject, I chose Professional Writing due to its flexibility and interesting curriculum. (Program Survey 2015)

From lawyers to editors, social media content developers to magazine writers, technical communicators to video editors, our graduates go on to a wide variety of careers within the broad range of writing studies. Perhaps because of our strong job placement too, professional writing is one of the only humanities majors in the university to be growing. From just five majors in August of 2011 (five of the sixteen BATSC students chose to switch majors, the rest finished their BATSC degree since they were one year or less from finishing), the professional writing major has grown to over 180 majors in December 2015.

FUNDING

As a major in the English Department in the College of Arts and Science, faculty lines (visiting and permanent) and TA lines are provided by the college. Classroom support such as ceiling-mounted LCD projectors, wall-mounted plasma screens, laptop-friendly furniture, and tech-support help for instructors is provided primarily by the University or the College, but we are fortunate to have one endowed classroom: the Walter Havinghurst Classroom. We are working with Development to create more endowed, named classrooms and, ideally someday, more named endowed professorships.

The program is currently provided a small budget ($5,000) from the English Department chair to bring in guest speakers, provide resources for student meetings/clubs, and to pay for such things as publicity materials, curricular development needs, and special student projects (such as field trips to community sites). Funding for more extensive projects may be sought from the department chair, the College of Arts and Science dean, or the Provost's Office, depending on the project. Key to any funding requests is to connect the funding project to the strategic goals of the department, college, and university, and to show that the return-on-investment, especially the benefit for student learning, will be worth it.

OPERATIONS

The professional writing major is a collaborative staffing endeavor among (as of this printing) eight tenure-line faculty, one full-time continuing contract lecturer faculty, six full-time visiting assistant professors, many doctoral students in Miami's PhD program in composition and rhetoric who teach six to eight sections of various courses per year, and administrative staff in the English Department.

The program is directed by a faculty member (tenure-line or lecturer) who has a one course-equivalence release, and in collaboration with colleagues in the program and in the department has a number of responsibilities:

- Advise and mentor students, including building workshop programming for majors.
- Market and represent the major both on- and off-campus.

- Foster off-campus and on-campus partnerships with other programs and with for-profit and non-profit organizations.
- Conduct assessment of student learning.
- Facilitate curriculum reviews and curriculum revision projects, including the development of new courses.
- Manage professional writing's allotment of the English Department budget (approximately $5,000 per year) for events and activities, such as off-campus trips, guest speakers, student projects, select software purchases not covered by Miami's regular computer process. (Note: the department chair handles big ticket budget items like faculty salaries and such.)
- Interview and advise the department chair on the hiring of visiting assistant professors.
- Communicate with English Department support staff for assistance in handling budget processing, the details of planning events, etc.

Faculty in the major also advise and mentor students, but given the growth of the major and the administrative commitments of more than half the faculty (director of PW, chair of department, director of the Howe Writing Center, director of the Howe Writing Initiative, director of composition, director of ESL composition), the most pressing challenge facing Miami's PW major is a shortage of permanent faculty. Of the forty-eight sections of PW courses taught in 2013–2014 (in fall and spring semesters), 77 percent were taught by temporary faculty/graduate assistants, and only 23 percent by permanent faculty (20% by tenure-line faculty, and 3% by lecturer faculty).

In our need for more tenure-line faculty, our program is not alone, given the decline of tenure-line positions in US institutions. Nearly every year we will continue to advocate for more lines and to gather data to demonstrate need.

ASSESSMENT

As part of Miami's efforts to assess learning in the majors, we have conducted a direct assessment of PW senior-level writing every year. We collect two major projects—one written to a specialist audience, one to a non-specialist audience—from every PW senior enrolled in the capstones. Because our program is relatively small—compared to, say, conducting assessment on a university-wide FYC program—collecting writing and conducting this assessment is easy. Faculty teaching the capstones de-identify the writing projects, send them to two colleagues who have not taught capstones that year, and working with the PW director and holding norming sessions, both readers read and score and then discuss the findings, writing a report that is shared with the university assessment office, the department, and all faculty in the PW program. These assessments have shown areas that we could improve upon in our curriculum, and after each assessment we have revised our curriculum and/or our program practices.

We also conducted a student perception survey in the spring of 2014, the third year of the major, and again in fall of 2015. In these surveys, we learned from students why they chose the major, what they liked about it, what they'd like to see changed, and further suggestions they had. We also surveyed graduates (something that will become more important as we have more graduates) to ask them what courses in the major proved most useful to them in their current careers and what suggestions they have for developing new curricula.

Collecting data on graduates is time-consuming; fortunately, Miami's Career Services is working to collect that data in more systematic and deliverable ways from every graduate, so with their help over the years we should be able to keep a robust database of Miami PW alumni.

MARKETING/PR

For the PW major at Miami, we pursue multiple marketing approaches to reach prospective students and parents, employers and community partners, and upper university administration.

To reach prospective students and parents, we have representatives and/or program information at all "Make it Miami" recruitment events. The information consists of two handouts: our list of courses and a PW "resume." This resume is key. It's a one-page description of what students can do with the major. We also put flyers for the major around campus, and thanks to the help of the Office of Residential Life, a flyer is posted in every hallway of every dorm on campus. (Miami has a two-year on campus living requirement.) Our flyer is very simple—white text on a solid color background. The text says simply: "Are you looking for a major? A second major? A minor? Consider Professional Writing. Tracks in Digital and Technical Communication, Editing, Public Writing and Rhetoric, Self-Designed See www.miamioh.edu/pw for more information." More than 25 percent of our majors say they first heard about the major from the flyer.

To reach employers and community partners we work with both Career Services and the Office of Community Engagement and Service. Faculty representatives from PW are often invited to meet with companies to talk about the program because employers in all areas have such a need for professional writers. As described below, in many of our courses, community-based partnerships and writing projects are a key feature of our major, and every semester students create print and/or digital communications for non-profit organizations.

Our best marketing, however, for reaching prospective employers isn't marketing per se—it's the quality of our students that we have who in class partnerships or in out-of-class summer and semester employment prove to be so strong; corporations and non-profit organizations come back seeking more Miami PW students. As we develop more and more students and alumni out in the field, those networks and connections will be key for building and sustaining the major.

To reach upper administration, besides the various encounters with the president, provost, and deans that happen in the course of our faculty and administrative work, we also write an annual report about PW every year that we send to the English Department chair. In this report, besides reporting quantitative data (such as number of majors), we also include voices of students, alumni, and, at times, employers, to show the impact of the major. It's pretty powerful to be able to share quotes like those that opened this profile, especially in a time and a region where universities are under more pressure to connect liberal education/humanities learning to careers and when the competition for enrolling students is fierce (especially in the Midwest with a declining college-age population).

We would like to do much more digital marketing of the major as well but, as of yet, given our shortage of faculty to guide such an effort, we have yet to do so. Our hopes are eventually to secure funding to provide paid internships to PW students to serve as the PW social media intern, but for now we're so busy still with curriculum building and career development programming for majors that Twitter, Facebook, and Instagram will have to wait a bit longer. Even though our program's digital marketing is not robust (to say the least), we do ensure that our students have robust, well-crafted digital presences—courses such as the required Digital Writing and Rhetoric and the electives Interactive Business Communication and Rhetorics of Digital Identity focus on that, as do our capstones working with seniors. For students, their digital presence has helped them both network and find jobs.

TECHNOLOGY

All on-ground courses are taught in laptop (bring your own) classrooms or in desktop labs. On the Oxford campus, more than 99.8 percent of students bring a laptop or tablet to campus. The PW major has priority scheduling (and basically exclusive use) of two computer labs—a Mac lab with an endowment that covers the cost of new computers every three years and a PC lab where we apply for a campus Student Technology Fee funding to replace the computers every four to five years. We also have access to and schedule classes in the College of Arts and Science computer labs. Until recently, we have always been able to secure any and all software we have needed. We try, where possible, to use open source/open access software, but we also recognize the pragmatic need to prepare students with industry-standard software, such as Adobe, as well. Given Adobe's latest pricing (fleecing one might say), we're working with university IT to figure out how to provide that software to students without putting the cost burden on to them.

We offer an increasing number of PW courses online, especially during winter and summer terms, but also during the semester as well. Many students report preferring the online format. So far we have found that all courses in our curricula can be taught online. We use combinations of synchronous and asynchronous communication technologies, including video conferencing. We're working with the university to try to provide students taking online classes (and thus not able to come to a hard-wire lab) access to required software.

ROLE OF RESEARCH

Central to the success of the PW major is the active, vibrant research community that Miami fosters among faculty and students (graduate and undergraduate). Miami faculty and graduate students research in, among other areas, digital media, e-publishing, community engagement, usability, gaming, rhetorical theory and histories (including comparative rhetoric), intercultural communication, business communication, workplace writing, composition pedagogy, online learning, research methodologies, writing centers, and writing across and in the disciplines. As described below, our research to-date in the major has primarily been assessment-based to help us build programming. But we also view all conversations and surveys with students and employers as valuable program-building research.

One area of need that we've heard expressed by employers and by former students and that we see in our own reading of professional publications is to better prepare professional writers for working within the increasingly global networks and intercultural communities that shape communications. We are in the process of building a new track in the major on "Intercultural Rhetoric and Global Writing," and we seek to integrate more global considerations in all of our core classes.

PEDAGOGICAL AND/OR ADMINISTRATIVE HIGHLIGHTS
Rigorous, Flexible, and Focused

A significant strength of our program is the range of courses we offer (see course listing in "Innovative" section below). In addition, we integrate our curricula with other programs in order to leverage combined strengths. Students in the major have opportunities to take courses in business legal studies, communications, creative writing, interactive media studies, journalism, linguistics, literature, and marketing. Students may also, with advisor support, petition up to two classes taken in any field in the university to count as track electives. Classes that have been petitioned include those in theater, computer programming, education, marketing, anthropology, psychology, and more. The diversity and flexibility of the major, and the way students work closely with their advisors to focus coursework tailored to their interests, are strengths of the major.

Innovative

Communicative contexts continually evolve, and in PW, we continually evaluate and develop our curriculum so as to provide students with needed theoretical frameworks and skills. Since the inception of the major, we have substantially revised many BATSC courses and designed many new courses, all of which are proving to be both popular and useful for students. We are developing new curricula as a result of our direct assessment of student writing, our surveys with students, and our research into other successful programs. Since 2011, new courses we have developed are:

- Rhetoric of Information and Data Visualization
- Writing for Global Audiences
- Interactive Business Communication
- Legal Writing
- Digital Media Ethics
- Digital Publishing (where students work with Miami Press to create e-books)
- Special Topics in Rhetoric (topics have included Queer Rhetorics, Rhetoric of Space and Place, Rhetorics of Digital Identity, and Rhetoric and Writing in Italy—for study abroad program)
- Environmental Communication

Courses we are in the process of developing include:

- Introduction to Professional Writing Theory, Practice, and Research (to be part of the core)
- Writing for Games and the Gaming Industry
- Writing Reviews
- Writing for the Sciences
- Issues in Medical Writing
- Special Topics in Community Writing (variable topic course, so it can have different offerings)

Experiential Learning Opportunities

PW majors have many opportunities to engage in experiential learning and career-development opportunities. Two of the required core courses in PW (ENG 411 Visual Rhetoric and ENG 415 Capstone in PW) always include client-based, community-based projects. A number of other courses also provide client-based opportunities (ENG 412 Print and Digital Editing, ENG 413 Grant Writing, and ENG 414 Usability and User Experience). Recent community partners for whom PW students created print or digital publications include a local YWCA, the Emery Theater in Cincinnati, the Limper Geology Museum at Miami, the Oxford Society's Salt Creek Sanctuary, and the Provost-initiated Writing at Miami project.

In every track in PW, ENG 340 Internship is a credit option for students who wish to earn internship credit (by completing the internship and related reflective and analytical assignments). PW students have held internships in a number of places on campus, including Career Services, University Communications, the Miami Art Museum, and the College of Arts and Science. Off-campus internships have included such companies as: Lorenz Educational Press (Dayton), *Cincinnati* Magazine, Bandito Brothers (Los Angeles), XA: The Experiential Agency (Chicago), London Computer Systems (Loveland, OH), America Multisport (Indiana), dunnhumby (Cincinnati), and PMK·BNC (London).

In our coursework and our out-of-class work with students (e.g., advising, workshops, employer presentations), we aim to connect learning and rhetorical theory and practice to "real-world" situations. Whether giving a speech, writing a grant, conducting usability, or designing a social media campaign, Aristotle's theories of rhetoric, for example, still matter—greatly. As one student said in the survey of majors, "The strength of the Professional Writing major is the focus on experience along with theory. My resume is overflowing with professional experience that I have gained from working on projects for clients in the community."

PRIMARY DOCUMENT (at writingprogramarchitecture.com)

Our "Revision to an Existing Degree" form was drafted by rhetoric and writing faculty with input from many colleagues across the university and has served as a foundational document to our program. A first draft was submitted in December 2010 to the English Department's Undergraduate Studies Committee. It was then revised and resubmitted in January 2011. It was revised again (the version included in the online companion) and eventually voted on and approved by the whole department and sent to the College of Arts and Science where it was approved. Then it went to the Council of Academic Deans and on to University Senate. As a revision to an existing major, it did not have to go to the state Board of Regents. The course list has been expanded and revised since this proposal and is available online through the university website.

WPA'S VOICE

What I hope comes through clearly in this profile, especially in the students' voices that I've shared, is this: WPAs can create opportunities to transform and positively impact lives—for students, for faculty, for the campus and off-campus communities. If you're not in program administration, seek out opportunities to become involved. If you are, take a moment to reflect—proudly—on all that you and colleagues have accomplished because of that work. What we do as WPAs matters and we make a difference in the world.

Now that is, I admit, the idealistic passion talking. There are too, of course, the hard slogs of WPA work. Building and sustaining programs are not easy tasks, especially in tight budget times or in contexts where you may be the lone (and lonely) WPA. To sustain ourselves and our passion, it's imperative as WPAs that we seek out and build support networks—and look widely across the university for those networks. Faculty, administrators, and support staff in other programs and divisions can be great allies. Reach out locally and nationally.

And in that reaching out we need to always (always!) keep what's best for students at the core of what we do and at the core of our messaging. Any argument we need to make to improve our programs can and should be tied to the mission of our institution, and for most institutions, especially when running a writing program, the core of that mission is academics and student learning. Students learn better with access to digital technologies; students learn better with well-trained, well-supported faculty who are paid a living wage and who have time for research and professional development; students learn better with experiential learning opportunities that can only arise with appropriate class sizes, etc.

And, lastly, we should never give up (although we may, at times, choose to walk away; see Yancey 2010). Any situation can be improved, perhaps not to the high level we strive for, but definitely improved. As WPAs we need to simultaneously hold to and strive for our ideals while also pragmatically taking what steps we can to get there. In innumerable ways, from large program-building acts like creating a new major to smaller but just as important acts such as taking the time to talk and mentor a new instructor, we can make a difference and we can make not just programs but lives better.

References

Adsanatham, Chanon, Phill Alexander, Kerrie Carsey, Abby Dubisar, Wioleta Fedeczko, Denise Landrum, Cynthia Lewiecki-Wilson, Heidi McKee, Kristen Moore, Gina Patterson, et al. 2013. "Going Multimodal: Programmatic, Curricular, and Classroom Change." In *Multimodal Literacies and Emerging Genres in Student Compositions*, ed. Carl Whithaus and Tracey Bowen, 282–312. Pittsburgh: University of Pittsburgh Press.

Johnson, Robert R., Pavel Zemliansky, and Heidi McKee. 2014. "Challenges and Opportunities Facing Programs: A Continuation of CPTSC Plenary Conversation." *Programmatic Perspectives* 6(2).

Miami University. 2009. "First-Year Class Profile, 2015." Web. Accessed June 20, 2016.

Ninacs, Michelle. 2009. "Crossing Over to the Multimodal Side: A Study of the Consensus Building Strategies Employed by Miami University in Support of a Multimodal First-Year Writing Curriculum." PhD diss., Indiana University of Pennsylvania, Indiana, PA.

Program Survey. 2015. "Professional Writing Majors: Perspectives and Experiences." Fall.

Yancey, Kathleen Blake. 2010. "Defining Moments: The Role of Institutional Departure in the Work of a (Feminist) WPA." In *Performing Feminism and Administration in Rhetoric and Composition Studies*, ed. Krista Ratcliffe and Rebecca Rickley, 143–156. New York: Hampton.

2

OAKLAND UNIVERSITY WRITING AND RHETORIC MAJOR

Greg A. Giberson, Lori Ostergaard, and Marshall Kitchens

Institution Type: Doctoral Research University

Location: Rochester, Michigan (suburban Detroit)

Enrollment: 20,000+

Year program was founded: 2008

WPA reports to: Department Chair

Program funded by: The program is funded through university general funds with the annual budget determined by the College of Arts and Sciences. Funding for activities is supplemented by grants from the Associate Provost for Undergraduate Education, the General Education Committee, and the University Retention Committee.

Description of students: We largely draw commuter students from Oakland and Macomb counties—largely white and privileged, but also including a large number of first generation college students and a significant number of students from urban school districts in Pontiac, Detroit, and Flint. Our undergraduates are mostly commuters and most work a minimum of seventeen hours a week, "more hours than both our peer group comparison and national norms," while carrying a twelve to sixteen credit course load (*Office of Institutional Research and Assessment n.d.a., n.d.b.*). *(Giberson 2015)*

PROGRAM SNAPSHOT

Our writing and rhetoric major is housed in an independent Department of Writing and Rhetoric and provides writing instruction grounded in rhetorical theory and based in best practices in the field. Students study the history and theory of rhetoric and its application to the production of print and digital texts. They also examine the role writing plays in public, professional, and academic spheres. Writing and rhetoric majors choose to focus their studies in one of three areas: professional writing, which prepares them for careers in business, industry, and nonprofits;

DOI: 10.7330/9781607326274.c002

writing for digital media, which provides students with competencies in digital and web productions; or writing studies, which orients students to the field of composition in preparation for graduate study.

WPAS' PROFILES

Greg

My position at Oakland University (OU) is my second tenure-track position, moving from Salisbury University (SU) in Maryland to OU in 2006. During the two years I was at SU, I served as the WPA, directing the first-year writing program, mentoring and overseeing a cadre of fourteen graduate teaching assistants while teaching undergraduate writing courses as well as graduate courses on the teaching of writing. I also served for a year as the director of the Eastern Shore Writing Project, a National Writing Project site. Although I had served for two years as the assistant director of composition while a PhD student at the University of South Florida, I found myself only marginally prepared for the complexities of running several programs immediately upon graduation—a topic Lori and I have written about before in *Composition Forum* (Giberson et al. 2009). While at OU I have not officially held a "WPA" position; it is more accurate to describe my work with the writing major as a "wpa" position, one with implied if not clearly defined administrative duties that suggest responsibility for the program with no formal authority to implement administrative prerogatives. We will discuss this in more detail below. My defined duties within the major are considerable, however. I am the official adviser for writing and rhetoric majors, chairperson for the department's Committee on the Major in Writing and Rhetoric (CMWR), and instructor of record for all internships and capstone projects for prospective graduates.

Lori

My first experience with program administration was as a doctoral student at Illinois State University where I served as an assistant WPA in the first-year writing program, observing and mentoring Graduate Teaching Assistants, helping to design professional development seminars, and co-teaching the practicum course for new instructors. During this time, I served as Doug Hesse's program assistant for the 2004 Conference on College Composition and Communication (CCCC) in San Antonio, and I learned a lot about the discipline and our national organizations as a result of that experience. I began working as an assistant professor at OU in 2006, and beginning in 2008, I received a single course release to assist with some faculty professional development and to observe and mentor part-time faculty. Over the years, I've served, with Greg and our colleague Jim Nugent, as an assistant editor of *WPA: Writing Program Administration*, and I've attended both the CWPA Workshop and Assessment Institute. In 2011, Marshall got permission from the dean to increase the number of course releases I received to create an official position for a first-year writing program administrator. I served in that capacity for three years, and I am currently serving as the department's second chair.

Marshall

During my pre-tenure years at Oakland University (2000–2006), I was a young faculty member in an aging writing program that was part of a triad department—Rhetoric, Communication, and Journalism. I was one of only two hires in nearly twenty years with no other new hires during my first five years in the program. Before I came to OU, as a PhD student at Wayne State University, I was the co-director of computers and composition in the writing program, helping to develop curriculum for composition in the digital age, managing the computer classroom, and working with a total of five funded teaching assistants (including myself) on issues around digital literacy. We developed sample web-building and Internet-connected assignments, offered a pre-CCCCs workshop on digital literacy, and wrote grants to refurbish the computer classroom, receiving $250,000 from the provost to do so. After I received tenure at OU, I took a one-year leave of absence to direct a writing program within an English Department at a smaller, local university, as well as oversee the writing center that served students in first-year writing. When I returned to OU in the fall of 2007 as a newly-tenured associate professor, I was named director of Writing across the Curriculum (WAC). The same year, the dean of the College of Arts and Sciences, Ron Sudol (a faculty member from the rhetoric program), separated the rhetoric program from communication and journalism and established it as a self-standing department—not without resistance from other departments and the faculty union. In the winter of 2008, I was elected inaugural chair of the new department, where I served for two three-year terms.

During my first term as department chair, I was also appointed chair of the General Education Committee, where I served for two years. This position was significant in that it allowed me to gain a better understanding of the general education curriculum at the university and the role that writing plays in that curriculum, both by developing courses to satisfy writing intensive requirements for students across the university and by developing courses to satisfy other requirements such as the Knowledge Applications requirement, the US Diversity requirement, and the Global Perspective requirement. We re-developed courses such as a course on ethnographic writing and one on peer tutoring to satisfy multiple general education requirements, drawing students into those sections so that we could begin offering multiple sections of upper-level writing intensive general education courses.

PROGRAM CONCEPTION
Department

In 1972, when a number of initiatives failed to improve student writing at OU, the university founded a new department of Learning Skills that was charged with administering five distinct remedial reading and writing courses. This skills-based approach to writing instruction ended in 1982, when faculty from that department joined with faculty in communication and journalism to form a new Department of Rhetoric, Communication, and Journalism (RCJ). Inspired by their new place in the university, the rhetoric faculty set to work eliminating some of the—now twelve—remedial classes, developing upper-level writing and rhetoric classes, and forming a site of the National Writing Project to provide outreach to teachers in the local community. In 2008, rhetoric split from RCJ to form a separate Department of Writing and Rhetoric to support both the first-year writing program and a new major in writing and rhetoric. Today the department administers the writing and rhetoric major and minor, a handful of graduate courses, a first-year program comprising the first (Composition I) and second (Composition II) largest courses at the university, and a variety of upper-level writing-intensive courses, including the tenth largest course (Business Writing) at the university.

The Writing and Rhetoric Major

While the authors of this chapter are responsible for the majority of the final structure of our major, a few other iterations of a proposal had been floating around the rhetoric program for the previous decade. In December of 2007, the associate dean of the College of Arts and Sciences approached the three of us and asked us to re-envision the proposal for the major that had been in process for the last decade. The then current version of the proposal had faced several roadblocks in the process due to a lack of focus, with one of the primary critiques being that it relied too heavily on courses already on the books, which were primarily service courses. The three of us were advised to start from scratch and construct a writing major with a clear core and a curriculum that was built around specific learning outcomes for students. We took on the challenge and over the next couple of weeks, during winter break, we rewrote the majority of the proposal building it around a curriculum consisting of three core courses and three different, yet interconnected, tracks: writing studies, professional writing, and writing for digital media.

The beginning of the fall semester of 2008 marked the birth of both our new major and our new department. We found ourselves facing the significant challenges of getting a new major off the ground combined with the extremely complicated task of creating a new and functional department. As a rhetoric program in RCJ focused almost exclusively on the first-year writing program, we approached program administration communally, with most major decisions being made after discussion and votes among the entire full-time faculty (harmoniously or otherwise). For the most part, we initially adopted the administrative and decision-making processes of the former rhetoric program by electing a chair and attempting to address departmental responsibilities and issues collectively. This led to a few problems. For example, our status as a new department with a new major meant that we had new responsibilities in terms of institutionally-mandated program assessment. Of course, assessment was required of the first-year program when we were a part of RCJ, but the new status and new major increased both the scope of the assessment we were responsible for as well as the expectations of the type of assessments we would perform. As had been the case in the past, a single individual volunteered to be responsible for guiding assessment; that individual was quickly overwhelmed by the task. The lack of administrative structure and support for this important and time-consuming service brought assessment efforts to a halt rather quickly. We also realized that our lack of formal structures, standing committees in particular, made it difficult to account for the contractually mandated service work required for contract renewal, tenure, and promotion. We have since constituted several standing and ad hoc committees, thus spreading departmental responsibilities around to smaller groups who report back to the full-time faculty.

POPULATION SERVED

The Department of Writing and Rhetoric serves a variety of groups. We are responsible for several first-year writing courses, including the

"Writing Foundations" course (Composition II), which is a general education requirement. We also offer multiple sections of WRT 382: Business Writing, which is a course available to majors as well as a service course populated primarily by students in the School of Business Administration. We also offer several 200–300 level courses that appeal to both majors and serve students looking to fulfill the "Writing Intensive Outside the Major" general education requirement. WRT 320: Peer Tutoring serves as initial training for students interested in working as tutors in the university writing center.

The major itself is designed to serve a population with a wide variety of interests and ambitions, and we've found that it certainly does. Over the first six years of its existence, the number of declared majors has fluctuated between thirty-five to sixty students. Unfortunately, we have seen a decline over the last few years, which we are working to reverse through a coordinated marketing and promotion campaign, which we discuss below. Some of our students come to us with a general interest in writing, or are disaffected former English majors more interested in the empowering act of writing than the analysis of literature. Others come to us more directly with existing ambitions to work as professional writers or interests in the rhetorical potential of new and emerging discursive media. Still others are interested in the teaching of writing and go on to pursue graduate degrees in rhetoric and composition. Recent graduates have gone on to work for a variety of different types of businesses and organizations including: Beaumont Hospitals, Volkswagen, Oakland Press, Tweedle Group, and Sugar Labs. Graduates have also been accepted into respected rhetoric and composition graduate programs and law schools around the country.

FUNDING

While the department's annual budget is over $2 million, the majority of that budget is for faculty salary, including salary and benefits for part-time faculty of around $1.5 million. Special Lecturers receive between $4,000 and $5,000 per course (plus benefits including partial healthcare and access to retirement accounts). This budget for salary and benefits is controlled by the College of Arts and Sciences, however, and is not negotiable in the annual budget.

The controllable annual budget is approximately $80,000, with portions set aside for supplies and services, student labor, faculty travel, and equipment. In addition, the department has regularly received grants from the provost's office and various university committees for retention initiatives, innovative learning initiatives, and teaching excellence initiatives. First year writing courses are particularly well positioned for grant funding from university sources as the sole course sequence taken by nearly all in-coming students. By focusing on elements important to university funding sources such as retention and high impact practices, we've been successful at developing proposals that demonstrate the impact of program development on student success at the university. Over the past seven years, we've received grants ranging from $5,000 to $25,000 for redesigning the first-year writing curriculum to include career exploration, integrating intrusive advising practices into online courses in first-year writing to improve retention, embedding peer tutors into basic writing courses, and assessing first-year writing with a goal of increasing student success. Grant funding sources include the associate provost for undergraduate education, the general education committee, and the teaching excellence committee. Finally, we periodically receive incentive funding for offering courses at branch campuses, typically ranging from $1,200 to $35,000. This incentive funding is used for professional development and program building, a summer stipend for the WPA, summer research grants for pre-tenured faculty, travel grants, new technology, and extra stipends for part-time faculty.

OPERATIONS

The department, major, and writing program are administered by a chair, WPA, associate WPA, and chief advisor. Each of these administrators is advised by a department committee and seeks advice and consent from the entire full-time faculty.

The chair is a tenured faculty member who receives one course reduction each semester for a 2–1 load and a stipend to cover summer duties. The chair is advised by an advisory council consisting of the chief advisor, the WPA, a representative from the assessment committee, and one elected faculty member on an ad hoc basis, and by the full-time faculty (seven tenured faculty members, four assistant professors, and two job-secured instructors) as a whole during monthly department meetings. With the assistance of various faculty members (most notably the WPA and chief advisor), the chair handles most administrative functioning— hiring and reappointment of part-time faculty, budgeting, purchasing, administering stipends for special projects, scheduling, fielding student complaints, determining committee assignments, mediating department disputes, and monitoring the tenure review process.

The WPA is a tenured faculty member who receives two course releases—teaching a 2–1 load—to oversee staffing and curriculum in four courses (WRT 102: Basic Writing; WRT 104: Supervised Study; WRT 150: Composition I; and WRT 160: Composition II). These courses are taught primarily by forty-five part-time faculty and serve about 2,800 students every semester. As WPA, Lori developed, with Marshall, the procedures for reviewing and reappointing part-time faculty. She also developed and chaired our new First-Year Writing Committee (FYWC), revised the curriculum in Basic Writing and Composition I, and led faculty professional development meetings and resource development.

The associate WPA teaches a 3–3 course load and his service obligations to the department are fulfilled through his work mentoring new faculty, reviewing and mentoring experienced faculty, conducting professional development, planning our annual Spring Seminar, and advising the WPA on issues related to the first-year program, its curriculum, and programs.

The chief advisor teaches a 3–2 course load with a one course reassignment for advising all majors and minors. He also chairs the CMWR and is a member of the First-Year Writing Committee. While the advisor is the most visible administrator for the major, the administrative responsibilities for the major have not been assigned directly to anyone in particular; they have been ill-defined yet shared between the chief advisor, chair, and the WPA. However, given Greg's role as chief advisor to the majors and chair of the Committee on the Major, he has felt a sense of responsibility for the major with no formal authority over it, sort of a wpa, as opposed to a WPA. As with several aspects of our young and developing department and major, we did not recognize a need for an official program administrator for the major and had assumed that it would somehow take care of itself. However, given our recent decline in majors, due at least in part to a lack of structural leadership, we are beginning to recognize the need for, at the very least, a formal structure for administering the major, as well as the need for full-department involvement in marketing and promoting the program.

Tenured and tenure-track faculty teach a 3–2 course load and are also responsible for maintaining an active research agenda and performing service to the department, college, university, and community. There is a total of eleven tenured or tenure-track faculty in the department.

Special instructors are full-time, job secure faculty who teach a 3–3 course load and who are also responsible for performing service to the department, college, university, and community. We currently have two special instructors in the department.

Special lecturers teach at least four classes during the regular academic year. These part-time faculty members receive some benefits from the university, teach on a two-year contract, and are a part of the faculty's American Association of University Professors (AAUP) bargaining unit. Over the last five years, Marshall worked to shift many of our special lecturers to 4–4–1 loads, ensuring that these teachers would be able to earn a living wage while developing a stronger connection to the department and the university. We usually have between forty and forty-five special lecturers working with us every year, but most of these colleagues have been with our department for more than six years.

Lecturers teach no more than three courses during the regular academic year and have one-year contracts for doing so. Some of our lecturers in the department are new instructors who need a year of mentorship to develop their practice. Others work full-time at other units on campus, for example, in the Writing Center or office of E-Learning and Instructional Support. We typically have between two and four lecturers working with us every year.

Our clerical assistant provides support for all department programs and staff, and on occasion we have a paid student assistant to help with paperwork, organizing and processing student evaluations, and the like.

ASSESSMENT

As mentioned above, our status as a new department with a new major meant that we had new responsibilities in terms of institutionally mandated program assessment. In 2013, the department's Assessment Committee turned its attention to the major for the program's first formal assessment, analyzing the most recent core courses, gateway courses, and capstone course syllabi from each instructor who taught these courses during the period from fall 2011–winter 2013. The committee also collected portfolios directly from students in the capstone course to analyze their direct, articulated knowledge of the history of rhetoric, theories of rhetoric, production of print texts, production of digital texts, the role of writing and rhetoric in the public sphere, and professional/academic possibilities for a degree in writing and rhetoric. In addition, the committee assessed students' abilities to

- apply rhetorical analysis to communicative practices, written or otherwise
- engage in appropriate research processes for the rhetorical situation
- apply writing processes (including invention, drafting, and revision)

- produce effective digital texts
- produce effective written texts
- engage in ethical collaborations
- connect classroom learning to service specific communities as civic-minded rhetors
- connect classroom learning to workplace applications
- connect classroom learning to pre-professional activities
- reflect upon one's growth as a writer

The portfolios required students to provide a variety of different texts they produced in core and other upper-level courses within the major, including texts produced in the capstone. The Assessment Committee began analyzing the results in summer 2014, and the final report of that assessment was due in February 2016.

MARKETING/PR

OU holds various recruitment events throughout the year, which we regularly participate in, and we try and work with student advising as much as we can to let them know what we offer and what types of students might be interested in our major. We also encourage our instructors to look out for students who are talented writers or who express an interest in more writing classes, and ask those instructors to refer students to the department's adviser. However, as others have noted elsewhere (see Bowden 2015; Livesey and Watts 2015; Ostergaard and Giberson 2010), marketing a new writing major in a new department that lacks the public recognition and institutional history of other departments can be difficult.

In our proposal, we estimated that during year one we would enroll ten students, maxing out after year four at twenty-five students. After year one, we had an approximate enrollment of thirty students (OU's tracking software does not account for double majors); after year three, fifty-three; and at the beginning of year six, we have fallen to approximately forty. While we are still comfortably above our estimated enrollment, we have since come to believe that we have the potential for it to be much higher. Throughout the existence of our program we have discussed how to market and promote it with the task being specifically assigned to the Committee on the Writing and Rhetoric Major (CWRM), but the committee has struggled to develop a broad approach that could be accomplished through the labor provided by the committee. Faced with falling numbers, the department, in the fall of 2014, decided to take an "all-hands-on-deck" approach to increasing enrollment and formed two ad hoc committees to support the struggling promotional work of the CWRM. The first ad hoc committee was charged with developing better promotional materials including fliers for specific and non-specific events and audiences. The second ad hoc committee was charged with developing a promotional video to be the centerpiece of the program's website. The video will also be a part of a broader promotional and informational program that will be rolled out in our first-year and service courses. The program will consist of an approximately ten-minute presentation to be delivered at the beginning of each semester in all FYC and service courses, and will consist of brief introduction to the department, the writing program, and the major. We have multiple goals for this program:

1. We want students in those classes to understand that the courses they are taking are a part of a broader, organized, and centrally administered program. In particular, we want students in FYC to know that their courses are part of a program and not some isolated, random course.

2. We want to inform students of the existence of the Department of Writing and Rhetoric, to increase our exposure on campus, and to promote the notion that we are the central hub for writing in the university. Sadly, students still come to our main office asking about their "English class" or looking for their "English instructor."

3. Obviously, we also want to take advantage of the large audience that FYC provides us for promoting the major. However, we are aware that we must walk a fine line with this sort of promotion. Many students already harbor some resentment that they are "forced" to take FYC, so we don't want to upset them further by making them feel like we are trying to sell them a time share. As we are writing this chapter, these programs are still being developed, so we have no information on how well they will work, if at all. We are hopeful, though.

ROLE OF RESEARCH

One of the first tasks our new department was charged with was the construction of our own policies and procedures for tenure and promotion. Early on, we recognized that the majority of program development, assessment, and administration would fall to untenured faculty in the new department. Following the lead of the Council of Writing Program Administrator's (1998) "Evaluating the Intellectual Work of Writing Administration," we encouraged those colleagues, and one another, to engage in the kinds of program research that is evidenced in this collection. Over the last eight years, Writing and Rhetoric faculty have compiled two edited collections related to the writing major (Giberson and Moriarty 2010; Giberson, Nugent, and Ostergaard 2015), and composed profiles of our writing major (Ostergaard and Giberson 2010; Ostergaard, Giberson, and Nugent 2015), professional writing track (Chong and Nugent 2015), and first-year writing program (Allan et al. 2015). We have collaborated on articles and chapters addressing our junior faculty's role in program development (Giberson et al. 2009), our first-year program assessment (Allan and Driscoll 2014), and our new Basic Writing curriculum (Ostergaard and Allan forthcoming). Our faculty have also written about our department's course offerings, publishing articles that highlight their work with students in our first-year writing courses (Kitchens 2006), and in our upper-level courses in Peer Tutoring in Composition (Driscoll and Kitchens 2014), Writing about Culture—Ethnography (Allan 2016), and Composition Studies (Ostergaard 2015).

PEDAGOGICAL AND/OR ADMINISTRATIVE HIGHLIGHTS

Our core is a three-course requirement including: WRT 342: History of Rhetoric, WRT 340: Contemporary Issues in Writing and Rhetoric, and WRT 394: Literacy, Technology, and Civic Engagement.

While the core is designed to provide students with a broad introduction to the discipline and its history, we also require that students take a gateway course specific to the track they elect. For example, WRT 329, Introduction to Writing Studies, was designed to provide students in our "Writing Studies" track with an introduction to the field. Students in the class study how this disciplinary community has been constructed through an examination of historical and contemporary artifacts. Students conduct research into the current state of the field by examining, among other things, the composition-rhetoric job list, CCCC program proposals, and undergraduate and graduate degree programs. They engage in a historical study of the field by researching institutional, individual, and published archives, relying on old course catalogs, textbooks, conference proceedings, student newspapers and literary magazines, and faculty files to create a snapshot of the field at a single moment in its history. This innovative, tiered core allows for both a general and consistent introduction to the discipline for all of our students while also providing a specific historical and theoretical context for their specialized track courses.

PRIMARY DOCUMENT (at writingprogramarchitecture.com)

The founding document of the writing major at Oakland University is our full proposal. While a version of it had existed for several years and had been circulated and rejected by various committees, this final version built a new program almost from scratch. It remains an important document for our young department as we continue to revise, update, and hopefully improve our program, as it serves as a reminder our original vision and goals.

Also important to the sustainability of our program is our video introduction to the Department of Writing and Rhetoric and the writing major at Oakland University; it is part of a broader promotional effort for both. After a couple years of rapid growth after first offering the major, the program experienced a dramatic reduction in declared majors, and we have since been looking for ways to reverse that trend. Instructors in all writing and rhetoric courses are encouraged to show the video during the first week of classes and encourage students who might be interested in learning more about the major to contact the department adviser. It is also an important component of our department homepage.

WPAS' VOICES

Greg

When we were writing the major proposal and developing the administrative structure of our new department, we did not spend a great deal of time considering how to administer the program. We tried to be as thoughtful and prospective as possible, but given that we had very little experience running a department it is not surprising that we missed a lot of things at first that we had to address as the department and program matured. As chief adviser, I wish I had consulted more with other advisers from other collaborated more with my own colleagues to develop and define the role of the department adviser. Doing that work alone was difficult and inefficient, so it took longer than I would have liked to develop the types of record keeping, advising strategies, and the like that established programs already have in place. Given a lack of a designated administrator for the major itself, it is not surprising that advising and the program were often conflated causing frustration and confusion for the department as a whole. Many of the issues that I encountered could have been avoided if we had foreseen the importance of having a dedicated administrator for the program.

Lori

My archival research examines the history of writing instruction in early normal schools and high schools, and I began my work at OU with an understanding of how history can shape current-day programs, departments, and institutions. As a new assistant professor, I paid close attention to the stories senior colleagues told about the rhetoric program. Until I began researching the university's archives and digitizing some of the Writing and Rhetoric Department's archives, however, I did not recognize how important my colleagues' stories were. The documented history of a program—told through committee meeting minutes, assessments, course catalogs, and annual reports—may provide a more accurate account of the past, but the stories our colleagues choose to tell and the ways they tell those stories offer insights into how they view their work in the context of the university and department. The histories they choose to repeat and embellish reveal their values as academics. I believe new administrators should be mindful that while the documented record of a program may contradict often-repeated department histories, effective administrative decision-making requires an understanding of, and sensitivity to, departmental lore.

Marshall

During its time as a unit within a larger department (Rhetoric, Communication, and Journalism), the rhetoric program itself had a fair amount of autonomy in its operations—from developing curricula and coursework to working toward a new undergraduate degree program in writing to faculty searches. However, a number of important operations were managed at the department level along with faculty from the other units, and the department had a long history of chairs from communication or journalism who made decisions about budgeting, requests for faculty, policy and procedure, and tenure. It wasn't until after I was elected chair of the newly created Department of Writing and Rhetoric in 2008 and gained a seat at the Council of Chairs in the College of Arts and Sciences that I understood the adverse impact that lack of voice in decision-making had on the program.

References

Allan, Elizabeth. 2016. "Ethnographic Perspectives on Student-Centeredness in an Academic Library." *College & Undergraduate Libraries*: 111–29.

Allan, Elizabeth, and Dana Driscoll. 2014. "The Three-Fold Benefit of Reflective Writing: Improving Program Assessment, Student Learning, and Faculty Professional

Development." *Assessing Writing* 21:37–55. http://dx.doi.org/10.1016/j.asw.2014 .03.001.

Allan, Elizabeth, Dana Driscoll, David Hammontree, Marshall Kitchens, and Lori Ostergaard. 2015. "The Source of Our Ethos: Using Evidence-Based Practices to Affect a Program-Wide Shift from 'I Think' to 'We Know.'" *Composition Forum* 32. http://compositionforum.com/issue/32/oakland.php

Bowden, Darsie. 2015. "DePaul University's Major in Writing, Rhetoric, and Technical Writing." In *Writing Majors: Eighteen Program Profiles* Greg A. Giberson, Jim Nugent, and Lori Ostergaard, 11–21. Logan: Utah State UP.

Chong, Felicia, and Jim Nugent. 2015. "A New Major in the Shadow of the Past: The Professional Writing Track at Oakland University." *Programmatic Perspectives* 7 (2): 173–188.

Council of Writing Program Administrators. 1998. "Evaluating the Intellectual Work of Writing Administration." *WPA. Writing Program Administration* 22 (1–2): 85–104.

Driscoll, Dana, and Marshall Kitchens. 2014. "Engaging in Communities of Practice: Supplementing Community-Based Service Learning with Online Reflection in a Peer Tutoring Course." In *Community Engagement 2.0: Dialogues on the Future of the Civic in the Disrupted University*, ed. Scott L. Crabill and Dan Butin, 41–55. New York: Palgrave Macmillon. http://dx.doi.org/10.1057/9781137441065_4.

Giberson, Greg. 2015. "Afterword—Finding the Bigger Picture: What Have We Learned?" In *Writing Majors: Eighteen Program Profiles*, ed. Greg A. Giberson, Jim Nugent, and Lori Ostergaard. Logan: Utah State UP.

Giberson, Greg, and Tom Moriarty, eds. 2010. *What We Are Becoming: Developments in Undergraduate Writing Majors*. Logan: Utah State UP.

Giberson, Greg, Jim Nugent, and Lori Ostergaard, eds. 2015. *Writing Majors: Eighteen Program Profiles*. Logan: Utah State University Press.

Giberson, Greg, Lori Ostergaard, Jennifer Clary-Lemon, Jennifer Courtney, Kelly Kinney, and Brad Lucas. 2009. "A Changing Profession Changing a Discipline: Junior Faculty and the Undergraduate Major." *Composition Forum* 20. http://compositionforum.com /issue/20/changing-profession-discipline.php

Kitchens, Marshall. 2006. "Student Inquiry and New Media: Critical Media Literacy and Video Games." *Kairos: Rhetoric, Technology, Pedagogy* 10(2). http://kairos.technorhet oric.net/10.2/binder2.html?coverweb/kitchens/index.html.

Livesey, Matthew, and Julie Watts. 2015. "Embracing the Humanities: Expanding a Technical Communication Program at the University of Wisconsin-Stout." In *Writing Majors: Eighteen Program Profiles*, ed. Greg A. Giberson, Jim Nugent, and Lori Ostergaard, 85–87. Logan: Utah State University Press. http://dx.doi.org/10.7330 /9780874219722.c007.

Office of Institutional Research and Assessment. N.d.a. "Spotlight on OU: NSSE Data Suggests Mixed Relationship between First Year Retention Rates and the Number of Hours that Students Work." Oakland University. Rochester, MI. Accessed December 2009.

Office of Institutional Research and Assessment. N.d.b. "Student Profile: Fall 2013." *Student Information and Enrollment History*. Rochester, MI. Accessed April 14, 2014.

Ostergaard, Lori. 2015. "Working with Disciplinary Artifacts: A Class in Composition Studies for Writing Majors." *Composition Studies* 43 (2): 150–171.

Ostergaard, Lori, and Elizabeth Allan. Forthcoming. "From 'Falling Through the Cracks' to 'Pulling Through': Moving from a Traditional Remediation Model toward a Multi-layered Support Model for Basic Writing" *Journal of Basic Writing*.

Ostergaard, Lori, and Greg Giberson. 2010. "Unifying Program Goals: Developing and Implementing a Writing and Rhetoric Major at Oakland University." *Composition Forum* 22. Retrieved from http://compositionforum.com/issue/22/oakland.php

Ostergaard, Lori, Greg Giberson, and Jim Nugent. 2015. "Oakland University's Major in Writing and Rhetoric." In *Writing Majors: Eighteen Program Profiles,* ed. Greg Giberson, Jim Nugent, and Lori Ostergaard, 78–84. Logan: Utah State University Press. http://dx.doi.org/10.7330/9780874219722.c006.

3

PURDUE UNIVERSITY GRADUATE PROGRAM IN RHETORIC AND COMPOSITION

Patricia Sullivan

Institution Type: Public Research University
Location: West Lafayette, Indiana
Enrollment: 38,000+
Year program was founded: 1980
WPA reports to: Head, Department of English
Program funded by: Department of English
Description of students: Drawn from an international pool of applicants, eight to ten new students enter MA or PhD programs each year, and there usually are forty-five to fifty students on campus with half taking courses.

PROGRAM SNAPSHOT

Purdue's graduate program in rhetoric and composition dates to 1980 and has 277 graduates (195 PhD and 82 MA). Students take courses in rhetoric and composition (focusing on history, theory, pedagogy, and empirical inquiry), linguistics, a language, a secondary area (such as ESL, professional and technical writing, writing program administration, feminist theory, and more), and complete written and oral comprehensive exams as well as a dissertation. At the time of this writing, fifty-three students are enrolled in the MA or PhD and also are on campus.

WPA'S PROFILE

I came to Purdue in 1985 while still an ABD (Carnegie-Mellon University [CMU]) with an appointment to direct technical writing service courses. I was classically schooled in Renaissance Rhetoric by Father Walter Ong, SJ, and when I returned to school at CMU, the panoply of emerging technologies caught my attention as potentially game changing for writing's identity and rhetoric's scope of influence.

DOI: 10.7330/9781607326274.c003

When I relocated to Purdue (where I completed my dissertation and rose to the rank of professor by 1996), my fascinations followed along. At the time, Purdue enrolled twenty-four thousand undergraduates with many of them majoring in engineering. In addition to its domestic students, Purdue attracted many Asian graduate students through its world-renowned agricultural and engineering programs. I had come from a technology-rich environment, so I worked to build technology into Purdue's teaching infrastructure. By 1989, all technical writing classes were taught in computer classrooms and by the mid-1990s, all business writing service courses and professional writing major courses were in computer classrooms as well. Because my roles were to direct technical communication, build computer capabilities, and teach graduate methodology, I shaped my scholarship to fit that work. The director of business writing left for industry shortly after I arrived, so I also inherited the development of a professional writing undergraduate major that was approved in spring 1985 but needed specialized coursework. Much of the next decade was spent building infrastructures—in technology and instruction and for undergraduate education in professional writing—pursuing projects, and penning a methodology book (*Opening Spaces* with Jim Porter [Sullivan and Porter 1997]).

Since January of 1998, I have directed Purdue's graduate program in rhetoric and composition. In that role, I oversee hiring, admissions, course scheduling, advising, and graduate student professional development. I also am responsible for advocating for faculty promotions. As a consequence of my work with graduate education I have focused on institutional processes and critique in scholarly work since beginning this position, and have had to reeducate myself in modern rhetorical history in order to teach a needed seminar. I still work with emerging and morphing technologies including the reimagining of video for a digital age. Thus, my recent scholarly attention has included rhetorical history, mentoring, disciplinary knowledge making, institutional critique, video, and emerging methodologies.

PROGRAM CONCEPTION

The early 1980s ushered in many new graduate programs in rhetoric and composition, and one was founded at Purdue University in 1980. As the story goes, Ed Corbett was serving on a committee to review the Department of English (and was asked if additions were needed for the department's fairly new PhD), and without skipping a beat he replied:

"Why don't you consider adding Rhetoric and Composition? Janice Lauer could come and direct it." Whether the Corbett quote is accurate or apocryphal, Janice Lauer indeed was hired to build a program (she arrived in 1982 about the time of the first prelims) and she fashioned an approach that her "Dappled Discipline" article might hint that she would (see "Constructing a Doctoral Program" [Lauer 1994] for her narrative of Purdue's early years). Originating faculty members were Leonora Woodman, Jeanne Halpern, Tom Gaskell, Irwin Weiser, and Janice, who directed the program from 1982 through fall of 1997. Since January of 1998, I have been director.

Janice Lauer (1984) insisted that multidisciplinary inquiry required community and cooperation. So this graduate program has been structured to build and sustain community, while at Purdue and beyond. Practically this means that the work of its director revolves around the progression of students, from prospective, to orientation, then coursework, preparing for exams, dissertation development, job search, and ultimately the transition to alumni/colleagues. Each stage has activities, checkpoints, and reflection. Faculty assists in this community building work both directly and through their scholarly and teacherly work, as do senior graduate students.

As a program we have come to believe (1) current and future literacy challenges—both in teaching and in theorizing—require multidisciplinary approaches, and (2) we learn together, so cooperation is a key to any successes we score along the way. These core beliefs have led us to establish a foundation of multiple inquiries for all students that require them to understand theory, history, issue formation in composition, pedagogy, and empirical research. Then each student goes deep in one of those areas with the support of coursework in theory and public rhetorics, in professional and technical writing, in digital writing and rhetoric, or/and in writing program administration. These current secondary (some would say cognate) areas were instituted between 1992 and 2005 and are inspired by (and adapted from) "Protean Shapes in Literacy Events" by Shirley Brice Heath (1988). Technology is an addition to the literacy domains that Heath does not feature, as technology was not on her radar at that time. But, in keeping with her ideas, our other secondary areas focus particular attention on school, work, or community/publics. In this way students can emplace their dissertation work in a family of inquiries and work to push the field along together.

POPULATIONS SERVED

Like most graduate programs in Rhetoric and Composition, our students come from many places. We also aim to include students who were born in or live in Indiana. Currently, 10 percent of our students are Indiana natives. Through the teaching of faculty and those graduate students who enroll at Purdue we also serve many of the undergraduate students at Purdue (in fall 2014, 29,255) through first-year composition, other writing courses, tutoring at the Writing Lab (WL) or materials from the Purdue OWL (Online Writing Lab). In addition, the work of undergraduates from across the university is featured at a yearly showcase that is sponsored by ICaP (Introductory Composition at Purdue) and PW (Professional Writing); not only can undergrads show their work, but teachers can as well and there are prizes (including a dean's prize).

FUNDING

Because Purdue's graduate program is a concentration in the Department of English, it does not have a line item budget (programs that are independent do have line item allocations). This makes it very poor in some ways. There also are ways this program is well funded in that it doesn't have to devote resources to administrative operations; its students teaching first-year writing teach two courses per year; and its students are funded for two years of the MA and for five years of the PhD. But this reasonable funding is not available in all needed sectors of graduate education.

To address its lack of administrative oversight, this program has focused on development and has targeted speaker series', scholarships, and dissertation awards to gather some funds of its own. The David Hutton Memorial Speaker series hosts five speakers in the fall semesters of even years; one of these speakers is local and one is a distinguished alumnus chosen by Janice Lauer who has endowed this series in memory of her late husband. In conjunction with the Hutton lectures we also host a prestigious scholar for the James A. Berlin lecture that is indebted for support to Jim's friends. The Crouse scholarships range from $2,500 to $5,000 and are awarded competitively to students in professional writing and editing (with one doing a special project in the Writing Lab and two working as editorial assistants for *Peitho*); if there is a Scotland trip, fewer and smaller scholarships are awarded so that the students (undergraduate and graduate) traveling to Scotland can receive support. Two writing awards are funded through the department's Literary Awards: the Hugh McKee award for undergraduate technical and scientific writing and the Grace Smart award for the best graduate paper in rhetoric and composition. Finally, alumni volunteer to read for the award that they generously support, the Lauer Award for Excellence in Scholarship. Each year, the prospectuses of current students are gathered and sent to a committee of alumni for selection as the Lauer Award winner.

The greatest needs for this graduate program (and probably many others) are for improved student stipends and travel. While it is inexpensive to live in Lafayette, IN, the program awards five years of funding for the PhD, which swells to seven years if you start as an MA student (the same time as it averages for graduation from the program). Although extra teaching or other work is available, the amount of our yearly stipend does not compare well favorably to some other programs' stipends. Students who fit well with this program sometimes decline to attend primarily for monetary reasons (which is frustrating). Also, departmental travel funds are normally restricted to students who are ABD, and this also figures adversely in decisions to attend.

OPERATIONS

Technically the staff for our graduate program consists of faculty, professionals, senior graduate students, and an undergraduate work-study student. The director receives a course reduction (and for that does advising, course scheduling, admissions, etc.); most faculty teach one or two graduate courses per year and then have other administrative assignments/duties. Because of this intermingling, no faculty member in the writing area is hired who cannot contribute to the graduate program. Currently, out of the nine faculty who regularly teach graduate courses, three faculty members have no assigned administrative roles. Also, faculty members in English education, second language studies/ESL, women's studies, and theory and cultural studies serve on dissertation committees and/or teach courses our students take. Three of the departmental secretaries spend part of their time doing for the graduate program, as does the assistant director of rhetoric and composition (who is a senior graduate student). In addition, there is a fulltime assistant director for ICaP, a secretary, five mentors for new teachers, two technology mentors to introduce both new and standard uses of technology for teaching writing, and a graduate student who does administration. For the Writing Lab, there is a faculty director, two fulltime professional staff (one traditional and one specializing in ESL and conversation), twenty graduate tutors, and a variable number of undergraduate peer tutors.

Many of the faculty have major undergraduate responsibilities. In 2014–15, Jenny Bay directed first-year composition, Michael Salvo

directed professional writing, Rick Johnson-Sheehan was acting director of the Writing Lab (Linda Bergmann had recently died and we were
searching for her successor), and Samantha Blackmon was developing
a video gaming minor. Harry Denny has joined the faculty in 2015 as
Writing Lab director and Krista Ratcliffe as department head. In addition, Jenny, Michael, and Sam monitor teaching technologies and
work to keep them up-to-date and correctly integrated with instruction
which carries on a tradition of innovating teaching with technology.
Because Purdue has a history of formally mentoring new teachers of
undergraduate courses, many of our faculty participate in preparing
future teachers.

Two types of work are needed to tend to graduate programs, recurring and ad hoc; further, some of the recurring work is predictable, and
other ad hoc work, not so much.

Each month there are recurring tasks that need to be addressed:
course planning happens in November and December; course scheduling in January and late August; orientation happens in August; admissions run from January to April; advising/course selection for new
students in late April; overseeing plans of studies and dissertation procedures meetings in September and October; student check-in and its
reports in May and June; mock interviews in December; reunion planning in February and March; coordinating of Lauer award in February;
job group starting in August; Smart award and Crouse scholarship judg-
ing in March. The director also serves on the departmental graduate
committee and advocate for the program's interests there, on the primary committee, and with the department head.

Ad hoc work includes working nationally with the Doctoral Consortium
(see Phelps and Ackerman [2010] to appreciate how important their
work is), answering requests for information (both locally and nationally), interfacing with prospective students, updating the program website and Facebook page, writing recommendations, proposing grants,
dealing with International Review Board (IRB) problems, and maintaining communication with alumni.

The assistant director plans the welcome picnic, helps out with ad
hoc tasks, works to stay ahead of resource room, directs the tasks of a
work-study helper, and helps with online communication. When the
Hutton Series is held (biennially in fall semesters), the assistant director helps with arrangements and oversees a modest reception that gives
students a chance to ask further questions of speakers. In years without
a lecture series the assistant director helps with a project that expands
the program; in 2015–16, Amelia Chesley and I are collaborating with

the Purdue Libraries to build an institutional repository for our graduate program research.

ASSESSMENT

Recently, the Doctoral Consortium of programs in rhetoric and composition[1] has stressed that every graduate program needs to assess
its students' progress/achievement regularly, though they have also
emphasized that the assessment needs to be driven by each program's
circumstances. Because our program has long been structured around
the students' journeys through this program, Purdue approaches assessment through several moves: early guidance, instruction in writing, and
systematic feedback. Assessment helps us keep students on track to move
through the program in five years (the amount funded). Purdue uses
a document that articulates how most students move through the program; it seeds writing practice for the preliminary exam into required
courses; and it provides written responses for PhD students' prelims that
aim to kick-start dissertation work. I also monitor grades each semester in order to be certain each student is thriving. In response to the
Consortium's urging for more formal assessment, I have instituted a
yearly student "check in" for all those who are in their second year or
later. At the end of the spring semester, each student submits answers
to six questions (new teaching or appointments for this year; activities on behalf of campus; conference presentations; articles submitted,
revised, or accepted; awards; plans for next year). After reviewing their
transcripts, I examine each document and write a response that con-
gratulates students on their accomplishments and suggests other things
they might do in the next year. To encourage the group, I also take the
answers to the questions and arrange them into a set of "wordles," so we
can be proud of what everyone is doing.

To establish a more general picture of the program, I also keep
records about admissions, course enrollments, attrition, time-to-degree,
and placement. I mention these records because they are the ones a university is likely to request of a graduate program.

MARKETING/PR

Marketing for most graduate programs aims to attract quality students.
This program's efforts are handled through pull moves (see Hagel,
Brown, and Davison's [2010] *Power of Pull*) rather than by pushing pro-
motional material. In part this approach was first dictated by a lack of

funds to market the program. Until the 1990s we had money to mail promotional flyers and alumni newsletters, but gradually the funds for mailing and then printing dried up. So, as quickly as we came to understand the Internet, we put it to use as a replacement for the printed materials we once produced and mailed. Beyond blanketing sites with materials, some graduate programs promote their programs through other routes. Some have fellowships under their control and others have monies set aside to fund a weekend to bring admitted students to campus. While our new students have been successful in winning university contests for fellowships for incoming PhDs (usually two/year), this program does not control any fellowships. Nor can it pay for campus visits. So some commonly used marketing strategies are unavailable to Purdue.

How do we pull interest and what do we do with it? Our website is a primary source of initial information for prospective students. Prospective students are invited to identify themselves, and Emily Legg (the assistant director) and I answer their initial questions, seek to understand their interests, and arrange for email exchanges for them with appropriate students and faculty. Individualized but respectful response is a key to our approach. We understand prospective applicants are making an important life decision and that fit is important to graduate study (particularly at the PhD level). So we work to be sure good students attend graduate school (e.g., we refer people who have little knowledge about programs to the Grad Consortium's list of schools in addition to providing information about Purdue), and we do not presume every good student should attend Purdue.

Secondary sources of marketing are our reunion at CCCCs each year, to which we invite newly admitted students attending that conference, and the OWL/WL that attracts many students to us as well. We also work to make visits to campus special (and this is one of the assistant director's main duties), by working out a schedule that includes meetings with faculty, attending classes (a grad seminar and a first-year writing course), lunching with grad students, touring the Writing Lab, and if possible providing a host for lodging. These personalized visits help prospective students decide (or confirm) the fit.

TECHNOLOGY

Technology is integral to this program's (and many others') conception of graduate work in both academic and work-a-day ways. We see technology as both infrastructural for teaching and a pervasive force for rhetoric to study. In cases where faculty positions are limited, a technology infrastructure can minimize distances through online conferencing, and can ease barriers to communication (though not erase it, as our love of writing groups attest).

Through the efforts of Professional Writing and ICaP at Purdue, the graduate program and its instructors have access to facilities (not only computer classrooms as needed but also a research lab), servers (for the OWL, for courses, and for discussion lists and redundant document storage), and support for both research and teaching (technology mentors for new teachers and technical support for infrastructure). Further, the Purdue Libraries, who are also committed to digital solutions, make digital copies of available books and scholarly databases accessible while on or off campus. While this work often is unglamorous, it is necessary for the support of graduate programs. It also inspires students to innovate with technology (e.g., Cody Reimer and Adam Strantz started and run the RhetComp subReddit to promote social media discussion, while Caitlan Spronk follows the traditions of OWL webmasters to program portable systems for key writing center recordkeeping, and Liz Lane is building a national site for CCCC to use in promoting local activism in the conference city) and to know that infrastructural improvements are grounded in philosophies of user experience.

ROLE OF RESEARCH

The task of advisors and the graduate director is to be sure that all students have opportunities to grow their interests and capabilities, through both coursework and participation in other projects. This means that students' developing interests need to be present in programmatic decisions related to course planning and to choice of participants, and the assessment plan our program has enacted improves our program's knowledge of where students' thinking/interests lie.

In the humanities, scholars enacting research set the dominant research agendas. Thus, in most graduate programs, faculty interests drive the research that swirls through the programs, and they involve students in traditional ways (and less traditional ones). Purdue is no different.

As faculty work on their scholarship, their work may involve graduate students in serendipitous ways. It may inspire a seminar such as the Burke seminar that Thomas Rickert (2013) taught that put Kenneth Burke into conversation with Martin Heidegger, served to ground a chapter in *Ambient Rhetoric,* and became an important part of some dissertation work. It may lead to travel and further research as Michael

Salvo's investigation of how technology uses encouraged postindustrial towns to reimagine work. It drew him to Scotland and through the research he started summer study abroad trips for professional writing students. Such serendipity also may result from study of curriculum as it did when Rick Johnson-Sheehan was named a fellow at the university's Research Park with a mandate to develop curriculum for a medical humanities MA, and already an undergraduate course in Writing for Health and Human Science has been launched and taught by advanced graduate students.

They also might plan projects, or join projects, that are intended to be cooperative and to channel many people's research energies. Samantha Blackmon, for example, involves graduate and undergraduate women gamers in her regular "Not Your Mama's Gamer" (Blackmon 2014) podcasts that discuss industry issues, game play, new games, new books, and so on. This award-wining series involves students in Sam's gaming initiative but also teaches them how alternative media can help them gain critical voice in other areas too. Jenny Bay, to offer another example, is ethnographically studying a local food pantry as she works with a number of graduate (and earlier undergraduate) students to run survey and interview projects that help this community partner learn more about itself and food insecurity.

Research projects may also derive from professional work as does work on tags and disciplinary knowledge making that is happening through the work that Jenny Bay and I are doing with the graduate students who are working with us to edit *Peitho* (the *Journal of the Coalition of Women Scholars for Research in the History of Rhetoric and Composition*).

We also start projects through our classes, as we did in Institutional Rhetoric. In that class, students worked to plan a partnership between the Writing Lab and the Purdue Libraries. That work prepared the way for our current initiative to store interim scholarship on rhetorical topics and pedagogical research in the Purdue Libraries' institutional repository (e-Pubs). Students too may instigate projects that faculty are invited into, as with the Berlin Project. In that project, eight of our students, under Don Unger's leadership, studied the cultural studies pedagogy Jim Berlin left in the archives, and they involved me to run focus groups. Don, Jon Wallin, and Kyle Vealey began interviewing Jim Berlin's former students, and as the project has unfolded the group has generated voluminous data from students, teachers, former graduate instructors, and archives; it also has attracted a small grant for expenses.

PEDAGOGICAL AND/OR ADMINISTRATIVE HIGHLIGHTS

We provide rich and diverse teaching and other institutional work to help theory and teaching percolate together into praxis, a departmental tradition that tracks back into the 1950s. These cominglings draw on Donald Schön's (1983) study of professionals' "reflection in action," an advanced professional skill that accompanies from analytic thought during action. So we too use diverse professional activities as a way to prepare for a life of reflection in action. Complementing coursework are teaching opportunities in many writing courses (first-year composition—with ten syllabus approaches and learning communities; community engagement composition; advanced composition; business writing; technical writing; healthcare writing), and in courses for the professional writing major. Graduate students may also tutor or do WAC outreach in the Writing Lab, and they also may teach for other units including second language studies' writing courses. Senior students also have opportunities to participate in the administration of the writing program, the professional writing major, the Writing Lab, the Online Writing Lab, and the graduate program.

We also actively pursue initiatives that expand our areas of disciplinary and public concern. Recent undergraduate projects have led to instituting "Writing for Health and Human Sciences," building hybrid summer experiential communication course that supports interns, offering a mobile technology class for the professional writing major, and developing a community engagement arm for composition. Curriculum-wise, we also are building a video gaming minor in cooperation with Computer Graphics Technology, who has a major in this area. Administration-wise, we are developing assessment tools for composition programs and collaborating with the Purdue Libraries to build an online repository starting with Writing Lab conference presentations.

We seek innovation and cross-level connections as we create new curricula. The proposed MA in medical humanities has ties to first-year (the Cancer Culture Community) and advanced writing (Writing for Health and Human Sciences) courses that already are underway, and extends their work through examination of ethics and ethos. The planned undergraduate minor in gaming has courses already being taught at the undergraduate level, including "Stories in Games," but is supported by a graduate course on the "History of Technology and Games." Further, community engagement redesign for honors-level first-year composition is supported by a graduate course on community.

Our innovations have to be thrifty, and one that is proving to be so is the Writing Lab e-Pubs Project. In many sectors of higher education, writing centers are being de-professionalized (and moved to student services), so we continuously seek ways to showcase the research being done in our Writing Lab. A new collaboration with the Libraries offers promise here. Purdue, like many other institutions, is developing a digital repository for the work done at Purdue but not formally published—librarians call it "grey literature." So the WL is working with the Libraries to highlight the research that writing center tutors, researchers, and staff conduct. One benefit we seek is to convince the public that research is both needed and produced in writing centers. This research is needed to support writing centers as research units (and supports arguments for keeping writing labs associated with academic units).

PRIMARY DOCUMENT (at **writingprogramarchitecture.com**)

As a model of an important primary document, I have included in the online companion the most recent copy of the student check-in distributed to the faculty in June 2015. This check-in details what secondary areas the students are completing and thus may predict some course needs. Covering one year, it also reveals how the students talk about their teaching and other appointments, work they do on behalf of the campus, conference presentations, articles in some stage of completion, awards they have received, and their plans for the next year. This document accompanies the individual feedback given to each student and is drawn from their submissions (a Google form or a highlighted CV), their transcripts, and any information shared with me by faculty. It may seem light hearted, but students have reported it also encourages them that everyone is hard at work and that we care about their success.

WPA'S VOICE

I can offer some advice about directing graduate programs:

Value Rank

Being/becoming a full professor undergirds a more stable graduate program. Those who administer graduate programs often stumble into the work. At a time when assistant professors are forging new administrative paths for writing programs (see Charlton et al.'s [2011] *GenAdmin*), graduate programs are more vulnerable than other programs because they often are more invisible (they may lack budgets, institutional stability, or controls over key resources), and so they depend more on the status of the director. Janice Lauer told me that her successor needed to be a full professor. I did not fully grasp why until bullets flew, and I had to learn how to use institutional rank to protect my program.

Try to Get It in Writing, Even if It's Email

While sounding defensive, this move can be the bedrock of stability for a graduate program.

Keep Close Track of Procedures and Precedents

Knowing the ways that procedures are handled and key forms are used is vital to program work. So I never pass up the chance to revise a form.

Universities prize fairness, and this value leads them to accept precedent as trumping evidence. This means that arguments can usually be won (or tabled) by citing precedents.

Expect the Best of Meetings, but Be Prepared

Most meetings can be productive, so I always attend with the expectation of cooperation and productive exchange. But I also prepare by examining agendas, taking notes on what precedents may need to be cited, and bringing data that may be needed.

Your Priorities May not Match Your Institution's

Keeping this in mind can limit stumbles such as one that happened to me when my assistant's appointment was reduced because of the recession. I declared that reducing support would mean we could no longer publish/mail a newsletter (leading to diminished alumni donations). The response was, "Ok." I had confused something I considered vital with an institutional priority, and thus I did not create the leverage I sought.

Put Aside Time to Free Plan

I keep a morning open to read about higher education and muse on how they might one day impact this graduate program (or the lives of alumni). I also think about emerging projects in order to build in activities for other levels so that I can prioritize projects in terms of which will contribute the most to graduate education. I sometimes call people during this time to gain their perspectives and enrich my own. This free planning makes the job intellectually stimulating.

Find the Part of the Program that Sustains You, and Never Short It

Participating in the intellectual growth of graduate students sustains me. When I find myself being drawn into waves of meetings or petty dramas, I step back and refocus on students. My job is to direct a program, but my calling is to help the program's students investigate problems that stimulate their passions. While much of the work of directing a graduate program is *work*, some is rewarding, and you need to focus on what sustains you. If you are fulfilled, less pleasant tasks that are needed to keep the program functioning are easier to complete.

Note

1. The Consortium maintains a website that assists prospective graduate students in locating programs. It also meets each year at CCCC and keeps in touch at other times through a discussion group.

References

Blackmon, Samantha. *Not Your Mama's Gamer* (blog), October 19, 2014. http://www.nymgamer.com/.

Charlton, Colin, Jonikka Charlton, Tarez S. Graban, Kathleen Ryan, and Amy F. Stolley. 2011. *GenAdmin: Theorizing WPA Identities in the Twenty-First Century*. Anderson, SC: Parlor Press.

Hagel, I. I. I. John, John Seely Brown, and Lang Davison. 2010. *The Power of Pull: How Small Moves, Smartly Made, Can Set Big Things in Motion*. New York: Basic Books.

Heath, Shirley Brice. 1988. "Protean Shapes in Literacy Events: Ever-Shifting Oral and Literate Traditions." In *Perspectives on Literacy*, ed. Eugene R. Kintgen, Barry M. Kroll, and Mike Rose, 348–370. Carbondale, IL: SIU Press.

Lauer, Janice M. 1984. "Composition Studies: A Dappled Discipline." *Rhetoric Review* 3 (1): 20–29. http://dx.doi.org/10.1080/07350198409359074.

Lauer, Janice M. 1994. "Constructing a Doctoral Program in Rhetoric and Composition." *Rhetoric Review* 12 (2): 392–397. http://dx.doi.org/10.1080/07350199409389044.

Phelps, Louise W., and John M. Ackerman. 2010. "Making the Case for Disciplinarity in Rhetoric, Composition, and Writing Studies: The Visibility Project." *College Composition and Communication* 62 (1): 180–215.

Rickert, Thomas. 2013. *Ambient Rhetoric: The Attunements of Rhetorical Being*. Pittsburgh: University of Pittsburgh Press.

Schön, Donald. 1983. *Reflective Practitioner: How Professionals Think in Action*. New York: Basic Books.

Sullivan, Patricia, and James E. Porter. 1997. *Opening Spaces: Writing Technologies and Critical Research Practices*. Greenwich, CT: Ablex.

4

ROWAN UNIVERSITY MAJOR IN WRITING ARTS

Sanford Tweedie

Institution Type: Public State University
Location: Glassboro, New Jersey
Enrollment: 17,000
Year program was founded: 1999
WPA reports to: Dean, College of Communication and Creative Arts
Program funded by: Division of Academic Affairs
Description of students: Accompanying the university's tremendous growth over the past few years, our student profile is becoming more racially diverse, international, and higher scoring, and we are attracting more out-of-area and out-of-state students.

PROGRAM SNAPSHOT

Housed within the six-department College of Communication and Creative Arts, the Department of Writing Arts offers a major with concentrations in creative writing, new media writing and publishing, and technical and professional writing. We also offer two minors, two sequences in majors from other colleges, a master of arts, and an accelerated 4+1 BA/MA (four years BA and one year MA). The department houses the First-Year Writing Program, and the Rowan Writing Center is affiliated with the department.

WPA's Profile

I obtained my PhD in English with a specialization in rhetoric and composition from the University of Wisconsin-Milwaukee in the mid-1990s. Having been in five English departments as a student and/or instructor, I had always perceived writing against the backdrop of literature. Being hired into Rowan's Department of Communications in 1994 moved me into an environment where curriculum and faculty focused on video,

DOI: 10.7330/9781607326274.c004

radio, television, and public speaking, in addition to all kinds of writing: public relations, advertising, journalism, creative, and academic. This represented a shift from what Robert Scholes describes as valuing writing via the consumption of texts (literary interpretation) to valuing their production. Scholes (1985) believes "as might be expected in a society like ours, we privilege consumption over production" (8). With my interest in composition studies, I immediately felt at home within this milieu that emphasized creation over interpretation.

The College Writing Program I joined at Rowan offered only the required first-year writing sequence and courses in business writing and advanced expository writing. From prior to my arrival until 2007, we had one WPA, Janice Rowan, who coordinated the College Writing Program and then served as the department's founding chair. Soon after we began offering our major and master's in 1999, Janice felt the chair's job had become too much for one person. She cleaved off three of her nine hours of reassigned time and created the position of first-year writing coordinator, asking me to serve in that capacity. In 2001, tenured and returning from a sabbatical that took me abroad, I inaugurated and defined the first-year writing coordinator position, creating the job as I went along and relying on Janice for mentorship and guidance, as I had had no graduate school training or experience in WPA work. After serving in this role for three years and with multiple obligations chairing senate and university-wide committees, I resigned my coordinator position when my term ended in 2004. By 2008, our major had grown to more than 350 students, necessitating more direct stewardship of that program. The position of undergraduate programs coordinator was created, and the department elected me to serve in this capacity from 2008 to 2013. Again, I shaped the position as I went along, determining what the priorities were and how they might be best achieved. In 2013, I was elected department chair and have served in that capacity since then. I ran with a five-goal platform:

- maximize communication
- act as a strong internal advocate for the department and its members
- act as a strong external advocate for the department and its members
- act as a strong advocate for students (potential, current, alumni)
- follow through on completion of already started initiatives

While I feel I have made progress in these areas, I spend the majority of time on other things: scheduling and staffing over two hundred sections each semester, resolving facilities issues, and dealing with and solving problems that often don't feel much like advocacy. Yet, as with the other positions, I have redefined the role to better align with department needs.

PROGRAM CONCEPTION

Implicit within the previous discussion is that my own changing situation parallels Writing Arts' shifting role—and department name—over the past two decades. From that first-year College Writing Program offering a handful of writing courses, we have grown into a department, that, in addition to teaching nearly every one of our freshmen at least twice a year, enrolls over four hundred undergraduates in several majors, minors, and other programs, and that offers an MA and graduate certificates to two dozen more students. Recent growth has been unprecedented. In fall 2015, the First-Year Writing Program filled 3,300 seats compared to 2,250 two falls prior, a 47 percent increase. The faculty has seen a parallel growth, swelling from 88 to 108.

When I arrived in 1994, Rowan was in the midst of reimagining itself thanks to the largess of industrialist Henry Rowan (no relation to Janice Rowan above), who two years prior had donated $100 million, at that time the largest single gift to a public institution. In 1996, the Department of Communications became the School of Communication consisting of five separate departments: College Writing, Communication Studies, Professional Writing (an umbrella term for Journalism and Creative Writing), Public Relations/Advertising, and Radio/TV/Film. In 1997, the state of New Jersey awarded university status to Rowan, and the School became a College of Communication. Graduates were awarded a BA in communication with a specialization from one of the departments.

Our undergraduate major began in 1999 when we assumed a group of majors who no longer fit into one of the specialization's curricular plans. Starting with fewer than thirty students and a set of non-cohesive course offerings, we revamped this into a writing-focused curriculum that appealed to more students. We also partnered with the College of Education to align our offerings with a state-mandated, subject-matter major for those pursuing early childhood or elementary education. Approximately half of our Writing Arts students are such dual majors. That same year, we created a parallel set of graduate courses and began offering an MA in writing with tracks in creative writing, composition and rhetoric, and journalism. With this expanded focus, the College Writing name no longer fit, and in 2001 we became the Department of Composition and Rhetoric. This nomenclature turned out to be short lived.

In 2004, the department was awarded a Certificate of Excellence by the Conference on College Composition and Communication during the award's inaugural year. More impactful was three creative writing faculty moving over from professional writing as Journalism became its own department. Our department welcomed this, as we already emphasized creative writing in both our undergraduate and graduate programs. We also changed our name to Writing Arts to reflect the department we had become.

In 2005, each specialization within the college became a separate bachelor's degree, a step that allowed us to become an even more independent program. With our own BA, we had the opportunity to further tailor our degree to meet the needs of Writing Arts majors. This led us to form the Discipline Committee, which met frequently over two years. As a result, in 2007 we introduced the core values into the major, added two required bookend courses—Introduction to Writing Arts and Portfolio Seminar—and overhauled the related electives banks. We also added a five-year BA/MA, a minor, and a Writing Arts sequence within a new liberal studies: humanities/social sciences major. Capping off this busy year, we opened the Writing Center, whose director is a member of our department.

In 2013, the Art Department was added to what was renamed the College of Communication and Creative Arts, a moniker that makes our Writing Arts choice a decade earlier seem prescient. And yet that Writing Arts name—and the perceptions that accompany our being an independent writing program—remains one of our greatest challenges. Too frequently, I find myself clarifying who we are and what we do for all kinds of people: administrators, staff, faculty, and sometimes even our own students. This discussion is pursued further in the "Marketing/PR" section.

POPULATION SERVED

Because our offerings range from an associated Intensive English Language program to a master's degree, the Department of Writing Arts serves the range of students who attend Rowan University. In addition to the First-Year Writing Program that includes associations with the College of Engineering, the Honors Program, and other departments, our undergraduate programs include:

- a writing arts major (with more than 210 students, half of whom are pursuing dual majors in education)
- two minors, one in writing arts and one in creative writing (each serving two dozen students)
- a sequence equivalent to a minor within the liberal studies: humanities/social science major (with more than 180 students)
- a twelve-credit focus within the literacy studies major that is targeted to elementary and early childhood educators (currently serving seventy-five majors but expecting immense growth in the near future)

These undergraduate, non-first-year-writing programs fill 1,500 seats per year. Graduates in the major average more than one hundred per year due to the large number of community college transfers who enter as juniors.

In addition to these formal programs, students can, for some majors, fulfill the university's writing intensive requirement with our courses. For instance, we offer Writing as Mangers, which serves students in the management major. Others meet the writing intensive requirement via Writer's Mind or Writing for the Workplace. We also draw students from other majors out of interest in the subject matter, especially in creative writing courses.

FUNDING

With salary and non-salary expenses, our department constitutes a nearly $3 million enterprise. While seemingly a large amount of money, almost 99 percent of this goes to salaries, something over which I have no control or oversight. And while Writing Arts accounts for 3 percent of the Division of Academic Affairs' annual expenses, we comprise over 5 percent of Rowan's total student enrollments. We are an academic bargain that supports more expensive programs and other university expenses.

Of our $32,000 total non-salary operating budget, over a third is dedicated to supplies and printing and another third to telephones, leaving the rest for supporting our graduate literary magazine, advertising, recruitment, and other smaller costs. We supplement this budget with revenues earned through graduate and summer programs. All graduate courses at Rowan are administered through our Division of Global Learning and Partnerships. These programs must be self-sustaining, and revenues are distributed to multiple constituencies: general fund, Provost's Office, Dean's Office, and the participating department. For Writing Arts, these revenues, along with summer offerings, bring in an additional $20,000–$30,000 per year, which the department can spend at its discretion.

We originally intended to use these revenues to augment the operating budget for items we might not otherwise be able to fund. However, an increasing portion is spent on items that other programs may fund or have funded differently. For example, we use the shared revenues to provide release time that coordinators would not otherwise receive or to pay them for summer work. We have given small stipends to Portfolio Seminar readers when they aren't under contract during the summer. More in line with our original intent, we provide funding for faculty projects through proposals made to the department revenue sharing committee. These include providing travel assistance, hiring undergraduates to create videos about the department, hiring students to assist with professor's research projects, and bringing speakers to campus. While this funding has been a great benefit to the department, the money is totally dependent on graduate and summer enrollments and ever-fluctuating accounting and distribution methods, and so lacks predictability from year to year.

Finally, I have undertaken to create alliances with University Advancement as I see this as a realistic possibility for department monies and increasing department awareness. I talk with my fundraising contact several times a semester to discuss ideas concerning potential donors, interested alumni, and faculty involvement. I give her ideas for donations—scholarships, travel funding for undergraduates, even a writer's house—which she can then pitch. In turn, she has taught me how to think about ways to increase alumni involvement, such as having them serve as contest judges, and how to promote department awareness that might augment her fundraising efforts. While the process can be lengthy and is ongoing, we have received an endowed graduate student scholarship and increased contributions from alumni.

OPERATIONS

The Department of Writing Arts started fall 2015 with 108 faculty in the department: 15 full-time tenure track, 30 ¾-time instructors, 56 adjuncts instructors who can teach up to two courses per semester, and 7 graduate instructors filling this newly created position. Since we are one of the university's largest departments and because we are spread across two buildings, we have two full-time administrative assistants.

Rowan is a unionized university. This means chairs remain part of the faculty. The only people I officially supervise are the secretaries. All other decisions—especially those concerning staffing and scheduling—are actually recommendations to the Dean's Office that they then have the power to enact, modify, or reject.

I receive two courses of reassigned time per semester, as do all chairs at the university. I have thus far been able to maintain an adjusted load award for scholarly and creative activity that gives me another course release. Currently, I teach one course, Introduction to Writing Arts, which allows me to maintain a connection to our majors.

The day-to-day work of the department is carried out by the department leadership secretarial support staff. The former includes the chair, the graduate, undergraduate, creative writing, and first-year writing coordinators, and the Writing Center director. This group, along with a ¾-time faculty representative, meets monthly to plan and execute department initiatives. I have contact with the first-year writing coordinator on a daily basis to address student issues and curricular and staffing needs. I meet with the undergraduate coordinator and graduate coordinator (who is currently also the creative writing coordinator) pretty much weekly to discuss similar situations. As the Writing Center is housed in the university's library and the budget comes directly from the Provost's Office, the director is more independent, but she provides me regular updates and reports, and we confer as needed. Our secretaries are, as in most places, the lifeblood of the department. Communication with them is vital and constant, whether in person or over email.

There are times when we have waves of work, especially near the beginning of the semester and more specifically fall semester. Last summer, for instance, we hired thirty new adjunct faculty and another dozen shifted from adjunct to ¾-time positions, requiring coordination of office space, phones, and computers, among other things. At the beginning of the semester, an overwhelming number of students need assistance in some way or another as they try to change classes, get overrides, challenge placement, and seek advising. A somewhat smaller wave hits at the end of semester, especially with student concerns about instructors and the need to accomplish things that have been put off during the semester. As chair, I also meet a completely different set of administrative deadlines, such as for scheduling, annual and semi-annual reporting, and hiring for both full- and part-time positions. Operating under the various calendars and with over a hundred faculty means that downtime in this position is limited, even during summer.

Long-term planning is accomplished via a combination of department meetings, May and August retreats, coordinator meetings I hold prior to department meetings and the department meetings themselves, meetings coordinators holds with interested faculty, and reviews such as the WPA self-study and assessment.

ASSESSMENT

Our Office of Analytics, Systems, and Applications (ASA) mandates that all programs submit an annual assessment report. Our challenge is not so much how to conduct assessment or where to focus it, but how to complete all the assessment we are being asked to do in our multiple programs: first-year writing, the major, the liberal studies option in Writing Arts, and our master's degree.

ASA requires that the annual report be presented in table form with additional narrative information. The columnar headings identify programmatic goals (we think of this in terms of what a student will be able to do five years after graduation); student learning goals and corresponding outcomes within each programmatic goal; the targeted level of quality we wish to obtain in the previous category; the assessment tools we use to measure that quality; our interpretation of how we met the targeted goal using a three-point scale; and proposed improvements based on all this.

While the format is burdensome, conducting assessment forces us to continually examine the effectiveness of our programs. Each year, we identify areas to focus our efforts. For the major, in odd numbered years we use the portfolio analysis statements that students create as part of Portfolio Seminar to assess how well they are meeting our core values. We choose three of the nine values to assess and, using random samples, ask a group of instructors to blind read these analysis statements to determine how well students are meeting our values. This has resulted in changes to the curriculum, including alterations to the core values themselves and to the supporting materials we provide students to help them understand these values. We have also created new courses as a result, most recently the one-credit Professions in Writing Arts: Post-Graduate Options, which gives students the opportunity to learn about available careers and graduate school. The effectiveness of this course has subsequently been assessed and found to be a worthwhile curricular addition.

In even numbered years, we use different means to complete the report. These have included using a student's survey of alumni and their satisfaction with the program and our own WPA self-study. Conducting a self-study requires that a program take an in-depth look at who it is and what it wants to become. Consultant-evaluators Barbara Cambridge and John Schilb provided us valuable critiques and ideas for moving forward. We have placed their recommendations into a chart with headings: *Recommendation, Response Action, Who is Responsible, When it Will be Completed, Notes, Status.* This is updated regularly and shared with the department so they can see where we have made and need to make progress. We know from the self-study that we also need to alter when we assess student progress to be developmental and not just terminal. Thus, our assessment is also teaching us how to better assess.

Outside formal and required assessment avenues, we employ empirical data, when available, to make decisions about numbers and types of curricular offerings and are currently using it to consider changes to the liberal studies option in the Writing Arts requirements. We also have had the instructors of a particular course meet to align goals and curriculum. While we are careful to retain academic freedom in how instructors can present their subject matter, this activity has allowed us to realign curriculum through revised course descriptions and goals.

MARKETING/PR

This is perhaps the greatest challenge we face. Since we are the only department in the country with the name Writing Arts, we have to put forth effort to make students aware of our existence, define who we are, and convince them that we are attractive to them. Of our current 200-plus majors, typically ten to fourteen enter as freshmen writing arts majors in fall. The rest arrive via internal or external transfers. The former come from other programs, such as English, since they know English via the high school structure that conflates literature and writing. Often our majors are early childhood or elementary education dual majors who don't realize that the state requires they complete a second major. They become attracted to writing arts after they arrive on campus because they seek a program that emphasizes relevant classroom skills. The external transfers come to us, in part, because they can graduate from our thirty-four-credit major in a timely manner.

While we will continue to serve these students, one of my main goals as chair is to transform writing arts into a destination major. I want to capitalize on our relative uniqueness as an independent writing program and our strong, flexible major to convince students that we are an attractive home for them *as freshmen*. Thus, I have implemented a set of initiatives that are, to borrow advertising terminology, marketing our department and increasing brand awareness.

In response to a 2013 WPA self-study and evaluator-consultant site visit, we created a vision to accompany our mission. Using epigrammatic vision statements as our model, we came up with the following:

MAKING WRITING VISIBLE

MAKING WRITERS MATTER

ROWAN WRITING ARTS

This vision, which also serves as a motto, gives us an internal and external touchstone we return to again and again when talking among ourselves, speaking with others on and off campus, and showcasing the department to the outside world. It suggests multiple levels of interpretation. We want to see writing through its multiple possibilities and actualities. We want to see the completed and the in-progress, the in-class and the out-of-class, the writing done by everyone and not just those considered Writers. We want writing to become demythologized. We want to demonstrate and have students show metacognitive awareness of their writing. We want to celebrate our own students' writing while they're with us. And we want our graduates, those who want to write for a living, have their writing become more visible. We want to make visible all writers—faculty, students, those we bring in to speak—through the various means available to us: our curriculum, our commitment to teaching, our dedication to continually assessing, reflecting on and altering our program to make it stronger. And as the department strives to make writing visible, we also make the creators of those texts—the writers—matter in everything we do. As a vision statement, I believe this can serve us for a long time.

My other major initiative is the *Write Rowan, Right Now!* Literary Writing Scholarship. With support procured from the Division of Strategic Enrollment Management, we offer incoming freshmen writing arts majors the opportunity to win scholarships of $20,000, $10,000, and $5,000 based on a portfolio of writing. These are given in addition to any other scholarship money they receive. We have teamed with Admissions to provide information about the scholarship to any student who expresses an interest in writing via the various web portals used to recruit high school students.

We believe the benefits of these outreach efforts to be many. First, we expect to attract more and stronger students to the program. We are already seeing results. The first class to receive the scholarship money nearly doubled the incoming class from twelve to twenty-two, had higher test scores, and included five Honors students. Second, these efforts put the Writing Arts name in front of people and so more will become aware of our program and offerings. We use press releases and directed emails/mailings to high school curriculum directors concerning the scholarship contest to increase exposure of our department within New Jersey and the Delaware Valley region. Third, we hope that as teachers become more aware of our programs they will not only promote us to their students interested in writing but consider the MA for their own professional and personal benefits.

We have also implemented other changes to attract students. We were recently selected as one of seven majors across the university to participate in a new initiative called *Degree in 3—Summers Free*. Students in this accelerated program live on campus and take courses during the summers following their first and second years that allow them to graduate in May of their third year. While students in our major could always accomplish this due to our multiple summer offerings, this program touts that it saves $25,000 on college costs and carves out an additional year of earnings potential.

A second minor change concerns the accelerated BA/MA. Previously only available to juniors, entering freshmen may now apply to and begin in the program. While we don't expect this to attract large numbers of students, it allows serious writers to plan their undergraduate and graduate paths while saving time and money. In the future, a 3+1 program combining this and the *Degree in 3—Summers Free* program may also occur.

Along with these initiatives, I have attempted to strengthen marketing possibilities already at our disposal. Rowan completely redesigned its website recently. When my colleagues complain they don't like the new look, I remind them, "It's not directed at you; it's for prospective students." The website no longer requires a digital pickax to chisel out information; it is a marketing hammer. With every university swinging a similar hammer, the noise can be deafening. Still, that web presence is crucial, and we make sure our department website is up-to-date, accurate, and informative. In addition, faculty member Drew Kopp works with our students to create short videos about the major. These provide prospective students information about the classes they might take. These are featured on a separate website linked from our homepage. We also maintain a social media presence, including a Facebook page and Twitter account, to increase awareness of events and provide information about the department.

More formal events also provide marketing opportunities. Open houses attract a small, captive audience of students—and parents—who are already interested in writing. To capitalize on this opportunity to sell our program, we have put together a PowerPoint and a bag of publications and information sheets that help any faculty member lead an open house. The bag includes the Writing Arts Advantage, a brochure emphasizing the strengths of our program; advising sheets; and copies of the undergraduate literary magazine, newspaper, and other student publications. Using these and the website while meeting in our newly remodeled computer classroom with a display case outside featuring faculty books, the presenter can give a fifteen- to twenty-minute introduction to the department that is consistent across open houses. We also use this venue to pitch the Writing Center as a place where a student can get practical experience, hone tutoring skills, and earn income all without having to leave campus.

Finally, we have several ongoing scholarships and awards that allow us to support student achievements, including a $1,000 award for a creative and entrepreneurial undergraduate; biannual Literary Awards in fiction, poetry, and non-fiction, each of which has separate funding; and an annual senior medallion given to the outstanding major in writing arts.

TECHNOLOGY

Several of our courses in the major—both required and optional—require that students write in digital environments. We don't teach the technology only, as we know it will change. We teach students about the history of writing technologies, how to implement representative contemporary technologies, and how to be rhetorically aware about and have the ability to critique technologies so they are more ready to adapt as new technologies emerge.

Most of this digital writing instruction takes place in a computer classroom that we had input on designing after seeing the original plan to create multiple rows of computers with students all facing the instructor. We created clusters of four computers with an adjacent workspace so that students can work online or offline, depending on the task. There are screens at both ends of the room, so projected images can be viewed without turning around. Due to our large number of classes, this classroom is filled almost continuously from 8:00 AM to after 9:00 PM. Courses taught in the computer lab include those one would expect to see there—Writing, Research, and Technology; Writing with Technologies; the Technologies and the Future of Writing module of Introduction to Writing Arts—and others that one would likely see there—Technical Writing and Writing for the Workplace. But we also offer sections of other undergraduate major courses there, such as Evaluating Writing and even creative writing, in addition to many first-year writing courses. Most instructors now see online digital research and writing as integral to their curriculum, and we often spill over into other computer classrooms and could easily fill a second one, were it available.

ROLE OF RESEARCH

While many of our faculty conduct classroom-based research and have presented and published about other parts of the department, especially our two-decade collaborative teaching of College Composition II with Sophomore Engineering Clinic (e.g., see Dahm et al. [2009] and two by Riddell et al. [2008, 2010]), several have written articles specifically about our undergraduate program:

- Deb Martin and Diane Penrod's (2006) "Coming to Know Criteria: The Value of an Evaluating Writing Course for Undergraduates" discusses our required Evaluating Writing course for a 2006 issue of *Assessing Writing: An International Journal.*
- Two chapters appear in Greg Giberson and Tom Moriarty's (2010) *What We Are Becoming: Developments in Undergraduate Writing Majors:* Jennifer Courtney, Deb Martin, and Diane Penrod's (2010) "The Writing Arts Major: A Work in Process" and Courtney, William Wolff, and my (2010) "What Exactly Is This Major?: Creating Disciplinary Identity Through an Introductory Course" (Tweedie, Courtney, and Wolff 2010).

PEDAGOGICAL AND/OR ADMINISTRATIVE HIGHLIGHTS

Our program has undergone dramatic change that has paralleled that of Rowan University over my two decades here. In 1999, we developed three classes—Writer's Mind; Writing, Research, and Technology; and Evaluating Writing—with which we launched this degree. A decade and a half later, the Writing Arts catalog numbers twenty-three undergraduate courses with more in the works.

Initiated by feedback from graduates via one student's senior project, in 2013 we shifted creative writing (either Creative Writing I or Writing Children's Stories) into the required courses and began offering three twelve-credit concentrations within the bachelor's degree:

- Creative Writing
- New Media Editing and Publishing
- Technical and Professional Writing

Students can choose to concentrate in one, two, or all three, or they do not have to declare a concentration at all, taking courses from among the three areas. We still do not feel the degree is fully realized. We know there is more we could do for our students in terms of professional preparation and internship opportunities. We've had to grow the program, sometimes slowly, as we've added faculty with different types of expertise and areas of interest. We will continue to do so.

Based on the marketing developments discussed above—including the "making writing visible; making writers matter" vision statement and the *Write Rowan, Right Now!* Literary Writing Scholarship—we anticipate a further increase in freshmen majors. Once students are here, we realize they still need to feel a sense of belonging, especially as they most likely won't take any major courses until their sophomore year. Thus, we have a learning community for freshmen. This includes students living together in the dorm, a section of College Composition I for majors, another general education course taken as a cohort, and a required one-credit course where majors learn about publications, careers, advising, and faculty. In addition, our Writing Arts Club serves majors. Among its many activities, members attend orientations and open houses to provide a student presence and perspective.

A new university-wide curricular initiative permits us to offer four-course certificates of undergraduate study both within and outside the university. We will begin with four. Two draw from our own concentrations—creative writing and technical and professional writing. We have a very strong children's writing program with high-achieving faculty and so will offer a third certificate, in conjunction with English, in that area. The fourth will be writing for educators, focusing on writing situations P–12 teachers face. Another outreach effort involves pairing with the county library system to offer a series of summer writing workshops for children.

When one of my daughters was younger, she frequently talked about things being "the same but different." Writing Arts is thusly so. We are the same as English because of our interest in writing, but we are different in that we do not focus on literary texts. We are the same as other independent writing programs in that we focus on production rather than consumption of texts as our primary methodology, but we are different because we have a strong commitment to creative writing and see it as equivalent to academic, technical, and professional writing. We are the same as the few writing majors that also prominently feature creative writing within their requirements, but we are different in that we are in a College of Communication and Creative Arts. And in this sameness and difference, we carve out who we are and what we offer to students, the university, the community.

PRIMARY DOCUMENT (at writingprogramarchitecture.com)

A document that has been important to our program is our self-study, written by faculty in the then-named Department of Composition and Rhetoric, which was followed by a site visit in April 2004 by Council of Writing Program Administrators' Consultant/Evaluator Service members Joan Mullin and William Condon. In one section of their report, they provided an evaluation of the major that motivated us to create what we called the Disciplinary Committee. This group met for over two years, sometimes weekly. The group created the major's nine core values and redesigned the curriculum, including both an introductory and capstone course, though these ended up looking quite different from the models suggested by Mullin and Condon.

WPA'S VOICE

Four myths and some advice about being a WPA.

1. It Doesn't Take a PhD To Do This Job

As you spend far too much time working on drudgery, you will ask yourself, "Does it take a PhD to do this?" Recall this: no matter the task, all those qualities that helped you get that advanced degree are the same ones that will help you survive—and perhaps thrive—as a WPA: perseverance, dedication, commitment, follow-through, meeting deadlines. But there is one quality from your graduate days you might need to relinquish: doing it all yourself. In reality, some WPA work doesn't require a PhD. For this, learn to rely on your administrative assistant(s). I say "learn" because few of us know how to use them well. Because you will work a lot, perhaps more than you ever have, you may feel that it is impossible to get everything done. Commit to making your support staff strong, and you will lessen your overall workload.

2. I'll Appear Weak if I Admit I Made a Mistake

You cannot be afraid to make mistakes. You will err; own up to it when you do. To limit these mistakes, you first need to know the rules. You cannot operate as a WPA without knowing what you can and can't do, which policies apply or don't. Rely on the people you work with to assist you. Ask questions. Listen. Confer. Communicate. And be sure to congratulate and thank people for doing good work—any work—that keeps your program strong or makes it better. They just might be more forgiving when you mess up.

3. Nothing I Do Will Change Anything

While academics are thought to prefer moving at glacial speeds, I have rarely found this to be the case. One of the most rewarding aspects of being a part of Writing Arts is that we never sit still. We have more ideas than we have the ability to implement or oversee. It is true we don't often make decisions without first gathering information, pondering, debating, revisiting, and even rearticulating the situation. Not surprisingly, this replicates the messiness, chaos and recursive nature of writing that results in a highly polished, finely wrought finished product. Of course, look at that product a few months or a year later, and you're probably not satisfied with it. Such is writing; such is being a WPA.

An admission: as a WPA, you are complicit in the system. If you don't want to be, don't be a WPA. I find discomfort in many of the ways the academic enterprise works. Still, there are ways to affect change from this position. To do so, you will need to support the changes you seek with data. If the real estate mantra is location, location, location, the WPA's should be data, data, rhetorical savvy.

4. The Problem with Students Today . . .

Frequently, a student shows up at my door saying, "*They* told me to come see you," accompanied by a vague hand wave toward somewhere. Often the student expects that I will know what to do without even knowing the circumstances. It can be frustrating for both the student and me. Above all, try not to send the student elsewhere to find the solution to his or her problem. As WPA, you have many more years of experience in the academic morass than this person. You know people. You know the internal paths, hierarchies, and networks. Make phone calls and send emails while the student is there—especially when he or she has already been sent from somewhere else. Try to have the student walk out with a sense of something accomplished, for you never know who will become your ambassador or your worst critic.

Paul could have become the latter. He walked into my office desperate to withdraw from his composition course and take it at a community college instead. My complicated response involved transfer credits, GPAs, and program requirements. Paul walked out frustrated and, I'm pretty sure, swearing under his breath. I wasn't convinced Paul heard everything in his anger, so I followed up with a clarifying email. I received this in response: "I really appreciate you taking the time to give me that information. Teachers taking a personal interest in me is something I need in school and have had had a hard time finding in college so far." Paul's frustration had subsided. As importantly, his wording reminded me that while this quasi-administrative position often requires dealing with an overwhelming amount of detritus, those of us in it remain, at heart, teachers. Recall this when interacting with students, faculty, staff, and administration, and you will be reminded often that the WPA position can be rewarding.

References

Courtney, Jennifer, Deb Martin, and Diane Penrod. 2010. "The Writing Arts Major: A Work in Process." In *What We Are Becoming: Developments in Undergraduate Writing Majors*, ed. Greg Giberson and Thomas A. Moriarty, 243–259. Logan: Utah State University Press.

Dahm, Kevin, William Riddell, Eric Constans, Jennifer Courtney, Roberta Harvey, and Paris von Lockette. 2009. "Implementing and Assessing the Converging-Diverging Model of Design in a Sequence of Sophomore Projects." *Advances in Engineering Education* 1 (3). http://dx.doi.org/10.1115/detc2006-99083 Accessed December 30, 2015.

Giberson, Greg, and Thomas A. Moriarty, eds. 2010. *What We Are Becoming: Developments in Undergraduate Writing Majors.* Logan: Utah State University Press.

Martin, Deb, and Diane Penrod. 2006. "'Coming to Know Criteria: The Value of an Evaluating Writing Course for Undergraduates.' *Assessing Writing.*" *International Journal (Toronto, Ont.)* 11 (1): 66–73.

Riddell, William, Jennifer Courtney, Eric Constans, Kevin Dahm, Roberta Harvey, and Paris von Lockette. 2010. "Making Communication Matter: Integrating Instruction, Projects and Assignments to Teach Writing and Design" *Advances in Engineering Education* 2(2). Accessed December 30, 2015. http://advances.asee.org/.

Riddell, William, Jennifer Courtney, Eric Constans, Kevin Dahm, Roberta Harvey, and Paris von Lockette. 2008. "The Connections between Engineering Design and Technical Writing in an Integrated Instructional Setting." *Design Principles and Practices: An International Journal* 2 (4): 37–44. http://dx.doi.org/10.18848/1833-1874 /CGP/v02i04/37575.

Scholes, Robert. 1985. *Textual Power: Literary Theory and the Teaching of English.* New Haven, CT: Yale University Press.

Tweedie, Sanford, Jennifer Courtney, and William I. Wolff. 2010. "What Exactly Is This Major?: Creating Disciplinary Identity through an Introductory Course." In *What We Are Becoming: Developments in Undergraduate Writing Majors,* ed. Greg Giberson and Thomas A. Moriarty, 260–276. Logan: Utah State University Press.

5

UNIVERSITY OF RHODE ISLAND WRITING AND RHETORIC MAJOR

Nedra Reynolds and Joannah Portman-Daley

Institution Type: Land, Sea, and Urban Grant Public Research Institution
Location: Kingston, Rhode Island
Enrollment: 16,000+
Year program was founded: 2006
WPA reports to: Associate Dean in College of Arts and Sciences
Program funded by: Division of Academic Affairs
Description of students: University of Rhode Island (URI) has 14,207 undergraduates, 57 percent Rhode Island students, 43 percent out-of-state; 21 percent of incoming freshmen self-identify as students of color.

PROGRAM SNAPSHOT

The Department of Writing and Rhetoric, an independent academic unit since 2003, is located within the largest of seven colleges, the College of Arts and Sciences, and is part of the Harrington School of Communication and Media, which includes five other academic units. The writing major is a thirty-credit bachelor's of arts degree that offers courses in a wide range of situational and professional environments, including Travel Writing, Technical Writing, Proposal Writing, Public Writing, Writing Health and Disability, and Writing Culture.

WPAS' PROFILES

Nedra

My WPA career began when I served for one year as acting director of composition at the University of Tampa, after spending two years directing the Saunders Writing Center there (at the time, I had an MA in English). Serving as a Writing Center director for two years, along with teaching basic writing and training tutors, did prepare me

DOI: 10.7330/9781607326274.c005

well for serving as a WPA—although I knew right away that I needed more experience and the credential of a PhD. My colleagues, who were mostly veteran tenured professors, did not take me very seriously as a WPA, but they did realize that I had more training in the teaching of writing than they did. Many years later, with that PhD and a specialization in rhetoric and composition, I am now a department chair and also served as director of the College Writing Program from 2002 to 2008. (Thanks to supportive colleagues, I was not asked or expected to serve as a WPA until after I had achieved tenure and promotion to associate professor.) The WPA role has shifted considerably as the "program" has become a "department," and as we added majors in writing and rhetoric, developed a curriculum to serve them, and took on all of the responsibilities of a degree-granting department. The shift from program to department meant, among other things, that we had an operating budget to manage, workload and assessment reports to file, and Annual Review procedures to establish and enact. Along with being responsible for tenure and promotion guidelines and strategic planning, we also began advising undergraduate majors and minors. Having served as both a WPA for a non-degree granting program and as a department chair for a degree-granting program, I now work more closely with deans and provosts.

Joannah

I began my PhD in URI's writing and rhetoric program in 2006 (we offer a specialization within the MA and PhD degree programs in the English Department). After finishing my course work, then chair, Libby Miles, asked me to serve as assistant director for the department, allowing me to learn firsthand about and assist with WPA responsibilities. The following year, I began work as associate director of technology, a position that asked me to design, create, and run a new technology lab for the department, as well as oversee technological administrative needs, all of which were in line with my doctoral interests and research. Upon graduation, Nedra hired me to work as digital pedagogy specialist, where I continued to run the technology production lab and manage the undergraduate majors who worked there as lab monitors. I also provided technology support for students, pedagogical consultation for faculty, and designed technology-based projects for several of our lab fee classes. Nedra asked me to coauthor this profile because she believes that new WPAs (readers of this collection) need to be prepared to address more issues related to teaching and technology than in the past.

PROGRAM CONCEPTION

The College Writing Program started in the 1970s as a way of allowing students to take flexible-credit writing courses through the English Department. When Nedra became WPA in 2002, the program had been ably guided for ten years by Professor Linda Shamoon, and, under her leadership, we had just concluded a self-study of our program using the Council of Writing Program Administrators' guidelines. Motivated by our frustration at being blocked from offering any new courses (viz. because members of the English Department were concerned about our "empire-building"—their term for our plan to propose new courses), we used the self-study to inform a proposal to the English Department and to the upper administration to become an independent academic unit, separate from the English Department. Because it wanted to be identified only with literary studies, the English Department favored the split and also supported our proposal for a major in writing.

So, the years 2002–2005 involved navigating that separation; this involved shepherding a fairly elaborate proposal through committees at the college and university levels and then seeking approval from the State of Rhode Island's Board of Governors for Higher Education. At this level, Nedra provided documentation that writing and rhetoric majors were being established at other colleges and universities but also that ours would be the first among the New England land-grant universities (a plus); she also illustrated to board members that the fields of literary studies and composition studies could be easily distinguished by their different academic journals and conferences. At least at URI, the traditional English Department did not give students substantial opportunities to study professional writing (although English houses the creative writing program and many of our students double major in English or take the creative writing classes). Once we had the approval to be an independent academic unit, all areas within the university were very receptive to developing an undergraduate major in writing and rhetoric and have been supportive of the changes as well as our accomplishments and contributions.

POPULATION SERVED

We serve undergraduate writing and rhetoric majors seeking a bachelor's of arts degree. Right now, we have eighty-seven majors. This number has grown considerably in the past five years, and we are hoping to grow it beyond the one hundred mark. We graduated twenty-five majors in May 2015 after graduating our first three in 2008. The relatively low number of credits required for this major (thirty) allows students to double major in another area, and we strongly encourage them to do so. As part of the Harrington School of Communication and Media, students majoring in the school's other areas—film/media, communication, journalism, and public relations—often choose to major in writing and rhetoric as well. Many students will also minor in leadership studies, public relations, sustainability, or dozens more. Recent graduates are working as professional writers at Hasbro, Blue Cross and Blue Shield, and Schneider Electric, just to name a few, and several are pursuing graduate degrees in law, editing and publishing, health communication, and other fields.

FUNDING

Our operating budget comes from the State of Rhode Island, via the Provost's Office and the College of Arts and Sciences. In addition to funding salaries, our operating budget provides travel funds for graduate students or candidates, office supplies, archival storage, telephones, keys, and a variety of printing costs.

In addition, we have a lab fee budget that comes from student fees assessed classes that have a specific technology learning or fieldwork component. Generally, these fees total over $35,000 each academic year, and that money goes to sustaining our lab equipment and consumables, as well as paying undergraduate majors to work as lab monitors.

OPERATIONS

Many people are responsible for the day-to-day success of our department. These include seven tenured and tenure-track faculty who serve as the department chair/WPA, the first-year writing coordinator, and the Writing Center director. We also have an office manager, who is a full-time staff member, and four to five office workers. We employ a dozen or more undergraduate students as office workers, peer tutors, and production lab monitors. The program has three full-time lecture positions, ten graduate teaching assistants, and twenty-five part-time instructors to staff primarily first-year writing.

The various operations that keep our program up and running every day include scheduling, hiring, classroom assignments, daily communication and administrative efforts, etc. In terms of planning and preparation, we hold all-department meetings a week before each semester begins. All faculty and instructors are required to attend. These meetings cover important administrative information, as well as promote faculty development by offering a workshop, breakout table discussions, and/ or a guest speaker (Cheryl Glenn came in September 2013). Recent faculty development efforts have focused on portfolio keeping, assessment, online peer review, and Sakai (our course management system) instruction, to name just a few topics. In addition, we hold department meetings on a bi-weekly or monthly basis (for continuing or permanent faculty), depending on the specific semester's agenda items.

Operations range across several elements of our department as well as annual events: Writing Center, Production Lab, Early Credit High School Program, a Portfolio Capstone Showcase, a Proficiency Exam for first-semester freshmen, Assessment reports, Curricular Changes, Search Committee work. Professional development for teachers is a priority, so as each new semester begins, colleagues come together to talk shop.

While the daily or weekly pace is rarely frantic, Nedra does bounce among a variety of tasks or deadlines: correspondence, departmental reports or proposals, meetings, committees, consultations with colleagues or staff members, advising undergraduates, and teaching one to two classes. A typical week includes several brief meetings with students from all across the campus, usually for the same reasons: they need prior approval for courses they want to take at other universities or in study abroad programs; they have a form that needs her signature (most often related to degree requirements); or they are hoping to sidestep a writing course and want her to know how well they write already! Nedra spends a lot of time quoting the University Manual, checking the AAUP contract or the Part-Time Faculty Union (PTFU) agreement.

We also rely on committees made up of permanent faculty and, occasionally, graduate students to oversee the aspects of our operations that don't necessarily need day-to-day attention, but whose results affect how the program runs on a day-to-day basis. Currently, we have a curriculum committee, responsible for revising current courses and adding new ones. The chair of this committee changes each year and depends on the classes in need of creation or revision. We have a Production Lab committee, which oversees the technology needs of our department's technology lab, the Writing Production Lab, and makes decisions about lab fee courses, technology purchases, and lab maintenance. Our Production Lab manager chairs this committee, in addition to supervising the undergraduate lab monitors who work there.

Advising for our eighty-seven majors is organized depending on the number of credits students have earned. Before thirty credits, students are advised through University College, and one of our full-time lecturers has one course release per year to work with those students, including students who are "undecided" but interested in writing and rhetoric or the Harrington School of Communication and Media. Once students have thirty-plus credits or are otherwise "official" majors, departments handle this advising differently. After experimenting for a few years with "everyone" advising (all faculty), we are going to try for next year to have only one academic advisor. While we thought it was a good idea to have all faculty teaching in the major familiar with requirements, electives, double-major issues, curricular modifications, and the all-important Intent to Graduate forms, we have discovered that advisors are more effective the more advising that they do! Advising five to ten students every week seems preferable to going for weeks at a time with no appointments. From this point on, then, the department's advisor will receive one course release per semester for this important position, which is increasingly valued by the administration in terms of annual reviews.

ASSESSMENT

From the time the state mandate for assessment was handed down (approximately 2009), our unit welcomed the opportunity to create our new major in writing and rhetoric by starting with learning outcomes. We were eager to see what student writing (e.g.) could tell us about what students should know and be able to do. We were one of the first departments on campus to develop learning outcomes and curriculum maps, which we began during a day-long workshop sponsored by the Provost's Office (with food, a small stipend, and some guidance from the state Office of Higher Education). Although the first task was to determine what writing majors should know and be able to do, we were also asked to develop, later, specific outcomes for our General Education courses. When we generated more outcomes than any program could reasonably deliver, we trimmed and modified them over the course of two to three years, revisiting them with our entire teaching faculty. In trying to make sure that our curriculum matched with our outcomes, we developed different final portfolio expectations in the first-year courses—from "revise three of the six projects" to "present evidence that you have met three learning outcomes." The loop of assessment continues to circle: to date, we have conducted one embedded assessment in the third required course in the core curriculum of our BA, and we have completed an assessment of our General Education writing courses—via final portfolios in all first-year courses. An analysis of our ratings of one particular outcome—"*Students reflect on the appropriateness of their choices for the rhetorical situation"*—showed that scores declined despite targeted professional development to address its importance. Our analysis suggested that high turnover among adjuncts might be one impediment; for example, in a three-year period, we had a turnover rate of nearly 60 percent.

MARKETING/PR

Our department relies heavily on our website as a marketing tool for recruiting prospective students. As our program offers a BA as well as specializations for MA and PhD degree programs (in English), we make sure to promote ourselves to students at varying levels of their educational journey. In doing so, we believe it is important not only to demonstrate what our department offers in terms of curriculum but also to show what faculty and students are doing with that curriculum. For example, we highlight the ways that faculty are using technology in the classroom, spotlight interesting projects, announce faculty and student achievements, and profile students who represent what a prospective student can experience and achieve as a writing major in our program. We put a lot of time and attention into the website, constantly updating it and making sure that it reflects the program accurately and appealingly. Recently, we completed our second overhaul in less than five years, situating our department as part of the larger Harrington School of Communication and Media and illustrating how prospective writing and rhetoric students can benefit from the reciprocity and interdisciplinarity of the other Harrington School departments.

While we also have a social media presence, the audiences for both our Facebook and Twitter accounts are largely current students and alumni. We generally use these platforms to make announcements and advertise new classes or special events.

As useful as the web and social media are for marketing efforts, they also present various challenges. Keeping the website current is a time-consuming responsibility and not all information gets posted or gets posted in a timely fashion. We are always trying to find a balance with our social media presence. We don't want to bug our followers with every last detail of every last announcement or event, but we do want to keep them aware and interested.

In terms of face-to-face marketing efforts, we hold information sessions for prospective majors each semester. Various faculty members represent our program at these events, talking with prospective majors and showing them examples of the kinds of writing experiences they can anticipate as a major. Since these sessions are usually held on the weekend, the main challenge is finding faculty who will volunteer to work them.

TECHNOLOGY

Technology is consistently changing the way we approach writing in terms of teaching, research, and administration. To keep our program and our faculty up-to-date, Joannah is dedicated to helping other faculty and instructors incorporate technology into their classrooms in current and meaningful ways. She offers occasional workshops on specific tools and practices, helps instructors move their courses to blended and online formats, and works one-on-one with department members who are looking to learn more about or enhance their pedagogy via any kind of digital technology.

Our program embraces the university's adoption of Sakai as a course management system and we require all instructors to use it as part of their course, at the very least to house their syllabus and for online portfolio submission. Joannah offers regular workshops on incorporating various Sakai tools into classroom pedagogy so those instructors who want to use it more heavily can learn how to do so in a writing-specific way. While we have encouraged Sakai as a means for online peer review, we have also used numerous online peer review platforms. Currently, our program is piloting the Eli Peer Review software.

As mentioned above, our website is targeted primarily at prospective students. However, we also use it to house important instructor resources. On a password protected page, faculty and instructors have access to standard syllabi, course specific in-class activities and rubrics, examples of student work, as well as general policies and other administrative information.

ROLE OF RESEARCH

A variety of research has been published on our program by both past and present faculty and graduate students. While we don't ask or expect our department members to research and publish on the program, we all seem to value the importance of reflecting on and improving upon our programmatic and pedagogical choices, so writing about them seems a natural part of the process. The majority of research published on our major thus far falls into two categories: curriculum development and delivery, and course-specific pedagogical approaches.

With regard to curriculum development and delivery, our department faculty, Linda Shamoon and Bob Schwegler, along with colleagues from other institutions, coauthored *Coming of Age: The Advanced Writing Curriculum* in 2000 (Shamoon et al. 2000). This book offers ideas for, and specific examples of, advanced writing courses, from our program and many others, that aim to prepare students for careers as writers. In 2010, Joannah, Jeremiah Dyehouse, and Michael Pennell explored the transition of our first-year writing course from a traditional delivery method to a hybrid model in "Hybridity in an Independent Writing Program," published in the Winter issue of *Academic Exchange Quarterly* (Portman-Daley, Dyehouse, and Pennell 2010).

In terms of the articles that focus on pedagogical approaches to, and implications of, specific courses within our program, there have been several. In 2009, Libby Miles and Michael Pennell discussed our Business Communication class as a platform for problem-based learning as a rhetorical pedagogy in "'It Actually Made Me Think': Problem-Based Learning in the Business Communications Classroom," published in *Business Communication Quarterly* (Pennell and Miles 2009). Several faculty members have written about our Writing in Electronic Environments course. In 2008, Michael Pennell published "Russia is not in Rhode Island": Wikitravel in the Digital Writing Classroom" in *Pedagogy* about a specific wiki-based project that focuses on writing within information ecologies (Pennell 2008); in 2009, Linda Shamoon, Jeremiah Dyehouse, and Michael Pennell published "'Writing in Electronic Environments': A Concept and a Course for the Writing and Rhetoric Major" in *College Composition and Communication* (Dyehouse, Pennell, and Shamoon 2009), which offers an overview of the course and explains how it meets the goals of our writing and rhetoric major; and in 2010, Joannah created a new project for the course and documented its goals with regard to digital literacy and civic engagement in the article "Reshaping Slacktivist Rhetoric: Social Networking for Social Change," published in *Reflections* (Portman-Daley 2010). Most recently, some of our faculty are researching Eli Review, both in writing courses and across the curriculum.

PEDAGOGICAL AND/OR ADMINISTRATIVE HIGHLIGHTS

Good writers are in demand in *any* organization or workplace setting, and that demand has increased as technologies for written communication expand. Our major prepares students to write well in all situations: academic settings, the public sector, private corporations, non-profit organizations, for their own pleasure or freelance writing career. Our writing and rhetoric (WRT) courses give them opportunities to write for specific clients or to partner with community organizations; in other words, majors write for and with *real* audiences.

Our majors also learn how to write with many different technologies. Our Production Lab houses the equipment necessary for both faculty and students to approach writing from multiple perspectives, as text, as image, as moving image, as virtual space, etc. Faculty members took opportunities of calls for proposals (CFPs) and wrote internal grants in order to fund the equipment; grants from the URI Foundation, the Provost's Office, the Honors Program, the College of Arts and Sciences, for example, allowed us to purchase twelve high-end Apple computers, all complete with various multimedia software packages, video capture capabilities, and wireless printing access. In addition, it houses a scanner, comb binder, laminator, a small library of resource materials, and several laptops, iPads, voice recorders, and digital video cameras for check-out purposes. Most recently, the lab acquired a Lynda.com kiosk and over fifty Lynda Pro licenses for faculty and students, so they may better learn how to teach and use the various software that enhance writing practices. Before turning the responsibility over to a graduate student, Joannah managed this lab, along with a staff of undergraduate lab monitors who not only help students with hardware and software needs, but who are also familiar with all of our courses and so can help with the invention, planning, and production stages of any writing process. We are able to pay these monitors, as well as purchase lab technologies and consumables to maintain the lab, because of fees assessed for a number of writing courses that have a high technology component. Students enrolled in those courses have access to the lab and all its equipment, and instructors who teach those courses work with Joannah or the production lab manager to create projects that ensure students are making good use of the lab and its resources.

PRIMARY DOCUMENT (at **writingprogramarchitecture.com**)

Our department's self-study—required every six years—was produced in 2014–15 for URI's Academic Program Review Committee, which provided guidelines, institutional reports, and funding for an external reviewer. Our process was hugely valuable because of the collaboration and input from all members of our unit, including per-course instructors and undergraduate majors. This document has been and will continue to be our North Star for the next five years; it captures valuable data and offers both practical and aspirational goals for our future.

WPAS' VOICES

While the roles of a WPA and a department chair differ somewhat, a WPA is nevertheless an ambassador for all-things-writing. This means "going public" with the role of writing and its importance to **learning**; it means being willing to serve on college and university committees and to share one's expertise—and to try to challenge assumptions and uninformed approaches to writing pedagogy. Successful WPAs walk a line between courting potential friends of writing and disabusing colleagues of their outdated or narrow views of what writing well means or how to get there. WPAs need rhetorical training to judge when to intervene in conflicts or (i.e., grade disputes) and when to let small fires just burn themselves out. Fire extinguishers might consist of a combination of well-crafted emails and judicious use of the phone (repeated as needed).

If new WPAs want to propose or consider proposing a new major in writing and rhetoric or a related field, it's important to recognize that writing is still considered a "skill" area on most campuses, and many colleagues in other disciplines may wonder how anyone can major in "writing." It helps to make the argument that such majors have a solid liberal arts tradition and are historically grounded in the art of rhetoric while they also prepare students through practice with a variety of tools and technologies (document design, web design, social media). Many of our stakeholders do not seem to understand the term "rhetoric," but we thought it was important to reference both the long tradition and also distinguish what we do from, for example, creative writing. Those who have the opportunity to become an independent unit will need to consider carefully their name: writing and rhetoric? Professional writing? Writing studies? It's important that everyone—from admissions' officers to fund-raisers and provosts—understands what the name stands for and what students are expected to know and be able to do in this major. In serving as the ambassador for all-things-writing on your own campus, new WPAs would do well to heed something Nedra learned from Richard Miller years ago: writing should be at the center of the curriculum, full stop.

References

Dyehouse, Jeremiah, Michael Pennell, and Linda K. Shamoon. 2009. "Writing in Electronic Environments: A Concept and a Course for the Writing and Rhetoric Major." *College Composition and Communication* 61 (2): 330–350.

Pennell, Michael. 2008. "'Russia Is Not in Rhode Island': Wikitravel in the (Digital) Writing Classroom." *Pedagogy* 8 (1): 75–90. http://dx.doi.org/10.1215/15314200-2007-025.

Pennell, Michael, and Libby Miles. 2009. ""It Actually Made Me Think": Problem-Based Learning in the Business Communications Classroom." *Business Communication Quarterly* 72 (4): 377–394. http://dx.doi.org/10.1177/1080569909349482.

Portman-Daley, Joannah. 2010. "Reshaping Slacktivist Rhetoric: Social Networking for Social Change." *Reflections: The SoL Journal* 10:104–33.

Portman-Daley, Joannah, Jeremiah Dyehouse, and Michael Pennell. 2010. "Hybridity in an Independent Writing Program." *Academic Exchange Quarterly* 14 (4). http://www.rapidintellect.com/AEQweb/cho4744.htm.

Shamoon, Linda K., Rebecca Moore Howard, Sandra Jamieson, and Robert Schwegler. 2000. *Coming of Age: The Advanced Writing Curriculum.* Portsmouth, NH: Boynton/ Cook.

6

UNIVERSITY OF WYOMING PROFESSIONAL WRITING MINOR

Michael Knievel and Meg Van Baalen-Wood

Institution Type: Public Research University
Location: Laramie, Wyoming
Enrollment: 14,000
Year program was founded: Fall 2001
WPA reports to: English Department Chair
Program funded by: University of Wyoming (UW) Department of English
Description of students: UW is the only public four-year university in Wyoming, enrolling over ten thousand undergraduate students (nearly fourteen thousand total) from all fifty states and more than ninety countries ("UW Quick Facts" 2016). Of these students, 74 percent are Wyoming residents, while the remainder, especially undergraduates, come from the West and Midwest, particularly Colorado (*UW Quick Facts 2016*). Given Wyoming's small population (under six hundred thousand residents) and vast geography, a significant number of students come to UW from rural or small town/city backgrounds (*"Wyoming"* 2016). In addition, the Outreach School offers educational opportunities for roughly two thousand students per semester (*Office of Institutional Analysis, University of Wyoming 2015*) who are site-bound and geographically dispersed around the state.

PROGRAM SNAPSHOT

The University of Wyoming's minor in professional writing is located in the Department of English, which is situated within the College of Arts and Sciences. Enrolling twenty to twenty-five students per semester from all over campus, the professional writing minor offers focused instruction in workplace communication that complements discipline-specific study in students' academic majors. The program requires eighteen credits, including a foundations course, two choices from six program courses (e.g., Editing for Publication or Writing for the Web), two elective courses, and a required capstone: Twenty-First Century Issues in Professional Writing.

DOI: 10.7330/9781607326274.c006

WPAS' PROFILES:

Michael

As the current coordinator of our professional writing minor, I can look back and trace a meandering path to this moment that likely started in graduate school. As a doctoral student, I mentored other graduate student teachers and served one year as a graduate assistant director for the first-year composition program at Texas Tech University (TTU). This gave me the opportunity to work with people like Fred Kemp, Becky Rickly, and Susan Lang at a time when great changes and highly experimental technology innovations were afoot within the program. I also was fortunate to take a seminar in writing assessment with Susanmarie Harrington, who was a visiting professor in the program at the time. It was enlightening to study and work in a context where composition and technical communication both had a significant programmatic presence. Simply observing these faculty mentors introduced me to the range of activity that can happen under the rubric of "writing program administration"—everything from overseeing first-year writing, to coding and developing an online/onsite hybrid model of first-year composition, to assessing programs, to developing a usability lab.

In spite of these positive experiences and great colleagues and mentors, program administration was not something I readily imagined myself doing; indeed, if memory serves, I somewhat passively *avoided* taking a seminar in writing program administration during my graduate coursework. Like many graduate students, I suppose, I imagined myself, first, as a teacher and a researcher, not as an administrator, and I could not yet feature the connections between and among these different roles. Looking back, such a view probably reflects little more than naiveté and my own inexperience. Given the growth in the field at the time, it did seem possible then (at least to me) to complete a graduate degree in a writing-studies-related field without seeing administration as an inevitable part of professional life. But I think I also knew at some level that such work would likely be a part of my career. All I needed to do was look around at my professors in composition and technical communication: almost all of them were involved in some form or fashion in the collaborative model of writing program administration that TTU featured at both the undergraduate and graduate levels.

When I applied for my current position out of graduate school, writing program administration at UW was mentioned as a future possibility for me, but until recently, all writing programs in our department were directed by a single faculty member. In 2011, we split up the consolidated director position, separating out coordination of first-year writing, university and state writing initiatives, and professional writing. So, when I succeeded Meg as professional writing coordinator three years ago under the aegis of this more collaborative, distributed model of administration, it felt, in some ways, like I was embracing an administrative identity that mirrored the model I had observed in graduate school.

Meg

Unlike many academics, I began my career in the private sector—working as a technical/professional writer in industries ranging from engineering to software development and consulting. Within ten years, my technical writing career expanded to include project management and independent consulting, both of which required some administrative skills, as well as a little bit of software design and development. I believe this early experience, augmented by a fierce interest in language, predisposed me to gravitate first toward teaching in the professional writing minor and then to coordinating it.

Like Michael's, my graduate training also helped nudge this trajectory. In a sense, I worked backward, first as a graduate student and later faculty, from *doing* to *teaching*. As I undertook this transition, my interests gradually shifted from discipline to pedagogy.

In addition to teaching Technical Writing in the Professions and several other courses in the professional writing minor, for ten years, I also coordinated the Professional Writing Internship, an elective that counts toward minor completion. My teaching is grounded always in the practical: how can I equip my students to communicate effectively and efficiently in an array of professional contexts? Growing that pragmatic classroom focus to a curricular scale was so natural it felt almost inevitable.

I served as the professional writing coordinator for the first year after we partitioned the WPA responsibilities in the department. During this year, I worked closely with Mary P. Sheridan and Michael as we reexamined many of the assumptions the department made about the minor when it was established, assumptions about student interests and demands, marketing the minor, the faculty composition, and most important, the focus of the curriculum itself. In that first year, Michael and I imagined we would alternate coordinating the minor. Subsequently, my interests in pedagogy and curricula led me to the Ellbogen Center for Teaching and Learning, the University of Wyoming's faculty development center, where I now reside full-time while Michael continues to coordinate the minor.

PROGRAM CONCEPTION

The professional writing minor emerged from a curious complex of factors. First and foremost, during the 1990s, a strong cohort of lecturers in the department were regularly assigned to teach English 4010, Technical Writing in the Professions, a senior-level service course taken by students across the university from a wide range of majors, including engineering, health sciences, education, and business, among others. Meeting regularly to share ideas, develop the curriculum, and assess student writing, these lecturers strengthened and regularized the teaching and activity surrounding the course. The lecturers' successes helped plant the seed for something more to develop, and in the late 1990s at a departmental retreat, the faculty voted to pursue a minor in professional writing, a decision that shaped the nature of a subsequent search for a WPA whose primary charge would be to oversee the first-year composition program but who would also be tasked with spearheading the development of the minor. Kelly Belanger was hired and worked with existing members of the technical writing cohort to devise a curriculum comprised of two new courses, Writing for Public Forums and Twenty-First Century Issues in Professional Writing (a title that made a lot of sense at that particular historical moment but which is now feeling its age!), and a handful of existing courses. While many students would satisfy the minor's eighteen-credit requirement entirely with courses we designated as "minor" courses, they could also opt to fulfill up to six credits with suitable writing-intensive courses in their home disciplines.

In the early days of the minor, our department, which has historically emphasized literary studies and, more recently, creative writing, was largely supportive but not without pockets of resistance. Some colleagues expressed concern about the vocationalism they thought a "professional writing" minor connoted and worried that the minor's name might suggest a specific career track to students that we would not be able to deliver. Even today, a few faculty retain these concerns. However, the estimable demand for the technical writing service course, a wealth of untapped professional technical writing expertise and experience within the minor faculty, and a nationwide trend to develop technical and professional writing courses went a long way toward assuaging these concerns.

Indeed, over the first few years, as the professional writing program slowly gained momentum around the university, it also gained enrollment. Kelly left in 2005, and for a couple of years, the program chugged along without direct administrative attention. In 2007, Mary P. Sheridan was hired as WPA and immediately began working to raise the professional writing program's visibility within the department and around the university, in part by developing two additional courses to bolster the curriculum: Writing for the Web and Writing for Non-Profits. Although Mary P. left the university in 2012, the distributed administrative framework established late in her tenure persists.

Overall, since we began coordinating the minor, we have found it to be largely in good shape, with the aforementioned new courses quickly finding a niche and minor numbers settling in where they remain today—about twenty to twenty-five students in a given semester. Together, we have worked to improve our program's web presence and general recruiting strategy, and Michael is currently working with others in the program to facilitate the transition of minor courses designated "writing-intensive" in our old general education program (University Studies Program or USP) to "communication-intensive" in our new USP, which blends oral, digital, and written forms.

At times, staffing courses has been difficult for problems both real and of our own making. For example, we have lost many of the original minor faculty to retirement and/or to administrative positions elsewhere in the university. Many of these faculty have been replaced by graduates of our own MA program. Since literature dominates our graduate program, as it does our undergraduate programs, this staffing solution has occasionally made for an uneasy fit leading to increased instability in our faculty. Departmental demands to staff the core curriculum and service courses exacerbate this instability by continually impinging upon our ability to staff—and therefore offer—the full array of minor courses.

Beyond these immediate concerns, we see the challenges we need to address going forward as threefold: (1) we need to develop a sustainable assessment model to position our program for long-term success. (2) We need to improve recruiting, not only in terms of raw numbers of students, but in terms of approach and scope. This means considering the ways in which our program speaks to students in the hard sciences, business, and other areas that we believe could benefit from it. (3) We need to carefully examine the ways in which we nurture a sense of community for our students to assure they have ample opportunities to realize the benefits of connection, idea sharing, and fellow-feeling that a community can provide. We discuss the first two of these challenges below in "Assessment" and "Marketing/PR," respectively. Due in large part to our minor status, the third challenge is elusive, especially regarding the "how." Despite most of our students' convictions that they identify more with their major cohorts than with other professional writing minors, those of us who teach in the minor maintain the conviction that a greater sense of programmatic community would enhance both students' and our own experiences.

POPULATION SERVED

Even as students and faculty in STEM disciplines and businesses recognize the need for additional preparation for the communication demands they will face as professionals, cultural factors and existing curricular requirements make it difficult to add our minor. As a result, far fewer of these students than we anticipated are part of the minor at present. In contrast, many English majors *are* interested in fleshing out their career prospects and see a minor in professional writing as a good way to do so. At present, 40–50 percent of all students enrolling in the minor are English majors.

Consequently, while we continue to monitor and respond to the needs of other student constituencies outside of English (especially in the social sciences), much of our curricular energy has been directed toward students from humanities backgrounds—and to a lesser extent, social sciences backgrounds—who seek to shape a marketable profile by completing our program. With that said, we are not content to stand pat with this student population and are currently studying the possibility of formally designating a 2000-level technical writing course geared toward students in the sciences and technology (Writing in Technology and the Sciences) as an alternative to our extant minor foundations course (Writing for Public Forums), with an eye toward giving students in the technical writing course a more "visible" pathway to the minor.

A recent alumni survey indicates that our graduates go on—perhaps unsurprisingly—to work in a wide range of workplace contexts with an impressive scope of communication challenges before them. Alumni reported working, for instance, as archivists, line cooks, project coordinators, copywriters, environmental consultants, insurance claim handlers, medical technologists, coaches, counselors, and teachers. While we were pleased to learn that our graduates are highly satisfied with our curriculum and teaching, the array of writing and communication work these alumni reported in the survey demonstrate that the curricular challenge before us—the challenge to position our students well for future workplace writing and communication success in a range of workplace settings—is formidable.

FUNDING

The primary cost of running our program is faculty and instructor salaries. All of our staffing comes from the Department of English. No one
who teaches for the program does so exclusively. A typical instructor
profile includes responsibilities in composition and/or literature, the
technical communication service course (which counts for the minor),
and the professional writing minor. The department, through the
College of Arts and Sciences, also funds adjunct hiring, which is usually
necessary to cover two to four campus sections of professional writing
and professional writing-related courses (most typically the technical
writing service course) per year.

Funding for other program endeavors is a curious and ambiguous
subject. Part of this has to do with our departmental culture and history
of entanglement with the composition program, whose modest annual
operational funds are sometimes, though rarely, used for writing program endeavors more broadly construed. The first-year program also collects modest royalties from its locally developed custom reader, which students purchase from the university bookstore. Again, these funds are not
the professional writing minor's funds, per se, and it is rare—very rare—
that the minor as a program looks in that direction for any operational
support. Fortunately, given the size and identity of the program, as well
as the aforementioned nature of funding for our instructional faculty,
these operational costs are relatively low, compared to many programs.

Occasionally, and sporadically, we have benefited from other small
internal and external funding streams. These opportunities have been
largely serendipitous. For instance, the program has applied for and
received modest internal grant monies, largely through an initiative of
our university's Ellbogen Center for Teaching and Learning to support
programmatic development and assessment. These funds have supported
occasional professional development activities for instructors. Over the
past three years, the Department of English has made $200 available to its
minor programs, with the stipulation that the money be spent on student
activities. Finally, a private, unsolicited $2,500 donation made explicitly
to the professional writing minor in the past year—the first of its kind—
has provided seed money for what we hope to be a more substantial
source of funding, one that might be used to attract additional monies
from donors and alumni. We hope to build the fund into something that
might support a modest annual support budget and professional development opportunities for faculty who teach in the program.

Finally, as noted earlier, we have had significant input in our MA program's L. L. Smith Speaker Series, which typically funds travel costs and

an honorarium for a small number of visiting scholars each year. For the past six years, faculty associated with the professional writing minor and writing studies have selected, invited, and hosted a leading scholar in technical/professional communication. In addition to presenting their research to students and faculty associated with the program and others from around the department and university, these scholars have also served as informal program consultants and advocates. Our collegial relationship with our department's graduate program has made this possible, and it has been a boon for the minor. Given our limited resources, we would not otherwise be able to fund a guest speaker.

OPERATIONS

As coordinators, we each have received one course release per academic year to oversee the professional writing minor. This shifts Michael's teaching load, for instance, from 3–2 to 2–2. His teaching responsibilities are typically distributed across different programs (e.g., Synergy program for conditionally admitted students, first-year writing, graduate program), with approximately 50 percent of his teaching committed to the professional writing program. For Meg, the course release also meant a course reduction, from a 4–3 to a 3–3 load. While all of her classroom assignments were in the minor, her load included one non-teaching assignment in the Writing Center each semester. The minor coordinator also serves as the student advisor for the minor. Students who are currently minoring in professional writing, as well as all of those who are interested in learning more about the program, are funneled to the coordinator via colleagues and department staff members who field such inquiries.

Courses in the minor are staffed by a combination of tenure-track faculty and what we call at UW, "Academic Professional Lecturers," some of whom are "extended-term" and others who are temporary. Extended-term lecturers undergo a process similar to tenure. Temporary lecturers are relatively few but remain crucial to our program. While technically only appointed for one year, it is not uncommon for temporary lecturers to work in this capacity for several years. In addition to their lower salaries, these positions are exclusively teaching-oriented and come without access to the rights and privileges (e.g., participation in departmental governance) afforded those in the extended-term line.

The number of tenure-track faculty who actively and regularly teach in the minor is relatively small—in recent years, two or three—including faculty with specializations in technical/professional communication, rhetoric, and creative nonfiction. Since our individual backgrounds are in technical and professional communication, a greater percentage of our teaching is regularly committed to the minor, with other colleagues' loads distributed disproportionately toward the department's major and graduate programs, as well as to other service courses.

We have no administrative staff committed, per se, to the professional writing minor; thus, the coordinator works with department staff to conduct our day-to-day business. Largely, though, we are a "resource-lite" operation, and if we want something done, we do it ourselves. Occasionally, we will hire a professional writing minor student as an intern to address an acute programmatic need, but that is rare. In short, day-to-day activities—scheduling, ordering food for events, making arrangements for guests, advising students, etc.—are part of the coordinator's responsibilities.

As coordinators, we develop itinerary for regular teaching cohort meetings, spearhead initiatives like the aforementioned USP transition, and map teaching schedules that will meet the needs of our students while working within our personnel constraints, in part by tracking enrollments and conferring with the chair to help allocate resources appropriately. Although we are not directly responsible for hiring within the program, we work in consultation with the department chair to analyze programmatic hiring needs and identify qualified candidates for adjunct appointments. In addition, we work with department staff to control enrollments as necessary, filtering enrollment in the capstone course and professional writing internship, for instance, and setting aside seats in the introductory course each semester to ensure that minors and prospective minors have opportunity to enroll. We also represent the program's interests to the department and chair and report annually to the chair to assist in evaluation and planning. In recent years, the professional writing minor program has benefited from a relationship with the MA program's L. L. Smith Speaker Series. Michael has taken the lead in identifying, inviting, planning, and hosting scholars' visits to campus.

In addition to the above operational responsibilities, we also keep an eye on the "bigger writing picture," monitoring, for instance, relevant curricular developments "around" the minor. For instance, our department is currently moving toward adding an English studies track within the English major, and it is important for the professional writing program to consider the proposal's repercussions for professional writing courses and staffing.

Finally, as a program, different issues pop up. Addressing them sometimes means that the coordinator responds. At other times, responding means creating an ad hoc committee (such as for curricular revision) or leaning on the expertise of others. For instance, Rick Fisher, a member of our teaching cohort, is the university coordinator for the new University Studies Program communications curriculum. We rely on Rick's work and insight to shape our program's adaptation to the new standards. In large part, the coordinator's job is to identify opportunities, occasions, and connections so that we can leverage our strengths and combine our individual work into a coherent, responsive whole.

ASSESSMENT

For the first several years of the professional writing minor's existence, program assessment was not given priority. Indeed, assessment remains an ongoing challenge, made difficult, in part, by the range of courses that comprise the program, as well as its elective component, which pushes a generous proportion of the total program curriculum outside the immediate ken of the English Department and program.

In recent years, we have borrowed from our first-year writing program's direct assessment protocols and conducted single-trait analyses using writing samples from across courses and sections. At the end of each academic year, professional writing faculty have gathered to read and evaluate samples from different courses in order to assess, for example, the effectiveness with which visual design elements were integrated in student writing. We attribute our faculty's willing participation in these assessment efforts to three things: (1) the cohort's stability and small size, (2) the faculty's strong sense of investment, and (3) the ownership our faculty feel in the program. However, difficulty with operationalizing key objectives in a manner that faculty find representative across the program curriculum has made this approach something of a challenge, and we are currently regrouping in order to improve our direct assessment process. As a first step, Michael has begun soliciting materials from individual instructors in the program with an eye toward developing a rich curriculum map that might enable us to better understand relationships between courses and how objectives are realized throughout the program.

Beyond these efforts, and partly in recognition of the ten-year anniversary of the program's first graduating class, we recently conducted the aforementioned alumni survey. The survey covered a wide range of program issues and enabled us to gather data illustrating where our alumni are currently employed, what kinds of communication work they are doing in the workplace, and how our program functioned as part of their professional preparation. Exit interviews constitute a second indirect assessment strategy. Each year, the minor coordinator interviews graduating seniors in order to get regular feedback about teaching, curricula, and recruiting.

MARKETING/PR

We have found marketing our program to be a challenge, one that we take seriously. While we have not received direct pressure to demonstrate a particular level of growth, we are sensitive to the importance of recruiting students and improving our visibility around the university, as doing so seems increasingly important. For instance, within the past year, our college performed a capacity analysis, with an eye toward identifying courses that fail to enroll at an acceptable level. Though we have yet to learn of any tangible consequences for low-enrolling courses, we are on notice, especially with regard to our required capstone course. While most courses in the minor fill with a combination of minors and other students who are seeking to fulfill university writing requirements, we have, in large part, screened out this latter population for the capstone in order to preserve a "capstone" experience and environment for declared minors moving toward completion of the program. As a result, enrollment in this course is consistently low—about half of its twenty-three-seat capacity.

Although we see this concentrated experience as valuable, we wonder how sustainable it might be in an institutional climate in which demonstrating value is of increasing importance for programs of all kinds. We are, it seems, faced with either opening up the capstone course's registration to make it more accommodating of students seeking only to fulfill their upper-division writing requirement—and thus diluting the capstone experience—or maintaining our stance and ramping up marketing in a significant way in hopes of building our student base in the minor. In the latter case, given our present numbers, we would likely need to double the size of the program to feel like the capstone course is on solid ground. Hitting that mark would constitute a significant marketing challenge.

Indeed, for a writing minor like ours, recruiting and attaining institutional visibility are likely different kinds of tasks than they are, for instance, for first-year composition programs. We have to beat the bushes a bit, as students *could* conceivably come from anywhere in the university. The key for us has been raising visibility and trying to identify and develop "new markets," so to speak. To that end, we have made presentations to student organizations and faculty in departments where students seem like a good fit for our minor. From time to time, we attend development fairs and staff an information table in our student union.

Beyond these moves, like most programs, we use digital resources with an eye toward making our program available and visible to various audiences. We maintain a Facebook page for current and prospective students, which we have had for a few years but which we use somewhat sporadically, mostly to circulate advising updates, course announcements, and occasional alumni and student news. We are working on developing a logo for our program that we can use in promotional materials and have redesigned our program website, a part of the Department of English's larger site, which we use to disseminate basic information about the minor's purpose and audience. In order to help students and potential students imagine possible futures emerging, in part, from our program as well as its curriculum and faculty, we also use the website to feature alumni. All of these efforts notwithstanding, we have found that on our campus, word of mouth, especially within particular majors, is significant, and so we rely heavily on our current students sharing their experiences with others.

An additional marketing effort has been to try and circulate information to prospective students through our freshman writing program. This has been a somewhat complicated practice, as it has oftentimes seemed that first-year students were not yet "ready" to hear about our program—enrolled in a compulsory writing course, many students could hardly imagine electing to minor in professional writing. However, incoming students seem increasingly attentive to their major decisions and their professional prospects. We are planning now to ramp up our first-year composition course recruiting by offering brief presentations by members of the professional writing cohort and sharing information around advising time. Of course, we also make every effort to share information about the minor in our own courses, especially by identifying students who might be enrolled in our courses in order to fulfill a university writing requirement but who might also demonstrate aptitude and interest in professional writing.

One last point: we are also becoming increasingly aware of the importance of writing "advocates" around campus. Their significance started to crystalize after a conversation with a couple of students in the minor capstone course, who discussed their parallel experiences in civil engineering and anthropology, respectively, with faculty members in their major departments who took writing more seriously than their other major faculty and who nudged them toward the professional writing minor out of a sense of writing's importance. Again, word of mouth matters: we can put the information in front of prospective students and try to sell it ourselves, but there is no substitute for a faculty mentor's endorsement and recommendation.

TECHNOLOGY

We do not have a devoted classroom, lab, or studio space for students, so in the same way that our software needs are managed through the centralized campus IT office, our classrooms are also centrally managed. In some ways, the lack of a devoted space is a problem, as it means a lack of control and all that control affords. But as campus IT has become more responsive, computer-based classrooms more plentiful, and free (or low cost) web tools more sophisticated and ubiquitous, some of these concerns have lessened, and not having the sundry complications associated with managing a lab frees us to do other things. Most teachers in the minor are now able to meet their classes' pedagogical needs by using Google apps, social media platforms, and various online research tools and website builders. In addition, our campus recently adopted Canvas (by Instructure) as its exclusive learning management system. The relative flexibility of Canvas and the ease with which it can integrate various apps and media make it a powerful addition for students and instructors in our program.

ROLE OF RESEARCH

As a minor staffed largely by instructional faculty whose job descriptions do not explicitly require research activity, research on and about our program has historically been of somewhat secondary importance to delivering our curriculum. With that said, members of our cohort have engaged in program-related research in recent years, and we have found this work to be both rewarding and useful for us as we continue to reflect and self-evaluate. Our research has centered on situating our local concerns within the broader disciplinary context of program development and administration in professional and technical communication. For instance, Kelly Belanger, Christine Stebbins, Julianne Couch, Colin Keeney, and Michael published a chapter about the professional writing minor's origins in Franke, Reid, and DiRenzo's *Design Discourse: Composing and Revising Programs in Professional and Technical Writing* (Knievel, Belanger, Keeney, Couch, and Stebbins 2010). Titled "Starts, False Starts, and Getting Started: (Mis)understanding the Naming of a

Professional Writing Minor," the chapter recounts the minor's origin story and investigates, more specifically, the rationale behind and consequences of choosing to name the minor "professional writing" at the time of its inception.

On a related note, Mary P. Sheridan and Michael published "Articulating 'Responsivity' in Context: Re-making the MA in Composition and Rhetoric for the Electronic Age" in *Computers and Composition* in 2009 (Knievel and Sheridan-Rabideau 2009). While this article's putative purpose was to examine our graduate program's proposed curriculum as a kind of telling case for other programs developing graduate curricula in the digital age, its curricular argument parallels, in many ways, the direction our minor has taken since its beginning, emphasizing curricular relationships between digital technologies and liberally defined constituencies for situated writing.

More recently, Michael and Meg authored a programmatic snapshot article that describes our origins and curriculum while characterizing local challenges ("What We Are (Not)" in *Programmatic Perspectives*) (Van Baalen-Wood and Knievel 2015). Additional research on our program as a "freestanding" minor—a minor writing program that exists without a relationship to a major program in writing—is in the planning stages, and we are keenly interested in learning more about our programmatic peers, as minors often remain largely invisible in broader conversations about writing programs. Both of these projects have emerged out of numerous conference presentations, particularly those we have delivered at the Council for Programs in Technical and Scientific Communication Conference and the Rocky Mountain MLA Conference.

PEDAGOGICAL AND/OR ADMINISTRATIVE HIGHLIGHTS

One of the most compelling things our program has to offer students is a significant range of writing experiences in a range of contexts for a range of different audiences. This comes about through our project-based, service-oriented approach that emphasizes team writing in real contexts. We are also fortunate to have some extremely strong instructors and curricular innovators working in our program. So, while all are united by a set of curricular objectives, the range of ways those objectives are satisfied is significant, a function of different instructors' interests—whether those are research interests, hobbies, business interests, or nonprofit affiliations. Our small town limits our network of opportunities in a quantifiable sense, but it multiplies it in the ways that our teachers are engaged with the university and community.

We think our minor program benefits to an extent from seeing itself as a major. By that we do not mean that we have an inflated sense of our importance or an outsized sense of our impact. But we think that because, since our inception, we have been *the* programmatic expression of writing studies in our department outside of first-year composition, teachers in the program identify strongly with it and take seriously the work we do. The minor does not get overshadowed by a major in writing, because there is no major. Consequently, we try to maximize our exclusive opportunity to develop a writerly disposition among our students. For instance, our capstone course, which Michael frequently teaches, features a final portfolio designed to give students not only an artifact to create and reflect upon, but also a way of talking about their writing as they seek employment. It is also important to note that our capstone course typically incorporates a heavy dose of usability testing practice and related instruction. This work tilts, perhaps, more in the direction of technical communication and is thus slightly at odds with the generalist bent of the minor. But it serves to instill an ethic and set of practices that make audience consideration an authentic, material practice that graduates can take with them, wherever they land as professionals.

Our other courses emphasize writing in context, writing that does work in the world, through a service-oriented, community-focused approach that balances the theoretical and practical. While such an emphasis may not register as particularly earthshaking, we value and try to steep our students in the belief that writing solves problems in civic and professional contexts and that they have the power to intervene in those problems by virtue of their training in the program.

PRIMARY DOCUMENT (at writingprogramarchitecture.com)

One of our most important primary documents is our annual report. Included in the online companion is a sample annual report, written by the coordinator of our minor each spring, and then submitted to the chair of the Department of English. In it, the coordinator outlines issues, challenges, and accomplishments; recognizes contributions made by colleagues; and charts a course for the subsequent academic year. Topics often include program-sponsored activities, curricular initiatives, enrollment, awards, recruiting, and assessment. Coordinators also use these reports to apprise the chair of program needs and other program initiatives. In short, the document provides a "big picture" that the chair can use in reports and conversations with colleagues, alumni, and administrators.

WPAS' VOICES

For those moving into administrative positions in writing programs, we would suggest, first, tapping into the national conversation on the subject. The most obvious incarnation of this conversation might be the Council of Writing Program Administrators (CWPA) Conference, held each summer. While Michael attended this conference only once, he was impressed with the knowledge sharing and goodwill that seem to be the conference's hallmark. As we both teach and research in technical and professional communication, we find that the annual Council for Programs in Technical and Scientific Communication (CPTSC) Conference fills a similar role for us, and the broad exposure to different kinds of programs and specific programmatic concerns within a one-day conference is unparalleled in this field. Like participants at the CWPA conference, the people who attend CPTSC are both deeply interested in the many iterations of technical and professional writing programs and generous about sharing resources and ideas with colleagues within and outside their own programs. Writing program administration is, in most institutions, a singular or near-singular status. Meeting other people who can relate to your circumstances and offer good advice rooted in experience is crucial, because odds are good that no one in your immediate institutional context, regardless of their familiarity with that context, can.

Subscribing to the WPA listserv, too (or, in technical communication, the ATTW listserv), whether you are a passive or active participant, allows you to witness a real-time, national and international conversation about the issues that matter in writing program administration. We are continually awed by the patience and generosity of the luminaries in this area who take so seriously their role as virtual mentors for others working in the field. Frankly, close attention to these lists might surpass in its utility any other kind of reading and research that one can do in this area.

With that said about the national conversation, so much of this kind of work is distinctly local. One thing we both wish we had done to prepare for this is to simply be more involved in our own college and university-level conversations about all matter of things. Doing so would better grease the wheels for helpful conversations with stakeholders around campus and provide more visibility for our program, in part because a minor in professional writing is a very different creature than, for instance, a first-year composition program. While public relations are meaningful for all writing programs, they seem essential in professional and technical writing, especially in a minor that depends heavily on the university community and a positive reputation when recruiting students.

At the end of the day, at our university, technical and professional communication remains something of an unknown, and therefore, somewhat illegible to our constituents. Our identification with English still elicits a range of associations on campus and conjures certain stereotypes that are hard to overcome with key constituencies—constituencies for which we believe we have something to offer. There is always room for formally approaching these constituencies. But more important than that is the informal publicity that accrues as an individual faculty member engages in casual conversations over *years*, leading into those conversations with "I teach in the professional writing program." So many good questions—and opportunities for informal education of colleagues—can start there and contribute to the growth, support, and health of a program.

References

Knievel, Michael, Kelly Belanger, Colin Keeney, Julianne Couch, and Christine Stebbins. 2010. "Starts, False Starts, and Getting Started: (Mis)understanding the Naming of a Professional Writing Major." In *Design Discourse: Composing and Revising Programs in Professional and Technical Writing*, ed. David Franke, Alex Reid, and Anthony DiRenzo, 19–40. Fort Collins: WAC Clearinghouse and Parlor.

Knievel, Michael S., and Mary P. Sheridan-Rabideau. 2009. "Articulating 'Responsivity' in Context: Re-making the MA in Composition and Rhetoric for the Electronic Age." *Computers and Composition* 26 (1): 24–37. http://dx.doi.org/10.1016/j.compcom.2008.11.003.

Office of Institutional Analysis, University of Wyoming. 2015."Fact Sheet, Fall 2015." October 26. Accessed January 12, 2016.

"UW Quick Facts." 2016. *UW Profiles*, University of Wyoming. Accessed January 10, 2016.

Van Baalen-Wood, Meg, and Michael Knievel. 2015. "What We Are (Not) and What We Might Be: The Professional Writing Minor at the University of Wyoming." *Programmatic Perspectives* 7 (2): 189–212.

"Wyoming." 2016. *State and County Quick Facts*. United States Census Bureau. Accessed January 10, 2016.

PART 2

Writing and Communication across the Curriculum

7

LOUISIANA STATE UNIVERSITY COMMUNICATION ACROSS THE CURRICULUM

Sarah Liggett

Institution Type: Land, Sea, and Space Grant Research University
Location: Baton Rouge, Louisiana
Enrollment: 25,000+
Year program was founded: 2004
WPA reports to: Vice Provost for Academic Affairs
Program funded by: Academic Affairs, Deans of Undergraduate Colleges, Grants, and Corporate and Private Donors
Description of students: Louisiana State University (LSU) enrolls approximately twenty-six thousand undergraduates and five thousand four hundred graduate students each fall at its flagship campus in Baton Rouge. Its ten undergraduate colleges and schools offer seventy-two undergraduate degree programs. Most undergraduates are Louisiana residents (82%); 72 percent identify as white, with black, Hispanic, and Asian students making up the next three largest groups. Due in part to tuition rates that are 15 percent below that of our Southern peers and to a state-supported scholarship program, LSU students carry 27 percent less debt than the national average for students in public institutions.

PROGRAM SNAPSHOT

A university-wide academic program, Communication across the Curriculum (CxC) is housed in Academic Affairs. The mission of CxC is to improve the written, spoken, visual, and technological communication skills of all LSU undergraduates while deepening students' understanding of discipline-specific course content. The five main components of the program are communication-intensive courses, CxC studios, a Distinguished Communicators certificate program, faculty development, and TEDxLSU.

DOI: 10.7330/9781607326274.c007

WPA'S PROFILE

My path to becoming a WPA began with an English Education degree as an undergraduate and continued with a master's degree and a doctorate in education, with several classes in the rhetoric and composition program, which was just emerging at Purdue University. There I gained valuable experience as a teaching assistant in first-year composition courses and business writing courses and as a writing center tutor trained by Muriel Harris; I also supervised student teachers. My dissertation, an empirical study of the impact of training students to dictate written communications, provided a research basis for my first book, *Computers and Composing: How the New Technologies Are Changing Writing*, coauthored with Jeanne Halpern (Halpern and Liggett 1984). Upon receiving my PhD, I was hired as an assistant professor in the LSU English Department where I have held various positions. First, I was the WPA of the first-year writing program for ten years, which led me to coauthor an edited collection, *Preparing College Teachers of Writing: Histories, Theories, Programs, Practices,* with Betty Pytlik (Pytlik and Liggett 2002). My next administrative position was director of the LSU Writing Center, and now I am director of the LSU CxC program. I've taught undergraduate and graduate courses in composition, research methodologies, and rhetoric, and instructed students in travel writing for the LSU in Paris program. I've served on dissertation committees, curriculum committees, search committees, assessment committees, and twice helped shape LSU's Quality Enhancement Plan for accreditation. I have enjoyed a rewarding career in teaching, faculty development, and writing program administration for more than thirty years. Did I plan and prepare for every role? Not exactly. But when asked to take on new assignments, I said "yes." I am glad I did because the challenges kept me learning.

PROGRAM CONCEPTION

I inherited the administration of the CxC program from Lillian Bridwell-Bowles, the first director and creative force behind the initiative. Lilly started the program in 2004 with a $2.5-million-dollar gift from the Gordon A. Cain Foundation (how this money was spent is discussed below under "Funding"). With input from key faculty advisors, she built a program from the ground up, winning faculty, departmental, and college support along the way. Through her guidance, CxC expanded beyond the typical WAC program to emphasize written, spoken, visual, and technological communications within

all undergraduate disciplines. Together, they drafted initial requirements for communication-intensive courses and the LSU Distinguished
Communication program. Through instruction at Summer Institutes,
frequent Lunch & Learns throughout the year, and one-on-one consultations with CxC staff, faculty became the champions of teaching communication in their own disciplines.

When I was appointed director in 2009, CxC was only five years old
and had just been named a CCCC Program of Excellence. Thus, it was
in great shape and poised to continue recruiting faculty and students. I
continued seeking guidance from an Academic Advisory Council composed of engaged faculty and key administrators, including representatives from Career Planning and Placement, the Center for Assessment
and Evaluation, and the Faculty Technology Center. I also formed a
Community Advisory Council to gather feedback from leaders in business, industry, and non-profit organizations as to what undergraduates
can do to be better prepared to communicate beyond the classroom.

CxC's biggest ongoing challenge has been financial stability. As private CxC monies dwindled, it became necessary to seek increased university (state) funding just as LSU's state appropriations were cut by
more than one-third. These very deep institutional budget cuts threat-
ened every program and department on campus. For example, the
Center for Excellence in Learning and Teaching and the LSU Writing
Center were eliminated. CxC was spared in part because of strong support by academic deans and its ability to demonstrate its increasing role
in faculty development (through activities such as the Summer Institute,
Lunch and Learns, and individual consultations with faculty regarding
course development and assessment) and student academic support
services (offered through our studios and conferences with peer mentors and staff), thus filling the void where some services had been cut.
Nevertheless, CxC staff is tasked with seeking private funding and grants
to supplement reduced state funding. But donors and granting agencies
are not as eager to fund day-to-day operating expenses and salaries as
they are to support programmatic growth and innovation that can only
happen if the day-to-day operating expenses and salaries are secure:
this reality is the catch-22 of a highly successful program built on non-
recurring funds.

POPULATION SERVED

CxC teaches nearly 40 percent of LSU's undergraduates each academic
year through its communication-intensive (C-I) classes; 506 courses were

registered as C-I in the most recent academic year, but the numbers keep growing. (LSU does not require that students take a minimum number of C-I classes to graduate; rather, students elect to take C-I courses even if they aren't pursuing Distinguished Communicator status.) Students also use CxC studios to work on communication projects, often with the help of peer mentors; together CxC studios logged more than fifteen thousand student sign-ins during a recent academic year. CxC faculty and staff also work one-on-one with nearly four hundred students who have enrolled in the LSU Distinguished Communicator program. Most recently, CxC named seventy Distinguished Communicators in a spring graduation ceremony, another number that keeps growing. Furthermore, the faculty who teach in the CxC program benefit from intensive in-service instruction through our Summer Institute, participate in monthly Lunch & Learns, and consult with area coordinators; to date we have certified more than five hundred faculty members to teach in the CxC program.

FUNDING

Although CxC was jump-started with a gift of $2.5 million (see "Conception" above), the donor stipulated that all funds were to be spent rather than invested. In the first years, donor funds covered everything: salaries, office equipment, start-up costs for studios, travel expenses to professional conferences, and honorariums for speakers for professional workshops. As CxC grew and established itself as a highly effective program, academic deans began to assume more of the costs, especially for studios within their colleges including the salary of the coordinator who recruits and consults mainly with their faculty and students. Ten years later, with nearly all of the initial gift spent, 60 percent of the current CxC budget comes from deans while roughly 40 percent comes from Academic Affairs. CxC occasionally receives gifts from corporate donors and foundations, mainly those who hire LSU graduates and recognize the importance of strong communication skills. (Development officers can be helpful in securing such donations.) Support from grants, including those from our State Board of Regents and from our Student Technology Fees, help us maintain state-of the-art studios. The annual budget for CxC is roughly $700,000 (including staff salaries, operating budget, technology updates, faculty stipends, and student workshops), not including variable income from grants and private funding.

Operations

As director of CxC, I have a half-time administrative appointment with the program and a half-time position in the Department of English where I am full professor, but those lines blur as I often feel I work full time in both arenas. My appointment is for the nine-month academic cycle, with additional compensation for one-month of summer work, although in reality (and through email) I am never completely away from work. I do, however, only teach one class each academic year, unless I opt to teach in a summer abroad program. My CxC job description indicates that I am mainly responsible for strategic planning and assessment, fund raising, and coordination of our academic and community advisory councils. Nevertheless, my job is anything but routine as I go from meeting to meeting with CxC staff, academic deans, and faculty; coauthor grants and write or review program materials; write or answer dozens of emails about CxC procedures and activities; or try to keep up with developments in discipline-specific and professional communication.

In addition to my services, the program operates with a full-time, highly skilled professional staff of eight: five area coordinators (two in engineering and one each in science, art and design, and humanities and social sciences) and three staff in the central office: an associate director who handles day-to-day operations of programming, budget, and staffing including supervision of studio coordinators and coordination of the TEDxLSU event; a program director who works mainly with the LSU Distinguished Communicator program and community outreach; and a technology/business manager. Each handles specific tasks and duties to make CxC work across the campus, yet we collaborate on nearly every aspect of the program. The synergy and collegiality make for an exciting and highly productive workspace.

Depending on grant funding, anywhere from one to four graduate teaching assistants have clearly defined project assignments. CxC studio coordinators hire and train peer mentors to help students with multimodal communication projects.

On a day-to-day basis, CxC's professional staff fulfills specific tasks and duties to make CxC work across the campus. Some of the work follows the natural rhythm of a semester: recruiting, mentoring, and certifying faculty to teach communication-intensive courses; overseeing day-to-day studio operations; coordinating the Distinguished Communicator program with its workshops, portfolio deadlines, and certification ceremonies. Meanwhile, our dedicated faculty members teach the communication-intensive courses and prepare LSU students for twenty-first century communications.

We hold staff meetings every two weeks, send steady streams of emails, see each other at events, and hold an annual retreat to reflect on our successes, identify what we can do better, coordinate new projects, and agree on long-term goals. We work side-by-side to plan and deliver an interactive three-day Summer Institute for faculty development and champion an annual TEDxLSU event, which, with themes such as Enact and Connect, engages the community and demonstrates the importance of innovation and communication. We also oversee a Student Creative Communications Team, approximately thirty volunteers, which helps us envision, plan, and execute various creative elements related to promoting, positioning, and hosting TEDxLSU. At the beginning of each semester and the summer, the central staff makes a multi-page to-do list of individual and collaborative responsibilities. Clear channels of communication are critical to such a large-scale communication program.

ASSESSMENT

The CxC program is assessed regularly through multiple methods. We administer course evaluations to learn students' and faculty members' sense of how C-I pedagogy influences communication skills and depth of content knowledge. (Ninety percent of LSU C-I faculty said their students gained a greater understanding of the course content because of the C-I activities they incorporated into the course. Two-thirds of LSU students say they will definitely use what they've learned about communication in the future, a positive finding given the lack of "relevance" that students attribute to college courses across the nation.) Whenever possible, we analyze data already gathered by faculty and departments to tease out the impact of the CxC program. For example, if two sections of the same course are taught, one C-I and the other not, and if a group exam is administered to both sections, we compare the grades of the two sections. Students in C-I courses tend to score higher. Or in a capstone course with a major communication project, faculty members may be asked to report final grades; we can then look to see if there are significant differences between students with two or more C-I classes and those who took only one or none. We have also used the university's large-scale portfolio assessment of student learning outcomes related to communication. Preliminary data show that a randomly selected group of students who have taken two or more C-I courses during their programs of study score significantly higher than a randomly selected group who took only one or none. We are now conducting a similar study of Distinguished Communicators. Finally, we have used findings from the

National Survey of Student Engagement (NSSE) and the optional questions provided by the Consortium for the Study of Writing in College to measure the impact of C-I courses on such measures as level of academic challenge, amount of active and collaborative learning, and degree of student-faculty interaction. We are also looking at the data for insights into how college students write, how college teachers teach writing, what students are writing in college classes, and the relationships among writing practices and engagement, persistence, and learning. In the future, we want to assess the long-term impact of our program by surveying our Distinguished Communicators one, three, and five years after graduation, and learning how they think CxC could better prepare students for workplace communications.

The challenges of assessing CxC are similar to those for any academic program. How can you isolate the impact of the program when so many other variables affect student learning? How do you find time to conduct meaningful assessment among all of the other programmatic demands? How do you weigh quantitative numbers against qualitative narratives? My advice is to look for places where faculty and administrators are already assessing the communication skills of their students (perhaps for accreditations purposes) and see how you can use the data to examine the effects of your program. Remember that you do not have to assess everything every year. Make assessment count; ask only those questions to which you honestly want to know the answers. Assessment is only valuable if you use the results to improve your program.

MARKETING/PR

Whenever given the chance to talk about CxC, we do: at orientations with students and parents, at meetings with faculty, at retreats with deans, at career fairs with employers, in private meetings with potential donors. CxC faculty and Distinguished Communicator candidates spread the word to fellow teachers and classmates about the value of the program. CxC faculty and students are often featured in "Highlights" on the main LSU web page. Our graduates send testimonials, which we then post on the CxC web page and blog contributing their success on the job with their strong communication skills. We encourage departments to add links to the CxC program and studios on their individual web pages. Finally, our work with TEDxLSU helps get our message out to the public and to potential donors.

Teachers of C-I courses are required to list the CxC goals on their syllabi and to encourage students to use the studios when working on their multimodal projects. The fact that students spent nearly twenty-six thousand hours in studios last academic year shows strong knowledge of the program.

But marketing and public relations must be as ongoing as the turnover is in administration, faculty, and students. Every semester brings the need and the opportunity to educate a new group about CxC.

TECHNOLOGY

Since CxC emphasizes technological communication as one of its four modes, we model the use of technology in our own communications. CxC maintains a website, a Facebook page, a blog, and a Twitter account. The TEDxLSU event we sponsor is a multimedia extravaganza. Our studios are equipped to best serve the students in particular disciplines—3D printers in engineering and art and design, and a presentation practice room with a video camera and a sound booth in the humanities, for example. We use technologies to track the students who use our studios. (*Appointy.com* is our online appointment/reservation system, and in the studios, we use the TigerCard office's TigerTracker system, a system specific to LSU). *KarmaCRM* is the Customer Relationship Management software application that helps us monitor the progress of our Distinguished Communicators. Our faculty submit course materials online when certifying their courses as communication-intensive. Our staff, including our student workers and peer mentors, keep the technologies working and train others to use them as well with the help of *Lynda.com.* Many workshops for faculty introduce them to the latest technologies to support teaching, including *Jing, Kaltura, Screencast-O-Matic,* and *iMovie* as well as *Final Cut Pro* for video editing in the visual mode. *Slack* has helped us coordinate communications in our TEDxLSU endeavors with community partners, students, and CxC staff.

ROLE OF RESEARCH

During the first decade of CxC's existence, we have focused on shaping the program and assessing its effectiveness at the departmental and university level. And while we have yet to identify a programmatic research project, several CxC faculty members, sometimes in collaboration with CxC staff, have published journal articles and presented conference papers describing the program and demonstrating its effectiveness (see Waggenspack et al. 2013 and Bosworth et al. 2012). Some CxC staff members have organized Wikipedia projects to engage students in communication projects with audiences beyond the classroom and shared their work at national and international workshops. The most comprehensive article on the original design of the program is by Lillian Bridwell-Bowles and coauthors, and an article in *Across the Disciplines* gives an overview of CxC's work in implementing the Student Creative Communications Team to support TEDxLSU (Bridwell-Bowles, Powell, and Choplin 2014). We would welcome research on CxC—especially by graduate students engaged in research for dissertations or by undergraduates seeking guided research projects. Programmatic research may well be the next venture for CxC.

PEDAGOGICAL AND/OR ADMINISTRATIVE HIGHLIGHTS

Three innovative initiatives within CxC strongly influence its success. First, CxC instructs students in written, spoken, visual, and technological communication, preparing them more fully for the multimodal communication challenges of the twenty-first century and appealing more broadly to disciplines campus wide. For example, students in architecture tend to be visually talented, but they often need help to translate their visions into narratives, while many students in the STEM disciplines need instruction in visual communication to translate complex projects into graphs and diagrams for a lay audience.

Second, the C-I courses in which students learn discipline-specific communication are taught by faculty members who agree to meet CxC requirements. While this arrangement means that not all sections of a course may carry the C-I designation, it does ensure that every C-I course has a faculty member whose pedagogy includes feedback on drafts and practice presentations and requirements for minimum number of graded assignments. No new courses were added to the curriculum or to students' plans of study to accommodate the CxC program. Rather if the student-to-teacher ratio is low enough (35:1), and the faculty member agrees to meet the CxC requirements for course certification, the course can be designated as communication-intensive and students' transcripts will carry the C-I designation.

Third, CxC supports an innovative program in which students seek certification as LSU Distinguished Communicators. In addition to taking twelve hours of C-I courses in their degree paths, these highly motivated students attend communication workshops; apply and reflect on their communication and leadership skills; and build digital portfolios documenting their skills. Throughout the certification process, the students are mentored by CxC faculty advisors and staff. Students' portfolios are assessed by their advisors and by a panel of CxC faculty to assure high standards across the disciplines.

CxC staff are currently working on increasing students' success in learning communication technology. We have recently entered a partnership with LSU's Information Technology Services to tutor students in the advanced technology they need for communication-related projects, creating a "one-stop-shop" for LSU students in our CxC studios.

PRIMARY DOCUMENT (at writingprogramarchitecture.com)

All of our most integral documents are housed on our website, which can be accessed by typing "CxC" into the search bar on the LSU homepage. Through it we communicate with faculty and students about CxC's many activities, offer resources, and publicize our successes. Here visitors can find the Distinguished Communicator Handbook, see our list of upcoming workshops, consult studio hours for mentoring on multimodal projects, print a rubric for a visual communication assignment, and more. CxC would not have been nearly as green or efficient without its website. Also, a sample agenda for the CxC Summer Institute is included on the companion website to illustrate the topics we cover and the means by which we deliver information. This three-day workshop is packed with ideas for teaching discipline-specific communication strategies and skills.

WPA'S VOICE

As a WPA, you soon realize that you did not learn everything you will ever need to know in kindergarten—or even in graduate school. You'll need to find ways to be:

- An effective fundraiser, or become good friends with your university's foundation officers.
- A savvy accountant who understands budget codes and can read financial spread sheets.
- An assessment guru who can analyze qualitative and quantitative data and to tell a convincing narrative about the value of your program as it relates to the university's mission.
- An expert in time management capable of weighing and juggling priorities, meeting deadlines, and recognizing when the workload is unrealistic and needs to be renegotiated.
- An astute delegator, one who knows how to tap the strengths of colleagues and locate campus resources to lighten the workload.

- A campus community player, one who uses work on university committees and involvement in campus-wide initiatives to publicize his or her own program while gaining a greater understanding of the campus culture and meeting colleagues from across campus who can serve as allies.
- A life-long learner in your professional field and in professional relationships.

While I have always been an active member of the National Council of Teachers of English (NCTE) and participated at the Conference on College Composition and Communication, I realize now I would have benefitted even more by attending meetings of the Council of Writing Program Administrators, the International Writing Centers Association, and the International Network of Writing-across-the Curriculum Programs. Each of these professional organizations offer educational opportunities geared toward those new to program administration. Some colleges and universities also offer faculty development for those who aspire to administrative positions. Much of what you'll need to know to be an effective WPA, you'll learn on the job, but there are many resources and mentors who are willing to help you shorten the learning curve.

References

Bosworth, Frank, Vincent Cellucci, and Marsha Cuddeback. 2012. "Nascent Narratives: Re-VIEWing Design Presentations." *International Journal of Literacies* 19 (1): 75–86.

Bridwell-Bowles, Lillian, Karen L. Powell, and Tiffany Walter Choplin. 2014. "Not Just Words Any More: Multimodal Communication across the Curriculum." *Across the Disciplines* 6.

Halpern, Jeanne W., and Sarah Liggett. 1984. *Computers & Composing: How the New Technologies Are Changing Writing.* Carbondale: Southern Illinois University Press.

Pytlik, Betty, and Sarah Liggett. 2002. *Preparing College Teachers of Writing: Histories, Theories, Programs, Practices.* New York: Oxford University Press.

Waggenspack, Warren N., Sarah Liggett, Warren R. Hull, David Bowles, and Paige Davis. 2013. "Development and Assessment of an Innovative Program to Integrate Communication Skills into Engineering Curricula." Presented at ASEE 2013 Conference Proceedings, Atlanta, GA, June 23.

8

MONMOUTH COLLEGE COMMUNICATION ACROSS THE CURRICULUM

Bridget Draxler

Institution Type: Liberal Arts College
Location: Monmouth, Illinois
Enrollment: 1,300
Year program was founded: 2005
WPA reports to: Advisory Committee and Dean of the Faculty
Program funded by: Academic Affairs, administered by Dean of the Faculty
Description of students: We serve many first-generation college students from downstate Illinois and Chicago. Monmouth College's all-undergraduate student body includes 26 percent American minority and 7 percent international students; business is the most popular major.

PROGRAM SNAPSHOT

The Communication across the Curriculum (CAC) program seeks not only to prepare students with basic skills in writing, speaking, and listening; it also frames communication as an exercise in critical thinking, a meaningful way to connect with the community, an instrument of change, and a foundational element of a liberal arts education. Students develop these skills in a series of six courses linked horizontally (first-year writing, first-year speaking, and a reading intensive first-year seminar) and vertically (a series of interdisciplinary courses taken each year that starts with first-year seminar). In addition, students develop communication skills in their major field of study through CAC department plans developed by faculty in each discipline.

WPA'S PROFILE

My PhD is in eighteenth-century British literature, and I had no formal exposure to or training in WAC methodologies during graduate school.

DOI: 10.7330/9781607326274.c008

So, when I saw the job ad at Monmouth College for a Communication across the Curriculum coordinator, I wasn't confident that I was qualified for the position. However, the school and the job seemed like such a good fit that I decided to apply.

The reality is, these types of positions—which involve both faculty and administrative roles—are positions that often graduate students may not feel qualified for, partly because they require such a diverse set of skills and experiences. My position is split between teaching three courses a year, coordinating the CAC program, and directing the Writing Center, along with expectations for research and service required of all tenure-track faculty. There are many hats to wear. But for me, that variety was part of the appeal.

What I didn't realize at the time was that my background as a graduate of a liberal arts college, my experience teaching several sections of first-year writing and speaking, and my service work in cohosting an academic conference, mentoring new graduate student teachers, and serving on the department textbook committee were all excellent preparation for the kind of work I do as CAC coordinator. Most important, my involvement with civic engagement turned out to be a surprising back door into writing program administration.

In my application to work at Monmouth, I wrote about "writing in community," and how the values that drive my commitment to civic engagement would transfer to the CAC program. These shared values, it turned out, were more important to the search committee than administrative experience. I had a vision of how a CAC program can build bridges across courses, within departments, and between the campus and community; I had an understanding of the role of communication as not just a skill but a mode of critical thinking within a liberal arts education; and I was an energetic and enthusiastic supporter of the immense reflection, collaboration, creativity, and intentionality that goes into good teaching. And ultimately, I believe these are the most important qualifications for this type of position.

Now on the job, I have sought out professional development opportunities to keep up with the field, attending and presenting at conferences like the International Writing across the Curriculum Conference, the Midwest Writing Centers Association Conference, the Small Liberal Arts Colleges Writing Program Administrators Conference, and the National Conference on Peer Tutoring in Writing. In addition, I have also continued to be involved in civic engagement organizations like Imagining America, since ideas of "writing in community" continue to inform the work I do as CAC coordinator.

PROGRAM CONCEPTION

As part of a curricular review over ten years ago, the Monmouth College faculty developed our signature Integrated Studies program: a four-year sequence of interdisciplinary general education courses covering Introduction to the Liberal Arts (ILA), Global Perspectives, Reflections, and Citizenship. In addition to this curricular revision, the college reemphasized the integration of our required first-year curriculum, including Fundamentals of Communication (first-year speech) and Composition and Argumentation (first-year writing) along with ILA (which emphasizes critical reading and college level discussion). These revised first-year courses were intentionally designed to provide students with skills in speaking, argumentation, research, and writing that would apply across the curriculum and specifically within the Integrated Studies sequence.

The CAC was developed in tandem with this curricular review. Its goal was to facilitate vertical and horizontal integration of this new general education plan through the incremental development of students' communication skills. Each of these six courses (the four Integrated Studies courses plus first-year speech and writing) introduces and reinforces a set of shared communication skills and shared vocabulary, which facilitate knowledge transfer of the writing, speaking, and listening skills that are taught within these courses.

From the beginning, even before its official launch in 2005, CAC was designed in collaboration between the departments of English and Communication Studies. They sought candidates in both fields, and I belong to both departments (though I will be tenured in English). Interestingly, and maybe unexpectedly, both my predecessor and I have happened to be eighteenth-century British literature specialists by training before taking the job at Monmouth. However, the position is decidedly interdisciplinary; even now, it is not physically housed in either the English or Communication Studies Departments, but is instead located in the Center for Science and Business, in the physics wing of the building. This unusual setup supports the original vision of CAC as a truly cross-campus initiative.

The CAC program had been without a coordinator for several years when I arrived, but through continued support by English and Communication faculty members, it was in a strong position. The shared communication skills and vocabulary had been developed by the two departments and revised by my predecessor, and the Integrated Studies program had hit its stride. In my first year, I hosted workshops for Integrated Studies instructors, interviewed each department to conduct a CAC inventory, and began developing a new CAC website. I also drafted a new mission statement and new goals for the CAC program:

CAC Mission Statement

Subscribing to the motto of "Learning to Communicate and Communicating to Learn," CAC promotes the integration of communication skills across campus, in both major and general education classes. It values communication as a way to facilitate developmental learning, active learning, integrated learning, and collaborative learning at Monmouth College. Students incrementally develop a variety of oral and written communication skills to engage course content actively, make strong arguments, and communicate effectively with academic and professional audiences.

Goals for the CAC Program

1. Students can **make an argument**, supporting it with reasons, addressing opposing point of view, and applying appropriate strategies for their rhetorical context

2. Students can **communicate in different genres**, including research, analysis, and reflection

3. Students can **communicate with an authentic audience**, including professional, academic, and community audiences

4. Students can **practice process writing and peer review**; they are capable of giving and receiving constructive criticism on their own and others' work through a multi-step composition process

POPULATION SERVED

Because Monmouth College is a small campus, and because faculty are expected to teach annually in the Integrated Studies program, the CAC program reaches almost all eighty tenure track (TT) faculty, and a handful of non–tenure track (NTT) faculty who teach in integrated studies (INTG) (75% of courses and 80% of INTG courses are taught by TT faculty). More than a third of our faculty are pre-tenure, so many CAC workshops have a combination of experienced faculty who have built the INTG program and new faculty with fresh ideas.

CAC primarily serves as a resource for faculty development, and historically, it has focused exclusively on faculty as teachers. In the past year, however, we have developed new programs to support faculty as writers, including faculty writing groups and writing retreats. We have found these programs to support faculty research have inadvertently increased interest in CAC programs related to teaching.

Because my position also includes directing the Writing Center, I am also the face of tutoring services to students. So although my role as CAC director focuses exclusively on faculty development, this linked position leads to obvious interconnection between CAC and the Writing Center, and between serving faculty and student populations.

The Writing Center has increased traffic in the past few years, from around six hundred sessions per year to over one thousand sessions in the 2013–14 school year. Of student writers who completed post-session evaluation surveys since 2014, 57 percent are first-year students, 19 percent are sophomores, 16 percent are juniors, and 7 percent are seniors (1% other). In fall 2015, one-third of student writers sought help for INTG courses and another 25 percent visited for first-year writing and speaking; just over half the sessions were for major courses with a handful of students seeking help with study abroad applications or other extracurricular writing tasks. Over half of survey respondents are repeat visitors, and nearly 20 percent are back for their sixth visit or more. Students identify seeking help with "organization" and "word choice/clarity" most frequently, and faculty encouragement is far and away the top reason students go to the Writing Center. More than 98 percent would recommend the Writing Center to their peers.

FUNDING

When I took over the program in 2011, there was no budget for the CAC program (aside from the half-time teaching reallocation to direct both the CAC program and the Writing Center). Working for the first three years without funding led to some challenges, but it also helped me to be creative. The ePortfolio assessment, for instance, is funded by the Integrated Studies program; this partnership provided an important excuse to talk about the connections and gaps between the content learning goals and the communication skills students develop in INTG. The guest speakers have mostly been in-house, which means that the faculty are hearing advice from people they know, and the speakers have an additional faculty development opportunity—especially if they didn't realize before that what they're teaching is a form of communication across the curriculum. Faculty members were given permission to use their development funds to pay for the writing retreat. I baked my own cookies.

In 2014, I applied for and fortunately secured an annual budget line for CAC through Academic Affairs, administered by the dean of the faculty. That budget includes:

Printing—$300

Travel—$1,000

Meals—$1,200

Speakers—$500

This new budget line will allow me to bring in more outside expertise to share with the faculty, and allow me to offer food at workshops—both of which are important next steps as we grow the program.

OPERATIONS

Our CAC program is a staff of one, although I work closely with an advisory committee that includes the chair of the English Department, the chair of the Communication Studies Department, the associate dean of Academic Affairs, and one outside member (usually representing the sciences).

The job duties for the CAC coordinator are twofold: first, to integrate the shared communication concepts and shared vocabulary into the first-year curriculum and interdisciplinary Integrated Studies courses; and second, to support the incremental development of communication skills (including writing, speaking, and listening) in the majors. I offer individual and departmental faculty consultations and frequent workshops on developing assignments, in-class activities, and assessments. In addition, I write a monthly report to the faculty, manage a CAC website, and maintain a library of reference materials. In partnership with the Integrated Studies coordinators, I have also begun developing a long-term vision and ePortfolio assessment plan for the program. In terms of teaching duties, I teach first-year writing, first-year speaking, and interdisciplinary general education classes within Integrated Studies, along with offering a credit-bearing tutor training course for the Writing Center. Finally, the position includes directing the campus Writing Center, which employs twenty peer tutors and provides around 1,200 tutoring sessions per year.

Beyond the job description outlined above, my day-to-day work is spent being a good listener and building bridges. When one department tries out a new strategy for senior thesis workshopping that is effective, I share that information with another department struggling with a similar issue. When one Integrated Studies course decides to change its prompt or rubric for the shared writing assignment, I talk with the courses immediately preceding and following it to see how they can anticipate and reinforce these new emphases in their courses. Most of the consultation work I do is informal, chatting before a job talk, after a faculty meeting, or over the Wednesday faculty lunches.

As CAC coordinator, I prepare about twenty-five workshops and work with three to four departments on CAC plans each year. I meet with my advisory committee every third week and meet regularly with coordinators of the Integrated Studies programs, members of the English and Communication Studies Departments, and new members of the faculty. I plan end-of-semester events for the faculty writing groups, including retreats. I also maintain the website, write reports to the faculty, manage advertising for upcoming events, and maintain an open-door policy to be available for my colleagues.

ASSESSMENT

In terms of internal assessment, I have tried to piggyback CAC assessment within broader assessment of the Integrated Studies program, in order to strengthen points of intersection between Integrated Studies program goals and CAC goals. For instance, as part of the new Integrated Studies ePortfolio assessment, student essays are evaluated both in terms of learning objectives and writing skills.

As part of the ePortfolio assessment, students upload to turnitin.com each semester the "shared assignment" from Integrated Studies along with a reflection about that assignment. The shared assignment differs in each year of the program: all sophomores in Global Perspectives, for instance, write a ten-page interdisciplinary research paper, while all juniors in Reflections write a three-step reflection paper.

Each course has developed a unique rubric to evaluate how well students have achieved the Integrated Studies learning goals for that course, and I have developed, in partnership with a member of the English Department, a rubric to be used across all four years to evaluate students' written communication skills. We will roll out this assessment plan one year at a time, beginning with students in Introduction to the Liberal Arts, then adding one course per year for the next four years.

The ePortfolio assessment will not only provide important assessment data on the writing skills of all Monmouth College students, but also create a faculty development opportunity for those who are trained each year to participate in the assessment. In addition to completing the rubrics, the faculty who assess the essays will also prepare a presentation to the faculty with patterns they noticed and recommendations for improvement, ensuring that our assessment results immediately feed into our teaching practices. The twinned results will also allow us to track correlation between student success in demonstrating knowledge of learning goals and proficiency in writing, building further connections between Integrated Studies and CAC program goals.

MARKETING/PR

CAC publishes a monthly report with information about what is happening in Integrated Studies, details on CAC department plans in progress, ideas and tips for writing instruction, and upcoming events. I also create a semester calendar of events, which includes twelve to fifteen workshops, discussions, and special presentations each term. Before each small-group workshop, I send reminder emails a week in advance and on the day of the workshop; for larger all-faculty workshops, I will send a paper advertisement a week in advance and an email to the faculty listserv on the day of the workshop. However, being an involved member of the campus community is the most important way I advertise for CAC.

Since developing our new website, I have also begun collecting resources for various constituencies, including materials for each of our Integrated Studies courses, resources for teaching the shared vocabulary concepts, and multimedia tools. The blog format of the site also allows me to post resources, articles, or tips on the homepage. These posts are fed into the college's homepage, which draws traffic to our site.

TECHNOLOGY

CAC workshops frequently include ideas for incorporating technology into communication instruction. Some workshops have included tutorials on Zotero, Prezi, Google Drive, WordPress, and YouTube Video Editor. As much as possible, I provide take-home tutorials so that we can spend the time in the workshop talking about pedagogy: ways that we can improve student learning by using social media in the writing process, using video or audio recording to give feedback on student papers/speeches, or using social annotation software to facilitate classroom discussion.

Our website includes a section devoted to faculty resources, which includes technology tutorials, handouts, and other materials specifically tailored to communication instruction at Monmouth College. For instance, we have a citation guide that uses examples from Monmouth College faculty publications and teaching ideas for each of the shared vocabulary terms.

ROLE OF RESEARCH

Conducting formal research to assess and report on the CAC program is not required for my tenure and promotion. However, I have had the opportunity to publish articles on several projects and collaborations that I have worked on at Monmouth, including an article on "Vocation in the Writing Center" in *Writing Lab Newsletter* (Jones, Becker, Riley, and Draxler 2015) I researched with three students, and an article coauthored with our Communication Basic Studies coordinator on "Strengthening Tutoring Communities with *They Say / I Say*" (Draxler and Walters-Kramer 2015), which will be published in an edited collection of essays titled *Communicating Advice: Peer Tutoring and Communication Practice.* Focusing on specific initiatives rather than overall program assessment, these research projects have allowed me to tie together my administrative roles as CAC coordinator and Writing Center director with my broader scholarly interests in the scholarship of teaching and learning.

In addition, I have continued to pursue research in eighteenth-century studies, though again with a focus on the scholarship of teaching and learning, and especially using public digital humanities initiatives to teach historical literature in undergraduate education. While this research may seem disconnected from my work as a writing program administrator, I find it valuable to engage with discipline-specific writing instruction in my home field of English as a way to connect with faculty who teach disciplinary writing to their own majors.

PEDAGOGICAL AND/OR ADMINISTRATIVE HIGHLIGHTS

Because the CAC program was imagined from the start as an interdepartmental collaboration, and as including writing, speaking, and listening, it holds a kind of interdisciplinary reach that may be more challenging for programs that focus exclusively on writing or are housed in a specific department. The distinction also lends itself more easily to multimodal communication and civic engagement, where writing, speaking, and listening skills are often overlapping and intertwined. Even among other CAC programs, ours is unique in including listening—an essential skill that can sometimes be overlooked in undergraduate education.

Our program is also distinctive for its shared vocabulary. For many students, it can be confusing to have Professor X ask for a thesis while Professor Y wants a main idea, or having Professor A want a works cited while Professor B wants a bibliography. The shared vocabulary supports knowledge transfer, as students hear the same language used in courses across the curriculum. And, using this shared vocabulary has also helped faculty: it gives us common ground to talk about how we teach communication skills and make connections across the general education and major curriculum.

Finally, our program is innovative in its emphasis on digital communication and civic engagement. Coming into the position with a background in these areas rather than in writing program administration, I have been able to widen the conversation from skill acquisition to larger issues of critical thinking, authentic audiences, and the liberal arts. I have hosted faculty development sessions on "Writing as Civic Engagement," "Making Projects Public and Meaningful," "Civic Reflection," and "Group Writing in Community," which have helped faculty embed communication instruction within civic engagement.

For instance, the senior Citizenship course in Integrated Studies prepares students for "conscientious action" in the community through "interpersonal and empathetic communication." I work with faculty in Citizenship to develop civic engagement projects that include writing and speaking as part of students' community involvement. Citizenship students have coauthored grant proposals with community partners and written reports that analyze economic development possibilities for local city government; they have created multimedia exhibits on community leaders and presented their research to local audiences; they have developed educational materials on information literacy and hosted public discussions and debates preceding national and local elections.

Because these projects are collaborative, with both peers and community partners, they allow students to negotiate their own voices as writers and speakers with the voices of others. Students discover new investment and value in their communication skills when this writing and speaking is embedded in public scholarship and service learning. These projects and partnerships have allowed me to connect CAC more closely with the institution's larger mission and my own research and teaching interests.

PRIMARY DOCUMENT (at writingprogramarchitecture.com)

Of primary importance to our program has been our Communication Skills Table, which serves multiple purposes: reminding faculty how a particular course fits into the bigger picture of communication skills in general education, signaling to the broader campus that writing skills are developed incrementally over time in multiple courses, and helping students transfer knowledge cumulatively between courses and contexts. The Skills Table was developed in 2010 by then CAC Director Steve Price.

WPA'S VOICE

If you're thinking about applying for or have gotten a position in WPA and don't have the administrative experience you think you need, remember that (like good writing) the skills don't matter if the ideas aren't there. Focus on the ideas about writing and pedagogy that your education and experience have given you, and you can catch up on the administrative elements of the job by going to conferences, researching institutional history, and asking lots of questions. I never imagined myself in a position like this one, but it's been a great fit for me. And in retrospect, my graduate studies prepared me in unexpected ways to succeed my current position.

Supporting student listening skills is a unique feature of our CAC program, but it's a skill that is essential for any WPA position. Spend lots of time listening.

While my joint position makes connecting to the Writing Center easy, it's an important connection to make: many of my department CAC plans have involved the writing tutors. For example, tutors lead senior thesis writing groups for students writing capstones for their major, and the tutors can often give an on-the-ground perspective of the writing skills that students in a particular course or major find most challenging. I also work closely with the director of our speech tutoring program, the director of academic support programs, and the coordinators of international student support and intercultural life. The faculty and staff in these positions are invaluable partners, and I could not do my job without them.

Finally, I encourage you to think about a position in writing program administration as a form of intellectual matchmaking. My position gives me a bird's eye view of communication instruction at the college, and some of the best work I do is bringing together people who are thinking about the same issues can work through these questions in conversation with one another. One department was thinking about helping its majors communicate about their field to a general audience, and I encouraged them to check out the weekly Science Seminar where biology, chemistry, and physics majors present their research to the public. A faculty member was struggling to get her students to give constructive criticism during peer review sessions, so I encouraged her to visit the monthly Art Critique in the Art Department, where students thoughtfully and respectfully give critical feedback to one another. The heart of my job, like communication itself, is about bringing people together.

Acknowledgment

Thank you to my colleagues at Monmouth College, especially Lee McGaan, who helped recover documentation and provide insights on the history of the CAC program.

References

Draxler, Bridget, and Lori Walters-Kramer. 2015. "Strengthening Tutoring Communities with *They Say / I Say*." In *Communicating Advice: Peer Tutoring and Communication Practice*, ed. Wendy Atkins-Sayre and Eunkyong L. Yook, 297–300. New York: Peter Lang Publishing.

Jones, Jessica, Lauren Becker, Alyssa Riley, and Bridget Draxler. 2015. "Vocation in the Writing Center." WLN: A Journal of Writing Center Scholarship 40(3–4): 28–31.

9

OLD DOMINION UNIVERSITY QUALITY ENHANCEMENT PLAN (QEP)

Remica L. Bingham-Risher

Institution Type: Public Research University
Location: Norfolk, Virginia
Enrollment: 30,000
Year program was founded: 2012
WPA reports to: Provost
Program funded by: Academic Affairs
Description of students: We are a metropolitan campus on the east coast of Virginia. The university serves largely Virginia-based native and transfer undergraduate students in equal numbers. More than 30 percent of the university's twenty-four thousand students (more than eighteen thousand undergraduates and nearly six thousand graduate students) represent a broad range of ethnic minorities, 48 states and more than 114 countries.

PROGRAM SNAPSHOT

Old Dominion's Quality Enhancement Plan (QEP) is focused on writing. Referred to as *Improving Disciplinary Writing* (IDW), the QEP has two major initiatives: faculty writing workshops and faculty action project internal grants.

WPA'S PROFILE

In 2002, I earned my bachelor's of arts degree from Old Dominion University (ODU) where I majored in English and minored in African American studies. In January 2005, I earned my MFA in writing and literature from Bennington College. My career as a WPA began unexpectedly. After I earned my MFA, I began looking for a job teaching English, but instead I found a job as an administrative faculty member—the writing competency coordinator—at Norfolk State University (NSU). I

DOI: 10.7330/9781607326274.c009

worked in the Department of Institutional Effectiveness and Assessment (IEA) to oversee a high-stakes writing exam, the Examination of Writing Competency (EWC), a graduation requirement for all undergraduate students. I tested over eight hundred students per semester and met with more than two hundred students individually throughout the term for tutoring on various aspects of writing. Each term, I oversaw the budget and spending for our initiative, analyzed the results of the EWC and of the EWC graders, provided information for curriculum feedback, and worked directly with faculty and staff concerning the EWC. Occasionally, I taught courses in my main fields of study—writing, literature, and poetry—as an adjunct.

After spending seven years at NSU, I was well-equipped to take on a larger position that became available at Old Dominion—the director of Writing and Faculty Development and an adjunct assistant professor at ODU. My major professional duties include overseeing the university's QEP: *Improving Disciplinary Writing* (IDW), which is an integral part of the Southern Association of Colleges and Schools Commission on Colleges (SACSCOC) accreditation process. As I was the first person to hold this position, beginning in August 2012, a large part of my job was establishing the IDW office by continuing the implementation of our initiatives. I work with faculty to implement techniques that improve student learning through writing to help improve individual courses and departmental disciplinary writing.

In addition to my work in education, I am also a practicing writer and teach one course each term in the master of fine arts program at ODU. My first book, *Conversion* (Bingham-Risher 2006), won the Naomi Long Madgett Poetry Award and my second book, *What We Ask of Flesh* (Bingham-Risher 2013), was shortlisted for the Hurston/Wright Legacy Award.

PROGRAM CONCEPTION

Our IDW program at ODU was conceived over a period of several years well before I was hired. Since it is a large part of the our accreditation process, universities governed by SACSCOC begin planning for the initiative some years in advance, as the plan has to significantly affect student learning and must run for at least five years. Old Dominion University's faculty and administration gave considerable thought to the selection of a QEP on disciplinary writing.

ODU's QEP emerged from analysis of the university's institutional effectiveness data and from campus and community-wide conversations with faculty, staff, students, alumni, and employers. Both sources supported the choice of writing as the focus of ODU's QEP. Skill in writing is demonstrated by six student learning outcomes that are assessed through evaluation of written artifacts. Students will be able to:

- clearly state a focused problem, question, or topic appropriate for the purpose of the task
- identify relevant knowledge and credible sources
- synthesize information and multiple viewpoints related to the problem, question, or topic
- apply appropriate research methods or theoretical framework to the problem, question, or topic
- formulate conclusions that are logically tied to inquiry findings and consider applications, limitations, and implications
- reflect on or evaluate what was learned (Old Dominion University 2012, 6–8).

As I am the first person to hold this position, my job was to begin establishing the QEP office by continuing the implementation of the QEP initiatives. In 2012, I was able to do this by collaborating with the ODU Office of Assessment, which oversaw the selection of the QEP topic along with the QEP Faculty Workshop Facilitators, faculty members in various campus departments.

As the Faculty Workshops were piloted in spring and summer 2012, I had the benefit of already having a basic formula for the workshops. The IDW program offers five-day faculty workshops on improving disciplinary writing across the curriculum. The campus reception to the program was overwhelmingly positive, due in large part to the fact that they had been included in the development of our QEP initiatives and those initiatives were well supported financially by the university. For instance, during the five-day workshops open to full-time faculty members, each participant receives a $2,000 stipend for participation as well as more than thirty hours of faculty development time. Accepted faculty from each of ODU's six colleges then learn from faculty facilitators with expertise in improving writing and write-to-learn practices.

Furthermore, I also revised and launched the call for proposals for the other major QEP initiative, the program-based Action Project grants. The IDW Action Project internal grant initiative focuses on building on the foundation laid in the IDW workshops by improving upper-division undergraduate students' disciplinary writing in departments and/or programs. Funding is available each academic year for program activities related to the IDW's goal of engaging upper-division undergraduate students in disciplinary writing that demonstrates a reasoning process supported by research and reflection on the problem, topic, or issue being studied. To complete this task, I worked with ODU's Research Development Office as well as the Center for Learning and Teaching (CLT) to design specific submission guidelines, a scoring process, and a scoring rubric for Action Project proposals. As a means of further assisting interested faculty, one of the major components added to the grant submission process was a guideline that all interested faculty had to meet with the director of Writing and Faculty Development prior to submitting an Action Project proposal. During these meetings, I speak with faculty about their possible projects, offer guidance about bringing said projects in line with the QEP mission and student learning objectives, and offer advice on proposal components such as the project budget and assessment plan.

POPULATION SERVED

Our program was geared toward a very specific group of faculty members: full-time faculty teaching upper-division (300 and 400 level) undergraduate courses. The impetus was placed on this group of seven hundred or so faculty members because it was hoped that the program would prepare students in their major courses for writing in their own fields of study (i.e., disciplinary writing). By focusing on full-time faculty teaching junior and senior-level courses, we hoped to, in turn, reach many of those students completing their upper-division (capstone and writing-intensive courses) that students are required to take prior to graduation but after they have completed their basic general education requirements.

FUNDING

Our program was originally funded with just under $3 million for the five-year program, with around $400,000 being spent annually. These funds were base budgeted by the university and, therefore, were allocated via Academic Affairs. However, my biggest challenge has been that the IDW budget was underfunded for the 2013–14 academic year, due to university streamlining of all units during a state budget cut. As the budget was not funded as was originally outlined, I had to spend much time and energy during the last year revamping programs while trying to maintain the integrity and efficacy of said programs, in an attempt to reallocate funds where possible. Ultimately, this was a setback for the program, as less faculty were able to participate in our initiatives, which in turn meant that fewer students would be able to benefit from them.

Departments currently do not contribute funding to the program and will most likely not be asked to do so by the university-at-large, even if the overall university budget decreases again.

OPERATIONS

The IDW staff includes an administrative assistant, a graduate student assistant, and me; the program reports directly to the vice provost. My role as the WPA is to oversee the IDW Faculty Writing Workshops and Action Project grants. My job is largely administrative though I do teach one upper-division course in English, but this is outside of my primary job description. Much of the red tape one must make their way through to begin to implement a large program like ours must be handled on a day-to-day basis, so ordinarily this is what I do. For instance, I encountered several issues during my first year in the position, most of which stemmed from the fact that very little of the foundation of the QEP office had actually been laid when I began. ODU's QEP team had done a wonderful job of developing a comprehensive plan for conducting the QEP; however, it was left up to the incoming director to figure out the missing nuts and bolts of that plan, while also trying to continue moving forward with the timeline that was prepared for the next five years.

Fortunately, over the next few years, I was able to acquire and train a graduate research assistant (GRA) and an administrative assistant for our program, both of whom have been invaluable.

Our graduate research assistant works primarily with the director of Writing and Faculty Development to assist with the ongoing implementation of ODU's QEP, *Improving Disciplinary Writing*, which involves collecting, maintaining, and analyzing data from QEP Faculty Development Workshops and Action Projects along with handling administrative responsibilities related to those activities. Specifically, the GRA works twenty hours per week year-round and assists QEP administrative faculty and staff with their tasks, such as marketing the QEP to the university community, compiling and maintaining information and data from faculty who participate in QEP workshops and action projects, cooperating in the maintenance and/or modification of assessment materials, including data entry.

Our administrative assistant works twenty-five hours per week and serves as the primary budget overseer for the program. The administrative assistant completes an extensive set of tasks, including but not limited to the following:

- oversee distribution of internal grants and workshop stipends from QEP budget
- interface with faculty and university staff about internal grants and faculty workshops along with other QEP initiatives
- distribute and provide instructions for completion of applications and other forms
- review forms for proper completion
- cooperate in the maintenance and/or modification of assessment materials, including data entry
- compile statistical information for QEP director and assist with completion of necessary assessment reports as requested
- receive and respond to inquiries by providing directions, instructions, promotional material, or other general information or referring such inquiries to the appropriate persons
- schedule appointments and reserve rooms for QEP functions
- schedule travel for QEP Director as needed
- order office supplies (including catering services)
- monitor inventory and help maintain office budget

I also worked with the four original curators of the Faculty Workshops (all full-time faculty members from various departments on campus such as English and Nursing), and I was able to infuse new faculty into the IDW workshops by identifying two former workshop participants to serve as facilitators for the workshops as well. I was also able to assemble a willing and capable group of university faculty and staff members from other university entities to serve on the QEP Advisory Board.

ASSESSMENT

Assessment of our IDW program began soon after I arrived. In 2013, the Office of University Assessment and the QEP GRA helped collect student writing from past and present courses of the workshop participants. An assessment process for these artifacts was designed using the IDW Writing Rubric as a basis for evaluating the written artifacts. In conjunction with the Office of University Assessment, our first annual assessment (a similar summit will take place for two days each year during the month of May) of post-workshop artifacts was held in May 2013. one hundred forty written artifacts randomly selected from courses taught by faculty who attended the spring and summer 2012 IDW workshops were assessed by faculty members, after a group calibration session using sample artifacts, based on ODU's IDW Writing Rubric. The assessment helped refine the workshops and began to address the student learning outcomes in writing across the curriculum at the university. The data is also generally shared with campus stakeholders such at the provost, vice provosts as well as the IDW workshop participants.

The assessment of the initial student artifacts from courses offered by faculty workshop participants led to my creation of an IDW Curriculum Matrix and workshop re-vamp with facilitators to ensure that all of the IDW student learning outcomes (SLOs) were being properly addressed in each workshop. Also, the Assessment Summit led to the creation of the first IDW Annual Assessment report. The report included the data from the summit as an overview of the summit process as well as the IDW programs and included recommendations for the future of the program. This document will serve as a basis for each subsequent IDW Assessment report.

Much work will also continue to be done to improve the IDW faculty workshops. I will take on a larger teaching role during IDW workshops, while continuing to revise each workshop session to make sure all of the writing SLOs are included, thoroughly explained, and emphasized in each iteration of the workshops. I will also continue to initiate and oversee the collection of pre- and post-test written student artifacts from participating faculty. Our preliminary data from our May 2014 Assessment Summit included pre- and post-workshop artifacts and is extremely encouraging, as it indicates that student learning has increased significantly in most of our focus areas. Though our assessment isn't necessarily tied to our funding, this data has helped to ensure continuous campus buy-in from stakeholders.

MARKETING/PR

Something that always serves as a challenge is continually finding new ways to market the IDW program. Well over one hundred full-time faculty members have taken part in the workshops or serve on an Action Project team, so most of the early adopters or those who have a personal interest in improving disciplinary writing have already come on board. Therefore, now I must continue to find new ways to be tied into the untapped potential of other faculty members who might not be early adopters of the program but who might enjoy the time spent on improving pedagogy, interaction with faculty outside of their discipline or other vital aspects of the IDW initiatives. One of the ways that I plan to do this is to work with other offices on the creation and implementation of smaller workshops in the new Faculty Writing Studio, where faculty in all colleges and of all ranks will be able to receive one-on-one help with improving their own disciplinary writing as well as that of their students.

The IDW faculty workshop and Action Project application deadlines are advertised via our campus email system, as there are currently more than four thousand faculty and staff members in our mass email list and it is difficult to reach out to them by any other means. As one of my major responsibilities is working with the university community to publicize the IDW program, this task is ongoing. One of the ways I keep our logo and write-to-learn principles in the forefront of our communication is by sending out QEP/IDW Weekly Writing Tips, which offer suggestions to improve disciplinary writing and increase the quantity and quality of student writing via concise, low-stakes writing exercises.

I am able to work with ODU's Information Technology Development to update the established QEP university website on an ongoing basis, especially adding an easily accessible repository of the IDW Weekly Writing Tips and successful Action Project grant proposals. The website contains information on the history of the QEP including the original full plan document, a database of all faculty who have participated in the workshops, a list of current Advisory Board members, as well as in-depth information about the faculty workshops, Action Project grants and Faculty Writing Studio.

TECHNOLOGY

Our website houses much of our general information as well as holds a repository of the Weekly Writing Tips and extensive information on Action Project proposals. All of our applications for our initiatives are created and housed in Qualtrics, an online survey system offered by our university, which I oversee along with University Assessment. We utilize Blackboard and set up a Professional Learning group for each set of faculty members taking part in the Faculty Workshops. In this group, we house daily materials such as PowerPoint Slides, links to articles or pedagogical resources, our group discussion boards and the faculty participants' revised course documents.

ROLE OF RESEARCH

Very little research has been done specifically about our program, though I believe it is very important for us to do so. I co-wrote a book chapter in *Accountability: Using the Work of Re/Accreditation to Improve Writing Programs* with Joyce Neff, one of the original Faculty Workshop facilitators entitled "Faculty Learning Outcomes: The Impact of QEP Workshops on Faculty Beliefs and Practices" (Neff and Bingham-Risher 2016). Also, many of the faculty members who have revised their courses using the write-to-learn principles emphasized throughout our workshops have gone on to present their work at national conferences and include it in their own research. Using our experiences and program as a basis, I worked with another of the original architects of the Faculty Workshops, Rochelle Rodrigo, to secure a Council of Writing Program Administrators (CWPA) grant to study the relationships between various WPAs at universities and their own writing-focused QEPs. Currently, I am working with the remaining Faculty Workshop facilitators on two comprehensive articles on our process and the results of our initiatives.

PEDAGOGICAL AND/OR ADMINISTRATIVE HIGHLIGHTS

Faculty feedback from those who have participated in our initiatives has been extremely positive, as they have noted the value gained from learning new pedagogy.

As of summer 2014, ODU's IDW program has held seven (at least two each term since 2012) five-day workshops in which 133 full-time faculty members were taught how to integrate "write-to-learn" practices into their upper-division undergraduate (300- and 400-level) courses. Since attending the IDW Workshops, these faculty members have reached at least 8,605 students at ODU.

We have continued to support writing in academic programs by awarding the Action Project internal grants with more than $150,000 awarded in grant funds since 2013. Among other departments and programs, grants have been awarded in all six colleges to benefit those in the Counseling and Human Services, Biology, Psychology, English, Teaching and Learning Modeling, Simulation and Visualization Engineering, and Information Technology and Decision Sciences Departments.

In addition, groups of IDW Workshop participants from various colleges along with the director of Writing and Faculty Development partnered with the Center for Learning and Teaching (CLT) to present the panels *Infusing Writing Into Our Courses: Success Stories* and *Improving Disciplinary Writing through Action Projects: Sparking Departmental Change* at the 2013 and 2014 Faculty Summer Institutes, where no less than six of the eighteen panels at the conference in 2013 and nine of the eighteen panels in 2014 included panelists who spoke about their participation in IDW initiatives.

One of the most exciting new IDW initiatives came out of a collaboration with ODU's Academic Enhancement Office: an IDW Faculty Writing Studio. To further improve student as well as their own writing, all ODU faculty are in need of a dedicated, physical space that will allow them to work individually or collaboratively on their own writing research and pedagogy along with developing and honing the best practices highlighted in the IDW Faculty Workshops and Action Projects. The Faculty Writing Studio opened in fall 2014 and serves as: (1) an external work space for faculty who are completing writing and research projects, (2) a meeting space for faculty interested in working collaboratively on writing or improving disciplinary writing, and (3) a conference space where faculty can receive one-on-one feedback about their writing and/or writing projects from the director of Writing and Faculty Development. In addition to work stations and spaces, the Faculty Writing Studio will include a comprehensive writing library with resources to assist with various facets of the writing process, developing writing ePortfolios, writing pedagogy, and multidisciplinary collaboration.

PRIMARY DOCUMENTS (at writingprogramarchitecture.com)

Documents most important to our program can all be found on our website, which can be found by typing "QEP" into the search bar on at odu.edu. There, readers will find out entire QEP proposal, student learning outcomes, rubrics, and Action Projects.

WPA'S VOICE

Anyone who has a writing degree might turn out to be a candidate for a WPA position and this is something that took me by surprise, though moving into the administrative realm of academia has been extremely beneficial for me. Everyone who is considering or is being considered for a role as a WPA would do well to learn something about the campus culture and how the writing program they might be attached to fits into it. Also, I've found that I've been most effective when I was still able to teach as well as serve as an administrator because, that way, I'm not able to lose touch with the long-term goal of most programs, which is ultimately to affect student learning. I'm also in tune with those I may be serving whether fellow faculty members or students. Another important aspect of administration is understanding that resources (mostly funding) will often dictate how much you are able to do, and this funding is often not indicative of the quality of your program. This can be discouraging, but focusing on the incremental results and the individual changes you are able to help others make helps to make any administrative job worthwhile.

References

Bingham-Risher, Remica L. 2006. *Conversion*. Twin Lakes, WI: Lotus Press.

Bingham-Risher, Remica L. 2013. *What We Ask of Flesh*. Wilkes-Barre, PA: Etruscan.

Neff, Joyce, and Remica L. Bingham-Risher. 2016. "Faculty Learning Outcomes: The Impact of QEP Workshops on Faculty Beliefs and Practices." In *Reclaiming Accountability: Improving Writing Programs through Accreditation and Large-Scale Assessments*, ed. Wendy Sharer, Tracy Ann Morse, Michelle F. Eble, and William P. Banks, 279–303. Logan: Utah State University Press. http://dx.doi.org/10.7330/9781607324355.c014.

Old Dominion University. 2012. *Improving Disciplinary Writing: Quality Enhancement Plan 2012*. Norfolk, VA: Old Dominion University.

10

UNIVERSITY OF MISSOURI CAMPUS WRITING PROGRAM

Bonnie Selting and Amy Lannin

Institution type: Research-Intensive, Land-Grant University
Location: Columbia, Missouri
Enrollment: 35,000+
Year program was founded: 1987
WPA reports to: Vice Provost for Undergraduate Studies
Program funded by: Provost's Office
Description of students: Because the University of Missouri at Columbia is the state's flagship campus, it enrolls many students from mid-size cities, small towns and rural communities throughout Missouri, along with those from large metropolitan areas, primarily from St. Louis, Kansas City, and Chicago, Illinois. In 2015, 6,191 of the undergraduate students were first year students, which is 22.26 percent of the undergraduates. In addition, international students make up about 7.1 percent of the university's undergraduate student body.

PROGRAM SNAPSHOT

The interdisciplinary Campus Writing Program (CWP) works with faculty who design and teach writing-intensive (WI) courses across the university curriculum. The CWP is contained within the division of the vice provost for undergraduate studies.

WPAS' PROFILES

Amy

In 2011, I came on as director of the Campus Writing Program at the University of Missouri (MU) and as an assistant professor of English education in the College of Education. I was familiar with the program by having attended workshops sponsored by CWP and from teaching

DOI: 10.7330/9781607326274.c010

writing-intensive courses for a number of years. My connections with Marty Townsend (CWP director from 1991 to 2006) were instrumental in my decision to step into this role.

I hold a bachelor's in English with a language arts education endorsement from Nebraska Wesleyan University (1986) and a master's in curriculum and instruction with a literacy focus from the University of Nebraska–Lincoln (1996). I received my PhD from the University of Missouri (2007) and have taught courses on the teaching of writing, literature, and media since 2002 in the College of Education. My research includes the impact of professional development on teacher practice and student achievement, program assessment, and writing across the curriculum. MU has hosted a National Writing Project site for almost forty years, and I have served nearly ten years as director of the Missouri Writing Projects Network, representing five National Writing Project sites in Missouri. Before coming to MU, I taught middle and secondary English language arts.

Bonnie

I became a coordinator in the MU's Campus Writing Program (CWP) in 2007. For ten years previously, I served as one of five faculty at the University of Central Arkansas (UCA) to design and develop a freestanding, independent writing program that is now a Writing Department offering an MFA, a writing major and minor, and a linguistics minor. This department served writing students across the campus, allowing constant opportunities to see the importance of WAC theories and pedagogies.

I hold a bachelor's and master's degrees from the University of Colorado, and a PhD from Purdue University in English with a rhetoric and composition specialty track. I worked with Janice Lauer, Shirley Rose, Patricia Sullivan, Patricia Harkin, and Muriel Harris in various areas of rhetoric and composition studies. My work with Harris tutoring students from disciplines across campus, plus online tutoring for the emerging Purdue Online Writing Lab (OWL) for students around the world, deepened an already strong interest in writing across the curriculum. At MU, I work closely with faculty from all disciplines by facilitating seminars, workshops, and retreats. I also consult one-on-one with instructors from chemistry, foreign languages, nursing, service learning, mathematics, health sciences, among others.

PROGRAM CONCEPTION

In the 1980s, the faculty of the MU's College of Arts and Science expressed concern over the inadequate writing skills of graduates and recommended a doubling of the composition requirement from one to two courses. In 1983, Milton Glick, MU's dean of Arts and Science, a chemist and a proponent of good writing, together with MU's provost, convened a Task Force headed by Dr. Win Horner and consisting of faculty from seven of the key schools and colleges on the campus. The Task Force was challenged to study the issue of composition skills at MU and other universities. As a result of its study, the Task Force proposed that MU create a Campus Writing Program (CWP). After the undergraduate colleges on campus debated and evaluated concepts and principles of such a move, the proposal was adopted. Dr. Doug Hunt, author of the then widely used composition anthology *The Dolphin Reader* (Hunt 2002) and at that time director of composition in MU's English Department, served as the founding director of the CWP from 1985 to 1988. The program offered workshops and weeklong retreats for faculty from every discipline on campus, and soon recruited many devotees to the concept of using writing across the curriculum.

Dean Milton Glick describes best the initial energy put into this program in his 1988 article for the *WPA: Writing Program Administration* journal titled: "Writing across the Curriculum: A Dean's Perspective" (Glick 1988):

> An essential element of the entire discussion has been faculty involvement and leadership. In particular, the faculty advocacy for the program has grown in ripple-like fashion. Initial advocates were members of the Task Force on Composition, later joined by members of subcommittees and by faculty named to the Campus Writing Board. These advocates were joined subsequently by faculty who volunteered to teach pilot writing-intensive sections, and, most recently, by the 150 faculty from more than 44 departments who have voluntarily participated in two ten-hour days of intensive workshops. (54)

Faculty at these gatherings helped determine the criteria necessary for a course to earn the WI designation (e.g., requiring at least five thousand words of writing, two papers that go through a complete revision process, and one that integrates several sources, among other criteria). Participants also learned new teaching ideas from their colleagues and were trained toward a better understanding of writing-to-learn and learning-to-write pedagogical strategies and principles. By 1988, faculty from more than thirty departments were on-board to redesign their courses to fit these criteria, and the university established a requirement that all students take at least one (extending to two) such courses to graduate. But the program quickly established itself as something more than an effort to improve writing. CWP became a center for faculty involvement and leadership. Its "Mission Statement" has changed little over the years and reads as follows:

> The mission of the Campus Writing Program is to support faculty as *the* primary agents of Writing across the Curriculum (WAC) theories and practices in educating students through principles of "writing-to-learn" and "learning-to-write." We believe that teaching by these principles will enhance students' critical thinking abilities and better engage them in complex problem solving while they learn to communicate with clear, effective language in discipline-specific ways. (University of Missouri 2017)

One of the aspects of CWP that we find unique and very successful is the organization and function of the Campus Writing Board. Since the beginning of this program, this eighteen-member board provides oversight of WI course guidelines, course reviews, and policy issues related to the teaching of writing and writing requirements at MU. Three subcommittees make up the board: Natural and Applied Sciences, Humanities and Arts, and Education and Social Sciences. Faculty who are invited to serve on the board commit to monthly committee and board meetings, reviewing of the proposals for their sector, and reviewing WI Project Award proposals.

POPULATION SERVED

The Campus Writing Program works with faculty who design and teach over four hundred WI courses and supervise approximately 170 Graduate Teaching Assistants a year. Because of the WI requirement that one of the two WI courses must be in the student's major, this program reaches every undergraduate discipline on campus. Faculty and teaching assistants are expected to attend at least one of the WI two-day workshops held the week before classes begin each semester.

WI courses are taught by a fairly even distribution between professor, associate professor, assistant professor, and other teaching staff. Thus, at any of the workshops, seminars, and retreats offered throughout the year, we find a range of faculty levels and experience.

FUNDING

The Campus Writing Program is strongly supported with funding from administration. Funding has been consistent, in part, because this program supports a general education requirement. In 2012, CWP met with approximately twenty departments across campus to review the number of WI courses and associated costs. We then shared this information with the provost, including the feedback from department chairs and WI faculty. The university, like most, had been and continues to face fiscal challenges. However, the provost meets the funding levels as enrollment increases and more WI courses and instructors are needed. The key to this funding and support has been the faculty involvement. Faculty started this program, faculty run the Campus Writing Board, and faculty help mentor and support one another in the teaching of WI courses. Such a model becomes a cost-effective way to reach faculty who teach the nearly 400 WI courses, the 170 teaching assistants, and 14,000 undergraduate students in WI courses each year.

Currently, WI courses receive $110 for every student over an enrollment of twenty (up to an enrollment of three hundred). These funds are meant for the hiring of teaching assistants (TAs) to assist teaching the course. The current budget for CWP is close to $1 million. Along with the graduate teaching assistants (GTAs) funds are Faculty Development monetary resources amounting to $85,000 allocated for WI faculty who propose projects that further the efforts to use writing as a tool for improving student thinking and learning skills. Some projects that have received awards include: the writing of a book edited by a WI class in Parks, Recreation, and Tourism; the institution of a WI course in which the science of mindfulness practices is studied; the design and implementation of technical writing modules for engineering students; the hiring of a to help build a website dedicated WI faculty teaching methods; and others.

It is important to realize the faculty involvement in this program and how that involvement leads to administrative support. From its inception, writing workshops have demonstrated to MU faculty the value of using writing-to-learn and learning-to-write theories and strategies. And, in turn, WI faculty have consistently appreciated opportunities to collaborate with colleagues on these teaching matters.

It is worthwhile discussing the relationship of the efforts to improve student writing and learning to the more general issue of faculty morale. Faculty burn-out and low self-esteem are important topics in the higher education community. These conditions relate, in part, to reduced support for higher education, to low faculty mobility, and to salary issues.

Evaluations of the faculty workshops have been filled with superlatives. A dean interested in faculty development is naturally pleased when he hears a veteran professor say that "the workshop was the most positive experience I have had with colleagues during my 20 years here" or a new assistant professor report that "the program was more than worth-while—it was exciting."

Even though this has been and continues to be a well-supported program, it is important to remember that this cross-disciplinary Campus Writing Program owes its success to the *faculty who built it from the ground up.* Without this sort of faculty engagement, administrative resources would be provided in a void. As history demonstrates, without intense, sincere, enthusiastic faculty commitment, writing programs often fail.

OPERATIONS

The CWP is run by a team of five: a director who is an assistant professor in English education, two coordinators (representing rhetoric and composition, literacy education and political science), a graduate research assistant, and an administrative assistant. The program resides in The Conley House, an 1860s home on the edge of campus. The location is excellent for meetings, small workshops, and faculty writing retreats. Indeed, WI faculty often choose to take advantage of the cozy, yet business-like atmosphere for attending these writing retreats, workshops/seminars and one-on-one consultations with CWP staff.

The program's director (Amy) is primarily responsible for administrative duties. This work includes facilitating weekly staff meetings, working with the chair of the Campus Writing Board to set agenda items and follow through on projects, and working with the coordinators to support the course review process. A portion of the director's load is for research, which includes research involving writing, assessment, and professional development. The role as a WPA includes opportunities for campus-wide outreach, which is accomplished through numerous campus committees, departmental visits, workshops, guest teaching, and varied projects.

As a program coordinator, Bonnie oversees two of the three subcommittees that together make up the Campus Writing Board. She reviews new and updated course proposals from WI faculty, and following this initial review, she works with faculty to make sure the proposals address the WI Guidelines and provide clear information for WI approval. After the subcommittee meetings, Bonnie follows up with faculty whose proposals may need clarification prior to being put before the full board for a vote. This process is repeated each semester when a course is taught as WI.

All of the CWP staff (director, two coordinators, administrative assistant, and graduate assistant) are involved in year-long professional development, such as leading monthly workshops and writing retreats, facilitating TA workshops and norming sessions, and running the two-day workshops at the start of each semester. In addition, most semesters the director and coordinators teach a course in their respective academic homes. This teaching is not required but is valuable for our work with faculty and students.

The program is not responsible for hiring the TAs that work with faculty in larger WI courses. This decision is made in the departments with funding support from CWP when a course exceeds an enrollment of twenty. CWP is, however, responsible for providing the training for TAs and offering additional workshops during the year as requested.

One of the helpful routines we keep is a weekly staff meeting at which we review the schedule, update one another on course proposals, Campus Writing Board agenda items, budget issues, and a variety of topics. Our administrative assistant provides careful record keeping, conference planning, budget updates, and vast institutional knowledge that keeps the program running smoothly.

Workshops

When Dr. Marty Townsend directed this Campus Writing Program, WI faculty development workshops went from two to three days. Through the years, however, and in response to participant evaluations, they evolved into what we have today—two seven-hour days of immersion in WAC issues and collegial interaction. Topics include disciplinary literacy, assignment design, responding to student writing, revision, WI courses that "work," and information on involving the Writing Center tutors. Also during this two-day workshop, CWP offers in-depth information on working with ESL students and building plagiarism awareness with students. We draw on Writing Center Director Rachel Harper, WI faculty who are willing to present on their own courses, librarians, the vice provost, the Campus Writing Board chair, and others.

Although CWP staff designs and conducts workshops and seminars, many are also led by cross-disciplinary WI faculty, themselves, who present ideas on WI issues, including peer review, responding to papers, using technology, designing assignments, and writing grants.

Retreats

CWP offers monthly, day-long faculty writing retreats in Conley House for which we furnish food and an enormously productive "writing" atmosphere. We also make available a two-day writing retreat in a historic, nearby hotel. Participants usually stay overnight at the hotel and spend two days immersed in their own writing projects. These retreats demonstrate to faculty across campus MU's dedication to helping them be part of a writing community. They highlight the value of writing in the campus culture, including its importance for learning disciplinary content.

ASSESSMENT

In November 2012, the CWP attended MU's Faculty Council in order to discuss programmatic policies regarding issues such as funding for WI courses. During this visit, two Faculty Council members asked CWP personnel the predictable question, "Do (WI) courses actually make students better writers?" along with the equally customary inquiry, "How can we know if WI works?" These types of questions have been around a long time, as have WAC programs like the one under discussion here. We are currently designing self-assessment methods to answer them as we shed light on ways in which this cross-campus writing program can operate as effectively as possible. Toward that end, CWP views program assessment as one of its chief responsibilities, and has solidified a design for a *Program Assessment Initiative*. This project is intended to understand the efficacy of using "writing-to-learn" and "learning-to-write" principles in our courses and to discover more about the ways we might further foster a culture of writing at MU.

In spring 2013, we put the assessment into motion by designing a pilot program. We have gained IRB approval and gathered data from two major disciplines on the MU campus: agricultural economics and biological science. The data are being collected in survey and interview responses from both students and WI faculty and in student writing samples and assignments.

We are also working with the Sinclair School of Nursing for an in-depth look at data being collected to study the proficiencies of professional nursing students in the WI course Evidence Based Practice 4930. A similar study is underway in the Human Development and Family Studies Department, analyzing data from one of the larger WI courses on campus. We expect these research projects to serve as models for future studies to help CWP better define challenges unique to WI course instruction and to determine what departments and programs need in order to improve implementation of writing in courses across campus.

Results of our Pilot Study will be presented at a variety of workshops and conferences and will serve to determine the best methods for finding answers to the type of questions asked by academics and community members alike:

- How well do students write?
- What types of writing skills are emphasized within WI courses?
- What types of discipline-specific writing do students complete?
- How can we create clear learner outcomes?
- How can we better understand the strengths and areas for improvement in student writing?

The multiphase approach we have chosen will be critical to ensure that the process of program assessment will be manageable and that relevant constituencies of the university will be involved with the assessment process. Although this assessment plan is formidable, we have already found essential information to support the notion that this program is highly valuable to the University of Missouri.

MARKETING/PR

A regular goal of the Campus Writing Program is to get the message out about who we are and what we do. We recently had our website redesigned (cwp.missouri.edu), which created a branding element that we have weaved into brochures, posters, and the like. Our brochures, posters, and advertisements make use of the same color scheme and the writing desk image that the website designer created. We also advertise in the *Mizzou Weekly* newspaper and Mizzou Announcements (through email), which reach the entire university community. Our position with the Vice Provost's Office connects us to other programs, such as Undergraduate Research, The Honor's College, Office of Service Learning, and Educational Technologies. This provides marketing through jointly produced materials. Our most used tool is our massive email list, which we use regularly to inform faculty of upcoming workshops, due dates for course proposals, and opportunities for awards. At least twice a year, we publish an online newsletter, *e-WAC*, which includes brief articles spotlighting WI faculty, offering teaching tips, and sharing information.

It is challenging to determine how well these various tools are used. As is all too common, we will send out the information and then have people ask us for the very thing we sent. It is obvious that in the deluge of emails and online access to seemingly everything, our CWP messages get lost. However, there is also quite a lot of response and at times we have to close events because we do not have enough space for all who wish to register. These workshops, plus one-on-one consultations with faculty, along with positive "word of mouth" recommendation among faculty have increased CWP's profile significantly on MU's campus.

TECHNOLOGY

As mentioned previously, our program has revamped the CWP website and uses this as an anchor of information. We keep this updated with events, news, and recognition of faculty. We also use a listserv and social media sites (i.e., Facebook and Twitter) for posting events, articles, and noteworthy items for the WI faculty.

Course proposals are submitted electronically to the CWP website, using Filemaker software. We maintain a database of all WI course information. Of the nineteen schools and colleges and 317 degree and certificate programs, approximately four hundred courses are writing intensive each year. This includes some online semester based and some "self-paced" courses.

CWP works closely with the office of ET@MO (Educational Technologies at Missouri). Both of our programs provide outreach and teaching support for faculty, such as with syllabus and assignment design. Most of our WI courses have some technology component, such as the use of a learning management system. We work to make sure faculty are aware of tools and applications they may find helpful for teaching, such as citation managers, plagiarism checking software, and tips for providing feedback on student writing. One of the CWP coordinators, Jonathan Cisco, regularly offers workshops on technology tools to help with faculty writing and the teaching of writing.

ROLE OF RESEARCH

It is important, as a writing program at a research institution, that we involve ourselves in research. As an assistant professor, Amy also conducts research in English education, focusing on writing across the curriculum and professional development. Her work with the National Writing Project's Local Sites Research Initiative has involved her in studies of middle and secondary writing instruction and assessment. Also, while working with the director of Service Learning, Bonnie, CWP coordinator, has investigated the connection between returning military veterans and Service Learning pedagogy. A report of this research is forthcoming in the book *Gen Vet* out of Oxford University Press and edited by Dr. Lisa Langraat and Sue Doe of Colorado State University (Selting 2014).

Historically our program has been featured in various research-based and scholarly articles published by our active WI faculty and CWP leaders. Just a few examples include Townsend, Patton, and Vogt's (2012) *WPA: Writing Program Administration* article on the history of the development of the internationally known and respected Campus Writing Program at the University of Missouri, Glaser's (2014) piece on peer critique in chemistry courses, and Patton's various articles referring to several years of working with the Engineering Department and the faculty dedicated to WI teaching (see e.g., Patton and Smith Taylor 2013).

A recent project is Marty Townsend's (CWP director from 1991 to 2006) collaboration with CWP staff to analyze and publish research on a study of TAs who worked in WI courses. These alums completed a phone survey, and findings from this data shed light on the positive, professional impact from serving as a TA (Lannin and Townsend, forthcoming in a special issue of *Across the Disciplines*, edited by M. Brooks-Gillies, E. G. Garcia, S. H. Kim, K. Manthey, and T. G. Smith). The CWP succeeds because of TAs, and we need to tell the story of this relationship between undergraduate and graduate education that is brought together in the Campus Writing Program.

Since 2012, the CWP has provided funds for Writing Intensive Project Awards. Faculty of WI courses can apply for these funds, and some of the funded projects have been to conduct research related to WI courses. In most cases, CWP works alongside the faculty member, providing help with assessment of writing, data analysis, and conference presentation. One example among many is Dr. Rainer Glaser's funding award to write a book, *Scientific Writing and Peer Review in Chemistry—An Assignment-Based Introduction*. Dr. Glaser is an internationally known chemistry scholar and devotee of using writing in his teaching. Among his numerous publications are several related to teaching students the complexities and value of peer review in science writing.

PEDAGOGICAL AND/OR ADMINISTRATIVE HIGHLIGHTS

Before every semester, on the opening day of our faculty workshop, Dr. Jim Spain, vice provost for undergraduate studies, welcomes the WI faculty and stresses the great importance of their role in student learning. Dr. Spain has taught a WI course for many years and draws on his own experiences to share the hard work and vital role of WI teaching. This administrative support has been instrumental to the success of the CWP.

Following the spring 2014 faculty workshop, two of the Campus Board members recommended that CWP provide mentoring for new

WI faculty. Based on this idea, those two faculty worked with the Campus Writing Board chair, Robert Bauer from geological sciences, to propose a mentoring program. The Board approved funds for this pilot project, which has involved ten faculty who spent time in the summer to prepare for and then attend the fall workshop. They were partnered with two to three new WI faculty to lead discussions and share ideas throughout the workshop. This created noticeable energy and naturally resulted in continued conversations.

Campus Writing Board

The function of the Campus Writing Board is key to CWP's success and an effective model for a productive faculty committee. Faculty who are appointed to this board serve a three-year term, and in the thirty years of this board's history, several faculty have served twice. We are fortunate in that so many faculty on this campus are involved in the WI process. For example, in 2011, CWP was contacted by Dr. Robert Bauer in Geology. Dr. Bauer had served on the board previously and wanted to return. When we asked him why, he explained that he learned so much by seeing what other faculty do in their WI courses. Another faculty member described the Campus Writing Board as one of the few (perhaps only) committees that he felt actually *did* something. Despite the work expected of Board members, we have found that faculty are eager to serve, committed to this program because they see the importance of student writing across campus and of the enhanced teaching when faculty engage students in writing assignments in WI courses.

Innovative Courses and Sequenced Curriculum

Beginning in 2012, the Campus Writing Program started recognizing faculty for innovative courses and outstanding WI teaching. These monetary awards are one way of highlighted effective teaching and student learning. With four hundred potential WI courses to recognize, we know that we have so far skimmed the surface of excellence. We offer two types of awards. One is a Writing Intensive Teaching Award in the amount of $500, which is given to six selected WI faculty at the end of each academic year. The other is the newly instituted Win Horner Award. In the name of the first CWP Task Force director, Dr. Win Horner, we offer an outstanding faculty $1,000 for their work. As an example of the pedagogical rigor involved with receiving one of these awards, we offer the story of our first recipient.

The first annual Win Horner Award (2012) was given to Dr. Louise Miller, a PhD nursing faculty member for her unique course in Evidence Based Nursing for practicing nurses pursuing their bachelor's degrees. Students in this course wrote research/persuasive papers, storyboards, scripts, and rebuttal papers all centered on producing a documentary video describing an evidence-based solution to a clinical problem. Audiences for these videos range from the student's own clinical workers to administration. Students learn the value of writing in nursing, the importance of audience analyses, the positive consequences of peer review, and more.

On our own campus, we have through the years, endorsed WI projects designed by departments themselves that do not strictly follow the Writing Intensive Guidelines, but serve students in the best sense of the WAC spirit. For example, our Geological Sciences Department proposed to the Campus Writing Program years ago to provide their own WI curriculum instead of one WI course. By working together, the faculty developed a four-course sequence with planned writing assignments throughout, but without one course "doing it all," so to speak. All geology majors take these courses, and at the completion when all writing assignments are completed, they actually exceed the WI Guidelines and requirements. We recognize that not all departments could offer this type of sequenced curriculum, but we have been sharing this model across campus in hopes that others will take advantage of this coordinated approach to a writing.

PRIMARY DOCUMENTS (at writingprogramarchitecture.com)

Our Writing Intensive Guidelines and course Proposal and Update forms are essential to MU's Campus Writing Program. The Guidelines can be found through the university website (Missouri.edu) by typing "writing intensive" into the search bar. These Guidelines have been the bulwark of this CWP since its inception. They have been revised through recent years to accommodate for digitalization of writing assignments, but their original purpose has remained: to emphasize writing as a prime teaching tool. The Guidelines are also used by the Campus Writing Board to review course Proposals and Updates. A sample form can also be found on the University of Missouri's CWP website under "Teaching Resources" enriched curriculum.

WPAS' VOICES

In 1993, Steve Weinberg, journalism professor and member of 1992 Campus Writing Program Internal Review Committee, wrote an article that appeared in "Opinion," *The Chronicle of Higher Education* (Weinberg 1993). Even at that early date CWP was viewed as a success story among WAC programs around the country. Thus, Weinberg attempted to account for the attributes that led to this success. He concluded there were six reasons:

1. The Campus Writing Program is a regular item in the campus budget, with what appears to be strong support from the provost.

2. The staff of the writing program is not housed in the English Department or in another specific discipline. Thus it is generally perceived as belonging to the whole campus.

3. The program's director, Martha Townsend, is a specialist in writing across the curriculum. She and her staff are intelligent, personable, and efficient. As a result, the pedagogy undergirding the program is clear, deadlines are met, and personality conflicts are minimal.

4. The training of teaching assistants and faculty members is carried out skillfully and regularly.

5. Students learn during their freshman composition course (housed in the English Department) what is expected of them in their later WI courses. As a result, many of the students enter the WI courses with a general understanding of how the extra work will benefit them.

6. Enough faculty members have seen enough rewards from the extra work that a seemingly permanent, enthusiastic core of teachers now is involved in the program, representing almost every major discipline on campus.

All those attributes are necessary, but it is number 6 that CWP still encounters every day at MU. It is important to stress the involvement of the faculty in this program. One quality that is shared from administration, WPA, Campus Writing Board, mentors, and on throughout the program is that we all are teachers of writing in our courses and use writing as a tool for learning. When approaching a consultation with a faculty member, facilitating a workshop, meeting with the Board, or any number of interactions with faculty, we approach this as colleagues working together for a shared goal. In addition, we as a writing program are stressing more and more the need to support our faculty with their own writing. Not only does it matter to the campus as a whole to have faculty with successful publishing and grant writing experiences, but we like to remind faculty that their teaching can be informed by their own writing practices. Making that pedagogical turn is important: when we pay attention to how and what we write, we can make better decisions about how and what to teach our students as they write.

In 2011–2012, when the CWP visited with about twenty departments across campus, we were exploring different funding models and wanted input from WI faculty and department chairs. We shared information and also gathered information from them. When we then shared this with the provost and budget director, we included input from the faculty and chairs. This proved very helpful in that it wasn't us as WPAs asking for continued support through changes in the funding models, but it was the faculty whose voice was heard. We, therefore, advise those in the early stages of WPA work to spend time listening to faculty, finding out their successes and concerns, documenting this, and using this information to guide the work.

References

Glaser, Rainer. 2014. "Design and Assessment of an Assignment-Based Curriculum to Teach Scientific Writing and Scientific Peer Review." *Journal of Learning Design* 7 (2): 85–104. http://dx.doi.org/10.5204/jld.v7i2.202.

Glick, Milton. 1988. "Writing across the Curriculum: A Dean's Perspective." *WPA: Writing Program Administration* 11 (3): 53–58.

Hunt, Doug. 2002. *Dolphin Reader*. 6th ed. Belmont: Wadsworth Publishing.

Lannin, Amy, and Martha Townsend. Forthcoming. "Graduate Student Perspectives: Career Development through Serving as Writing-Intensive GTAs." *Across the Disciplines*.

Patton, Martha. 2011. *Writing in the Research University: A Darwinian Study of WID with Cases from Civil Engineering*. New York: Hampton Press.

Patton, Martha Davis, and Summer Smith Taylor. 2013. "Re-evaluating Directive Commentary in an Engineering Activity System." *Across the Disciplines* 10 (1). http://wac.colostate.edu/atd/articles/patton_taylor2013.cfm.

Selting, Bonita. 2014. "The Value of Service Learning for Student-Veterans: Transitioning to Academic Cultures through Writing and Experiential Learning." In *Generation Vet: Composition, Student Veterans, and the post 9/11 University*, ed. S. Doe and L. Langstraat, 240–256. Logan: Utah State University Press. http://dx.doi.org/10.7330/97808742 19425.c011.

Townsend, Martha, Martha Patton, and Jo Ann Vogt. 2012. "Uncommon Conversations: How Nearly Three Decades of Paying Attention Allows One WAC/WID Program to Thrive." *WPA: Writing Program Administration* 35 (2): 127–159.

University of Missouri. 2017. "Mission." Campus Writing Program. http://cwp.missouri .edu/about/index.php.

Weinberg, Steve. 1993. Opinion. "Overcoming Skepticism about 'Writing Across the Curriculum (WAC)'." *Chronicle of Higher Education* B2–3.

PART 3

First-Year Composition and Introductory College Literacy

11

ARIZONA STATE UNIVERSITY WRITERS' STUDIO ONLINE

Angela Clark-Oates

Institution type: Public metropolitan research university
Location: Four campuses around the Phoenix, Arizona valley, and EdPlus: ASU Online is considered a fifth campus
Enrollment: 15,224 enrolled in EdPlus: ASU Online
Year program was founded: 2011
WPA reports to: Dean of the College of Letters and Sciences
Program funded by: EdPlus: ASU Online
Description of students: The majority of ASU Online students reside in Arizona. The average age of this student population is thirty-two with the majority of the students classified as juniors and seniors. Sixty-four percent of ASU students classified as white and 63 percent are classified as female. The top five degree programs are psychology, nursing, criminal justice, communications, and liberal studies. The Writers' Studio is also available to students seeking face-to-face degrees. Institutionally, 80 percent of the students at ASU are undergraduates. There is almost equal representation of men and women in both the graduate and undergraduate populations, but there is a much larger international graduate student population. On the "Quick Facts Sheet" published by the University Office of Institutional Analysis in spring 2015, 36 percent of undergraduates and 22 percent of graduate students are categorized as minority (Office of Institutional Analysis 2015).

PROGRAM SNAPSHOT

ASU Online offers forty-six undergraduate degree programs and forty-one graduate degree programs. The Writers' Studio is housed in the College of Letters and Sciences. It is a fully online model of first-year composition (FYC), and unlike other FYC courses at ASU, it is available to any campus-based student or any ASU Online student. In the Writers' Studio, we offer our courses (ENG 101, 102, and 105) in either

DOI: 10.7330/9781607326274.c011

a seven-and-a-half-week or fifteen-week semester in an asynchronous online learning space.

WPA'S PROFILE

I began my WPA work in a writing center as a doctoral student when I was hired as a management intern to grow the writing center at ASU on the Downtown Phoenix campus (DPc). Although, at the time of my hire, there was a Writing Center director who organized initiatives across all four ASU campus writing centers, I reported directly to the founding director of University Academic Success Programs (UASP) at DPc, which was indicative of the organizational structure within the university-wide UASP unit.

Within a year of my hire, I was asked to move the writing center from a shared space with the other tutoring service to a stand-alone center to meet the founding director's strategic growth plan for the DPc. This move also helped align the DPc writing center practice with the other three writing centers at ASU. The move also increased the visibility of the center—another goal of the strategic plan—allowing the center to more than double the number of students it served. In my second year, I led a team to design and implement an online writing-tutoring center for all students at ASU. The exigency for an online writing center emerged from the needs of students participating remotely in degree programs, the growth nationally in online writing centers, and the strategic plan for EdPlus: ASU Online. This online writing center along with other online tutoring services won the ASU President's Award for Innovation. Based on my expanding roles and responsibilities, I was offered a full-time coordinator position at the end of my second year in the writing center.

As the center grew, so did my commitment to providing better professional development opportunities for the writing tutors, constructing a culture of writing on the Downtown Phoenix campus, addressing issues of access for our diverse student population, building partnership with area high schools, and designing writing-in-the-disciplines initiatives with the College of Nursing, the School of Social Work, the Mary Lou Fulton Teachers College, and Barrett, the Honors College. After four years in the writing center, I moved my WPA practice to an online FYC program when I accepted the position of course manager for the Writers' Studio.

I completed my doctorate at Arizona State University in May 2013, a PhD in curriculum and instruction from the Mary Lou Fulton Teachers College with an emphasis in language and literacy. Pursuing scholarly curiosities from an interdisciplinary perspective was valued in my college, so my program of study included graduate coursework in rhetoric and composition. I also explored the field of composition studies for my comprehensive exams and used composition theory and scholarship to inform my dissertation. I earned an MA in literature with a minor in technical communication from Texas State University and a BA in English with a secondary teaching certificate from the University of Texas at Austin.

PROGRAM CONCEPTION

The idea for the Writers' Studio emerged in spring of 2011 when Duane Roen proposed an alternative design for delivering instruction in first-year writing at ASU. Roen conceptualized the FYC redesign at ASU as an emporium-style classroom for campus-based students. For a host of reasons, it was ultimately offered online only in the College of Letters and Sciences. The Writers' Studio did not replace the campus-based or hybrid FYC courses already being offered in the college but was presented to students as another option for completing their FYC requirement.

Seven months after Roen proposed the idea, the Writers' Studio piloted in fall 2011. An instructional team that included Tiffany Bourelle, Sherry Rankins-Robertson, Andrew Bourelle, and Duane Roen worked collaboratively to redesign first-year composition "to accommodate a large number of students in a fully online environment where teachers work as a team to collaboratively facilitate and assess student learning" (Bourelle et al. 2013, para. 1). This model would not only inspire collaboration among the instructors, it would also champion the importance of embedded writing tutors in FYC courses. The instructional team used instructional assistants to support the teaching and learning in the classroom (Bourelle, Bourelle, and Rankins-Robertson 2015).

We do require all campus-based students to receive departmental consent before enrolling in ENG 101, 102, or 105 in the Writers' Studio. I review all campus-based student enrollment request forms, survey their academic history and placement indicators, and, in some instances, speak to them face-to-face to determine their eligibility.

By the end of the first year, the members of the instructional team had accepted new positions at other universities. Their move opened up an opportunity to re-conceptualize the organizational structure of the Writers' Studio. Duane Roen would remain the faculty head, but a new three-person administrative team would be hired to manage, coordinate, and teach in the program. I was hired as the course manager, and Allyson Boggess and Ebru Erdem were hired as course coordinators. We began our positions in June 2012.

Students navigate Blackboard using a structured course calendar, reading project material, dialoguing with classmates on discussion boards, watching videos, reading chapters and crafting invention work in a digital textbook, and participating in synchronous online team activities. Our faculty uses the same syllabus and assignments, generated collaboratively during professional development workshops and mid-semester meetings. To connect synchronously with students, faculty and writing fellows offer one-on-one conferences and office hours using Skype or Google Hangout.

We use outcome-based assessment in the Writers' Studio. To demonstrate their learning in our courses, we ask students to complete two projects and an ePortfolio using Digication. Both major writing projects include a substantial print-based academic essay and a multimodal component designed to extend the rhetorical strategies, concepts, and writing styles covered in the project unit. In addition, students are required to write a substantial reflection for each of the multimodal projects explaining their rhetorical decisions, their use of design principles, and their choice of audience. Finally, for each of the projects, the students also reflect on their learning through the lens of the WPA Outcomes and Habits of Mind from the Framework for Success in Postsecondary Writing.

The ePortfolio in Digication is an archive of the writing the students have crafted during the semester. It is an electronic document that they curate in Digication, and this archive gives them an opportunity to demonstrate what they have learned during the semester by reflecting on their experiences inventing, drafting, revising, seeking feedback, and editing, as well as some broader core skills and knowledge. They use the Outcomes Statement and the Habits of Mind as frames for these reflections. Through these projects and the Digication ePortfolio, the students have the opportunity to hone their ability to develop ideas, express ideas effectively, and engage in multiple literacies. Using a process-based pedagogy, the students are required to invent, draft, and seek feedback from their peers, their writing fellow, and the ASU Writing Centers. This means the writing fellow program—a course-embedded writing tutor program—is integral to the students enrolled in FYC in the Writers' Studio.

A campus-based version of Writers' Studio ENG 102 piloted in spring 2015 on the Downtown Phoenix campus, a course that resembles Roen's original idea for an emporium-style composition classroom. Like its online counterpart, face-to-face Writers' Studio is housed in the College of Letters and Sciences and marketed to campus-based students seeking degrees on Downtown Phoenix campus.

POPULATION SERVED

Writers' Studio is available to any campus-based student on any of our four physical campuses or any ASU Online student. Campus-based students must submit a registration form and receive department consent to enroll. We have approximately 1,800 students enroll per year in the Writers' Studio, but the majority of our students are enrolled in degree programs offered by EdPlus: ASU Online. Due to a partnership between EdPlus: ASU Online and Starbucks, the Writers' Studio experienced a 40 percent increase in enrollment during the 2014–2015 academic year.

FUNDING

EdPlus

ASU Online funds the Writers' Studio through the College of Letters and Sciences. The funding is directly linked to the enrollment numbers in the program because the majority of the program cost is tied to faculty and staff salaries. For other funding needs (e.g., catering for faculty development, conference travel, Digication), I request financial support from the dean of the College of Letters and Sciences.

OPERATIONS

Writers' Studio consists of an administrative team, full-time and part-time instructors, and undergraduate and graduate writing fellows. In a typical semester, we have approximately thirty people teaching in our courses. This includes five full-time instructors, a pool of fifteen to twenty faculty associates (adjuncts), and fifteen to twenty writing fellows.

The administrative staff for the Writers' Studio includes my position as course manager, two course coordinator positions, and a faculty head. The course manager and course coordinator positions are university staff classifications and work on a twelve-month contract.

As the course manager, I supervise the course coordinators, the full-time and part-time instructors, and the writing fellows. The course coordinators are each responsible for one of the courses in the required two-course sequence: ENG 101 or ENG 102. They are responsible for the day-to-day operations of the online classroom, ensuring our curriculum is organized for the learning management system, coordinating the full-time and part-time faculty teaching in the course, completing daily administrative tasks for the course, and monitoring the students' and instructors' experiences in the online collaborative teaching space. As a

team, we co-design curriculum with the full-time and part-time instructors, problem solve student and faculty issues, engage in research, and
conduct programmatic assessments.

My duties and responsibilities include scheduling and staffing all sections of ENG 101, 102, and 105. I also hire and mentor the instructors
as well as manage and supervise the writing fellows program. In working closely with the faculty head, I also attend meetings at the university
level, working with instructional designers at EdPlus: ASU Online and
the university technology office. I also work with the other WPAs, department chairs, and faculty heads across ASU who offer FYC courses at
ASU. Finally, as an instructor in the program, I teach online FYC courses
and the writing fellow internship course; outside of my position, I have
also taught young adult literature courses for the English Department,
worked with the Central Arizona Writing Project in various roles, and
collaborated with the Mary Lou Teachers' College.

I also review each campus-based student's request to enroll in the
Writers' Studio before granting departmental consent. This process
includes comparing the requests to academic and retention data, speaking to the student on the phone, corresponding via email, and in some
cases reaching out to the student's academic advisor.

I also work very closely with the administrative staff in the College of
Letters and Sciences who work directly with payroll, human resources,
and the bookstore. I also work with issues related to classroom scheduling like updating the college's central record of teaching, preparing
funding percentages related to teaching loads, and ensuring all instructors have access to the administrative tools for teaching like grade ros-
ters and the learning management system.

Our entire administrative team works closely with an instructional
designer from EdPlus: ASU Online. For the first three years of the program, Writers' Studio faculty used Pearson Learning Studio as the learning management system (LMS), but in the fall 2014, after EdPlus: ASU
Online announced it would not renew its contract with Pearson, the
administrative team moved our online classrooms to Blackboard. Our
relationship with the instructional designer ensures that our curriculum
is streamlined for online learning and our videos are professional, informative, and succinct. She also helps us troubleshoot any issues with our
LMS and advocates for our needs and the needs of our students to the
university technology office. Finally, she assesses our courses using the
Quality Matters Rubric.

ASSESSMENT

The assessment criteria in the Writers' Studio emerge from three documents: the WPA Outcomes Statement, the Habits of Mind from the Framework for Success in Postsecondary Writing, and the Quality Matters Rubric.

Using an outcomes-based approach to assessment, the first two documents support the articulation of what the student should learn over time and what evidence should be collected to show this learning has occurred. We use a process-based pedagogy to assess how students engage their academic and digital literacy practices for particular writing purposes and different audiences. For each project, the student must seek out at least three people to provide feedback. Typically, they include a peer, a writing fellow, and the instructor. Through each iteration, they are encouraged to collect the revisions as evidence for the claims they will make later about their learning. Students also spend the semester designing and crafting ePortfolios, where they reflect on their learning using the language from the Outcomes Statement and the Habits of Mind.

The third document, the "Quality Matters Rubric," is used to assess our online curriculum. Each year we work closely with an instructional designer to apply the rubric to each of our courses to ensure our curriculum promotes student engagement and provides tools and resources that encourages student success (Crawford 2012).

In spring 2015, we also completed a programmatic assessment. We collected data—students' written/digital artifacts and reflections—for fifteen months through Digication, the ePortfolio platform. Working with the Digication data team, we gathered a randomized sample of 10 percent of our students' portfolios across four semesters. We evaluated the ePortfolios using a rubric that was designed to assess the students' claims about learning, students' selection of evidence to support those claims, and students' explanation of the critical connection between their learning and the evidence. The purpose of this programmatic assessment was to better align our teaching practices and evaluation practices.

MARKETING/PR

With such a variety of FYC courses offered at ASU, Writers' Studio relies on academic advisors to make recommendations for what program might be best suited for particular students. We also use our Writers' Studio website as a marketing tool. I am currently working with an instructional designer to develop an infographic for our courses. The graphic will be added to our website and embedded in our courses to engage students visually in understanding the structure of the online FYC classroom. Finally, I participated on a committee with other WPAs, department chairs, and faculty heads to build a writing commons website that would give students a better understanding of the different FYC courses offered at ASU.

TECHNOLOGY

In the Writers' Studio, the instructors are encouraged to use technology to facilitate asynchronous and synchronous learning. In this way, their practices honor the curriculum design. As a result, many of us use a variety of technologies to provide audio feedback to students, including screencasting technology and iAnnotate. We also use video lectures—recorded using Camtasia or produced in a studio at ASU—to provide an overview of tasks or to focus specifically on recurring writing issues.

We also use Google Hangout, Google Chat, and Skype to meet our students for office hours and one-on-one conferencing. Another powerful tool to foster collaboration has been the Google Community I created for all instructors and writing fellows.

ROLE OF RESEARCH

With its innovative approach to teaching FYC, Writers' Studio has been an optimal site for research since it piloted in fall 2011. We have a standing IRB that allows us to collect student artifacts, instructor-student interactions, peer-to-peer interactions, and writing-fellow-to-peer interactions from the virtual classroom for research purposes. We ask all students to sign a consent form to participate in research, but signing the consent form is not mandatory.

The instructional team who designed and piloted Writers' Studio has published four articles on the Writers' Studio (T. Bourelle, A. Bourelle, and Rankins-Robertson 2013; T. Bourelle, A. Bourelle, and Rankins-Robertson 2015; T. Bourelle, Rankins-Robertson, A. Bourelle, and Roen 2013; Rankins-Robertson, T. Bourelle, A. Bourelle, and Fisher 2014). The four articles cover a range of topics: assessment in the online composition classroom, employing multiliteracies to prepare the twenty-first-century student, constructing multimodal instruction, and using embedded writing tutors to enhance learning in online classrooms.

In my first two years as course manager, my research agenda was focused on two areas: (1) the articulation of writing pedagogy between high school English classrooms and FYC classrooms, and (2) the professional development of FYC practitioners. In pursuing these topics for research, I coauthored pieces with the faculty head and course coordinator, presented at conferences with Writers' Studio instructors, and published single authored book chapters. During these studies, I also relied on the Framework for Success in Postsecondary Writing as a lens for my research.

More recently, my research agenda in the Writers' Studio has been focused on pedagogies of revision. I am conducting two studies in the Writers' Studio focused on the feedback practices of the writing fellows. One is a collaborative study, with an associate professor in technical communication in the College of Letters and Sciences, focused on the content of the writing fellows feedback on FYC students' multimodal projects. My co-researcher and I received an International Writing Centers Association (IWCA) grant to support the pilot study in fall 2013 and were awarded a Council of Writing Program Administrators (CWPA) grant for 2014–2015 to continue our research. We presented our preliminary findings at Computers and Writing in summer 2014. The second study is focused on technology-mediated pedagogies of revision. In this study, I co-designed a multi-institutional project with two professors at different universities across the country. The study is focused on examining how peer-to-peer feedback is impacted by the use of screencasting technology. My co-researchers and I presented our findings at CCCC in spring 2015.

PEDAGOGICAL AND/OR ADMINISTRATIVE HIGHLIGHTS

Writers' Studio is a unique redesign of FYC. As a fully online program, it develops students' academic literacy practices and digital literacy practices by asking students to craft both traditional academic essays and multimodal projects.

Using writing fellows in FYC courses is integral to student success. In the Writers' Studio, this program not only provides rich mentoring and professional development to aspiring teachers and researchers, it also becomes a reflective lens for the instructors teaching in the Writers' Studio.

Moreover, the curriculum in the Writers' Studio is innovative and engaging. For example, in an ENG 101 project, we engage students in issues surrounding local and global food justice. To do this, we ask students to craft a visual analysis in response to one photograph from *Hungry Planet: What the World Eats* (Menzel and D'Alusio 2005) by responding to guiding questions that will support them as they explore the photographs for their rhetorical weight, explaining how the photographer appeals to the audience, conveys meaning through photograph beyond its individual parts, and argues for its relevance in both a global and local context. The students are also required to research and discuss the context, history, and social and cultural norms of the subjects of the photography. Their analysis must also show an understanding of the economic significance of the price of food in the photograph and the nutritional value of the food itself, but the majority of the analysis will focus on what story and argument the photographer is trying to share with the viewer through the camera lens.

For the second part of the project, the students are required to design, stage, and photograph their own picture, focusing on their own weekly food consumption. They are asked to consider design elements like arrangement, color, and focus to make an argument (and tell a story) about the role of food in their lives. Then, they craft a reflective analysis that challenges them to put these two photographs into dialogue with each other.

PRIMARY DOCUMENTS (at writingprogramarchitecture.com)

Of essential importance to the history and development of the Writers' Studio are (1) our initial FYC Redesign proposal, (2) the updated proposal submitted by an implementation team four months later, and (3) the syllabus for our online FYC course. These primary documents allow readers to grasp the evolution of the Writers' Studio as it was being conceptualized by various stakeholders across the university. Unique to the program was also the design of the course manager and course coordinator positions; the job advertisement is also included in the primary documents collection.

WPA'S VOICE

Using the habits of mind—curiosity, openness, engagement, creativity, persistence, responsibility, flexibility, and metacognition—to guide my work has been as important to my practice as a teacher as it has to my practice as an administrator because these habits encourage me to be an active administrator.

My goal when working with practitioners, whether students or professionals, in a writing center or a FYC program, is to offer them opportunities to be agents, to provide rich professional development opportunities, develop a deeper investment from faculty, and construct collaborative spaces where the value of teaching and learning are renewed.

This renewal and investment can also foster safe spaces for risk-taking. I support risk-taking by viewing the systematic and intentional actions of the practitioners—faculty and writing fellows—in the Writers' Studio as professionally informed actions, ones that emerge from their disciplinary knowledge, writing expertise, and varied teaching experiences. In taking this position, I also invite the practitioners to articulate their action through the same critical lens because informed action and calculated risks are integral to the growth and sustainability of a program. Innovation, learning, and growth emerge from ethical risk.

References

Bourelle, Tiffany, Andrew Bourelle, and Sherry Rankins-Robertson. 2013. "Employing a Multiliteracies Pedagogy through Multimodal Composition: Preparing Twenty-First Century Writers." *Computers and Composition Online* (Fall 2013).

Bourelle, Tiffany, Andrew Bourelle, and Sherry Rankins-Robertson. 2015. "Teaching with Instructional Assistants: Enhancing Student Learning in Online Classes." *Computers and Composition* 37:90–103. http://dx.doi.org/10.1016/j.compcom.2015.06.007.

Bourelle, Tiffany, Sherry Rankins-Robertson, Andrew Bourelle, and Duane Roen. 2013. "Assessing Learning in Redesigned First-Year Composition Courses." In *Digital Writing Assessment and Evaluation*, ed. Heidi McKee and Danielle Nicole DeVoss. Logan: Computers and Composition Digital Press/Utah State University Press. http://ccdigitalpress.org/dwae/12_bourelle.html.

Crawford, Steven. 2012. "Quality Matters Overview." TeachOnline: Resources for Teaching Online. Arizona State University Online.

Menzel, Peter, and Faith D'Alusio. 2005. *Hungry Planet: What the World Eats.* Napa, CA: Material World Books.

Office of Institutional Analysis. 2015. "Reports." Institutional Analysis. Tempe: Arizona State University.

Rankins-Robertson, Sherry, Tiffany Bourelle, Andrew Bourelle, and David Fisher. 2014. "Multimodal Instruction: Pedagogy and Practice for Enhancing Multimodal Composition Online." *Kairos* 19(1).

12

JOHN JAY COLLEGE OF CRIMINAL JUSTICE FIRST-YEAR WRITING PROGRAM

Tim McCormack and Mark McBeth

Institution type: One of eleven undergraduate senior colleges in the City University of New York (CUNY) system.
Location: Manhattan
Enrollment: 13,000
Year program was founded: 2005 (in current form)
WPA reports to: English Department Chair, although consults frequently with Dean of Undergraduates
Program funded by: releases supported by Dean of Undergraduates and Provost
Description of students: 39 percent Hispanic, 28 percent white, 21 percent black, 12 percent Asian, 33 percent foreign born, 47 percent first generation, 75 percent commuter

PROGRAM SNAPSHOT

Program offers about one hundred courses per semester (two ESL, one basic writing and a two composition course sequence) taught by 75-percent part time and 25-percent full time faculty. The current curriculum is grounded in the core literacy principles of inquiry-based research, writing in a variety of genres/disciplines, the ability to read and write rhetorically, and intense reflective practice.

WPAS' PROFILES

Tim

During my own undergraduate years I worked as a pool manager and deli manager. After college, I spent a decade in public relations, where I managed a million dollars in client accounts with a staff of five. When I first switched careers to academia, it seemed completely natural to be asked to manage writing programs. As an adjunct professor, I directed

DOI: 10.7330/9781607326274.c012

the faculty development and tutoring services for the College Now High School Program. As I finished my PhD a few years later, I was a full-time lecturer at New York University's General Studies Program and directed their small tutoring program, chaired the department faculty senate, and was under consideration to become the assistant dean. Instead, I took a tenure track job at John Jay in 2007 to focus on teaching and research, but, just two years later, I "volunteered" to direct its writing program when no other faculty member with any composition and rhetoric or management experience was available to take the job. Though I may not have intended it, I was drawn to writing program administration, and, in many ways, I was expected to fulfill that role.

Though my PhD program did not offer any coursework in writing program administration, my management-based work history should have prepared me for directing a first-year writing program. However, writing program administration is unlike any other "managing" because of the highly political nature of the work of literacy, and because WPA work at our college is underappreciated in terms attaining tenure and promotion. In addition, similar to most colleges, John Jay's first-year writing program has a university-wide role but a localized workforce and management structure and no direct or explicit funding. My WPA work has required an intense second career's worth of knowledge and practice that crosses with but also sits outside of my scholarship focus on ethnography and basic writing. WPA-work needs to be: grounded in theory, theory which I had to learn on the job; carried out in written policy documents, a kind of writing that I was not prepared for in graduate school; and validated by writing program assessment practices, which meant not only learning assessment theory and processes, but "reacquainting" myself with long lost numeracy skills. I have tried to take on the role of "change agent" in my WPA work, evaluating the status quo and looking to make slow, progressive changes that can be accomplished given the program's limited access to staffing and funding. There have been many successes during my time as WPA (building an annual program assessment, creating an ENG 101 summer bridge course, designing tutoring workshops to support the writing program), but dedication to WPA work has overwhelmed my ability to meet the publishing requirements for tenure and promotion at my college. I have written about the difficulties and successes of WPA work in two recent pieces: "Boss of Me: When the Former Adjunct Runs the Writing Shop" in *WPA: Writing Program Administration* (McCormack 2011) and "Equal Opportunity Programming and Optimistic Outcomes Assessment," the latter with my coauthor here, Mark McBeth (McBeth and McCormack 2016).

Mark

I arrived in academia and into the position of WPA in a circuitous route that deserves mentioning only for the fact that many of us land in this field from multiple trajectories and with a multiplicity of accumulated perspectives. I earned a Bachelor of Fine Art in painting and printmaking after which I worked as an artist professionally for twelve years. During that time, I also worked administrative jobs to supplement my starving artist career, and in those positions as lower-level administrator, I learned a lot about organizational strategies of nonprofits, budgetary constraints/planning, and program development. When I finally moved to New York City, I had one such position at City College as the Assistant to the Composition Program, working with Barbara Gleason, Mary Soliday, and Fred Reynolds. I worked on issues of placement, problems with scheduling, other day-in-day-out duties, and had a lot of contact with students. Both Barbara and Mary recognized my affinity with students and asked me to take classes in the City College of New York (CCNY) Language and Literacy Program, after which I could be enlisted to teach composition courses. As a result, I worked my administrative job in the day and would then teach an evening freshman comp course while also taking graduate courses. Eventually after a period of really enjoying teaching, I phased out of the process of art-making and into the process of meaning-making through writing.

After five years at CCNY, I was promoted to the director of the Writing Center where I coordinated a group of twenty-five student tutors and computer lab assistants for five years. During this time, I finished my master's in language and literacy and, subsequently, began my PhD studies at the CUNY Graduate Center, working with Sondra Perl. Once I finished my PhD in 2001, I then started in a tenure-track faculty position at John Jay—at that point, the only comp/rhet appointment within the English Department. The college hired me with the understanding that after a year, I would become the writing program director, which I did under my departmental colleagues' careful protection as I was not yet tenured. From 2003 to 2009, I assumed this FYC directorship, acted as WAC coordinator, and developed a number of advanced literacy initiatives at the college (i.e., Pre-Law Boot Camp and a graduate course in writing for public administration majors). I also published a coauthored book and numerous articles and, as a result, became tenured and promoted. Since then, I have also acted as English Department coordinator of assessment, chair of general education, as well as began teaching in the CUNY Graduate Center PhD Program in English.

PROGRAM CONCEPTION

The first-year writing course sequence at John Jay has always been offered by the English Department, and as of 2002 (when our process of writing program revision began) consisted of six courses: a two-course ESL sequence, a two-course basic writing sequence, and a two-course composition sequence. In all of its sequences, the prior curriculum followed a linear model of literacy learning, one that placed heavy emphasis on current traditional rhetoric, learning fragmented skills (sentence and grammar work, vocabulary building) leading to standard five paragraph expository argument essays. Students were evaluated almost entirely on their final products, with no learning objectives related to writing process or reflection. Since the ESL and basic writing courses were all aimed at passing the university required "placement" exam, the curriculum placed a heavy emphasis on using personal experience and logical reasoning to support generalized claims about commonly debated topics of the day, a curriculum that was a direct "backwash" from the required CUNY writing exam that students needed to pass before accumulating sixty credits and continuing into the core curriculum. ENG 101 and 102, taken after passing the exam, consisted mainly of expository essays with literary fiction as the majority content and thematic reading as the primary source for development of the essays. All of these courses were taught, not as a cohesive unit with a scaffolded curricular design, programmatic support, and ongoing program assessment, but rather as ad hoc classes loosely based on the course description but without learning objectives or curricular guidelines that could make the different sections of the course consistent or coherent as students moved through the sequence. Because there was no curricular structure, the second semester course ran much like a repeat of the first since ENG 102 faculty would not know what their second-semester students had done in ENG 101. Because of the dedicated, talented and thoughtful full-time and adjunct faculty in the department, we found that many of the courses offered good teaching and good assignments, but, because the courses had no real sequence or scaffolding, and no theoretical spine of consistent tasks or repeated coherent objectives, the student experience was ad hoc and teacher dependent, a mere "bedlam of good intentions."

Into this all-too-common story arrives the newly minted PhD in composition and rhetoric, Mark McBeth, who after one year on the job, is asked to take over the writing program in the fall of 2003. Since there was little departmental desire to change the curriculum and little faculty familiarity with recent, evolving composition and rhetoric theory and researched-based literacy practices, Mark looked outward to the

WPA Outcomes Statement and later to the *Frameworks for Success in Postsecondary Writing* (Council of Writing Program Administrators 2011) to devise a new curriculum that offered a stark alternative to the current set of courses. In addition, Mark looked inward to the current faculty and students to understand what kind of writing was valued in our local context. Mark's research led him to design a new curriculum focused on writing as a process and one that foregrounded research and rhetoric, giving students early opportunities to work in a variety of genres and to revise and reflect on their work in a portfolio-based system.[1] Mark set down a set of principles for first-year writing at John Jay. The new writing curriculum:

- Serves a writing community largely comprised of English-as-second-language and English-as-second-dialect students who need extended periods of instruction and rehearsal to master reading and writing skills.
- Addresses the writing needs of a mission-based college, primarily sociologically and scientifically oriented, while still providing the rhetorical sensibilities for a well-rounded liberal arts undergraduate.
- Approaches writing as a means of analytical and organizational thinking rather than mere reporting of information.
- Presents writing as a scaffolded sequence of manageable, interrelated tasks.
- Integrates college resources (i.e., Center for English Language Support, Writing Center, and the library) into the curriculum to reinforce the activities that occur in the writing classroom.
- Emphasizes (and consistently reinforces) the habits, techniques, and strategies necessary to compose a college-level piece of writing.
- Introduces students to the cross-disciplinary aspects of writing, which teaches them how to apply their writing skills in a variety of academic and rhetorical writing contexts.

It took three years of design and piloting, numerous department and college-wide persuasion sessions, and a good bit of political finagling, but eventually a new curriculum was designed and presented to the frequently contentious college curriculum committees for approval.[2] All three courses had undergone separate (yet interdependent) departmental scrutiny, curriculum committee revisions, and college council debate; this seemingly endless process finally resulted in a governance-sanctioned writing/research curriculum that was authorized through college policy rather than mere proclamation of the English Department-based faculty. In the fall of 2006, the writing program launched its new series of courses: English 100, English 101, and English 201, and the initiation of this new curriculum coincided with the arrival of two new tenure track faculty members in composition and rhetoric.

POPULATION SERVED

Not only is John Jay College a majority-minority institution, but our students also differ from national trends for college students in many ways: they more frequently hold jobs while attending school (63% work more than twenty-one hours per week); they have more dependent care responsibilities (64% care for a dependent at least part time); they have lower household incomes (72% earn less than $50,000 per year and 25% less than $15,000 per year); and they have above average commutes to school, the majority via the NYC public transit system.[3]

As WPAs who set out to build a writing program, we took in these local, contextual factors and made them key design considerations for the broader, academic and professional literacy goals of our program. Because of their limited income and time constraints, our students need to have a sturdy foundation in reading and writing that also expands upward to their majors, and they must accrue their "starter" literacy skills quickly, with a consideration of their time to graduation (and, therefore, their post-college employment or further education) as well as their governmentally-regulated and time-restricted financial aid allowances. More importantly, because we recognized that our students come to John Jay with strong rhetorical knowledge in a variety of languages and cultural contexts, our writing program needed to move beyond a curriculum based in a narrow view of skills attainment, and instead immediately challenge the students by showing them how to apply their already existing rhetorical fluency and dexterity to the college academic writing context.

FUNDING

The writing program at John Jay has no budget that is directly managed by the program administrator; our funding is allocated by upper administration without any input from us. The writing program director and WAC director earn a nine-hour reduction in a twenty-one-hour teaching load for their WPA work. There is no summer salary. The college's investment in tenure track and lecturer lines in composition and rhetoric remains the sole funding commitment to the writing program, which has a course enrollment cap of twenty-seven students per class. Our writing program has access to the English Department coordinator and a department administrative assistant, but both of these administrators are also responsible for the requests of the three hundred students in our major and fifty full time and sixty adjunct faculty members. We do most of our own day-in-and-day-out paperwork, such as the administrative work of outcomes assessment, uploading of website materials, correspondence, copying, and filing. We have come to learn that our plight as WPAs without supporting staff is fairly common in the field.

OPERATIONS

Currently John Jay has four tenure-track composition and rhetoric faculty members and ten full-time lecturers dedicated to the writing program. Our lecturer lines are full-time lines with expected contributions to administrative and teaching needs of the program. Lecturers can earn a tenure-like Certificate of Continuous Employment after five years at the college. Still the majority of our courses (75%) are taught by adjunct faculty, who are only allowed to teach two courses per semester. Most of our adjunct faculty have been with us for many years, as we do provide office space, schedule accommodations and faculty development, and the union provides health care and other benefits.

Our primary work as WPAs is to be proactive stewards of the curriculum. We must not only enact the learning objectives, prescribed assignments and pedagogical focus in our own classrooms, but also facilitate these core goals in all of the writing program courses. This involves hiring and mentoring adjunct faculty (we currently have thirty-six adjunct faculty members teaching in the writing program), staffing writing courses (more than ninety sections per semester), facilitating faculty development, conducting program assessment, and building curricular innovations and initiatives that support students and faculty in the classroom. In addition to this work in first year writing, we also direct a WAC program for the college, where we train faculty in other disciplines to teach writing in their courses and design and facilitate the work of graduate student writing fellows, who are loaned out to departments to work on writing curriculum and pedagogy in their departments.

In any given week, our management duties can involve working with the testing director regarding incoming placement exams, meeting with an unhappy student in a writing course, providing guidance and materials to a first-time writing faculty member, attending a curriculum committee meeting to put through a course revision, designing a workshop on disciplinary writing for faculty development day, reviewing a pile of adjunct faculty observations, and working with the admissions office, registrar and the office of financial aid on why incoming ESL students should have the entire six hours of their ESL course time counted toward their credit hours.

In addition to these ongoing and incessant parts of WPA work that are directly connected to the teaching of first-year writing, WPAs are perceived as the go to experts on campus for the development of literacy initiatives outside first-year writing. In the last five years, our writing program faculty initiated a WAC push that requires the certification of Writing Intensive faculty, designed a legal-writing initiative, which was eventually named the Pre-Law Boot Camp, to better prepare students for law school; and developed courses and outside the classroom interventions to improve the writing of graduate students. These college-wide initiatives are guided by the same theoretical underpinning of literacy and language development of our first-year writing program, so our students will encounter a repeated set of literacy tasks and practices during the accumulation of their 120 credits at the college.

ASSESSMENT

Each academic year, the First-Year Composition Assessment Committee stipulates target goals for the assessment process, which both confirm reforms we have put in place as well as suggest additional improvements. Our assessment process includes: designing research methods for each assessment; collecting and evaluating quantitative and qualitative data; analyzing and triangulating data; discussing the overarching implications of our findings; instituting changes to curriculum pedagogy or programmatic practice based on the findings; conducting faculty development to encourage suggested programmatic alterations; and re-evaluating the changes to see if improvement has occurred. This program assessment cycle is analogous to the type of writing revision we expect students to perform while producing their portfolios; we are not afraid to continuously reimagine our processes and practices each year. While we attempt to always fulfill the data-supported validity and reliability requirements of outside program assessors, we also never fail to meet self-imposed goals for programmatic growth and innovation.

In the past our assessment practices have included reviewing program syllabi, student and faculty focus groups, student and faculty surveys, and learning outcomes assessment through portfolio review. All are done anonymously, not as critiques of individual student's performance or faculty teaching ability but as a program assessment that we use to modify curriculum and enhance learning practices. The portfolio assessment remains the focal point for the outcomes assessment portion of our assessment practice. The data allows us to formulate claims about our program, and show evidence of what students and instructors have accomplished. Based upon the multivalent information that comes out of the portfolio evaluation, we can pose a variety of inquiries about student writing, verify our claims through actual student projects, and make educated, well-informed speculations about what programmatic moves to make next. To ensure that faculty and students are willing to participate, the WPA alerts faculty early in the semester of the assessment process and explains how student portfolios are randomly chosen, how all identifying information is redacted from the portfolios, and how the assessment goal evaluates the program as a whole rather than individual instructors or courses. While this rich assessment process guarantees anonymity of instructional staff, it does provide the necessary data for beneficial faculty development opportunities. Since full-time and part-time instructors complete this portfolio reading as a collective force, they can see the variety of ways that students compile portfolios, teachers develop creative assignments, and administrators implement supportive policies and procedures. The collective effort thus demystifies the often-tacit procedural coordination for writing faculty and illuminates the problems that may arise from administrative decisions for the WPAs who make them. After each reading session, a discussion is held where these ideas are shared, posited as potential improvement, and imagined as already instituted policy. So, even in the cases where quantitative results may be judged to be insignificant or counter-productive, the time spent reading and discussing student portfolios works as faculty development, as the faculty return to the classroom the following semester with new knowledge, fresh assignments, and inspired teaching approaches.

MARKETING/PR

In terms of marketing our writing program to students, we don't need to, as the two main courses—English 101 and 201—are required parts of the students' general education requirements, and students are placed into the ESL and basic writing courses through testing. However, we invest our effort of marketing to faculty outside of English, so that they know what types of writing experience and rehearsal students receive prior (or concurrently) to arriving in their classrooms. Thus our first-year writing curriculum is linked to other writing initiatives at the campus. For example, our WAC coordinator runs across-the-disciplines workshops each semester about how faculty members might appropriate and adapt our exercises, assignments, and writing objectives to the purposes of their own courses.

Going a step further, in 2008, the college instituted an incentive for this extracurricular faculty work. In an effort to establish some requirements for writing-intensive courses, the WPA and dean of undergraduates designated criteria for writing intensive courses as well as a procedure that faculty could become certified to teach these courses. Instead of certifying each individual course, faculty members who would teach across the curricula would attend faculty development workshops, prepare course packets, and develop evaluations of their own teaching. Instead of a previous policy that set quantitative measures for different levels of writing intensive courses (i.e., 100 level = ten pages of writing; 200 level = twenty pages, etc.), this proposed and eventually ratified policy would reset more descriptive quantitative minimums for both low- and high-stakes writing assignments as well as include qualitative requirements:

- integration of "low-stakes" and "high-stakes" writing assignments
- integration of peer review of writing assignments
- integration of self-reflective writing

The integration of these teaching criteria would introduce students to the varying elements of academic writing, offer them the rehearsal of the processes and methods commonly used by effective writers, and afford them a variety of writing tasks and scenarios. These WAC marketing endeavors helped the college to move beyond thinking of first-year writing as the inoculation that cures all student writing woes.

TECHNOLOGY

The university has long imposed Blackboard on all faculty, and many faculty use it with varying degrees of success. Some faculty complain about the prescriptive nature of this technology and the lack of student control and creativity the software provides—especially for working with and "publishing" writing. The college has been interested in mandating an ePortfolio software package as well. But this too has met with resistance. Currently, individual faculty in the writing program use a number of technologies that have led to ePortfolio or blog development in writing courses through WordPress and Squarespace, among others, that are in complete student control. Many faculty are experimenting with multi-genre, visual text work and these are often featured in our faculty development sessions. Other faculty members use Digication and some use Turn-It-In as a repository for portfolios.

The technology piece of the WPA workload is extremely difficult and time consuming, as it requires an intense knowledge of a rapidly changing field, but also a firm understanding of how technologies can be used to enhance existing curriculum and pedagogy, without turning writing courses into technology courses. Rather than impose a universal technology that may not be appropriate or useful, we have, so far, encouraged the use of digital technology based on faculty and student need and desire. Technology should not be imposed on faculty but developed with faculty. This stance has put us in conflict with the college and university, who too often prefer universal and static implementation of technologies without considering curriculum and learning outcomes.

ROLE OF RESEARCH

As a means to explain the varying aspects of our program, Tim McCormack and Mark McBeth have coauthored "Apologia without Apologies: A Local Lecture on Full-Time Lecturers," which offers a rationale and justification for our full-time lecturer lines, and "Equal Opportunity Programming and Optimistic Program Assessment: Writing Program Design and Assessment at John Jay College of Criminal Justice" (McBeth and McCormack 2016, 2017), which profiles and explicates our curriculum design as integrally related to our assessment efforts. In "Queering the Institution: Politics and Power in the Assistant Professor Administrator Position," Tara Pauliny (2011) has described the disruptive potentials of an untenured WPA, based on her role as John Jay WAC coordinator.

All of our tenure track composition faculty members began their careers at John Jay with established scholarly paths (educational history, race pedagogy, writing and gender studies, and the ethnography of basic writing). While Mark McBeth has done archival work in international contexts (*Teacher Training at Cambridge: The Initiatives of Oscar Browning and Elizabeth Hughes*, coauthored with Pam Hirsch [McBeth and Hirsch 2004]) as well as localized CUNY biography ("Memoranda of Fragile Machinery: A Portrait of Shaughnessy as Intellectual-Bureaucrat" [McBeth 2007]), offering him insights that informed and foregrounded his curricular designs, the John Jay writing faculty has paused and reflected upon various aspects of their pedagogical and bureaucratic initiatives. In "Arrested Development: Revising Remediation at John Jay College of Criminal Justice," McBeth (2006) described and reported upon his developmental course design; this curriculum later won the 2007 Conference of Basic Writing National Award for Innovation in Basic Writing Curriculum. The John Jay faculty has on numerous occasions been called upon to present as invited guest speakers about our writing curriculum as well as its relation to our WAC program and support services, including at the WPA and CCCC's national conferences, and at writing conferences at the University of Connecticut and LaGuardia Community College.

In reviewing the collective work of our writing faculty, one notices the recursive cycle of our scholarly efforts: a close attention to an aspect of the program and/or student composers, a collection of data through applied administrative labor, and then reflection upon the work and the evidence produced during those pedagogical or administrative efforts. These applied intellectual labors alongside our subsequent publications have followed the resolutions of our national flagship organizations in the field of comp/rhet. In "Evaluating the Intellectual Work of Writing Administration," The Council of Writing Program Administrators (1998) has defined the varying ways that WPAs "produce knowledge" through program creation, curricular design, faculty development, program assessment and evaluation, and program-related textual production. The joint work of writing faculty mirrors their definition but has also enriched and improved our ongoing curricular efforts. Upcoming collaborations between our faculty cohorts will yield even greater understanding of our particular population of student writers and the institutional conditions in which they learn.

PEDAGOGICAL AND/OR ADMINISTRATION HIGHLIGHTS

Since students' ability to write well is a college-wide concern, WPAs must work with other stakeholders to develop programmatic supports for the curriculum. Fortunately, at John Jay we have many amenable colleagues with whom we have collaborated to advance the writing curriculum: first the Writing Center director, a fellow English Department faculty member, quickly understood our new writing program objectives, altered tutor training to fit the curriculum, and began workshop and special initiatives to support students in the composition classes. In addition, the Student Academic Success Programs (SASP) office,[4] whose interest in first-year student success aligned with our own, designed effective initiatives, such as peer mentoring, that were integrally related to student achievement. SASP fully supported and advocated for the writing program curriculum since it provides the literacy foundation for student success and achievement, a key component of their student retention mandate. In 2010, the writing program, writing center, and the SASP office began to collaborate on curricular and co-curricular programs for students.

EARLYstart

In the fall of 2011, we built an ENG 101 bridge course that would start in the summer months and carry over into the fall. This program serves sixty to one hundred incoming students whose low scores on testing and below average high school grade indicators designate them as "at-risk" students. Based on our basic writing course (ENGW100), the enhanced ENG 101 course provided (1) sixty hours (four mornings per week for three hours per day) instead of the forty-five in the traditional semester setting, (2) a veteran writing center tutor and a student peer mentor assigned to the classroom, (3) extracurricular common events and field trips, and (4) a "stepped back" and "move forward" curriculum that began with a series of literacy building activities, a completion of the standard ENG 101 curriculum in an intensive summer session, and additional one-on-one and small group meetings in the fall semester used by the professor to mentor the students on the required end-of-course portfolio, advise them on writing assignments in other courses, and prepare them for the subsequent ENG 201 course. Now in its fourth year, the EARLYstart program consistently achieves higher course completion rates (near 100% as compared to 85% for the general population), higher first semester credit accumulation rates (up to two credits higher than the rest of their first-time freshmen cohort), and higher GPA in ENG 101 (5 percentage points higher than the general population).

JUMPstart

With the same cohort of stakeholders (the writing program, the writing center, and SASP), we designed intervention options for not only those students willing to self-select into a summer 101 course, but also those first-time, first-year students who may have "passed" the entrance exam, but whose triangulated testing data indicated basic writing challenges. Rather than single out these students for an additional course that they might view as an expensive tuition-costing delay and unnecessary obligation, we developed an early intervention to keep these students mainstreamed in ENG 101. Working with input from faculty, the Writing Center created a series of Freshman Composition workshops in four crucial areas: developing ideas; close reading; summarizing/ paraphrasing; and sentence fluency (basic sentence level skills in terms of intelligibility, sentence integrity, coherence/clarity). The Writing Center constructed each workshop to focus on students' writing assignments and, thus, asked students to bring their writing drafts so they could apply the workshop's particular concentration directly to their work. This early intervention structure maximizes students' connections between the workshops and the 101 courses and used the Writing Center tutoring services early in the semester when they often go under-used. Now in its third year, the results have surpassed expectations: though these students' challenges could potentially overwhelm them in the rigorous ENG 101 curriculum, close to 95 percent of JUMPstart students pass the course, more than 7 percent higher than the general population.

The First-Year Showcase

Three years after the launch of the new curriculum, the SASP office came to the writing program with the idea of linking ENG 101 courses to disciplinary courses, subsequently named Learning Communities. Given that our curriculum introduced students to interdisciplinary writing, this initiative again aligned with our aims. In this partnership, the WPA would run faculty development workshops to help faculty pairs cultivate pedagogical and curricular connections between their linked courses. Ostensibly, the linked communities helped introduce WAC into freshman composition, yet an even more innovative programmatic support emerged at the college as a result. As composition faculty representative in the Learning Community advisory group, Kim Helmer proposed that the Learning Community sections of English 101 participate in a late-semester First-Year Showcase, where students would present their "in process" research to the college community in a variety of formats: posters, digital presentations, or presentation panels. The ENG 101 faculty, working with their faculty partners, helped curate the show by guiding students on how to exhibit their research and talk about their work; the SASP office provided upper level undergraduate peer mentors to help the students design their materials (including professionally printed color posters); and the writing center held workshops on presentation software, and worked with students to edit and proofread their texts for the showcase. In each year after the initial showcase, SASP has reserved a larger space for the Showcase, which now attracts hundreds of students, faculty and administrators who peruse the "research aisles," where eager first-year students engage them in discussions about their topics as well as the rhetorical strategies and research methodologies they implemented to create their research projects.

Each of the cross-campus initiatives described above involves the WPA moving beyond the role of curriculum taskmaster and logistical controller of the writing program. In the role of collaborative innovator, the WPA coordinates with stakeholders throughout the college to enhance literacy practices that connect securely to the freshman writing curriculum yet, ultimately, reach well-beyond first-year writing.

PRIMARY DOCUMENTS (at **writingprogramarchitecture.com**)

We have included the proposal to our college curriculum committee for our ENG 100 course. As a means to illustrate the initial steps in developing the John Jay writing curriculum, these governance-required protocol documents represent the curriculum design description and rational as it was first proposed to our English Department faculty, to the college-wide curriculum committee, and to the College Council, who would finally ratify the curriculum as institutional policy in 2005. These types of documents represent the labors of carefully articulated rhetoric that a WPA must finesse to convince a department, a campus faculty, and an upper administration of the value of sound writing curriculum. Note that the tone, word choice, and style of these documents is aimed at this larger audience and does not at all resemble the documents we would go on to create to introduce the curriculum to our writing faculty or to writing program administrators within and outside the university. In taking this document out of the archive, we also notice that the current curriculum with its decade-long evolution barely seems recognizable in these now historical accounts of its original design and planning.

WPAS' VOICES

During the design, implementation, and assessment of our curriculum over the past decade, we have often heard colleagues aver that "our students can't do this or that," normally referring to some literacy task for which they presumed our students incapable yet without ever offering them the opportunity to succeed, fail, or do some intermediary adequate attempt. The work of WPAs, especially when it involves designing or revising a new curriculum, remains politically difficult work that is too often viewed by colleagues as a simple problem to solve. In *Lives on the Boundary*, after providing a close reading of his life as an administrator of educational programs, Mike Rose (1990) announces:

> What began troubling me about the policy documents and the crisis reports were that they focused too narrowly on test scores and tallies of error and other such measures. They lacked careful analysis of students' histories, and lacked, as well, analysis of the cognitive and social demands of the academic culture the students now faced. The work I was doing in the Tutorial Center, in the Writing Research Project, and in the Summer

Program was guiding me toward a richer understanding of what it meant to be unprepared in the American Research University. (187)

Like Rose, we realized the direct consequences of the shallow representation of educational programs, teaching life and students, and we looked to overturn those overly simple analyses by investing our knowledge into the daily practices of running a writing program that understands the world of college literacy as "messy and social and complex" (200). New WPAs should resist the urge to become "Bartleby the Compositionist," sucked into the vortex of enrollment numbers, book order memos, and daily staffing concerns, while ignoring the curriculum design, formative assessment measures, literacy initiatives and faculty engagement that the WPA ought carry out as theoretically-based practices of intellectual labor and possible scholarship (Rose and Weiser 2002). Looking back now, it is clear to us that viewing WPA work not as practical and logistical tasks but as theoretically grounded scholarship of practice played a major role in our winning the CCCC's Certificate of Excellence Award in 2013.

For example, at the "high" theoretical level, our curriculum framed our classrooms as "contact zones of proximal development," thus interweaving Mary Louise Pratt's (1991) cross-cultural interchanges (which recurred in our highly diverse, urban contexts) with Lev Vygotsky's (1978) understanding about the judicious "stretch" that students would need to make to challenge their learning development (which our students had often been denied in test-saturated educational experiences). Blending these abstract learning theories with the on-the-ground research done by CUNY scholars such as Kenneth Bruffee, Marilyn Sternglass, Mary Soliday, Barbara Gleason, and Sondra Perl (a nonexhaustive list), we devised and revised our curriculum to reflect this accumulated knowledge about advanced, postsecondary literacy in a public university. Our work is also constantly shaped by the administrators who oversaw the college, by the instructional staff who taught the courses and, most important, by the students who enrolled to acquire the advanced literacy abilities expected of them at college. These "primary source" practitioners provided the local knowledge and institutional context so critical to our success. It is ongoing, theoretically progressive and academically meaningful work that too often goes unrecognized and unrewarded by the college.[5]

Herein lies the challenge of writing program administration: a well devised curriculum demands active listening to a heteroglossia of voices, insights, and stances that must add up to a completed vision, which must be revised (really *ad* infinitum) based on changing needs of the institution, its faculty, and its students. It is a never-ending, and almost all-consuming task. We are buoyed by the understanding that our work provides our urban, multilingual, multiracial, multi-gendered, multi-sexually-oriented, multi-(dis)advantaged (again a non-exhaustive list) the curricular and pedagogical opportunities for advanced literacy practice and strong intellectual habits of mind. These WPA-created opportunities enable what we refer to as an equal opportunity writing program.

Notes

1. The portfolio-based curriculum also afforded the means for valid and reliable programmatic assessment, another key change to existing practice.
2. Note that although based in the English Department, the writing program courses receive a high degree of scrutiny at all levels and in all departments, since college writing courses are often seen not as discipline courses, but college-wide service courses.
3. All college statistics provided by the John Jay College Office of Institutional Research annual reports.
4. This office is often called First-Year Experience (FYE) at many colleges.
5. While we understand what we do as applied scholarship, our college has yet to recognize our work when considering tenure and promotion. All WPAs are advised to become very familiar with "Evaluating the Intellectual Work of Writing Administration," written by a subcommittee of the Council of Writing Program Administrators (1998), which explains writing program work as applied scholarship and can be used by WPAs involved in battles over tenure and promotion.

References

Council of Writing Program Administrators. 1998. "Evaluating the Intellectual Work of Writing Program Administrators." Accessed February 1, 2015. http://wpacouncil.org/positions/intellectualwork.html.

Council of Writing Program Administrators. 2011. *Frameworks for Success in Postsecondary Writing.* Accessed February 1, 2015. http://wpacouncil.org/framework.

McBeth, Mark. 2006. "Arrested Development: Revising Remediation at John Jay College of Criminal Justice." *Journal of Basic Writing* 25 (2): 76–93.

McBeth, Mark. 2007. "Memoranda of Fragile Machinery: A Portrait of Mina Shaughnessy as Intellectual Bureaucrat." *WPA: Writing Program Administration* 31 (1/2): 48–64.

McBeth, Mark, and Pam Hirsch. 2004. *Teacher Training at Cambridge: The Initiatives of Oscar Browning and Elizabeth Hughes.* London: Woburn Press.

McBeth, Mark, and Tim McCormack. 2016. "Equal Opportunity Programming and Optimistic Outcomes Assessment" *Composition Forum* 33.

McBeth, Mark, and Tim McCormack. 2017. "Apologia without Apologies: A Local Lecture on Full-Time Lecturers." In *Contingency, Exploitation, and Solidarity: Labor and Action in English Composition,* ed. Seth Kahn, Amy Lynch and Bill Lalicker. WAC Clearinghouse Perspectives on Writing Series. Fort Collins: Colorado State University.

McCormack, Tim. 2011. "Boss of Me: When the Former Adjunct Runs the Writing Shop." *WPA* 35 (1): 163–4.

Pauliny, Tara. 2011. "Queering the Institution: Politics and Power in the Assistant Professor Administrator Position." Accessed February 1, 2015 *Enculturation: A Journal of Rhetoric, Writing, and Culture* 10.

Pratt, Mary Louise. 1991. "Arts of the Contact Zone." *Profession* 91: 33–40.

Rose, Mike. 1990. *Lives on the Boundary.* New York: Penguin Books.

Rose, Shirley, and Irwin Weiser, eds. 2002. *The Writing Program Administrator as Theorist: Making Knowledge Work.* Porstmouth, NH: Heinemann Boynton/Cook.

Vygotsky, Lev. 1978. *Mind in Society: The Development of Higher Psychological Processes.* Ed. Michael Cole, Sylvia Scribner Vera John-Steiner, and Ellen Souberman. Cambridge, MA: Harvard University Press.

13

ONONDAGA COMMUNITY COLLEGE WRITING PROGRAM

Malkiel Choseed

Institution type: An open admissions, two-year college, part of the State University of New York (SUNY) system
Location: Syracuse, New York
Enrollment: approximately 12,300
Year program was founded: 2003
WPA reports to: English, Reading, and Communication Department Chair, Provost and Chief Academic Officer
Program funded by: Provost and Chief Academic Officer (funds are administered through the English, Reading, and Communication Department budget)
Description of students: Very diverse, including many under-prepared and non-traditional students. Approximately 20 percent place into basic writing.

PROGRAM SNAPSHOT

The Writing Program consists of two first-year writing courses (ENG 103 and ENG 104) and our single non-credit, developmental writing course (ENG 099). Prior to 2003, these classes were simply referred to as "English" classes. With the establishment of a WPA position, the identity as a writing program became more well-formed within the Department of English, Reading, and Communication.

WPA'S PROFILE

When I entered the University of Pittsburgh (Pitt) in the fall of 1997 as an MA student, I was interested in studying literature with an emphasis on cultural studies. I was introduced to the formal study of composition through a mandatory teaching seminar and practicum my first two semesters at Pitt. My interest piqued, I took more and more courses in composition as I pursued my PhD, eventually getting a PhD level

DOI: 10.7330/9781607326274.c013

certificate in composition, pedagogy, and literacy, and working as a mentor for new teachers of composition. All the while, I was teaching a mixture of FYC and introductory literature courses and regularly presenting at the Conference of College Composition and Communication (CCCC). While the topic I chose for my dissertation may not have been a traditional composition topic (an historical analysis of the teaching of Shakespeare in American higher education and its link to the development of English as a discipline), pedagogy played a central part in it. I also spent a few semesters working as a tutor in the Pitt Writing Center.

When it was time to go on the job market, I was ideally looking for a position at a community college where teaching and service were emphasized over research. Geographic and family considerations took me to the Syracuse area and Onondaga Community College (OCC). I was hired as an assistant professor of English and immediately went to work teaching the standard load of five courses per term. The first few semesters were spent teaching FYC exclusively. I began working with the then Writing Program coordinator (WPC) on a number of projects, especially around assessment of SUNY general education requirements and professional development. My knowledge of composition history, theory, and practice made me a useful addition to the department, as most of my colleagues were generalists or literature focused (although we all taught FYC). At one point, the WPA arranged to "share" one credit (the equivalent of a third of a course) of her release time with me so that I could coordinate one of the general education assessment projects, essentially arranging for a stipend for me to take charge of the project. In retrospect, I see now that she was giving me a chance to try out the role.

Soon thereafter, she stepped down from her WPA position, and I took on the role, beginning the year that I earned tenure. I didn't go on the job market looking for a WPA position, but my background and experience made me a candidate for one. It helped also that Onondaga, like many community colleges, allows for tenure relatively quickly; I received tenure in my fifth year of employment. While I did need to be conscious of them, I did not have to worry too much about internal, departmental power struggles or the rigors of WPA work getting in the way of my tenure bid. My work as WPA was counted as departmental service (another benefit of the community college environment), and my innovations were, by necessity, gradual; thus minimizing ruffled feathers.

The best thing I ever did to prepare for the WPC position was attend the CWPA workshop in Denver in 2008. That gave me the tools to start implementing practical changes, and I recommend it to anyone even interested in WPA work. I made a special appeal to our college president for funding and was lucky that she saw the value in it.

PROGRAM CONCEPTION

The Writing Program at Onondaga Community College came into being with the creation of the position of Writing Program coordinator (a WPA position). The position was created, advertised, and hired so that it began in 2003. At the time, the senior administration wanted someone to try to bring consistency and uniformity to course delivery and content of our required two-part FYC sequence and our developmental writing course. The formation of the Writing Program coordinator position called into being the "writing program." Prior to that, we simply had English classes. Everyone taught FYC, and there were some faculty members with extensive backgrounds in the theory, history, and practice of composition, but there was no sustained conversation around teaching composition, no sense of the disciplinarity of it, no program per se. Faculty members, both full and part time, had an extraordinary degree of autonomy in the way they taught their classes, with little oversight aside from required observations necessary for reappointment or promotion. Course outlines existed with specified learning goals, assignment types, page minimums, and the like, but the way in which these were interpreted varied widely, and the concept of what college level writing is or could be varied from instructor to instructor, section to section.

Based on conversations with the outgoing WPA, she saw her role as laying the foundation for future innovations by introducing the department to theory and the larger discipline of composition. The members of the department were simply not used to someone taking a sustained interest in their pedagogical choices, nor were they used to professional development or engaging in a disciplinary conversation outside of their own classroom experience or talk around the coffee maker. The former WPA established reading groups, resource libraries, assignment exchanges, and a host of professional development opportunities (e.g., introducing an organized, discipline-specific adjunct orientation). In addition, the department was responding to new mandates for general education and course-level assessment imposed by SUNY and Middle States, our accreditor. Most important, the WPA took part in hiring committees and tried to steer the committees to hire faculty who had more formal training in composition (people like me).

Many full-time and part-time faculty had a lot of experience teaching composition, but, because they were trained in creative writing or the study of literature, that teaching was often done without reference to the larger fields of rhetoric and composition. The presence of a new WPA who was hired from outside the college did throw some people off balance. Before, everyone operated with almost complete autonomy. Now there was someone who had it as part of her job description to ask questions about what happened in everyone's classrooms. Some people saw it as another layer of oversight, or as threatening, either to their identity as "good" teachers or literally to their job security. The person hired came from a nearby research university with some renown for its composition program. This helped set up an "us vs. them" mentality that never really went away. There was some explicit resistance to the position and even an official compromise in which the position went from being appointed by the president to being voted on by the department and limited by three-year terms.

Throughout this profile, I refer to the department, the English discipline, and/or the Writing Program. I use these terms somewhat interchangeably because at OCC, the boundaries are themselves somewhat malleable. When a faculty member teaches a composition course, he/she is a *de facto* member of the Writing Program. Since only English faculty are eligible to teach composition, all are considered part of the Writing Program, whether they acknowledge it or even know it. Generally speaking, writing tutoring has been considered as part of the Writing Program as well.

POPULATION SERVED

At Onondaga, we do not have traditional majors. A student interested in getting a four-year degree majors in a broader program, such as liberal arts: humanities and social sciences. Upon transfer to a four-year school, students select the appropriate major. All students regardless of their program take at least one level of FYC. If they are enrolled in a transfer program, they usually take two. This may be in addition to the non-credit, developmental writing course, which approximately 20 percent of our incoming student body is required to take. The FYC courses also play a role in satisfying various SUNY general education requirements (allowing students to fulfill college requirements in humanities and communication as well as SUNY-wide requirements).

As such, our FYC courses are composed of a cross-section of our students who range in age, experience, preparedness, goals, and learning (dis)ability. For example, in one FYC section, I had a recent Cuban immigrant who was still learning English, who was sitting next to a

returning veteran "trying out college," who was sitting next to a traditional student seeking transfer, who was sitting next to a disabled, former truck driver coming back to school for re-training/credentialing as
well as to pursue his passion for creative writing.

FUNDING

Approximately 80 percent of operating costs at Onondaga come from
salaries and benefits. The department budget comes from the college
by way of the provost and chief academic officer's office. The chair
oversees this, and there are no separate budget lines for the Writing
Program *per se.*

It takes a tremendous amount of money to fund the English department at Onondaga. In the fall of 2014, 61 sections of ENG 099 were
taught (21 by full-time faculty and 40 by part-time faculty), 105 sections
of ENG 103 were taught (52 by full-time faculty and 53 by part-time faculty), and 57 sections of ENG 104 were taught (32 by full-time faculty
and 25 by part-time faculty). In the spring of 2015, 28 sections of ENG
099 were taught (16 by full-time faculty and 12 by part-time faculty), 68
sections of ENG 103 were taught (41 by full-time faculty and 27 by part-
time faculty), and 73 sections of ENG 104 were taught (32 by full-time
faculty and 41 by part-time faculty). Based on information from our
interim provost and our assistant vice president of Financial Services, we
can estimate that an average section taught by a full-time faculty member costs the college approximately $9,178 (including fringe benefits).
There are two pay scales for adjunct instructors depending on seniority, but the average cost per section is $3,660. The total cost for all of
these sections over the 2014–2015 academic year was approximately
$2,505,212.

To put this into perspective, only 33 courses out of a total of 266
taught in the fall 2014 semester were not developmental writing or part
of our FYC sequence. In spring 2015, only 33 courses out of a total of 202
were not developmental or part of our FYC sequence. That is approximately 12 percent and 16 percent, respectively. We offer a smattering of
journalism, creative writing, and literature courses, but they are small
compared to writing. At many community colleges, there is no real distinction between writing faculty and literature or creative writing faculty. Everyone, full and part time, teaches writing courses. Unlike many
four-year universities where various factions jockey for resources, composition comprises the bulk of our offerings. In that sense, funding for
instructors is not an issue.

It is an issue, however, when it comes to funding pilots and special projects. Generally speaking, there is no budget to support innovation. Recently, we have relied on internal and external grants to support the development and implementation of special projects (see "Pedagogical and/or Administrative Highlights" section). If our administration was not receptive to funding our ideas, it would be that much more difficult to get these programs established. The college as a whole values assessment and continues to support it by paying readers for their participation from a budget line earmarked for that purpose. For example, in fall 2015, we received approximately $2,000 to fund a four-hour reading/scoring session that included adjunct and full-time instructors. So far, the support has been stable, but we are keenly aware that the budget lines for these projects exist outside of our direct control. If the administration were to change priorities, there is no guarantee that funding would continue.

Until recently, the WPC oversaw the budget for the Writing Skills Center. We employ approximately twenty-five professional tutors who staff approximately 175 hours (spring terms) to 225 hours (fall terms) per week. In addition, we have an e-tutoring option that runs concurrently with face-to-face tutoring. We also offer summer term tutoring hours. In the 2014–2015 academic year, tutor salaries amounted to approximately $156,000, not including secretarial or WPC salaries.

The WPC does not have a budget for professional development or marketing for the Writing Program. Possibilities exist for the WPC to partner with existing campus entities (like the office that funds our assessment readings) or apply for grants through our campus Teaching Center. We have, through a Teaching Center grant, brought Rebecca Moore Howard to campus to speak about her work with the Citation Project in April 2013. Before the Writing Skills Center joined the new learning commons, there was a modest budget for promotional items, maintaining a small library of professional resources, etc. Now, the administrator in charge of the learning commons handles all budgetary matters.

OPERATIONS

There are many individuals who have a hand in making the department run on a day-to-day basis: the department secretaries, the department chair, and the writing program coordinator. Within English, the Writing Program coordinator (a WPA-type position) is voted into a three-year term. The WPC at OCC receives nine hours of release time from a fifteen-hour load each semester. Three hours are for overseeing the writing tutors, three are for overseeing general education assessment, and three hours are for overseeing curricular innovation. Much of the WPC's time is taken up by planning and overseeing assessment.

The two department secretaries are our front-line staff, directing student questions and requests to the appropriate person or office. The department chair also spends much of her time answering student questions and complaints. The WPC deals with questions related to placement testing and occasionally course transfer and the like. In terms of the discipline/program, committees of full-time faculty do the bulk of the work. Adjunct faculty are sometimes invited to participate, but given the fact that they are not paid for their work, participation is very low. The WPC has limited authority to simply implement change; hence, any large-scale change must be discussed and voted on by the English discipline and then the department as a whole (made up of English, Reading, and Communications). While this does slow down the process, it does ensure at least some degree of buy-in.

The standard load for a full-time faculty member at OCC is fifteen credit hours per term. Many teach up to eighteen credit hours. Full-timers are also required to advise and perform service to the college, usually in the form of committee work. Adjunct faculty are paid only for teaching duties and are contractually required to attend only one college-wide meeting/orientation per term.

The chair of our department is responsible for vetting, hiring, and evaluating adjunct instructors, although in recent years the chair has asked the WPC to sit in on interviews for FYC instructors. This is a courtesy to the WPC but also has a practical benefit for both the chair and the WPC. The chair uses the WPC's experience and disciplinary expertise in decision making. The WPC gets a chance to influence the chair's decisions, establish a connection with new hires before the semester starts, and get a sense of incoming staff and their needs. Ultimately, the chair has authority in hiring.

All members of the English Department teach at least half their load on the 100 level or the remedial level. This translates into everyone teaching FYC, from the most junior faculty member to the most senior. The majority of our adjunct instructors are hired to teach FYC or our developmental course. At any given time, between 50 and 60 percent of our courses are taught by adjunct instructors.

The WPC does not directly oversee adjunct instructors but does oversee writing tutors in what is now our new learning commons space, the Learning Center. The writing tutors in the Learning Center are all under the title of "Professional Tutor." To be a professional tutor, a person must have the same credentials as an adjunct or full-time faculty member: an MA in English or a closely related field.

The WPC has no dedicated office or administrative staff. I do, however, have access to the departmental secretaries. From a practical standpoint, this means that I can ask one of the two secretaries to forward me an updated list of adjunct instructors and class assignments or to reserve a room for a meeting, but "department" business takes precedence, and much of the day-to-day work of the WPC is done by the WPC.

ASSESSMENT

Like most colleges today, Onondaga has assessment and effectiveness as institutional priorities. As such, the department has received a lot of pressure to assess courses and programs. For us, that has manifested primarily in the assessment of general education requirements and our two-course FYC sequence. The first course, ENG 103, helps students satisfy an institutional and system-wide requirement in communication. The second course, ENG 104, a "writing about literature" course, helps students satisfy an institutional and system-wide requirement in the humanities. Other assessment efforts in English are generally modeled after the system developed for these two courses.

Prior to the WPC position being created on my campus, assessment was only done in response to a program review or accreditor visit, and even then, the college was primarily demonstrating that assessment was being done, not that it was used in any way to foment change. As the need for more and sustained assessment of student learning outcomes was mandated by outside groups and then eventually our administration, various assessment models were tried. When I became WPC, the system was very cumbersome, with every full-time and adjunct faculty member teaching a given section of a course expected to contribute a sample assignment set from his or her entire class for the first course in the sequence, or a quiz on literary terms for the second part of the sequence. Participation could not be enforced, and submission rates by faculty were low. When we did generate data, we had no assurance that the data gave us a valid measurement or a complete picture.

My goals were to create a simpler, more streamlined process that led to more authentic assessment of student writing. As such, we decided to randomly sample 20 percent of sections of a given class. Of those sections, we randomized the course list and selected 20 percent of the students in the class. These percentages were chosen in consultation with our office of Institutional Planning, Assessment, and Research. We now ask faculty from only those selected sections to turn in sample papers from those selected students. These papers are collected, anonymized by the WPC, and assessed. In ENG 103, the papers are assessed according to a rubric developed and vetted by SUNY for their Strengthened Campus Based Gen Ed Assessment. In ENG 104, the papers are assessed according to a rubric developed by the English discipline. Every semester the WPC organizes a reading/scoring session for the samples collected the previous semester. The college has recognized and supported our assessment efforts by paying adjunct and full-time faculty members in English $30 per hour to score the essays in sessions organized once per term. Lunch is also provided. This has turned into a wonderful community building and professional development event with adjunct and full-time instructors getting to see a range of assignments and student work from across the department, often for the first time. We begin each session with a norming exercise and each assessment paper is read twice in a double-blind assessment.

We enjoy support by our Office of Institutional Planning, Assessment, and Research and other campus entities that randomize the course lists, provide pay by the hour for assessors, and lunch. Since most of the people doing the assessment readings are adjunct instructors looking for a little extra money, the readings and the conversations they engender actually serve as a *de facto* professional development opportunity. On a personal note, I am very proud of this assessment model and am gratified to hear that other departments on campus may adapt it.

In the Writing Skills Center, we used a modified version of the system described above. In order to establish a "value added" assessment, we ask those students who have attended nine or more tutoring sessions in a given semester to turn in a paper they have written early on in the term and one at the end of the term. We score each paper against the SUNY rubric used in the communication general education assessment and, if their sessions in the Writing Skills Center have helped them become better writers, we should see an increase in the score. We are still refining this process.

Overall, the biggest issue related to assessment at Onondaga is "closing the loop," in using the assessment data to direct substantive change. Our new assessment model has finally given us a reliable baseline and consistent assessment results so that we are now in a better position to make real changes. For example, based on our assessment results, we are in the process of revising our course outlines for both ENG 103 and 104 to better define and emphasize revision.

MARKETING/PR

Given that we don't have traditional English majors and that the bulk of our courses in any given semester are either developmental or FYC, the department is not under much pressure to advertise to students. Almost every course offered in our department fulfills some sort of curricular, general education, or transfer requirement. In short, the students come to us.

The department does try to maintain a web presence and a social networking account. These are, however, targeted mostly toward our adjunct faculty and act as a platform for sharing information and professional development (see more on this under "Pedagogy/Innovation").

TECHNOLOGY

Onondaga recently transitioned to the Blackboard course management system. Each instructor has a lot of freedom to use the technological tools or not according to his or her discretion. Some faculty make use of other, supplemental technologies, like Dropbox or Google Docs.

ROLE OF RESEARCH

As a representative of the Writing Program, I have referenced our ongoing work, especially around assessment and program development, at numerous presentations at CCCCs, Two-Year College Association Northeast (TYCA-NE), and the SUNY Council on Writing. In terms of publications, I discuss the program at some length in a book chapter published in Goodburn, LeCourt, and Levernz's (2012) *Rewriting Success in Rhetoric and Composition Careers* (Choseed 2012). Another chapter manuscript, which explores aspects of the program in detail, is currently under review for publication in an anthology focusing on assessment.

There is, however, a sustained research effort that has a mostly internal audience. My arrival at Onondaga coincided with the push both nationally and SUNY system-wide for ongoing assessment of student learning outcomes. While this has been onerous at times, the assessment process itself (as discussed above) has provided me as a WPA (with often uncertain authority and sometimes-hostile constituents) with a set of tools to help measure student success and teacher effectiveness and implement change and professional development. Both as a WPA and an engaged faculty member, I want to know what we are doing, why we are doing it, and how it is or is not working to help students write better. The assessment mandate has helped us do this.

PEDAGOGICAL AND/OR ADMINISTRATIVE HIGHLIGHTS

The pace of innovation at Onondaga is slow. As a faculty member, the WPC has no direct authority to enforce procedures, policies, or curricular changes. Everything has to be discussed and voted on. Consequently, any substantive change to the program occurs very, very slowly, sometimes frustratingly so.

It is important to note that much of my time as WPC coincided with the institutional drive for assessment, which allowed a lot of our work to progress. If I received pushback, I could always claim (truthfully) that the administration, SUNY or whoever, was forcing us to do this, so we might as well do it right.

At Onondaga, we are proud of our assessment mechanism. Although it was developed "in house," parts of it were inspired or adapted from programs at other colleges (e.g., the idea for randomized course lists was inspired by Professor Curt Nehring Bliss from Finger Lakes Community College). Our goal is to take what works, adapt it to fit our context, and improve it when we can.

Some of the most exciting innovations we are experimenting with have to do with developmental education. At the time of this writing, we are scaling up Accelerated Learning Program (ALP) sections (developed at the Community College of Baltimore County) in which students take their required developmental education course simultaneously with their FYC course. Almost a quarter of our developmental sections are ALP and we plan to continue the expansion.

We are also in the first semester of piloting an ALP-type course specifically for our Mechanical Engineering and Technology (MET) majors, which combines the ALP methodology with the content of Washington state's Integrated Basic Education and Skills Training Program (IBEST) system. In this FYC course, students in the MET program read their engineering textbook and write lab reports, chapter summaries, etc. along with academic essays related to MET content.

We have also started giving students who place into our developmental English course the opportunity to take a three- to four-hour refresher workshop on basic skills and test taking strategies and then retest. This was inspired by an existing program at Erie Community College. Our program significantly shorted the length of time of the workshop. We have approximately 60 percent of retesting students changing their placement to FYC.

Finally, in terms of professional development, we partnered with SUNY Oswego to offer graduate seminars in composition theory and practice on our campus. The class is free to our full-time and adjunct faculty and carries master's level credit. The course has been offered twice so far, and we hope to have enough interest and support to offer it again. While our program ended up being quite different, the idea to offer a free course to faculty was inspired by a program developed at Mesa Community College by Jeffrey Andelora.

Ongoing and sustained professional development for both adjunct and full-time instructors has been our biggest challenge. Many of our instructors have years of experience teaching FYC, but relatively few come to us with coursework in composition or a working knowledge of the field. Professional development is necessary to ensure baseline knowledge and even a chance at a consistent practice across sections. The problem is that with a program as big as ours, it is exceedingly difficult to gather a critical mass for training or discussion. Neither full-time nor adjunct instructors are paid for professional development other than participation in assessment sessions. Whoever attends does so out of his/her own desire.

In recent years, the department has begun discipline-specific mentoring programs pairing incoming adjuncts and full-timers with experienced full-time faculty. Even though participation cannot be mandated, the program has been successful in at least establishing multiple points of contact between newcomers and representatives of the discipline where none might have existed before.

Although we have accomplished a lot during my time as WPC, we still have a long way to go. I see my role as modernizing practice and helping to cement the gains made by the former WPA. Based on what I learned at the CWPA workshop, I began forming committees to work on a mission statement and a learning outcomes document (based on the CWPA Outcomes for First-Year Writing) and revamping our course outlines for the FYC sequence. Once these documents were in place, we moved on to the other, more ambitious projects outlined above. We continue to return to our course outlines to adjust and update based on assessment data.

I faced some of the same challenges as my predecessor (distrust, unease, suspicion), but they were mitigated by the fact that I came from within and, perhaps, my gender. I was a known quantity, at least as far as the full-time faculty were concerned, and the fact that they voted me in (and could potentially vote me out) might have made me in the WPC role more palatable.

PRIMARY DOCUMENT (at writingprogramarchitecture.com)

One document that has been central to our program is a memo regarding our first bi-annual assessment. The memo was circulated to full- and part-time faculty who were selected for this assessment of student learning outcomes using a random sampling method. While somewhat dated, the memo and the accompanying documentation lay out the basic outline and rationale for our assessment method as it has evolved over the years. The paid scoring sessions and the data provided by these assessments have given us a foundation for professional and program development.

WPA'S VOICE

Every program and department is different and operates in its own context, but if I had to give some advice to a new WPA, here it is:

Have a vision. Stay connected to the discipline of composition. Be prepared to teach yourself what you don't know. Expect resistance to change. Understand the limits of your authority. Be patient and willing to compromise. Explain why you do what you do and seek the changes that you seek. Understand that most people want to do a good job but may not be sure how to do it. Recognize that change is hard for everyone. Protect yourself, but take risks. Remember that, ultimately, you work for the students. Try your best to always work in their interest.

It may be fairer, though, to call this the condensed version of what I have learned in my time as WPC at Onondaga Community College rather than "advice." The most important part of what I have learned is about having a vision. By this, I mean that even if the WPA position at your college or university does not have explicit authority, it is still a leadership position. Your colleagues in the faculty and administration will look to you for guidance and direction as you work together to move your program forward.

While the changing landscape of higher education and the growing "accountability" movement may ultimately bring changes, our department currently enjoys a remarkable amount of autonomy. In order to maintain that autonomy, however, we need to be more focused on student learning and success, and this "vision" must come from the WPA. This is especially true at community colleges with high rates of attrition. It is often possible to get the support of administrators just by using words and phrases like "student success," "increased persistence," "learning outcomes assessment," etc. in your presentations and reports.

The need for a WPA to have vision is especially true for those programs in which the majority of faculty are either minimally or not trained in composition. You need to help set the goals and trajectory of the program. For example, if there is an assessment mandate at your school, the WPA, given his or her background, needs to at least have a hand in designing the assessment. Your colleagues will look to you to help explain why the assessment matters, and why it matters how you do it. The same is true for curricular changes, or textbook selection, or portfolio review, or whatever the current project is.

Having a "vision," however, does not mean that input from others should not be welcome. Some departments establish a WPA because the rest of the full-time faculty do not want to be bothered with FYC, but, even in these environments, most of them will want input into decisions with wide ranging impact. The same is true for adjunct instructors and, when practical, students. The process for stakeholder input, even though it can be laborious, usually does lead to workable compromises, establishes some faculty buy-in, and can even improve the overall "vision." Good leaders, after all, are responsive to the needs of their constituents.

Ultimately, WPA work can be compared to classroom teaching. Even on the days when it leaves you unbelievably frustrated, there are usually moments of profound satisfaction and even joy. It is a difficult, but ultimately a fulfilling and rewarding job.

References

Choseed, Malkiel. 2012. "Moving Up in the World: Making a Career at a Two-year College." In *Rewriting Success in Rhetoric and Composition Careers*, ed. Amy Goodburn, Donna LeCourt, and Carrie Leverenz, 18–31. Anderson, SC: Parlor Press.

14

OUR LADY OF THE LAKE UNIVERSITY QUEST FIRST-YEAR WRITING PROGRAM

Candace Zepeda

Institution type: Catholic liberal arts and science university
Location: San Antonio, TX, and satellites campuses in Houston and La Feria
Enrollment: 3,173 with half undergraduate and half graduate students
Year program was founded: 2011
WPA reports to: Vice President of Academic Affairs and Dean of College of Arts and Science
Program funded by: Academic Affairs and Our Lady of the Lake University (OLLU) Board of Trustees
Description of students: Designated as a Hispanic Serving Institution, 77 percent of our undergraduate student population identifies as a minority population, with 64 percent of our student body identifying as Mexican American. Our campus also serves a growing rate of first-generation, freshmen students (46%) who come from families in which neither parent has received a college degree. Moreover, 67 percent of our student body receives Pell grants, compared to 24 percent nationally.

PROGRAM SNAPSHOT

The program redesigned developmental writing courses into what are now identified as Intensive (INT), credit-bearing Composition I courses. Classes meet four days a week with two of those days serving as a lab/writing studio. The founding values of the university—community, integrity, trust, and service—encompass the design of the QUEST First-Year Writing Program and our culture of *comunidad* (community) with other campus partners including the Library, Student Success, Writing Center, and Academic Center for Excellence (ACE).

WPA'S PROFILE

My WPA career began in the most unexpected way; it was a position that I was able to create in my role as Quality Enhancement Plan (QEP)

DOI: 10.7330/9781607326274.c014

director at my current institution. In 2012, I was invited to join the English, Drama and Mass Communication Department as a visiting professor of English. The semester I joined my department, our campus was about to initiate year one of our Quality Enhancement Plan. By the end of spring 2013, our former vice president invited me to serve as QEP Director considering my research focus and academic training.

The heart of my academic training begins with my graduate studies at Texas A&M Corpus Christi (TAMUCC) where I concentrated my scholarship in the field of rhetoric and composition; it was at TAMUCC where I also taught for the nationally recognized First-Year Writing Program under the direction of Dr. Glenn Blalock (now chair) and later Dr. Susan Wolf-Murphy (the current WPA). The graduate program, faculty, and leadership of Drs. Blalock and Wolf-Murphy inspired me to continue my studies and apply for doctoral programs in rhetoric and composition. My scholarly interest in how Hispanic Serving Institutions (HSI) are pedagogically "serving" first-generation, Latino/a students in the writing classroom led me to apply to the PhD English program at the University of Texas at San Antonio. Their program was unique and offered concentrations in rhet/comp and Latino/a literary and cultural studies.

In retrospect, my academic training (or what I consider my academic awakening) in rhetoric and composition at the graduate and doctoral level, prepared me for my current position as both QEP director and WPA. I was able to redesign the writing curriculum and market it as a First-Year Writing Program. The success of our program earned me a tenure-track English faculty position and a three-quarter release every semester to serve a dual appointment as QEP director and Writing Program coordinator. I report directly to the vice president and associate vice president of Academic Affairs on many levels, but most recently I cooperate with Academic Affairs in faculty development sessions. My unique administrative roles have provided me the opportunity to be innovative and bring writing-enriched curriculum across our campus.

PROGRAM CONCEPTION

The QEP was centered on eliminating all non-credit, developmental courses and redesigning them to be credit bearing. The decision to eliminate all non-credit, developmental courses was our campus' response to increase access and on-time completion for underrepresented, underprepared, and low-income students. The QUEST First-Year Writing Program was implemented as part of our QEP, which redesigned developmental courses into an INT (and credit bearing)

Composition I model, with classes meeting four days a week with two of those days serving as a lab/writing studio.

The curriculum was redesigned to enhance student learning for first-time, first-year students in order to help them build and demonstrate mastery of the foundational knowledge and skills necessary for academic success. Changes to the curriculum included scaffolding of major writing assignments, writing activities that encourage students to explore their own literacies and discourse communities, transparent rubrics, metacognitive activities, integrated library instruction, integrated library modules, and lab time for students to develop their projects in an environment that encourages drafting, revision, and peer editing.

Early challenges faced by the program included: a) finding computer lab space across campus for the mandatory two day a week writing labs, b) training faculty to feel comfortable with new writing curriculum that moved away from developmental models of instruction, and c) training faculty to learn how to work with and utilize writing coaches during the lab time. To address these challenges, I first worked closely with Student Success advisors and our English Undergraduate Program coordinator, when creating the course schedule to ensure computer lab space for all INT Composition I courses a semester ahead of time. I also developed a mandatory Summer Teaching Workshop for all QUEST English instructors and Writing Coaches. During our annual Summer Teaching Workshop we met to introduce the writing assignments, discuss writing theories, introduce culturally sensitive pedagogies, and best practices. Writing coaches were also introduced to their writing instructors in order to strategize on classroom interaction with students during lab time. In addition to the Summer Teaching Workshop, I am working to develop a Winter Teaching Workshop to help instructors prepare for the spring semester.

POPULATION SERVED

The QUEST First-Year Writing Program is tailored to serve our population of incoming freshmen students (approximately 375 every academic year) and/or transfer students (approximately 20 students) who need to fulfill our general education requirement of Composition I. With the significant majority of our incoming freshman students placing below proficient on in-house writing placement exams, all students are automatically placed into what are now recognized as INT Composition I courses. OLLU's Office of Institutional Research and Effectiveness shows the percent of first-time, first-year students who placed into developmental courses grew from 66 percent in the fall of 2008 to 86 percent by the fall of 2011. This increase was a significant factor when considering the topic of our QEP, and justified to our QEP committee the need to eliminate and redesign developmental courses.

FUNDING

The operating budget of the university and Academic Affairs provides funds for the implementation of the QEP, which spawned the QUEST First-Year Writing and Math Programs. The Board of Trustees of the university approved the budget for the QEP. The projected budget for the QEP for the next five years is $120,000 annually. This budget includes course release for the director, writing coach student budget, stipends for course overloads for faculty to cover the additional lab/writing studio period that falls outside their normal contract, promotional stipends, travel, computer equipment, faculty development, promotional material, and equipment/supplies. As director, I manage the entire budget and determine how monies are allocated annually. My base salary is still covered by the College of Arts and Sciences and falls under the English Department salary line item.

OPERATIONS

Our QUEST First-Year Writing Program is situated in the English Department. My staff includes one graduate assistant and two undergraduate work-study students. Of the sixteen sections of INT Composition I courses, we currently have two full-time faculty members and six part-time faculty members. Two part-time faculty members are recognized as graduate teaching fellows who have reached eighteen hours of graduate level work, and they are enrolled in a required Composition Pedagogy and Theory graduate course that I teach every fall.

One unique feature of the QUEST First-Year Writing Program is our mentoring/coaching model. Two days a week (Tuesday and Thursday) during lab/writing studio, and under the direction of the English faculty member, writing coaches provide supplemental assistance for students. Although each faculty member determines how to best utilize the class time, writing coaches are known to support the course with the following types of services: peer-to-peer mentoring, reviewing papers during the writing process, mini-writing workshops, student success encouragement talks, and group work leadership. Writing coaches are upper division, English majors or minors with at least a 3.50 GPA.

The culture of comunidad is a significant theme of the QUEST First-Year Writing Program model. Rather than exist as an isolated program, our program model works as a unified circle of partners that collaborate on multiple levels in order to better serve our first-year freshmen. Key partners include staff and faculty members including the dean of Student Success, director of Writing Center, librarians, Undergraduate Program director coordinator, retention officers, and academic counselors. These QUEST Partners work collaboratively to ensure that freshmen enrolled in INT Composition I courses are provided a network of resources to assist them throughout the semester. Although I can provide many examples of our community partnership, it is our collaborative work with the library that best exemplifies our comunidad model.

ASSESSMENT

Our Lady of the Lake University is currently at year four of our QEP (fall 2015). The QEP has four specific learning outcomes (SLO) associated with the first-year curriculum that include: (1) analytical reasoning, evaluation, and reflection; (2) writing process and organization; (3) research process; and (4) knowledge of writing conventions and style. These outcomes were determined and approved by OLLU's QEP Advisory Committee and reflect common standards that are frequently assessed at other First-Year Writing programs. The Southern Association of Colleges and Schools—COC (SACSCOC) required a minimum of two learning outcomes to assess through the duration of our five-year report. As director, I selected SLO 2 (writing process and organization) and SLO 4 (knowledge of writing conventions and style) to accumulate data for SACS-COC at three different times during a semester including pre-diagnostics, mid-term, and post-term.

Our pre-diagnostic assessment is given during the first-week of the semester and is a basic essay (title "A Letter to My Instructor"), which evaluates students using an in-house designed rubric on the following areas: introduction, thesis, subject, descriptions/examples, organization, transitions, conclusion, sentence structure, MLA basics, and grammar/syntax. Our post-assessment evaluates students' second major writing assignments on the same measures as the pre-diagnostic essay, but it also evaluates students' attention to documentation. The in-house designed rubric is on a five- or ten-point scale that measures students under the following categories: mastery, proficient, competent, ability, developing, and not clear. Additional assessment measures also include monitoring students' overall GPA, successful course completion, and their persistence rate after their first year.

MARKETING/PR

Because INT Composition I is part of our general education curriculum, our Writing Program does not advertise. However, the College of Arts and Sciences and OLLU marketing often promote our unique program and nationally recognized award to recruit prospective freshmen students.

TECHNOLOGY

Our Writing Program operates under our campus portal system with all INT Composition I courses using Blackboard-Learn course shells. Faculty members' shells include a common syllabus, course assignment package, assessment measures and rubrics, and sample writing samples. One area of technology that our Writing Program takes pride in showcasing is our Library Modules that are designed by our librarian partners. The Library Modules, designed using software called SoftChalk, introduce students to information literacy and research skills during lab periods.

ROLE OF RESEARCH

Because our Writing Program is relatively new and under the umbrella of the QEP, I am eager to begin publishing on our innovative program and comunidad model. The success of our redesigned curriculum has earned us some great attention as a small writing program. To explain, early fall 2013 our program was awarded the Council of Basic Writing (CBW) Inny Award for innovative curriculum and program model design. I presented a brief presentation of our curriculum and program model at the Conference on College Composition and Communication (CCCC) in Indianapolis in 2014, and we were invited to lead a Wednesday workshop at the 2015 CCCC for the CBW. In partly due to the national recognition, our program was encouraged to apply for the CCCC Writing Program of Excellence. Our QUEST Writing Program Curriculum Committee just recently submitted a nomination package to this award committee where we emphasized our comunidad model and progressive curriculum design.

PEDAGOGICAL AND/OR ADMINISTRATIVE HIGHLIGHTS

QUEST revaluates college readiness and developmental/remedial writing by redesigning our freshman writing courses into hospitable environments that are credit-bearing and support longer sessions designed to encourage students to develop academic writing at a comfortable pace. The QUEST First-Year Writing Program is unique in our commitment toward encouraging first-generation and minority student populations by means of our interdisciplinary curriculum that emphasize students' spatiality.

Although my role is to integrate students into a traditionally exclusive academic culture and to introduce students to academic discourse, it was imperative that our curriculum employs students' experiences as a method to stimulate personal motivation in the classroom. The design of our writing curriculum places great emphasis on the home and community in order to assert how these places and spaces contribute to students' epistemologies. By re-envisioning writing classrooms into safe and/or familiar community spaces (spaces of comunidad), students are capable of bridging home-based knowledge with academic experiences, thus earning an authority that empowers them in an institutional culture. By inviting students to study their own spaces, we are also strategically introducing an alternative writing agenda, far removed from basic drills of traditional developmental, non-credit, writing courses.

Our assignment package includes three major essays, one research project, and a final portfolio. The first three assignments build into the research project, leading to the final portfolio.

- Writing Assignment One (Literacy Autobiographical Narrative-Study of Self) invites students to study their literate practices, beginning with their experiences as a child.
- Writing Assignment Two (Writing for Social Inquiry: Study of a Local Space; Cause and Effect) helps students gain a better understanding of the social issues impacting their environments/communities and to further develop their sense of civic awareness by discovering cause and effect circumstances.
- The Discovery Project is a great example of QUEST's comunidad model. In a collective effort with our library partners, the assignment introduces students to research strategies (using tailored virtual modules) that they will need as they continue their assignments.
- Writing Assignment Three (Solutions: Exploring an Issue) invites students to explore solutions to these issues (or controversies) exposed in their previous assignment. This project informs readers about the problem and attempts to convince readers to share the writer's position by providing reasons and evidence.

- Final Portfolio invites students to revise major assignments and submit a final reflective piece of their overall learning experience and growth as a writer.

Every assignment description is paired with associated rubrics that provide a comprehensive breakdown of Student Learning Outcomes:

- SLO 1: analytical reasoning, evaluation and reflection (5pts)— Labeled a "reflective overview," meta-cognition is encouraged for students to evaluate their learning process and active engagement with the writing assignment. Students complete a one- to two-page reflection on their process of writing and a self-evaluation. This area of assessment is also a pedagogical tool for instructors to reflect on their understanding of assignment outcomes.

- SLO 2: writing process and organization (60pts)—Rather than provide a generic (and holistic) description of the writing process, this area of assessment provides a comprehensive breakdown of the expectations of the writing assignment. For instance, a well-developed "introduction" that engages the reader and creates interest earns five points (mastery). The rubric was designed as a checklist for students to acknowledge all areas of the writing process before submitting the assignment. This outcome includes: introduction, thesis, subject, description/examples, organization, transitions, conclusions, sentence structure, and drafts and peer review.

- SLO 3: research process (10pts)—In collective efforts with QUEST's library partners, each assignment integrates the research process that assesses a series of library modules tailored for our student population. The modules are interactive, high quality, and designed to be entertaining while reviewing significant research areas such as: scholarly vs. non-scholarly, evaluating a book for value, developing a research journal, and what is a literature review?

- SLO 4: knowledge of writing conventions and style (25pts)—Outcome includes: MLA style, grammar/usage, flow, and documentation. By separating this outcome from the writing process, students understand this SLO assesses areas of writing that are necessary to develop in academia but does not reflect the entire writing process.

The assignments and rubrics provide an example of how our Writing Program reevaluates traditional/developmental writing curriculum and emphasizes our students' experiences in the context of the curriculum. The success of our curriculum is significant if you evaluate the growth of our students' writing by studying our course complete rates. Fall 2014 we had 84 percent course completion rates, compared to fall 2013 at 81 percent and fall 2012 (the pilot year of the QEP) at 66 percent.

PRIMARY DOCUMENTS (at **writingprogramarchitecture.com**)

We have added two documents to the online companion that have both been important to our program. The first is our 1313-INT Quest English syllabus. All part-time faculty and graduate teaching fellows are provided a sample of this syllabus. They are encouraged to add personal touches to the syllabus including quotes and links to classroom social media sites. The second document is a flyer promoting a summer book club that was well attended by faculty and staff. The QUEST First-Year Writing Program encourages ongoing faculty development through our Pedagogy Playtime sessions. Ongoing professional development, like the summer book club, is open to any campus faculty or staff member.

WPA'S VOICE

Although our curriculum places great emphasis on students' "funds of knowledge" and encourages students to study their personal and collective experiences, our assignment sequence and assessment measures are tailored for *our* campus and student population. The curriculum does not provide a universal model for all writing programs, and *nor should it.*

Our curriculum model does address the need to accommodate a population of students who are more than likely not going to complete four years of college for a variety of reasons, including their feelings of alienation, insecurities, or fears. The QUEST First-Year Writing Program inspires to improve students' understanding of writing and encourages them to include their own subjectivities in the writing and research process. This progressive vision offers endless opportunities for new scholarship on curriculum design and the future of our Composition II courses. Currently, administration and the Board of Trustees are supporting the redesign of our Composition II courses. We are actively considering an alternative intensive model proposal that would foster a Writing in the Discipline curriculum for the sciences, social sciences, liberal arts, and social work.

15

ST. LOUIS COMMUNITY COLLEGE ESL PROGRAM

Lisa Wilkinson and Heather McKay

Institution type: largest community college in the state of Missouri
Location: The college is spread across four campuses: in North St. Louis county in Ferguson, Missouri; east in Forest Park; the Meramec campus in suburban Kirkwood, Missouri; and in downtown St. Louis, the human resources and upper level administrative functions are centralized in the Cosand Center. The four campuses together are accredited as a single college and are known as the St. Louis Community College "district."
Enrollment: 15,000
Year program was founded: 1993
WPA reports to: English Department Chair and Division Dean
Program funded by: English Department
Description of students: 39 percent of students on our campus are under the age of twenty-one. English as a Second Language students, both immigrants and international students come from a variety of countries including: Albania, Bosnia, France, Eritrea, Ethiopia, Somalia, Mexico, Korea, China, Vietnam, Sierra Leone, Kenya, Nigeria, Brazil, Colombia, Uzbekistan, Moldova, Russia, Syria, Afghanistan, Iraq, Saudi Arabia, Nepal, India and Pakistan.

PROGRAM SNAPSHOT

The ESL program is located within the English Department and thrives at two campuses in our district: Meramec and Forest Park. The third campus, Florissant Valley, lost its ESL program through retirement of the coordinator and a significant drop in enrollment. In addition, a Federal grant, The Cooperative Association of States for Scholarships (CASS), later renamed Scholarships for Education and Economic Development (SEED), which had sustained the ESL program for many years, was ended. Each of the remaining two campuses has an ESL coordinator who receives released time to perform the duties of hiring

DOI: 10.7330/9781607326274.c015

adjuncts, developing a schedule, and responding to campus and community inquiries about the ESL program and its students. The program consists of three ESL courses: ENG 050, 060, and 070.

WPA'S PROFILE

Lisa

I earned my master's in TESOL in 1992 from Southern Illinois University at Edwardsville, and I continued my graduate coursework in writing pedagogy and eventually received a graduate certificate in the Teaching of Writing from University of Missouri St. Louis and the Gateway Writing Project. Initially, I worked as an adjunct at St. Louis Community College (STLCC) and in an Adult Education program in University City, Missouri. Eventually, I committed myself completely to STLCC, and taught for ten years as an adjunct faculty member in ESL while assisting with placement. Over the course of that time, I taught almost every course offered by our program.

In 2002, I was hired as the ESL specialist, a professional position that no longer exists due to budget cuts. I left the specialist position when a rare full-time faculty position opened due to an unexpected tragic death of a colleague. I was hired full-time and immediately became the ESL coordinator, at first in an interim capacity due to a colleague's sabbatical. A year after her return, she stepped out of the position, and I assumed it. As of this publication, I have been ESL coordinator for over five years

PROGRAM CONCEPTION

Starting in 1993, Sharon Person was hired as the ESL coordinator for the entire STLCC District, all four campuses. Along with two founding faculty members, Dr. Heather McKay and Dr. Grace Liu, she taught across the district. Of course, these faculty members had a hard time driving around St. Louis to teach at the various campuses. From their stories, there were also some issues in being fully integrated into the English Departments on the various campuses in terms of service and meeting attendance.

However, their hard work eventually built a program. In 2000, the District ESL coordinator position ended, and an ESL coordinator was assigned to each of three campuses at that time: Forest Park, Meramec, and Florissant Valley. By this time, Forest Park had four full-time faculty members, and Meramec had two. In 2014, there was an adjustment and both Forest Park and Meramec each had three faculty members. As previously noted, the program had already ended at Florissant Valley.

In the beginning, STLCC adopted a "fluency first" approach in its core writing courses district-wide. All courses were run with exploratory course numbers and tweaked before going through curriculum committees on all three campuses. Sharon Person also worked hard at marketing the growing program internally at the college in functional areas such as Admission, Advising, and Assessment, working to develop relationships and referrals to the program. This type of work is ongoing today on both campuses.

Since that time, our curriculum has shifted to a whole-language theory approach, which is more fully described below under "Pedagogical Highlights."

POPULATION SERVED

The ESL program district-wide serves approximately four hundred students including recent and long-term resident immigrants, F–1 visa students, Generation 1.5 students and au pairs, a visa type that includes a required educational component, usually in a community college. While the percentage of ESL students is about 1.7 percent of the district student population, they account for about 10 percent of the English Credit Hour enrollment at the Meramec campus.

Funding

Because we are happily housed within the English Department at STLCC, most of our operating costs fall under the English Department's budget management. Faculty salaries and adjunct payroll are all managed through College and Division allocations, and are not part of my daily responsibilities. The estimated combined cost of our program is around $200,000 for full- and part-time salaries. Each full-time faculty member is entitled to $1,000 a year for professional development activities and may request up to $2,000 over that amount.

In addition, we do have a small budget that we can control of $1,200 for special materials such as colored markers and large Post–it poster paper, and our teacher book copies for the writing classes that must be purchased since they are not textbooks but trade books.

Finally, there are costs associated with hiring people to do interviews for placement and for the exam itself, but again the English Department and the Assessment Office absorb most of those. The test costs about $10 for each student, and we test almost four hundred students a year.

OPERATIONS

The staff is comprised of the chair of English, a coordinator (the role I am currently in), two other full-time faculty, and between nine and fourteen ESL adjuncts per semester depending on enrollment. On both campuses, we work with English Department chairs and a Division dean. Currently, Francine Sigmund, a full-time faculty member, handles placement, and I do scheduling and general inquiries. There is also a shared secretary with another department, who refers students to my office, double checks our workloads from the Division Dean's Office, handles payroll for adjuncts and accounts payable for our professional development fund. Finally, we work with the academic division secretary for hiring and scheduling classrooms, and we occasionally work with the supplemental instruction coordinator to clarify recommendations for students.

In my role, in addition to teaching nine credits per semester, I assist the English Department chair with the ESL part of the English schedule. I hire ESL adjuncts and provide them with teacher texts and other teaching supplies. I train all new ESL teachers on my campus and orient them to their classes and the campus. I am responsible for the details of their hiring packet such verifying their I–9. We prefer to only hire adjuncts who have a master's in TESOL or Applied Linguistics.

I observe the adjuncts and deliver their student evaluations. I provide professional development for the adjuncts each year along with my other full-time colleagues, especially at our August district meeting but also at meetings throughout the semester on my campus. I develop and update curriculum and course profiles, sending them through the appropriate department, campus, and district committees.

I am also sometimes asked to explain non-native speaker testing, placement, and curriculum to New Faculty orientations for campus and district faculty from many other disciplines. I serve on committees on which I am expected to be the voice of the adjuncts, the ESL program, global issues, and international students. I sometimes act as a consultant to departments or faculty who are having a problem with an ESL student. In those cases, I do research on the student, and I may seek out him or her to rectify the situation, even in a non-ESL class. I have met with departments such as nursing to try and understand the issues of non-native speakers of English in their programs; in addition, I provide a resource for Advising and Admissions who have questions about special cases.

Finally, I deal with student inquiries, new students, and enrolled students. I listen to complaints, mediate teacher-student disputes, and deal with student behavior issues referred to me by teachers. I read papers with teachers to identify error patterns or plagiarism. I am authorized to put in overrides for students in our Banner database system. I input notes about student recommendations and resolutions.

Classes continue every day because of the efforts of my full-time and part-time colleagues. The faculty in the classroom and secretaries help with the schedules, supplies, and office management. Placement and tutoring staff members meet the needs of new students and those who need help with course work. ESL students on our campus are heavy users of the learning centers.

Moreover, we have an extensive and intrusive placement process in which students take an adaptive computerized test, write a thirty-minute writing sample, and are interviewed by a teacher in the program. Placement responsibilities include scheduling and training other teachers in the program to ask the right questions and interpret the scores so that students will be placed into the right courses for their level. The questions on our interview form highlight a student's past schooling and whether it was in an English medium environment. We also want to ascertain if students had periods of interrupted schooling due to residency in refugee camps, or war; in addition, to their schooling experiences in the United States. Many Generation 1.5 students come to us with minimal ESL support in their K–12 experience, so we try to get at that as well. We ask for fluency and literacy self-assessments in other languages as many students are multilingual, and we believe it enhances our understanding of their literacy overall and their facility with learning languages to know this information. We also ask the names of favorite books in English, something that they can write well in English, and how much they understand from TV or radio without closed captioning. These self-reports are combined with the objective listening and grammar scores as well as the holistic writing score to determine placement in one of our three levels.

ASSESSMENT

The main program assessment that we use is our portfolio process, which happens across the district in partner teacher pairs. Before the process begins, students produce work for the portfolio in the following ways:

ENG 050

In-class writing is asked for and collected in class. It may be typed or handwritten. The prompts for this class in response to fiction is often in the form of a letter to a friend telling them about a specific section of the book, or a request for students to take the point of view of a secondary character or animal in the story. Their writing must have a beginning, middle, end, and verb tenses must be at least 60 percent correct.

ENG 060

Students write three pieces in class: the first is a response to the semester themed book in health care, diversity, poverty, or education. They are given analytical prompts that require them to use support from the book in a formal essay. The second is a research essay on a topic they have chosen within the above themes. They read articles on this topic, turned in research notes and summaries, and created an outline. Finally, they write a reflective cover letter. This writing needs a main idea, clear support that shows evidence of reading comprehension and research, and grammatical structures should be 75 percent correct.

ENG 070

Students write a standard academic essay on a book the class has been reading all semester, such as *The Warmth of Other Suns* by Isabel Wilkerson (2010), *The Big Burn* by Timothy Egan (2009), or *The Immortal Life of Henrietta Lacks* by Rebecca Skloot (2010). Analysis, compare/contrast, descriptive, and explanatory prompts dominate this level. More than seven errors might fail a student in this level. Although prompts are shared by the teacher over the semester, each teacher is free to develop his/her own prompts. We invite ENG 101 professors to read the essays at this level because students will be coming to that level if they pass. They use a similar rubric to asses ENG 070 students' readiness for ENG 101.

In each case, the process is as follows: students choose the writing sample that they think is the best. The teachers collect and copy these to send to two other partner teachers in that course across the district. The partner teachers read alone, then meet and discuss, rating the work on a rubric on a pass/fail basis. They translate the rubric score for each student onto a Scantron sheet, which is submitted and later processed in our Assessment Office.

We submit the forms for each level on a district basis. We can clearly see which areas of the rubric are weak and which meet our goal of at least 70 percent proficiency. Students pass or fail the piece and the class if they do not meet those learning outcomes.

We have a mini-midterm and full final portfolio exchange in this manner each year. Then, at our August district meeting, teachers start semester preparations with a discussion of portfolio results from the previous year. For instance, since the areas of support and reading comprehension have been lower than we wanted for several years, we invited an area colleague, Rosa Brefeld, who had been working on her dissertation topic of improving student discussion around reading, to hold a presentation on her research and specific strategies for scaffolding and supporting ESL student speech and comprehension. In short, because of our portfolio process in these classes, we know the student learning outcomes for each of our courses.

We have also delivered a student survey several times in the ESL section of ENG 101 College Composition. The survey asks students questions about skills they learned in the ESL program and tries to assess satisfaction with the ESL program and also any practical learning transfer that students can identify.

MARKETING/PR

Since our program is well-established, we benefit greatly from word of mouth. Many extended families have attended our program. An oldest brother may start and then cousins, mothers, aunts, uncles, younger siblings, and so on. We also have information about our program on the college website with the names and phone numbers of current coordinators. F–1 visa students are informed by Admissions of the language requirements. Students often call to get information or just come to see me directly.

We are invited by Recruitment Management directors to attend Red Carpet Events for local area high schools, which host special days for ESL students, and finally the college has produced a brochure that is distributed at such events and to interested parties in the ESL Office or Admissions. We also communicate with potential high school ESL students though Enrollment Management staff and on days when ESL students from service area high schools are brought to our campus directly.

TECHNOLOGY

Our listserv/email list is a main tool we use, especially in coordinating our assessment process (described above). The email list is actually part of our course management system, Blackboard Learn-Community. ESL coordinators or staff in the Center of Teaching and Learning add colleagues. Teachers create and share materials across the district in this way. In addition, we use Scantron machines/computers to run our assessment forms, which are delivered to assessment staff at the Meramec campus and then returned to us.

ROLE OF RESEARCH

Although we are not required to do research that must be published, we do have a strong culture of assessment on our campus that allows us to measure the relationship between our teaching and student learning outcomes. As such, our individual research activities are most often contained within the frame of sabbatical leave and published mainly within our institution.

For instance, on my sabbatical I followed six ESL students to their general education/mainstream classes. I attended classes and observed the level of vocabulary and lecture styles across the disciplines. I interviewed faculty and my focus students, and I tracked the students' grades. I have also conducted a focus group in an ENG 101 class reserved for non-native speakers, and I delivered a survey on the perceptions students had on the ESL program after exiting it. Finally, I visited other ESL programs in our area and observed classes and interviewed coordinators.

My Forest Park colleague, Keith Hulsey, is currently engaged in a study of the ESL programs in our service area high schools and community programs. In the past, another ESL faculty member, Sharon Person, worked at a community service provider for victims of torture, learning how to work with our traumatized refugee student populations. In addition, one of our past adjuncts completed her doctoral research with our student population by delivering a survey to assess ESL students' motivation in classes. All of these research endeavors were highly informative for our institutional setting and our teaching. Currently, we have a survey in the works for our own English Department at the Meramec campus, which will attempt to measure English Department perceptions of the ESL program and its students.

This research, as with our assessment, informs the assignments we create, the books we choose, and our interactions with students. For instance, Keith's work revealed that many of our service area high schools have a culture of no homework. Since our program requires a lot of homework, we will clearly need to explain and mentor our students more in this area, or they aren't going to be successful. I discovered that the main assessment mode in general education courses on my campus are multiple choice tests, which overwhelmed many of the strong students I followed. We learned that we need to introduce strategies and present multiple test items whenever appropriate in our program; for example, in grammar or note-taking classes.

PEDAGOGICAL AND/OR ADMINISTRATIVE HIGHLIGHTS

The approach of our curriculum was originally developed at CUNY City College by Rorschach and McGowan-Gilhooly and is grounded in whole language theory in 1993. This sets the traditional, atomistic approach to teaching ESL writing on its head. Instead of moving through a course sequence, which focuses first on the construction of sentences, then paragraphs, and finally, essays, with attention to accuracy as the primary concern at each level and reading restricted to carefully constructed model texts, students who place into any level of the ESL reading/writing sequence engage immediately "with authentic texts and produce extensive writing which is meaningful to them" (Wilkinson and McKay 2012).

In the three-part reading/writing course sequence, primary attention is always given to the communication of meaning; however, the focus moves from the students' ability to get their meaning across in descriptive and narrative modes (fluency) in the first level (050), to organizing ideas/academic content to make the meaning as clear as possible (clarity) in the second level (060), and finally, to eliminating patterns of error (accuracy) in the third level (070). At all levels, teachers build from strength, starting with what the students already know; in addition, the students' writing acts as the primary text through which the teacher is able to identify and respond to students' needs. These needs may be addressed in mini-lessons and/or individual conferences, depending on the number of students who share a particular need. Some of the basic tenets that underpin our program are discussed below.

Writing is a Process

In keeping with a fluency first approach, writing is taught as a process with multiple cycles of drafting, feedback, revision, and editing. Ongoing formative feedback is provided by the teacher and by peers, and the criteria for final evaluation are established in advance. Through reflection and discussion, students build an increased awareness of their own writing process.

Targeted Discussion with Peers Facilitates Writing Improvement

In our program extensive use is made of pair and collaborative group work. Early in each course students participate in community building activities. Once trust is established, group members act as a sounding board for each other's ideas during the prewriting process; this allows the students to rehearse orally the language they will use in their writing. After writing drafts, group members work together on the revision process, providing an authentic audience for each other's work. Finally students work together on the editing process. For ESL students this combination of talking and writing is especially important as it fosters a range of skills that will allow them to thrive in mainstream college classrooms.

There Is a Symbiotic Relationship between Reading and Writing

The close relationship between reading and writing puts ESL students who have had little exposure to extended written texts in English at a major disadvantage. They lack input to call upon when they are creating their own texts. They lack the exposure to vocabulary and grammar in context that reading can provide. For this reason, at each level of the program, our students engage in large amounts of extensive reading outside of class. They respond to this reading in double entry journals, which form the basis of group discussion and of further writing. It is not unusual for students in our first level reading/writing class (ENG 050) to tell us that these are the first books that they have ever read in English. In the six-credit hour 050 course, students read and journal about approximately eight hundred pages of fiction during the semester; in the six credit 060 class, students read and journal about eight hundred pages of popular non-fiction; and in the three credit 070 class, students read and journal about three hundred pages of academic texts.

When It Comes to Writing, More Is Better

In the same way that the students at all levels of the ESL program engage in extensive reading, they also engage in extensive writing. Our students spend a great deal of time inside and outside of class writing. The type of writing varies somewhat according to the level of the class, with 050 students producing a writing project based on personal narrative and description, while 060 students produce a research-based writing project and ENG 070 students focus on fine-tuning essay writing, with fewer essays and more development in both in-class and take-home assignments. Writing effective article summaries is also an important component of the course. However, in each level the students' writing will also include journals, personal reflections, self-assessment, free writing, and timed writing. In the 050 and 060 classes students produce a total of twelve pages or more of writing a week. In the ENG 070 class students produce about ninety pages each semester by completing approximately six pages of written practice each week, including reading, vocabulary, and grammar assignments, free writing, and revised and edited pieces.

Students Need to Develop a Repertoire of Writing Strategies

Teachers encourage their students to reflect on their writing process at the macro-level to see what works for them. This includes developing strategies that can be brought to bear at different stages in the writing process. According to the needs of the students, teachers develop mini-lessons to teach brainstorming strategies and also monitor and support their use.

Other mini-lessons are developed by teachers as needed by each individual class. For instance, if students all perform badly on a piece of writing, or a test, teachers will prepare a strategic mini lesson to address the problem. Several teachers combine these ideas. When a set of free-writing comes in, we read and respond to it but try to avoid correction. However, we pull error-filled sentences from the writing, retyping it anonymously to create a worksheet to use in a think-pair-share activity or mini-lesson in class. It is time consuming for the teacher, but students attend much better to their own authentic errors than they might to a worksheet.

ESL Students Need to Develop an Awareness of the Different Conventions at Work When Writing in Their First Language and in English

Languages differ not only in vocabulary and grammar at the sentence level but also in the ways that texts are typically organized. While affirming the student's first language knowledge, teachers need to help students work through a process of identifying differences in the ways texts are constructed in the two languages.

For instance, students who have a Russian speaking background have been known to struggle with sentence word order. They tell us that word order choices are much more optional in Russian at the sentence level. As well, Arabic speakers might have trouble organizing a narrative in a North American fashion. Farsi speakers might use more conditional structures than others. Punctuation marks and their use may also vary widely across languages. However, these kinds of attributions to error type by language should be avoided. Many students actually speak several languages and teasing apart the influence of each is frankly impossible. Although rhetorical patterns may indeed vary in a variety of countries, English models dominate in most countries of recent immigrants.

ESL and composition students today have such varied language experience and ability that attempting to overgeneralize is not actually going to be helpful. While some students may not have studied writing in their own countries at such an advanced level, others may have done graduate theses in English. Therefore, having students write about their own language background, or write in their own language and then write the same piece in English and analyze it, will yield much more helpful results for both the student and the instructor. In ENG 070, our pre-college level, many instructors have students write a literacy autobiography as a first assignment, which will inform an instructor much more directly about some of these issues.

The outstanding thing about our program is that we have continued to do the portfolio evaluation for over ten years and that we involve ALL of our faculty in the process from new part-timers to twenty-year teaching veterans. Our continued use of bestselling fiction and non–fiction as opposed to adapted texts or textbooks also is a strength of our program. A sample of each of the texts used in the fall 2014 semester is as follows: our first level used *Hunger Games* by Suzanne Collins (2010), our middle used *Waiting for Superman* edited by Karl Weber (2010), and our highest level used the *Warmth of Other Suns* by Isabel Wilkerson (2010). Our Service Learning Office, CCCC, and the State Department have also noted our campus for integrating Service Learning successfully into ESL classes. This is documented on our college website in a small presentation I did after one ENG 060 semester project at a food bank. Also, of course, it is notable that we were recognized as a Writing Program of Excellence by CCCC.

PRIMARY DOCUMENT (at **writingprogramarchitecture.com**)

The portfolio exchange, in which in-class, ungraded student writing is sent to other teachers in that class level with all identifying student information removed, is central to maintaining the student learning outcomes of our program. Included in the online companion is the document that describes the process to faculty. This involves meeting other teachers to discuss papers, and completing the rubric for each level, systematically collecting the data from those rubrics, and then sharing that data and generating teaching strategies around the results is central to the integrity of what we do in the St. Louis Community College ESL program. We also included a report of results from our spring 2015 portfolio rating, which we use for discussion among instructors. In addition, we frequently exchange syllabi, assignment prompts, and other teaching materials via email, and we consider these primary documents and our sharing of teacher-created curriculum to be fundamental to our program.

WPA'S VOICE

ESL program coordinators will be considered as experts in their fields by their hiring institution and so need to be well aware of theory and pedagogy in the field. They should become members of TESOL International and their local TESOL affiliate. Membership in CCCC is also a good choice as are CEA, NCTE, and if in a two-year college, TYCA. A program coordinator must utilize every bit of professional development funding provided by the college. This includes funding that will allow you to attend conferences and take classes.

I wish I had known that a program coordinator has to be willing to fight for a program much more than I would have expected. Upper level administrators in your institution may know very little about the needs or activities of your teachers and students; however, they will make decisions that create personal and professional difficulty for you in your work, so you must argue against seemingly unfortunate decisions. Some of the issues that we have encountered were sudden changes in workload for full-time faculty, sudden increases in class size, disputes over released time allocations, and loss of staff positions. Nonetheless, institutional structures often limit your success, and you just have live with the results.

Finally, a coordinator needs to be organized and to try to manage time within the limits of the released time that they are given; at the same time he/she should be aware that this is very difficult to do, and that there will be late nights and lots of time worked over the released time. Being clear about your availability to both students and teachers is vital to maintaining your sanity.

References

Collins, Suzanne. 2010. *The Hunger Games.* New York: Scholastic.

Egan, Timothy. 2009. *The Big Burn: Teddy Roosevelt and the Fire That Saved America.* Boston: Houghton Mifflin Harcourt.

Skloot, Rebecca. 2010. *The Immortal Life of Henrietta Lacks.* New York: Crown.

Weber, Karl. 2010. *Waiting for "Superman": How We Can Save America's Failing Public Schools.* New York: Public Affairs.

Wilkerson, Isabel. 2010. *The Warmth of Other Suns: The Epic Story of America's Great Migration.* New York: Random House.

Wilkinson, Lisa, and Heather McKay. 2012. CCCC Writing Program of Excellence Award application.

16

UNIVERSITY OF NOTRE DAME
UNIVERSITY WRITING PROGRAM

Patrick Clauss

Institution type: Catholic Research University
Location: Indiana, ninety miles east of Chicago
Year program was founded: 1997 in an earlier form; 2007 in current form
Enrollment: 12,000
WPA reports to: Dean of the College of Arts and Letters
Program funded by: College of Arts and Sciences
Description of students: Our student body is drawn from all fifty states and nearly
ninety countries. The majority of undergraduates live on campus, and many are
active in service learning and community volunteer activities. Approximately 90
percent of our students were in the top 10 percent of their high school graduating class, and just over 80 percent of our students identify as Catholic. We do
not have any social fraternities or sororities. Instead, the residence halls serve as
the focus for social, religious, and intramural athletic activities.

PROGRAM SNAPSHOT

The program consists of a first-year course: First-Year Writing and
Rhetoric. In addition to the traditional course, students can also take
Community-Based Writing and Rhetoric or Multimedia Writing and
Rhetoric; all three courses share the same goals. The mission is to introduce students to the practices of academic discourse and ethical argumentation. Students are taught how to conduct research, frame claims,
provide evidence, consider alternative views, and write in language
appropriate to intended audiences and purposes. We teach these skills
as necessary constituents of academic writing and ethical practices. In
addition, we situate these skills within the context of Catholic Social
Teaching: students may study the rhetoric of issues such as the dignity
of the human person, the options of the poor and vulnerable, and the
rights of workers. Our courses offer Notre Dame students opportunities
to participate in rich conversations while preparing them for academic

DOI: 10.7330/9781607326274.c016

life and raising questions about what it means to be an ethical writer
and speaker.

WPA'S PROFILE

I earned my doctorate in rhetoric and composition at Ball State University, writing a dissertation about the influence of Stephen Toulmin's
(1958) *The Uses of Argument* on the teaching of writing.

Just out of graduate school, I was hired as an instructor at Butler
University, teaching first-year writing and advanced composition. One
year later, I was promoted to direct the Peer Tutoring Program in
Butler's Writers' Studio, a position equivalent to directing a writing center. In addition, I began teaching a wider range of courses, including
rhetorical theory and a senior-level tutor-training and English education
course. As the director of Peer Tutoring, I recruited, trained, and supervised approximately twenty-five undergraduate and graduate tutors each
year. I also served as a campus resource for writing across the curriculum
and writing in the disciplines. With two other Department of English
faculty members, also trained in rhetoric and composition, I led faculty
workshops and was involved in other faculty development initiatives.

After eight years at Butler University, I applied for my current position at the University of Notre Dame. I was hired as the associate director of the University Writing Program (UWP); I have since been named
the director of First-Year Writing and Rhetoric. As an administrator and
faculty member in the UWP, I am fortunate that my love of argument—
studying argument, that is, not necessarily engaging in argument or
being argumentative—has sustained my interest and continues to serve
my work in a program that places academic argument at the heart of
our mission.

PROGRAM CONCEPTION

In the mid-1990s, Dr. Eileen Kohlman, then dean of Notre Dame's First
Year of Studies, chaired a task force to address student writing at the
university. While Notre Dame's Department of English offered a small
number of first-year writing courses, they were largely introduction to
literature courses: writing about literature, with a strong emphasis on
grammatical correctness. Members of the task force determined that the
existing structure and curriculum did not sufficiently address students'
needs, teaching them the writing skills necessary to succeed in college
and beyond. A national search was undertaken, and in 1997 Dr. Stuart

Greene was hired to design, staff, and direct the UWP. Greene's initial program had two closely related components: a first-year writing course, one focusing on academic argument; and training and support for graduate students (doctoral candidates in English and American literature) teaching the course. At the time, the university had no writing center, so soon after he was hired, Greene convinced administrators to hire Dr. John Duffy to found and direct Notre Dame's University Writing Center. When Greene was appointed associate dean of Undergraduate Studies in 2007, Duffy was appointed Francis O'Malley director of the UWP.

At Notre Dame, the UWP and Writing Center are independent from the Department of English. Though Greene and Duffy are tenured faculty in the Department of English, and we enjoy a productive, collegial relationship with English faculty, from the beginning of our program through today we have had a great deal of freedom to determine our own direction. We report to the dean of the College of Arts and Letters, not the chair of the Department of English. Consequently, we are not seen, as is sometimes the case at other institutions, as a sort of servant to the English Department. While some in English and across the university undoubtedly see Writing and Rhetoric as a service course, we embrace our mission, goals, and autonomy.

Although our program's curriculum and structure have undergone a fair number of changes since the late 1990s, we still use a portfolio approach similar to the one Greene implemented. We have, however, modified other structures and procedures. For instance, in recent years we have hired four full-time, "core" faculty with PhDs and/or extensive experience teaching writing to undergraduates. We have emphasized the professionalization of graduate students in recent years as well. In addition to staffing first-year writing classes with graduate instructors from English, we also offer competitive teaching fellowships to five graduate students from across the humanities and social sciences. When our Graduate Teaching Fellowship was originally designed and implemented in the late 1990s, the UWP offered teaching fellowships to ten doctoral students from disciplines such as philosophy, sociology, theology, and history. The **graduate teaching fellows** (GTFs), all of whom were sixth- or seventh-year doctoral students, would teach one section of Writing and Rhetoric in the fall and then return to their home departments in the spring, teaching an introductory course in those disciplines. We realized, however, that we were investing significant time and energy training these graduate students to teach writing. Each spring we would lose many excellent teachers after only one semester in our program. Thus, we modified the GTF program: we now award the fellowship to five advanced doctoral students, not ten, and those five stay with us for the full academic year. We have also implemented, in recent years, other curricular and structural changes to our program, including, but not limited to, the following: expanding the role of digital technologies; promoting community-based learning throughout our courses; and engaging more with the wider Notre Dame community. We have exciting plans for the future of our program and its role in the first year and across the university.

POPULATION SERVED

We serve first-year undergraduates, about 450 students per semester. (Because of Advanced Placement [AP] and International Baccalaureate [IB] credit, about half of incoming Notre Dame freshmen do not take our course. We are working to change this.) Perhaps indirectly, we serve another population as well: the graduate students teaching in our program. In a typical academic year, we have seven full-time faculty and approximately eighteen graduate instructors. As Notre Dame does not offer graduate coursework in rhetoric and composition, the majority of our graduate instructors will not devote their careers to scholarship and research in these areas. Most are doctoral students in English or American literature, but we are also joined by doctoral students in other disciplines from our College of Arts and Letters. All graduate instructors take a one-semester teaching practicum the spring semester before they teach for us. There, they are introduced to the fundamentals of rhetorical theory and composition pedagogy. Most have little teaching experience. Plus, because they will eventually teach their own courses across the liberal arts—at Notre Dame and beyond, after they graduate—we realize that we are charged with inculcating within them good practices regarding writing across the curriculum and writing in the disciplines. Our teaching practicum and other faculty development initiatives are likely the only training these faculty will have in composition theory and pedagogy, not only while in our program but also in their careers as well. Consequently, we eagerly embrace our responsibilities to introduce these nascent scholars and teachers to sound composition practices and pedagogies.

FUNDING

Most of our funding comes from our College of Arts and Letters, our academic home. However, several initiatives and aspects of our program are funded through other university departments or offices. For instance, five of our graduate instructors each year are Graduate

Teaching Fellows. Funding for the GTF program comes directly from our Graduate School. In addition, another UWP initiative, our Writing Tutorial (discussed in more detail below), is funded through our Provost's Office. All together, including not only faculty and graduate student salaries but also money for writing center tutor salaries, travel expenses, copying, office supplies, and a host of other costs, our annual budget usually runs about $675,000 a year.

OPERATIONS

There are three administrators in the UWP: John Duffy, the O'Malley director of the UWP; Matthew Capdevielle, the director of the University Writing Center; and I am the director of First-Year Writing and Rhetoric. In a typical semester, we have approximately twenty-five faculty total: the three administrators just mentioned; four other full-time, core faculty; two or three adjuncts teaching one to two sections each; and fifteen graduate instructors, each of whom teaches one section per semester.

As the director of First-Year Writing and Rhetoric, I am primarily responsible for the day-to-day operations of the program. For instance, one of my duties includes designing and implementing our program's course schedule. We usually offer about thirty sections of Writing and Rhetoric, our first-year course. Starting in late August or early September, I begin building the spring schedule. This process includes communicating with deans and staff members from across the university, as we have to be able to project, accurately, how many students will need our course. Closely related, then, are staffing and classroom concerns, which I also handle. Projecting hiring needs, based on enrollments, may be one of the most challenging aspects of the job. Quite frequently, students who need our course appear at their advisor's door at the last minute. While such cases can usually be absorbed into a course schedule already in place, when the numbers become too high, it is then necessary to open additional sections. This, in turn, starts the whole process all over again: communicating with deans, finding classrooms, hiring qualified instructors, ensuring that book orders are placed, and so forth. I also facilitate communication between Writing Program faculty and their students' advisors in Notre Dame's First Year of Studies; I observe classes and meet with teachers individually afterwards; and I work closely with campus librarians, ensuring that our faculty and the librarians work together to best serve students.

In addition, we are fortunate to have a graduate student assistant director, or GSAD. This position is typically filled by our best graduate student instructor from the previous year. Our GSAD helps with many "behind-the-scenes" sorts of things, including, but not limited to, website development and maintenance; faculty development initiatives; classroom observations; and other teacher-support activities. Full-time faculty teach three course per semester—or their equivalent. Many of us have course releases for administrative work, including writing center or program administration, coordinating our Writing Tutorial, or editing our online journal of award-winning student writing from across the first year, *Fresh Writing*. Finally, we have two full-time support staff members: a program coordinator and a staff assistant.

In addition to our program's three administrative faculty, the remaining full-time, core faculty are also involved in many of our day-to-day operations of our program. An important aspect of our program is the professionalization of the graduate student instructors who teach with us each year. To support these efforts, each core faculty member serves as a mentor group leader. Mentor groups typically contain between three to five members each, and they meet every three to four weeks to discuss pedagogical concerns and practices. A mentor group meeting may involve discussions of sample student papers (e.g., "what feedback would you offer about this draft?"), discussions of classroom management, or discussions of recent teaching accomplishments. All full-time, core faculty members are involved in various UWP committees as well. Among other topics, we currently have committees devoted to assessment, technology, community-based learning, and faculty development.

ASSESSMENT

Assessment in our program is an ongoing and evolving project that has taken a variety of forms in recent years. Within the last three years, efforts have been focused through the work of the UWP Assessment Committee, convened in fall 2011 to address two broad questions: is our program working, and are we doing what we say we do? Our assessment efforts fall under two general, related categories: assessing the quality of our training and support for our graduate student teachers and assessing the quality of our undergraduate writing.

Graduate Instructor Training and Support

Among other preliminary tasks, UWP Assessment Committee members drafted and administered a graduate student instructor survey, measuring satisfaction and soliciting feedback regarding teacher training, support, and mentoring in our program. Since the spring of 2012, we have administered some version of that survey at the end of the academic year, just before our graduate instructors leave our program to return to teach in their home departments (e.g., English, Theology, etc.). While responses vary from year to year, and disparate answers are sometimes hard to summarize or generalize, several trends have emerged, and we have tried to respond appropriately. For instance, our mentor groups routinely receive high marks from graduate instructors. Among other aspects, they appreciate the chance to share teaching successes and challenges with a small group of their peers, led by experienced writing program faculty. Thus, we have increased opportunities for mentor group meetings by scaling back on full-faculty meetings. Recent survey respondents have also remarked that they would appreciate more support regarding program teaching resources—for example, handouts regarding sample assignments, grading rubrics, and lesson plan ideas. To respond, we have increased our efforts to collect and make available such documents, storing them in several easily accessible online locations, such as our program's Sakai site.

Undergraduate Writing

While our recent assessment committee work addressed training and support for our graduate instructors, most of our assessment efforts have focused on our first-year writing courses. The committee has issued the following recommendations concerning program assessment. We believe we need to

- study our aspirational peers (e.g., Duke, Stanford, Harvard) to determine how they manage their writing programs and requirements
- compare our program's goals, assignments, and procedures with guidelines recommended by WPA, CCCC, AACU, and NCTE, ensuring we are consistent with discipline-specific standards
- begin to use data from items we are assessing to generate programmatic improvements
- solidify and centralize our core course values (articulated across a variety of sites: our website, our *Guide to Teaching*, various syllabi, etc.)
- generate new questions for end-of-semester student evaluations
- study IB and AP exempted students to determine the quality and quantity of writing instruction in students' courses, during their freshmen years and beyond

Most recently, our UWP Assessment Committee drafted a plan for the summers of 2014–16, a long-term study requiring the collection, reading, and scoring of randomly sampled research papers from every section of Writing and Rhetoric from three academic years. A common rubric developed by the Assessment Committee will be used for this assessment. In an attempt to compare the performance of students required to take writing and rhetoric (WR) with that of students exempted from the requirement on the basis of IB or AP credit, we plan to use the same rubric to evaluate a sample of papers written by exempted students in Notre Dame's University Seminar course. We also have several preliminary assessment measures in place for the University Writing Center, which we plan to develop in the coming years. We recognize the need to expand our efforts to institutionalize a meaningful, systematic assessment program.

We are also piloting electronic portfolios across in curriculum. As of this writing, two full-time, core faculty are using Notre Dame's ePortfolio site, with plans to roll out the site across our program next year. Though undoubtedly a challenging task, such efforts would be beneficial in a number of ways, our primary concern here relating to a program-wide assessment of student work: compared to hard copies of student essays, ePortfolios are more convenient to collect, organize, access, and archive for future research. Along similar lines, previously our program collected hard copies of students' midterm evaluations of our teachers. The documents were scanned before being returned to the individual teachers; program directors had access to the scanned documents in a private database. While collecting midterm evaluations online is not inherently better simply because the mechanism is electronic, after piloting electronic midterm evaluations in one section in the fall of 2014, we are moving to electronic midterm evaluations this semester, spring of 2015.

While we have invested a great deal of time in researching assessment methods, cataloguing program components, and planning measures, we face several challenges to implementing the full-scale assessment system we believe is necessary to ensure excellence in the program. The biggest challenge we face is lack of sufficient time. Since most of our faculty carry a 3–3 teaching load (or equivalent), finding time to plan and implement large-scale assessment measures is difficult. Graduate instructors are with us for one year only, so their contributions to assessment projects are necessarily minimal and limited primarily to aiding in data collection. We are at present exploring possibilities for funding the required release time and/or summer funding for faculty to conduct the assessment measures we have identified as relevant to our needs.

MARKETING/PR

When I was a graduate student, I would not have considered marketing and PR to be an important component to a WPA's job. I likely would have wondered, "What is there to market? Don't students just sign up for required classes, and that's about it?" After having worked as a writing center director and now a writing program director for the last fourteen years, I recognize that marketing and PR are important aspects of program administration. Even though our first-year writing classes are required, we do market, to some degree, to students and parents (e.g., our program website, brochures and information tables at orientation meetings, etc.). Perhaps even more so, we must continually communicate our mission and goals to advisors, faculty, and administrators from across the university. About once a week, it seems, I find myself explaining to a well-meaning faculty member or administration that, no, the UWP and the University Writing Center are not the same thing.

Two common and potentially frustrating assumptions WPAs face are that a first-year writing course is "just a skills course" and that a first-year writing course can solve all of the problems under-prepared or struggling writers face. The same is true, of course, with writing centers: directing the writing center at Butler University, I would occasionally receive communications from faculty that went something like this: "My student visited the Writers' Studio for help on her ten-page history paper about the war in Vietnam; why were there still two comma splices in the paper?" Very quickly, I learned to remind faculty, as tactfully as possible, that writing is a complex, multifaceted activity, also observing that we do the best we can with the skills and motivations students bring to us. I recognize that I am an ambassador for not only my program specifically—who we are, what we do, why we do it—but also for good composition pedagogy in general.

TECHNOLOGY

While we make use of the sorts of technological tools that are now likely standard across most writing programs—for example, Sakai, a program website—we are especially proud of a new digital initiative in our program, *Fresh Writing*. Edited by UWP faculty member, Dr. Erin McLaughlin, *Fresh Writing* is an annual collection of the best multimodal writing from across Notre Dame's First Year of Studies. The online publication is a required text in all first-year Writing and Rhetoric courses, thus serving as a model of effective arguments across a variety of media and modes. Essays are chosen for their engaging prose and the extent to which they successfully execute the conventions of writing genres students may encounter in other academic, civic, or professional contexts. In addition, however, students are encouraged to make use of what Aristotle terms all the available means of persuasion. For instance, students' arguments can include not only alphabetic text but also text more broadly understood: images, sound, etc.

Our use of *Fresh Writing* coincides nicely not only with our Multimedia Writing and Rhetoric sections but also with a relatively new requirement across all sections in our program: we now ask all instructors, no matter which particular course type they are teaching, to include at least one multimodal assignment. Perhaps the most popular assignment is the audio narrative. While this assignment manifests in different forms, depending on the particular class's curriculum and focus, most instructors ask students to compose a three- to six-page essay, as a sort of script (e.g., a narrative argument, an evaluation argument, etc.), which they then record using audio software. Students get in-class, hands-on practice with software such as GarageBand or Audacity, and instructors demonstrate not only how to save and export audio files but also how to incorporate sound effects as well. After students have worked through a draft of their essays, including receiving feedback from peers, they record themselves reading their work. Our program has two homemade sound booths available (essentially, each is a foam-lined, plastic storage bin turned on its side, large enough to hold a microphone plugged in to a laptop computer). Notre Dame's Center for Digital Scholarship, conveniently located in our campus library, now has a sound-proof booth faculty, staff, and students can reserve for private use. After recording the audio files, students then submit written copies of the essays via Sakai or some other file-management system; they also submit the audio essays as MP3 or .WAV files.

ROLE OF RESEARCH

Notre Dame faculty fall into two general categories: teaching and research; and special professional faculty (also known as SPFs.) Because our six remaining core faculty members are SPFs, they are not necessarily required to publish as part of their contracts. However, we are each active at the state, national, and international levels regarding conference presentations and other contributions to our field. Our full-time, core faculty regularly present at CCCC, National Council of Teachers of English (NCTE), and Computers and Writing, just to name a few. Our areas of expertise include digital and multimodal literacies, writing center theory and administration, writing in the disciplines, argumentation theory and practice, and community-based learning initiatives. Our individual research agendas, it must be noted, arise out of and are a result of our shared work in the program. For instance, recent SPF presentations at CCCC and other national or international conferences reflect not only our research interests but also our program's emphases on virtue ethics, academic argument, and digital rhetoric, among other areas. No matter our particular, individual research interests, our scholarship and teaching are closely related, with activities in one domain informing, complementing, and energizing activities in the other.

PEDAGOGICAL AND/OR ADMINISTRATIVE HIGHLIGHTS

Because we are a Catholic university, we are uniquely situated to incorporate not only Catholic Social Teaching (e.g., students may study the rhetoric of issues such as the dignity of the human person or the options of the poor and vulnerable) but also, more broadly speaking, the role of virtue ethics in the writing classroom. The university touts its mission as providing "a distinctive voice in higher education," one "that is at once rigorously intellectual, unapologetically moral in orientation, and firmly embracing of a service ethos" (University of Notre Dame 2017). Thus, our mission is to introduce students to the practices of academic discourse *and* ethical argumentation. Virtuous rhetoric, in many ways, serves not just one's own needs but also the larger needs of the community or culture as well. Our courses offer Notre Dame students opportunities to participate in rich conversations while preparing them for academic life and raising questions about what it means to be an ethical writer and speaker.

In addition, another important aspect of our program is the latitude we give instructors regarding the particular type of first-year writing course they teach. While we have a common syllabus—common goals, learning objectives, assignment types, etc.—we allow instructors to choose from three varieties of classes when they design their individual courses and syllabi:

WR 13100: Writing and Rhetoric

Our standard Writing and Rhetoric course is designed to help students identify an issue amid conflicting points of view and craft an argument based on various sources of information. The course stresses the identification and analysis of potential counter-arguments and aims to develop skills for writing a research proposal, for conducting original research, and for using print and electronic resources from the library. Students are taught to see writing and speaking as ethical activities that contribute the moral development of the individual and the health of the wider community.

WR 13200: Community-Based Writing and Rhetoric

Community-Based Writing and Rhetoric courses offer students a unique opportunity to learn skills and strategies for effective research and written argumentation through investigating social justice issues and performing community service. In partnership with the Center for Social Concerns, instructors connect students with local venues where they perform approximately ten to fifteen hours of community service over the course of the semester. Students integrate their service experiences into readings, research, writing, and discussion about the meanings of community, citizenship, and social justice in contemporary America. In some sections, the students write about their service. In other sections, the students' writing is the service (e.g., case studies, biographies of clients for the sites' various promotional or grant needs, etc.). As is the case with our standard WR course, these courses emphasize the ethical dimensions of speaking and writing.

WR 13300: Multimedia Writing and Rhetoric

Digital culture and new media have dramatically affected reading, writing, and research practices. Consequently, multimedia sections of Writing and Rhetoric teach students to apply rhetorical principles across a variety of media. Students learn both print-based and screen-based literacies that address the complex realities and challenges of composing ethical, reasonable, and conventional arguments in the twenty-first century. Students do not need prior technological skills to be successful in these courses, but they should anticipate learning to use a variety of multimodal authoring technologies (which may include blogs, wikis, web editors, video editing software, and so on). Multimedia sections of Writing and Rhetoric teach students how to make the most of a wide array of technological resources and address the challenges of composing in the twenty-first century. Students in the Multimedia Writing and Rhetoric course address the unique challenges and opportunities of communicating ethically in a digital environment.

In addition to serving first-year University of Notre Dame writers via the above course offerings, we also serve a similar population of students via a relatively new course in our program, WR 12100: Writing and Rhetoric Tutorial. This is a one-credit, supplemental, elective course that can be taken in conjunction with or subsequent to WR 13100, 13200, or 13300. The Tutorial offers individualized instruction and writing process coaching to students who need additional support and guidance as they transition to reading and writing at the college level. Weekly meetings are scheduled around students' and instructors' availability. Registration is by recommendation and instructor-approval only. While we currently serve twenty-four students per semester in the Tutorial (three sections, capped at eight students each), plans are underway to enlarge the size and the scope of the program, serving as many as forty writers per semester.

PRIMARY DOCUMENT (at writingprogramarchitecture.com)

Our faculty handbook, *Guide to Teaching Writing and Rhetoric*, is an important resource for teachers in the UWP at Notre Dame. With sections addressing our pedagogical and theoretical approaches, the guide also includes sample syllabi, program policies, and other relevant materials. While more recent versions of the guide exist, as we revise and update it each fall, we offer the 2014 edition as a model in the online companion because it is a stand-alone PDF. More recent versions contain numerous links to documents that are password-protected or are located in drives on our university's intranet.

WPA'S VOICE

About two years out of graduate school, I was fortunate to be selected to direct the writing center at Butler University. This was more a case of being in the right place at the right time, really, as the current writing center director was moving across the country because of her spouse's job. Fortunately, I eagerly accepted that position, growing tremendously as a teacher and administrator in the next seven years. Those skills served me well when I joined the University of Notre Dame as the associate director of the UWP in 2008 and was then named director of First-Year Composition (now, Writing and Rhetoric) in 2009. I have learned a great deal in recent years, perhaps most importantly the benefits of cultivating strong relationships with faculty and staff from across the university. In graduate school, I could not have predicted how much of my work day would be taken up with meetings about curriculum issues, phone calls about finding classrooms, emails about registration snags, and a wide variety of other tasks. So much of what I do involves other people; very rarely am I the solitary scholar, toiling alone in the stacks as I did in graduate school and imagined I would do for most of my career. Having established productive and positive relationships with people from other programs and departments helps a great deal.

In addition, I have learned—and am still learning—the importance of knowing when to trust my instincts on certain issues and when to let go of ideas or beliefs that are wrong-headed, outdated, or not relevant in a particular case. Knowing when to say, "I'm not sure we should do that; I think this is a better route" versus when to say "You're right; that is a better plan," is never easy, but it is an important skill for any university faculty member—especially, however, one working in administration. I am fortunate to work with teachers and scholars who care very much about teaching and scholarship, which makes these sorts of moments much easier to identify and respond to.

Finally, I want to offer a few words about what is known as "imposter syndrome," the nagging feelings many of us have that we are somehow not qualified enough, able enough, or skilled enough to be in our present position. Any good teacher has undoubtedly dealt with such anxieties while standing in front of a class or enforcing a class policy, for instance. While explaining a concept or offering a definition, it can be somewhat unnerving to watch a classroom full of students dutifully write down our every word. In graduate school, we learn to question assumptions, to consider issues from multiple angles, and to interrogate pretty much every construct or belief. It is perhaps only natural, then, that these attitudes and practices would carry over to estimations of our own talents. I am certainly not advocating unabashed bravado or a false sense of one's own abilities. Sadly, academia, like any profession, has its share of such people, people who seemingly love to hear themselves talk. I do believe it is important, then, especially for beginning writing program administrators, to have confidence in their own abilities. A critical self-awareness is vital, but so is a genuine recognition of one's own strengths and talents. I sometimes tell my students, when I sense they are struggling with the demands of college, "Notre Dame wouldn't have accepted you if you couldn't handle the challenges. You can do it." Privately, I sometimes tell myself, "Notre Dame wouldn't have hired me if I couldn't handle the challenges. I can do it."

References

Toulmin, Stephen. 1958. *The Uses of Argument.* Cambridge: Cambridge University Press.

University of Notre Dame. 2017. "About Notre Dame." https://m.nd.edu/notredame/about/_/about_notre_dame.

17

UNIVERSITY OF WISCONSIN– EAU CLAIRE UNIVERSITY WRITING PROGRAM

Shevaun E. Watson

Institution type: mid-sized regional comprehensive university; one of thirteen four-year universities in the University of Wisconsin System.
Location: Eau Claire, Wisconsin
Enrollment: 10,500
Year program was founded: 1960s
WPA reports to: Department Chair
Program funded by: Department of English, College of Arts and Sciences
Description of students: primarily from Minnesota, Wisconsin and northern Illinois; small but growing populations of first-generation, veteran, nontraditional, international, multilingual, and nonwhite students.

PROGRAM SNAPSHOT

The University Writing Program, which is called the "Blugold Seminar in Critical Reading and Writing," is housed in the Department of English within the College of Arts and Sciences. The program consists of one five-credit-hour course with a two-credit-hour course option for some students, either of which satisfies the University Writing requirement. All courses follow a standard curriculum focused on rhetoric and inquiry. The infrastructure of the program includes professional development, placement, and a "flipped" staffing model.

WPA'S PROFILE

During graduate school, I was always interested in writing program and writing center administration, though my dissertation research focused on the history of African American rhetoric and literacy. I actively pursued a broad research agenda that encompassed multiple areas of the

DOI: 10.7330/9781607326274.c017

field. I was fortunate to take a course in writing program administration and to have significant administrative duties as a graduate student. In my master's program, I served as the assistant director of the writing center, and as a PhD student, I worked in the first-year writing program and with various WAC initiatives. In my final year of dissertation writing, I worked at another institution in its upper-level writing (writing in the disciplines [WID]) program. All of these opportunities provided me with invaluable experience in different kinds of writing centers and programs, teacher training and mentoring, program assessment, large-scale portfolio programs, faculty development and campus outreach, and qualitative and empirical research on writers.

After several years in a tenure-track position at an R1 university, I was motivated for personal reasons to look for positions in other areas of the country, and ultimately I was hired to direct the composition program at the University of Wisconsin–Eau Claire (UW–Eau Claire). UW–Eau Claire offered a unique situation that compelled me to devote my intellectual energies more to WPA work. First, all tenured and tenure-track faculty in the English Department teach first-year writing at least once, and usually twice, each year. I believed this arrangement afforded me as WPA some rare opportunities. I had witnessed first-hand at several institutions how divorced English faculty were from the composition programs in their own departments, and how that in turn hampered the efforts of the WPA. But this wasn't the case at UW–Eau Claire. I was working with faculty colleagues who all had extensive experience teaching first-year writing, and that changed the nature of the conversations about composition in the department.

Second, the faculty was primed and ready for change when I arrived. It was clear from my early discussions with colleagues that everyone wanted an infusion of new ideas and new energy in the writing program. There was a strong sentiment that a larger vision for the program was missing, and that the development of one could bolster everyone's efforts in the classroom. Finally, there was another factor making this a kairotic moment: there was the possibility of capturing a significant amount of money to facilitate major change. The university raised tuition for the first time in decades, and those new monies were designated exclusively to support improvement and innovation. So, I was presented with a fantastic opportunity: colleagues who all taught composition, broad support among them for programmatic change, and the money to make it happen. Today, as a tenured WPA, I oversee an exciting first-year writing program and collaborate with many wonderful colleagues in my department and across campus.

There was also the opportunity to work closely with the Center for Writing Excellence (CWE). The CWE offers one-on-one peer support in reading, writing and research to all students on campus. Because the scope of the CWE extends far beyond composition, the CWE is housed in Academic Affairs, but its faculty director works in English. The CWE and the first-year writing program work together to deliver a variety of WAC/WID programs and support on campus.

PROGRAM CONCEPTION

The composition program at UW–Eau Claire began along with the inception of the English Department in the 1950s. A decade later, a unique one-semester, five-credit writing course was introduced as an alternative to the typical two-course, six-credit composition sequence. This five-credit course has long been a distinctive feature of the composition program because it allows for more intensive writing practice and student-faculty contact during one semester. Another longstanding and noteworthy aspect of the program is that no graduate students and relatively few adjuncts teach the first-year writing course; instead, all English faculty are committed to composition as a core component of their regular teaching load.

I arrived in 2009, when the English Department was beginning to address an array of issues pertaining to the composition program that had been accruing for years. Overall, the program was in need of fresh perspectives and approaches. For over two decades, internal and external department reviews expressed serious concern about class size: twenty-eight students (and often overloaded to thirty) was the highest composition enrollment cap in the entire UW–System, including all of the two-year colleges. The course curriculum and goals existed in a tenuous and unclear balance between faculty autonomy and pedagogical coherence, which made program assessment extremely difficult. Student success in composition and the transfer of writing skills to other courses were impossible to identify or track. The non-credit basic writing course had become ineffective and marginalized in the department. The issues facing the writing program at this point were varied and complex.

At this same time, the university created a competitive grant-like process called the "Blugold Commitment," whereby faculty applied for funds to create major innovations that would contribute to the university's distinctiveness in clear and substantial ways. I collaborated with the English Department chair to apply these new funds to revamp the writing program, receiving significant additional annual funding (approximately $250,000 each year beginning in 2011 and thereafter) to build, pilot, roll out, and maintain what would become the Blugold Seminar (BGS) in Critical Reading and Writing. This additional money augments the existing budget allocation for first-year composition, paying for additional sections and instructors due to the decreased class size (lowering the course cap to twenty from twenty-eight meant offering approximately thirty more sections in a year and hiring about five new instructors to cover those).

This infusion of money and innovation yielded an entirely new writing program, involving the following changes:

- **New array of equivalent courses.** (See chart below. The five-credit course model was retained, but different versions of it were created to accommodate students' different needs. Any one course fulfills the new University Writing requirement.)
- **Lower course caps.** (Fifteen to twenty-two students, depending on the course, but most classes at twenty. See table 17.1.)
- **Updated placement mechanisms**, including a portfolio option to "test out" of first-year writing available to all students (to replace AP, IB, and CLEP credit options).
- **One additional tenure-track full-time equivalent (FTE)** to assist with the increased number of sections that resulted from the lower course caps.
- **Four visiting assistant professor positions.** (Offered two-year, one-time renewable contracts, as a new way to staff more sections without needing to rely on additional adjunct instructors.)
- **Full-credit basic writing course** (WRIT 114) replaced non-credit ENGL 099 class.
- **"Flipped" staffing model** where the most experienced and effective faculty teach basic writing (WRIT 114) and transfer students (WRIT 120), populations most at risk not to graduate.
- **Standardized rhetoric- and inquiry-based curriculum** populated by themed sections (see table 17.2).
- **Updated information literacy and digital literacy** learning outcomes.
- **Paid professional development.** (Offered year-round for all faculty, including non-tenure-track.)
- **Program and curriculum assessment.** (Ongoing, multimodal, and recursive; includes longitudinal study, student surveys and focus groups, faculty surveys, blind review of students' portfolios, etc.)

POPULATION SERVED

The BGS serves about 2,200 first-year and transfer students on campus, typically offering over one hundred sections of composition each year. The university is located in western Wisconsin and draws about

Table 17.1. Blugold Seminar Course Array

WRIT 114	Intensive BGS	5 credits	15 students
WRIT 116	BGS	5 credits	20 students
WRIT 118	Accelerated BGS	2 credits	22 students
WRIT 120	BGS for Transfers	2 credits	22 students

Table 17.2. Sample Blugold Seminar Themes

WRIT 114	Tourism and Public Memory
WRIT 114	New Orleans after Katrina
WRIT 116	Representations of Disability
WRIT 116	Street Art
WRIT 118	Animals in Visual Culture
WRIT 118	Privacy
WRIT 120	Nursing Dilemmas
WRIT 120	Questions in Communication Disorders

90 percent of its students from Wisconsin (many from rural areas), Minneapolis/St. Paul and its suburbs, southern Minnesota, and northern Illinois. The student body lacks significant ethnic and racial diversity, with only a little less than 10 percent of students identifying as multicultural or students of color. Nearly 20 percent of students at UW–Eau Claire are low income, though about half of all students receive financial aid. More than a third (36%) come to Eau Claire as first-generation college students. Numbers of transfer, nontraditional, veteran, and international students continue to increase each year. We work closely with many units on campus, particularly the Center for Writing Excellence, the Center for International Education, and the ESL program, to help all of our students succeed in the BGS.

FUNDING

Since the first-year writing program is housed within the English Department, there is not technically speaking a separate budget for the BGS. In the past, the department was simply allocated a certain amount of funds to staff the first-year writing courses based on past offering and anticipated needs. Currently, financial support for the program is provided through special tuition dollars ("Blugold Commitment" funds; see "Conception" section), which involves an annual application detailing the use of monies and the efficacy of the program to request funding for the next academic year. Through this process, the first-year writing program has received substantially greater fiscal support from the university, and given the demonstrated success of the BGS, these funding levels are expected to remain in place for the long term. Currently, the program receives about $250,000 (not including fringe) in addition to the regular English budget to sustain current enrollment and staffing levels, plus other funds (about $42,000) for summer salaries, faculty development, travel, and/or services and supplies. The department chair has full discretion over how those extra (non-instructional) funds are used.

OPERATIONS

I served as the director of the writing program from 2009 to 2015. I received a 50 percent course release for this administrative work, which means that I usually taught five to seven credits each semester (e.g., two three-credit courses, or one five-credit class and a one- or two-credit course). In addition to teaching in the BGS, I offered courses in our rhetorics of science, technology, and culture major, and in composition studies for our small MA program. There is no assistant director and graduate students do not teach or serve in any capacity in the program. As the director, I served as the main contact on campus for first-year writing, assisting students, parents, faculty, advisors, and staff with any number of issues and questions. I was the primary instructional mentor and support for all BGS faculty, collaborating with them regularly to devise course materials, classroom resources, writing assignments, rubrics and evaluation guidelines, theme-based supplements, and rhetoric content.

I also collaborated closely with the department chair and administrative assistants to attend to the daily operations of the writing program. I see this work as involving three distinct components of planning and problem-solving.

1. One is the immediate context and current term, which includes things like working with students (schedule problems, placement issues, complaints, inquiries, course equivalencies, etc.), supporting faculty to teach the course (one-on-one meetings, impromptu consultations, professional development workshops, technology assistance), and helping faculty and staff across campus with issues that come up about first-year writing (student advising, curriculum information). At least half of a regular week is devoted to addressing an array of immediate needs and questions. Because these issues are relatively urgent, I needed to prioritize them in my daily schedule.

2. The second component of operations is short-term planning. Along with the department chair, I was always thinking one to two semesters ahead for things like scheduling, offerings, staffing, budget, assessment, and faculty evaluations. Fall meant planning for summer and the next fall, spring meant planning for fall, and so on. At certain points in the academic calendar, I needed to be prepared to make a variety of decisions for the following term or year, and I relied on a variety of people in and outside of the English Department to provide necessary information and data (such as enrollment numbers, budget updates, scheduling needs, teaching evaluation).

3. Finally, the last major element of operations is long-term planning: three, five, ten years out. At this level, my planning was devoted to "big picture" issues on the program and campus levels, such as using assessment data and research to implement revisions to the curriculum; rethinking what faculty development looks like and how it's delivered; setting long-range goals for things that require piloting, careful consideration, or broad faculty buy-in; and working with units on campus to further university initiative and goals (liberal education reform, college readiness, external grants). Another aspect of long-range operations is articulation between our writing program and those of "feeder" schools, both secondary schools and two-year colleges. I worked to share information about the BGS to area teachers and administrators to promote the program, learn about questions or concerns, and create a smoother transition for students.

ASSESSMENT

I undertook significant amounts of program assessment in an effort to meet three goals: first, to understand how the curriculum of the BGS was and was not working; second, to make data-informed decisions about the program; and third, to meet the university's need for assessment of liberal education courses (of which the first-year writing program is a part). Since 2010, the writing program has been collecting massive amounts of data through qualitative, ethnographic, empirical, quantitative, and experimental measures to meet our assessment and research goals. I involved more than a dozen English and psychology majors in university-funded research grants to conduct some of our program assessments. The projects listed with asterisks below indicate those funded in all or part by the university's undergraduate research grants program. Specifically, I gathered data through the following measures:

- **Surveys** (Some semesters, students were asked to report their perceptions about the course and college writing in general.)

- **Focus groups** (Most semesters, small groups of students were gathered for focus groups to provide direct feedback about the course.)
- **ePortfolios** (All students in the BGS are required to submit an electronic version of the four major course projects each term. Twenty percent of each year's portfolios are randomly selected to review in the summer. A group of faculty in and outside of English evaluate these portfolios to determine achievement of course goals.)
- **Self-assessments** (Most semesters, students were invited to assess their own learning and achievement of course goals, and these were compared to ePortfolio data.)

MARKETING/PR

There were audiences both on and off campus that I regularly communicated with. I worked with University Communications, Admissions, Advising, the College of Arts and Sciences, the Center for Writing Excellence, and the English Department to get the word out about our award-winning program. This included websites, social media, and print materials, in addition to talking face to face with administrators, faculty, staff, students, parents, and alumni whenever possible. Our YouTube video, for example, helped promote and explain the program to various audiences. I offered regular workshops through our Center for Excellence in Teaching and Learning to educate faculty about the writing program and to support them in building on the curriculum when teaching writing in their own courses. I worked one-on-one with as many faculty as I could manage, and I tried to get into individual departments or programs to answer questions and provide updated information. All of this work created a positive "buzz" on campus about the BGS. The value of this kind of "leg work" and relationship-building cannot be overstated.

TECHNOLOGY

The wholesale revision of the writing program was motivated in part by the need to update the curriculum in relation to twenty-first-century literacies. Digital literacy is one of four main learning outcomes for the course. Several factors facilitated the widespread buy-in among faculty for these changes. First, a new tenure-track digital literacies position was created to support the new curriculum in scholarly and theoretical ways. This faculty member works closely with the WPA to provide a research-based perspective on multimodal composition, digital literacies, writing technologies, etc. Second, we have adopted the "T+1" approach (Brooke 2013) whereby we set the expectation that faculty and students alike will try one new technology-related thing in their courses each year. This appeals to faculty with all levels of familiarity and comfort with technology, and we provide a great deal of on-the-ground support for doing this. Related to this, we emphasize that "trailing" technologies are as useful or relevant as "leading" technologies. Third, I collaborate very closely with our Learning Technology/IT specialists on campus to expand the kinds of technologies they officially support on campus, as well as the kinds of one-on-one and in-class instruction they offer faculty. Finally, the BGS curriculum offers a variety of ways that faculty can teach and engage the digital literacy outcomes; they don't have to do a major multimodal project but can instead focus on teaching students how to read multimodal arguments, and so on. Each of the four main segments of the course offers faculty choice and flexibility with how to integrate technology into their individual classes.

ROLE OF RESEARCH

Doing research on first-year writing is invaluable to me as a WPA. It not only helps me think about the necessary demands of curriculum and assessment, but it deepens my intellectual engagement with my day-to-day work, so that I am always going between the minutiae and the big picture, policies, and pedagogies, and local and disciplinary contexts. I pursued two major research projects during my time as WPA at UW–Eau Claire.

One involved information literacy. I collaborated with library faculty on campus on a national information literacy project (part of the Association of College and Research Library's [ACRL] Assessment in Action program), where we investigated ways to improve students' information literacy learning in the first-year writing program. We looked at curriculum, faculty development, and student work in order to understand more deeply how and why students struggle with finding, evaluating, and using source materials in their writing. For example, I developed "research-intensive" sections of the composition course in an effort to prepare and motivate more students to pursue undergraduate research. These sections involved more hands-on instruction in broader information literacy concepts and skills, as outlined in the ACRL's new Framework for Information Literacy. Students' work in both "research-intensive" and "regular" sections was collected and reviewed for assessment data.

The second research pertained to stereotype threat, a thread of robust research in social and educational psychology. Stereotype threat is a pervasive phenomenon wherein a person is worried about confirming a negative stereotype related to group to which s/he belongs (e.g., a female student worrying that she will 'prove' the stereotype that women are bad at math). I became interested in the role of stereotype threat in writing classrooms, such as assumptions that certain kinds of people are "bad at writing", and the ways that this might impact individual student performance in college writing. There are a variety of interventions shown to be effective at countering stereotype threat in and outside of the classroom, and I tried to understand how these interventions might mitigate the experiences and performances of basic writers specifically. I completed several empirical studies of writers within the composition program to understand how, if at all, stereotype threat might explain the underperformance of some groups of writers. I am now collaborating with colleagues at Florida International University to develop a multi-institution study of stereotype threat in first-year composition.

PEDAGOGICAL AND/OR ADMINISTRATIVE HIGHLIGHTS

Many of the innovations undertaken with the development of the new program, the BGS, are discussed previously. Some of the most distinctive features of the program include excellent faculty development opportunities, a unique information literacy curriculum, and what I called a "flipped" staffing model. First, BGS faculty get paid $500 to participate in a week-long teaching workshop in August (about twenty faculty participate each year), in addition to a $200 stipend for a two-day workshop in June to "debrief" teaching the BGS at the end of the year and to offer recommendations on curriculum, professional development, instructional materials, and other issues to the WPA and department chair. Faculty also get paid $500-$1,000 to participate in summer assessment projects, which all have professional development components and benefits. BGS faculty share resources with one another via a campus listserv and an online (intranet) program site, in addition to volunteers who showcase their lessons and materials by inviting colleagues to visit their classes. As the WPA, I offered a number of workshops throughout the year to support faculty teaching the curriculum, and I brought a leading teacher-scholar to campus each year to do workshops with faculty as well.

Second, based on recent research on information literacy and related reading and writing issues (e.g., Citation Project, Project Information Literacy, Assessment in Action, etc.), I collaborated closely with colleagues in the library to develop an innovative information literacy curriculum. Together, we created a new library session for all first-year writing students through a "lesson study" and published our results. From there, we shifted the curricular emphasis from writing research papers and doing research to teaching meta-level thinking about research and research processes. We focus on understanding and tracing "information cycles," identifying and analyzing source types from a rhetorical perspective, interrogating issues of credibility with greater nuance, and promoting information-literate "dispositions" among students (e.g., persistence, creativity, etc.). Library faculty no longer teach first-year writing students how to use databases; that instruction is provided via online tutorials. Instead, they teach students more "foundational" information-literate concepts, such as how information is organized on a macro scale, and some even visit writing classes to workshop students' exploratory "research" projects.

Third, the common curriculum allows for greater flexibility in staffing; certain versions or "levels" of the BGS are the exact same as others in terms of content so faculty can teach anywhere in the program (see table 17.2). I considered this flexibility a key factor in the program when we decided to "mainstream" basic writers. I wanted that new course (WRIT 114) to be a desirable one to a variety of faculty so that teaching struggling writers was no longer marginalized in the department. I used the flexibility of the standard curriculum to staff WRIT 114 sections with our most experienced, most popular, and best trained writing faculty, thereby "flipping" the typical staffing model for such a course. This has yielded several benefits: students do very well in this course (higher grades and rates of passing than before), and there is no stigma attached to teaching these students. Rhetorically, on the campus level, this approach to staffing communicates that we value this course and take these students' needs seriously.

PRIMARY DOCUMENTS (at writingprogramarchitecture.com)

Well-compensated and well-planned faculty development was crucial to the success and sustainability of the curriculum as the BGS was first conceived. A key component of the week-long faculty workshop each summer was the "Segment Guides," which outline for instructors the overarching rationale, key concepts and goals, suggested readings, supplementary materials, digital options, recommended projects, and other instructional support information for each of the four main segments of the curriculum.

WPA'S VOICE

I have used a great deal of what I learned in graduate school about establishing, assessing, and maintaining a vibrant first-year writing program.

Like others, I regularly rely on the advice, support, and wisdom of colleagues in the field, via listservs, conferences, and professional relationships. But the success of the BGS specifically can be attributed to two factors beyond our disciplinary expertise: collaboration with the department chair and cultivating working relationships with faculty and units across campus. When a writing program is situated within an English Department, the role of the chair and the relationship between the chair and the WPA are absolutely central to effecting any kind of substantial change or garnering any kind of substantial campus support. Put simply, I could not have achieved what became the BGS without the unconditional and unflagging support of my department chair.

In addition, efforts to building relationships with all kinds of people and programs on campus become incredibly valuable as you seek support and input from outside the department. For me, this meant "cold calling" people to request meetings, inviting small groups of people to lunch, going to other department meetings, attending campus events, and just generally being visible and "on people's radar" so that I could build support among people when I needed it. The collaborations have not just benefitted me in terms of campus politics, but more important, they have deeply shaped how I think about the role of first-year writing on our campus.

References

Brooke, Collin. 2013. "New Media Pedagogy." In *A Guide to Composition Pedagogies*, 2nd ed., ed. Gary Tate, Amy Rupiper Taggart, Kurt Schick, and H. Brooke Hessler, 177–193. New York: Oxford University Press.

18
UNIVERSITY OF WISCONSIN–SUPERIOR BASIC WRITING

John McCormick, Heather McGrew, and Jamie White-Farnham

Institution type: Public liberal arts college
Location: Superior, Wisconsin, a city of 25,000 located on the western tip of Lake Superior
Enrollment: about 2,500
Year program was founded: Basic Writing has existed since at least 1960
WPA reports to: Chair of Writing and Library Science Department
Program funded by: Academic Affairs and campus developmental education funds
Description of students: Students at UW–Superior are mainly described as economically disadvantaged. For instance, 29 percent of students in a recent incoming class were awarded Pell Grants, higher than the UW–System average of 20 percent ("Educational Attainment" 2010). Many are also first-generation students. Students largely hail from the surrounding area in Wisconsin or Minnesota, although about 10 percent of an incoming class are international and from as many as forty-three countries. Students who are placed into the Basic Writing course score 18 or below on their ACTs. These students comprise about 20 percent of any incoming class.

PROGRAM SNAPSHOT

Basic Writing at UW–Superior consists of a three-credit developmental course, WRIT 099: Fundamentals of Writing. The course is offered face-to-face by two dedicated full-time instructors. The curriculum helps students develop strategies to recognize and employ a critical process for both reading and writing in a variety of contexts. The two instructors, John McCormick and Heather McGrew, work as a team along with the WPA, Jamie, in continuous improvement efforts on the course.

WPA'S PROFILE

Jamie
I earned my PhD at the University of Rhode Island (URI) in 2011. While my coursework and research were decidedly focused on rhetorical

DOI: 10.7330/9781607326274.c018

theory and research, I always considered WPA work to be my other half. I came to the field as an undergraduate, working as a tutor in the Writing Center. As a master's student at my alma mater, Bridgewater State University (then College), I served as a graduate assistant at the Writing Center, where I learned a bit about hiring, scheduling, running professional development sessions, and collecting and using in-house statistics. This was a great entrée for me, and I fully intended to become a Writing Center director after my PhD program.

Later, at URI, I served as the graduate assistant director of the Writing and Rhetoric Department. The elements of WPA work I practiced first-hand included assessment, curriculum development, textbook selection by committee, and scheduling. By then, I had widened my sights on the type of job I was interested in, but I hoped for a balance between research, teaching, and administrative work. While on the job market, I actively looked for jobs that featured WPA work either eventually or immediately. I felt very confident coming into my job at the University of Wisconsin-Superior.

I suppose I am a rare bird, given that many WPAs in this collection did not expect or even imagine that they would become WPAs. I seem to be a member of GenAdmin. I am good at the work, and I like it. This is not to say that the contextualized nature of WPA work has not made for some real challenges for me in my five years on the job. Indeed, working at a very small university like UW–Superior has taught me many lessons, about which I explain in the "WPA Voice" section below.

PROGRAM CONCEPTION

Some form of Basic Writing has existed since as early as 1960, when our campus was named Wisconsin State College-Superior (the UW–System was unified in 1971, and the campuses were renamed with their UW–prefixes). The catalog reads:

> 1a. Freshman English. Required of all freshmen. A course designed to improve effectiveness in analytical reading, listening, note-taking, and expository writing [...] During freshman registration, the English department administers an English Placement Test to all freshmen. On the basis of the scores made in this test some students are assigned to sections meeting four times per week instead of three. The work in these special sections is planned to meet the needs of students whose Placement Test scores show them to be deficient in the language skills which are prerequisite for doing college work. ("General Catalog 1960–1962" 1960, 71)

Only a bit more is said about the content of the course, which is the "same as those for the three-hour sections," and that the "earnest student has the opportunity to remove his deficiencies" (General Catalogue 1960, 71).

At some point, probably around 1975, the model of the course changed into the "pre-credit" type, an arrangement much maligned for its unethical dimensions. Particularly, students pay for a class that doesn't earn them credit even with a passing grade (though it does affect their GPAs). Placement practices remained relatively similar to those mentioned in the catalog, although the UW System first tested its own placement test in 1975 ("Background of the Test" 2016). So, at our campus, students are placed either by their ACT score, or, in absence of one or to try for a better placement, the Wisconsin English Placement Exam. This exam is reviewed and maintained by a committee of representatives from each campus and administered by the Center for Placement Testing in Madison.

At UW–Superior, the course Developmental English continued to be administered by the English Department in a routine way. Its course description by 2002 read:

> Fundamentals of academic writing: active reading strategies, writing processes, revision, audience awareness, full development of ideas, adherence to rules of standard edited English. ("General Catalog 2002–2004" 2002)

This description suggests an apt and fair curriculum. Its only "crime" is that it is not quite distinguishable from the actual first-year writing courses; indeed, in the two-course sequence that follows (WRIT 101 and 102), WRIT 101's course description reads:

> Fundamentals of expository composition; writing of short papers; critical reading.

The distinction between "fundamentals of academic writing" and "fundamentals of expository writing" alongside the focus on active and critical reading in both classes is blurry, to say the least.

In 2010, the Writing Program (including basic writing, first-year writing, other general education and service courses, and the minor/major) was administratively reorganized into a new department with the Library Science and ESL programs. English remained a department with the foreign languages and English Education. The course's new appellation became WRIT 099: Fundamentals of Writing. Upon Jamie's hire in 2011, the program was able to spend human resources (Jamie) on some attention to WRIT 099: its enrollment trends, how students fare after

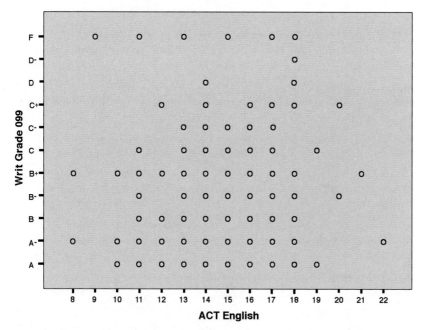

Figure 18.1. ACT scores and WRIT 099 grades, 2010–14

the course, and other concerns of the administration, including adjunct spending and student retention.

POPULATION SERVED

In our small college, an incoming class is about four hundred students. Generally, the profile of an incoming class includes the fact that about one-third of the students will have graduated at the bottom half of their high school class ("Fact Book 2015–16" 2015, 19). More particular to writing, 20 percent of them—about eighty each fall—will arrive having been placed in WRIT 099. Across the building, our colleagues in math will seat about 40 percent of the class in a two-course developmental sequence.

In terms of preparedness, we know that WRIT 099 students score anywhere from an 8 to an 18 on the ACT. Although we know that test scores are not the strongest way to judge writing skills, we are pretty confident that this cut-score tells us something about the ability to succeed in the course. For instance, the scatterplot above (Figure 18.1) features the ACT scores and grades of students enrolled in the course from 2010 to 2014. There is no significance between them, but the pattern suggests to us that no one who scored above an 18 failed the course. Of course, the two students who scored an 8 also passed, so this is not a perfect measure, but it gives us a general sense that the placement suits the students.

We also know, based on observation, that the students are native speakers of English. For one thing, a separate (credit-bearing) ESL Writing course exists. Colleagues in the ESL program teach these courses, and they relate to the first-year writing sequence in a similar way to WRIT 099. After some years of confusion in terms of appropriate placement, now, very few ESL international students end up in WRIT 099. In addition, those students who place into WRIT 099, again from our observations, seem to struggle with one or two particular things: either they have reading difficulties or they have not yet developed any college skills.

True, many of them will write ungrammatical sentences in first drafts. But, we believe that the inability of a student to do well is based more on a lack of understanding reading materials, including assignment sheets or reading assignments to spark conversation and invention, than with his or her ability to express his/herself in writing. Students also do not do well when they do not come to class, do the work on time, or pay attention. When this happens, instructors work hard to set clear expectations for these skills and practices, and they treat early mistakes as learning opportunities for the students.

FUNDING

The budget for developmental courses and projects related to them on our campus is a deep well. Perhaps surprisingly, that is both bad and less bad news. On one (bad) hand, this account is separate from the general university budget because the students who are placed into developmental courses are basically funding these courses themselves; fewer tax dollars are used there.

On the other (less bad) hand, this is how our department was able to successfully argue for two full-time instructors in Basic Writing. In fact, their lines are split between the developmental account and our department budget. It's a two-for-one on both sides. The whole scenario is a rock and hard place for us: the funding source seems unfair to students, but we really do spend it working hard to do right by them.

In addition to the salaries of our instructors, we are able to request and secure funding from this developmental account (simply by asking the dean or provost) when professional development opportunities arise. The instructors have attended CCCC, NCTE conferences, and presented at regional and UW System conferences. We buy ourselves books and watch webinars that might be helpful to our continuing work. Between our departmental budget and the development allotment, the Basic Writing budget totaled around $125,000 last year.

OPERATIONS

The day-to-day operation of our Basic Writing course is almost completely indistinguishable from the rest of the Writing Program. Daily, the focus is on teaching courses and communicating with students. As a team focused on Basic Writing, our meetings and progress take a slower pace: semester to semester, we are reading, discussing, looking at our assessment statistics, writing our reports, advocating for the changes we wish to make (to such bodies as the Faculty Senate) and cooperating with other units (such as Enrollment or Advising for instance) to plan our next move. The WPA facilitates these meetings and conversations, working within the teaching schedule of the instructors. The other people involved include:

Fulltime Instructors

John and Heather are true workhorses. They teach a 4-4 load, half of which is Basic Writing and the other half of which is an assortment of first-year and business writing courses. We share an informal but generally agreed upon position that Basic Writers should have face-to-face conferences on every major project in the course. So, much of the instructors' time outside of class is taken up with these meetings for each of eighteen students (times several sections) each semester. With their focus on researching and improving Basic Writing, they have shown themselves to be passionate believers in the advocacy function of Basic Writing, affording students who otherwise might fall behind early in mainstream classes the time, patience, and academic reading and writing practices necessary to stay in the race. Their efforts have paid off greatly, as we will explain in the "Assessment" section.

Mentors

Mentors are Writing Center consultants (usually) who are looking for a heightened and/or more focused assignment as they continue to learn about responding to students' writing. They are hired when they have enough experience in the Writing Center to meet the responsibility of face-to-face consultations over the course of a semester with an entire class and when their schedules match the course meetings. Mentors work with the instructors to understand the assignments and plan out when and how the students' conferences will take place. Typically, the instructors ask them to come to class only on certain days, such as when a new project is assigned. Their face-to-face consultations are, as one would expect, various and customized to each student's needs.

WPA

Jamie's role on the Basic Writing team is mainly facilitative. She has organized the meetings, research, and decisions related to Basic Writing. She communicates the needs and wants of the team up the chain to the dean and provost, and in turn, relates any pertinent information from the administration to the instructors. As readers will see in the "Assessment" and "Marketing/PR" sections, she represents Basic Writing when meeting with other campus units to gain helpful information as well as publicize the success of our efforts. These responsibilities are less daily than periodic. Daily, Jamie will check in with John and Heather and help if any problems arise.

Chair

This is our most senior colleague, who also happens to be the campus Writing across the Curriculum (WAC) coordinator as noted earlier. She is a great champion of Basic Writing and has led the way in requesting funding from the developmental account to boost our efforts. In addition, even when her own WAC budget was cut, she was keen to be sure that the mentors would remain in place for WRIT 099.

Department Associate

This is our staff person who supports all the work of the chair, but is actually only half-ours. Her time is split 50/50 with another department. In terms of Basic Writing, her support and patience has been necessary as we revise the credits, names, and descriptions of the course; she inputs all the logistics into the PeopleSoft scheduling system. Her understanding of our plans makes rolling the course out to students all the smoother.

ASSESSMENT

In our relatively short time of attending to WRIT 099, we have relied on two indirect assessment measures. This is for the time being, as we settle on a sustainable curriculum and course structure. However, this information has been helpful in understanding the students and monitoring the results of the changes we have made in quick succession. They include:

1. Retention rates. This is really our ace in the hole. Our Office of Institutional Effectiveness runs reports that they tell us are statistically significant and which have shown the following progress for students who have enrolled in WRIT 099:

   > Fall 2012 cohort: 53 percent retained
   > Fall 2013 cohort: 71 percent retained
   > Fall 2014 cohort: 77 percent retained

   We couldn't be happier that these students are retained. The first increase was so sharp that we had to allow for chance or a fluke. However, the third cohort's improvement is no mistake: there has been a positive effect on WRIT 099 students' retention since our efforts began.

2. Student feedback. As is typical, students evaluate the course and the instructors at the end of the term. A repeated theme in each year's feedback is mention of the mentors. Notably, the question on the evaluation reads: "what were the most valuable aspects of the class?" and, for each of the three years, students have mentioned the mentors without prompting. Here are examples taken from recent sections:

   "I really liked having the confrences [*sic*] with either the professor or the mentor. The feedback from those meetings helped with revising my major assignments throughout the course." (Fall 2015 section 001)

   "The most valuable aspects [*sic*] of this class was the ability to sign up with the writing center and meet with them to check out papers. It helped that we had a specific mentor as well." (Fall 2015 section 002)

   "I think the most valuable thing about this class was that we had hands on face to face time with a teacher/ writing mentor to help us better our papers." (Fall 2015 section 005)

MARKETING/PR

Marketing for a required and sometimes misunderstood class is not aimed at the people one might suspect. In fact, the students are not the audience at all. Instead, we have discovered the need to communicate extensively with two units in particular: Academic Advising and the Orientation staff. The communication has become routine, both in writing and face-to-face. First, the WPA meets the advising staff each spring to explain the placement process, cut scores, and content of WRIT 099. This is necessary because of the high turnover in the position of academic advisors on campus. There is always someone new. We also emphasize our retention and grade statistics because we've felt that advisors in the past sometimes explain WRIT 099 in 1960-terms: that there is something wrong that needs fixing. We emphasize the academic support and one-on-one attention that students receive.

It is also necessary to market ourselves to the Orientation staff because it is mainly made up of students. And, because Orientation is a day well-known for being hectic, it has happened that entire rooms full of students have been told they need a placement test (or not), which has caused some confusion about who needs what (this was especially problematic one year when ESL international students attended orientation for the first time together with domestic students). The Orientation staff now delivers placement information in the students' individual packets, and we provide the cut score chart and course descriptions of WRIT 099 and the mainstream courses in the orientation booklet.

Finally, a third audience has been our campus generally. Often, as we will describe, changes come down the line that we have little control over. We therefore "publish" the results of our work everywhere that can draw attention: our annual report, in informal emails, and in meetings with other units. Presenting at national conferences and publishing on our program also draws positive attention.

TECHNOLOGY

The instructors in WRIT 099 use technology quite robustly in the classroom, including using the course management system (D2L) as a course site and using our two twenty-two–computer labs to engage students in the writing process during class time. However, in terms of the administration of the Basic Writing course and its attendant projects, technology does not play a special role. Generally speaking, we use a shared space in D2L to share documents, Google Docs to write collaboratively, and email to communicate.

Recently, however, the PeopleSoft scheduling system has become an important feature to help us transition into a new course structure. Students placed in WRIT 099 are co-enrolled in a mainstream course, and the WRIT 099 hours serve as a lab that supports the work of the mainstream course. Seeing the courses paired with matching numbers makes all the difference to understanding this arrangement. In other words, those students placed in WRIT 099 are offered very narrow choices among the long list of section options in a semester.

The Registrar helped us greatly by linking the reserved mainstream sections to the lab sections in the PeopleSoft system, so that one forces the other; students can't complete their enrollment process until the counterpart course is added. In addition, our IT staff merged the courses' separate D2L sites so that the instructors and students share a single space for "both" courses.

ROLE OF RESEARCH

Research has played a different role than initially expected in terms of our work in Basic Writing. As someone trained in traditional scholarship, Jamie came into our work in WRIT 099 believing that the theories and practices published in our discipline would lead the way. That was true to a certain extent. Although we were inspired by, especially, the work of Susan Naomi Bernstein, one of the contributors to this volume, our context is so particular that we had to get creative. Therefore, research plays out in the following ways:

1. Scholarly inquiry: Reading and sharing our points of view on Basic Writing scholarship played an early and important role. Our small team organized a book club over one semester, and we read *Teaching Developmental Writing: Background Readings* by Bernstein (2012). We took notes during our conversations and kept track of what recurring themes or interests seemed to ring especially helpful for our students. These conversations developed into a conviction that reading support was as essential as writing to the class.

   Another inspiration came from the work of Downs and Wardle (2007) on Writing about Writing (WAW). John in particular was motivated to use this approach in Basic Writing. He did so in one semester as a SOTL project (scholarship of teaching and learning) with funding from our Center for Excellence in Teaching and Learning. He surveyed two sections of WRIT 099, one with a WAW approach, the other without, gleaning the students' thoughts on and confidence in their college reading and writing. He also kept, for anecdotal purposes, notes on their successes in their assignments. He found, impressively, that the students who engaged in the more difficult reading of the WAW approach did no worse and felt no less confident than the students who did typical readings for a Basic Writing course from the textbooks. In the end, we believed there was an inherent value and satisfaction in reading the more difficult readings without any more challenge than would otherwise have existed.

2. Internal statistics: As we intimated in the "Assessment" section, in-house statistics get the most play on our campus. This is what administrators care about and what persuades them. Disciplinary scholarship, in our experience, is important for our conceptions, but not our arguments about our choices.

3. Publish or perish? Research and publication is not more important than quality teaching at our small regional campus. It is not required at all

of instructors like John and Heather, though it is to a certain degree for Jamie, who is on the tenure-track. Still, publishing articles about our writing program (developmental courses and otherwise) does go some way toward establishing our ethos on campus. When an article has been published about our larger Writing Program, we seek attention for it on the campus homepage or in the newsletter of our Center for Excellence in Teaching and Learning. Because the scholarship of teaching and learning is valued on our campus, we are able to point at these articles as evidence that our curriculum and pedagogy generally are high-quality enough to merit publication.

PEDAGOGICAL AND/OR ADMINISTRATIVE HIGHLIGHTS

Based on some long-time neglect of the curriculum, the statistics we have at our disposal, and our observations of our students, in the past three years, our small team has undertaken some major changes to the curriculum and the pedagogy of the course. These changes are inspired by a fundamental shift in perspective on Basic Writing—a point of view far different than "removing deficiencies," of course. We have adopted a point of view inspired by Meyer, Rose, and Gordon's (2016) ideas of "universal design" for learning: academic literacy is not a hierarchy to be climbed or even a discourse community into which students are initiated; instead, students are invited to participate in the difficult but rewarding reading and writing of the university. The instructors don't expect them to perform at a "higher" level, but help them succeed in the expected reading and writing in developmentally appropriate and explicitly process-orientated ways. More particularly, here are the steps taken from that point of view:

Year One (2012–13)

Two fulltime instructors are hired to teach Basic Writing. Professional development is supported with developmental funds. We spend the first year researching best practices and curriculum ideas for the course. We also collaborate with our campus Writing across the Curriculum coordinator (also our chair) to secure funding for dedicated writing mentors.

Year Two (2013–14)

We implement the new curriculum with balanced attention to reading and writing. Mentors are hired and conduct thirty hours of conferences with students throughout the semester. During this year, John also experiments with the Writing About Writing model.

Year Three (2014–15)

Maintain curriculum and mentors. Prepare for potential changes in the state of Wisconsin (following other states) regarding developmental education.

Before moving forward, some explanation is called for in regards to the future of developmental education in the state of Wisconsin. Specifically, president of the UW–System Ray Cross has called for a decrease in the number under-prepared students in the system, both by working with K–12 colleagues and by putting more and better measures into place at the college level to help developmental students persist and graduate (Herzog 2014, par. 1). Attention has been on decreasing the number of students placed in remedial math courses from 21 percent to 14 percent, and the same type of goal will be expected of English and Writing in the near future (Herzog 2014, par. 3).

As a unit, we are especially concerned that Wisconsin's legislature will follow Florida's 2013 example by ending mandatory placement in developmental courses, essentially leaving this choice up to students (Smith 2015, par. 7). Of course, this would curb the practice of admitting under-prepared students and then enrolling them in non-credit courses, but the students and their challenges will remain. In mainstream courses, without the support of a separate developmental budget, it is possible they may fare worse than other students, as they have in math courses in Florida (Smith 2015, par. 12).

This is all to the point that by trying out the co-enrollment/lab model of Basic Writing that accompanies the mainstream course now, we may be able to argue for its effectiveness should we lose our lines dedicated to teaching Basic Writers.

Now we are in year four (2015–16). We are piloting a co-enrollment model in which students take two hours of WRIT 099 as a lab to complement their work in WRIT 101 as a mainstreamed student.

This structural change looks a lot like the course did in 1960, where the students earn credit for the mainstream writing class while getting additional support each week on reading, drafting, or whatever is called for (minus the idea or any statements about "deficiencies"). Our state politics have prompted us to test this structure, which might be able to survive a cut to the developmental education budget. This is where our basic writing concerns lie in 2016.

PRIMARY DOCUMENT (at **writingprogramarchitecture.com**)

Our primary document is the proposal we used to change the credit hours in WRIT 099 from three to two and allow students to "co-enroll" in WRIT 099 and the mainstream course, WRIT 101. The main piece of persuasion we relied on was that the changes we made in the previous year in terms of professional development, curriculum, and pedagogy had increased students' retention dramatically. In the proposal, we describe how co-enrollment would work and that we expected even more benefits to students. There was no university template for a credit-change, so we wrote this as professionally and simply as we thought was appropriate. The credit-change was granted by our department and then the Undergraduate Curriculum Committee. We then worked with the Registrar informally to ensure a smooth transition for students.

WPA'S VOICE

Jamie

As a self-described confident WPA, I still must confess that there are days when I am disappointed, when something I was sure would be great ends up a mess, or when I make honest-to-goodness mistakes. Given my emphasis on how small our campus is, one might ask: what is there to get wrong? In terms of how a WPA might find success while working on a small team, here is how I (strategically) use my voice:

- Talk with your colleagues about more than work: not only are we all physically together every day because of our heavy teaching loads, we also have no one else to work *with*. It's just us. So, a little attention to each other as other than teachers goes a long way. Cheerful "good mornings," interest in each other's home lives, the occasional holiday card or new baby gift. These may seem like lame workplace clichés, but it makes as much of a difference as it does when you make an effort to get to know your students.

- Lead with numbers: in meetings outside of your program or department, share your numbers. This is where having a small student population is great. Even a non-math person can calculate percentages out of four hundred easily. Know how many students you serve, how many pass, how many place into the higher course, how many were retained last year. Use them as examples. Use them to answer the question: "how's it going in writing?" A simple: "Great! Our pass rate was up to 85 percent last year" will stick with those colleagues in other departments whose support you might need down the line. It also, I have found, helps to improve the tone in a meeting or a project when success is expressed as not only the goal but the norm.

- Befriend the support staff: befriend and genuinely appreciate not only your own department associate, but those of other departments, and especially those in the library, bookstore, athletics, the administrative offices, and units such as Academic Advising. I have found that the ability to know support staff in offices by name not only creates for a pleasant work environment but also helps expedite the small, everyday tasks of the WPA: problems with scheduling, opening or closing a section, adjuncts contracts, ordering more books, etc.

- Ask for deadlines: I overheard this sage comment once: "there are no academic emergencies." While the work is important, while students depend on us, there is hardly ever a reason to do more than you can do reasonably in one day. Time management habits aside, I am speaking of the "drop everything" mentality that sometimes accompanies the requests made of WPAs. I often wait an hour or until after my next class to respond to an email from a person whom I suspect wants me to drop everything. Another strategy I use is to ask for a deadline: does Thursday work? The person nearly always realizes they are acting like there's an emergency and becomes reasonable again.

- Listen more than you talk: this is the hardest one for me for two reasons: one, because I am gregarious and like to make friends (as the above suggests); and, two, because people expect me to know what to say. Still, I force myself to stick with this advice, even saying it to myself as a mantra sometimes. One situation in which it's better to listen than to talk is when colleagues outside of writing express unwelcome perspectives on what constitutes good writing or a good writing curriculum. Listening and affirming their negative experience or their tiredness of bad student writing is all you can and should do. Once processed outside of the context, perhaps this information can be useful to you. But, in cases of simple kvetching, remember that informal grievances have little bearing on a good decision-making process.

Another situation in which this approach has worked more productively than as a defense mechanism is within my program. For instance, to solve a problem, I will research and compile two or three ideas or resources and lay them out for the group to consider. I try not to emphasize my own perspective too much, again listening more than I talk. When a solution does not rise naturally or there's not a clear preference, we vote. I have been surprised more than once at how the choices the group makes together are nothing like those I would have chosen on my own, but are still good, solidly informed decisions. That's when I know that our process is collaborative and that I have truly facilitated our team.

References

"Background of the Test." 2016. *University of Wisconsin System Center for Placement Testing.* Accessed February 1, 2016.

Bernstein, Susan Naomi, ed. 2012. *Teaching Developmental Writing: Background Readings.* 4th ed. Boston: Bedford.

Downs, Doug, and Elizabeth Wardle. 2007. "Teaching about Writing, Righting Misconceptions:(Re)Envisioning 'First-Year Composition' as 'Introduction to Writing Studies.'" *College Composition and Communication* 58 (4): 552–584.

"Educational Attainment." 2010. University of Wisconsin–Superior. March 3. Accessed February 1, 2016.

"Fact Book 2015–16." 2015. University of Wisconsin-Superior. December. Accessed February 1, 2016.

"General Catalog 1960–1962." 1960. Wisconsin State College. 63, 4 (January).

"General Catalog 2002–2004." 2002. University of Wisconsin–Superior. Accessed February 1, 2016.

Herzog, Karen. 2014. "UW spotlights 'tragedy' of students needing remedial help." *Milwaukee Journal Sentinel*, August 22.

Meyer, A., D. H. Rose, and D. Gordon. 2016. *Universal Design for Learning: Theory and Practice.* Wakefield, MA: CAST Professional Publishing.

Smith, Ashley A. 2015. "When You're Not Ready." *Inside HigherEd*, June 25. Accessed February 1 2016.

19

UTAH VALLEY UNIVERSITY DEPARTMENT OF LITERACIES AND COMPOSITION

Jacqueline Preston and Deborah Marrott

Institution type: Public open enrollment university
Location: Orem, Utah
Enrollment: 33,000
Year program was founded: late 1970s
WPA reports to: the Dean of University College
Program funded by: State funding and tuition
Description of students: Most students at Utah Valley University (UVU) are resident Utahns, drawn from our three-county "service region"—Utah, Wasatch, and Summit Counties. Having no on-campus housing, per se, UVU is exclusively a commuter campus. The majority of students are white, between the ages of eighteen and twenty-three, who self-identify as "middle-class."

PROGRAM SNAPSHOT

Utah Valley University has a "unique educational mission" mandated by the Utah State Office of Education to provide graduate and undergraduate education, including classes and programs for students who would commonly attend a community college. The university sponsors an independent pre-core department made up of eight tenured and tenure-line faculty who share not only a background in composition and rhetoric but also a commitment to the students who enroll in these courses. The department has long rejected curriculum and pedagogy that would place strong emphasis on surface level error and has for some time now committed itself philosophically to social constructivism. Drawing on the work of post-compositionists and a foundational theory of the writing space as an assemblage, instructors take up a project-model based curriculum and pedagogy. Our published mission statement reflects these philosophies and pedagogical commitments:

DOI: 10.7330/9781607326274.c019

The Department of Literacies and Composition understands that all students bring with them rich and diverse histories, knowledge, skills, and literacies that can be applied to the literacy work they will take part in as college students at UVU. We are committed to providing opportunities for students to recognize their own oral, written, and visual literacies as relevant to the academic setting and to helping them develop these literacies for the work they will do in the academy, in the workplace, and in their personal lives.

The department offers two courses, English 0890 and English 1000, Composition and Literacies across the University and Composition and Literacies across Communities respectively. Sections are offered in three formats: face-to-face, hybrid, and fully online.

WPAS' PROFILES

The traditional duties of a WPA are the primary responsibility of the department chair. The Faculty InService coordinator assists in those duties at the request of the chair.

Deborah

I joined the department's full-time faculty in 1992 with a master's degree in English studies. I had happily been teaching English majors for several years at an elite private university, but when I taught a writing course at UVU one summer, I knew I'd found a vocation. I fell in love with the students and the department and obtained a full-time position in the department the next year. Since my previous teaching and educational emphases had been literature and advanced composition, my learning curve was fairly sharp, so I immersed myself in basic writing literature and attended every WPA and basic writing conference I could. Largely because I had formal training in rhetoric and composition, I was asked to chair the department after only four years on staff. At the time, the department was transitioning from a program focusing on sentence-level accuracy to one emphasizing reading-to-write for academic purposes. After serving a five-year term as department chair, I began working on a doctoral degree at the University of Utah in education, culture, and society, a program uniquely devoted to social justice in education. There I trained as an educational linguistic anthropologist with a focus in non-oppressive literacy instruction, specifically basic writing instruction. I started my second full term as chair in 2009. By that time, the department had adopted a social constructivist philosophy of reading and writing as situated social practices. This highly rhetorical approach allowed the department to move beyond a pedagogical focus on correctness, grammar, spelling, syntax, and uniform style and arrangement toward a pedagogy that emphasizes writing within diverse contexts. However, the complexity of a more rhetorical focus also necessitated new curricular and faculty development approaches since the majority of our part-time faculty members have formal training in literature studies and current-traditional approaches to composition instruction. In 2011, when Jacque joined our full-time faculty, the department created the position of InService coordinator to assist in developing curricula, mentoring new and adjunct faculty members and providing true professional development for these part-time instructors.

Jacqueline (Jacque)

In 2011, I completed my doctorate in composition and rhetoric at the University of Wisconsin–Madison (UW–Madison). While at UW–Madison, I completed a three-year longitudinal study, which explored how students tapped into both familiar (home) and emerging rhetorics to negotiate transitions between the university and their home community. The study examined how college students returning to their communities of origin interacted with members of their home community, specifically how individuals used language to negotiate sociocultural shifts. This research contributed to more recent scholarship, research, and publications exploring approaches to teaching writing and theories of the writing space that could acknowledge the important work that goes on in the writing space beyond representation. At UVU, I found support for these ideas and ample opportunity as the Faculty InService coordinator, to move forward, developing curriculum and pedagogy, model syllabi, online courses, and continuing research. The small program and concentration on serving a very particular population was fertile ground for my continued development as both a scholar and administrative support.

Prior to taking a position at UVU, I held the position of assistant director of the English 100 Writing Program at UW–Madison, then under the direction of Morris Young. As part of a leadership team, I provided support to over forty graduate assistants and assisted in the ongoing development of UW–Madison's first-year composition program. I worked closely with graduate teaching assistants, providing formal instruction via weekly seminars, conducting classroom observations and mentoring both new and experienced instructors in the classroom. As a graduate student, I recall that I was in the awkward position of overseeing other graduate students from across the English spectrum, graduate students seeking terminal degrees in creative writing, literature, and composition and rhetoric. What I soon realized, however, was that while instructors charged with teaching first-year writing may very well regard themselves as accomplished writers, many lacked confidence in their ability to *teach* writing. This realization, along with my personal experiences teaching as both an adjunct and a TA, are at the center of my administrative philosophy. While seasoned faculty have had years to hone and tweak a philosophical and theoretical approach to teaching, new and part-time instructors welcome a well-articulated philosophical and theoretical framework and a solid curricular and clear pedagogical approach, upon which they can begin to craft assignments and rubrics for assessing student work. As the Faculty InService coordinator, at UVU, I believe that some of the most important work that I do is to provide these kinds of supports. At UVU, I continue to work in writing program administration, coordinating our Faculty Seminar, assisting with curriculum development for online, hybrid, and face-to-face classes, as well as developing texts and materials for the English 1000 course.

PROGRAM CONCEPTION

What is now the Department of Literacies and Composition at UVU started in late 1970s as the Department of Developmental English. The department was originally tied to the institution's Learning Enrichment Center (later renamed University College), which housed all non-credit and "remedial" courses on campus. Freshman English and other credit-bearing composition courses were (and still are) housed in the English and Literature Department, a separate program in a separate college. Until the late 1980s, the English and Literature Department dictated the content of the Developmental English courses: it was assumed that these courses should focus exclusively on sentence-level accuracy (grammar, usage, punctuation, and mechanics) and that true writing instruction should be left to faculty outside the Literacies and Composition Department. By the time Deb joined the department in 1992, short modes-based writing assignments had been added to the curriculum in both courses, but course content remained focused on editing issues.

From 1992 until 2002 the department worked steadily to shift from a developmental English approach to an approach that reflected the most current scholarship in basic writing, eschewing textbooks and curricula that promoted a deficit or "building block" model of writing (i.e., the idea that students should first learn to write perfect sentences and paragraphs before moving on to "whole texts.") At this time, the pedagogical and curricular approach by the department was characterized as academic or "essayist" literacy where students focused on writing short essays in response to or incorporating written sources.

The department, known then as the Department of Basic Composition, experienced its greatest growth from 2002 through 2008 after the institution received university status. Programs were encouraged to hire tenure-track faculty with terminal degrees. In addition, the department moved to hiring exclusively faculty from Rhetoric and Composition or Literacy Studies graduate programs.

Concerned that the departmental name, Basic Composition, did not accurately describe the content of our courses and referenced deficit theories of pre-core students, in 2015 the department proposed a name change to the Department of Rhetoric and Literacy. This name was strongly opposed by the leadership of the Department of English and Literature. In light of this opposition, the department proposed the name the Department of Literacies and Composition, which was approved in 2016. The department continues to be housed in University College, which allows us to be responsive to student needs and disciplinary trends through administrative and instructor support. However, common misunderstandings about pre-core students and our separation from the program that teaches First-Year Composition (FYC) on our campus continue to create unique challenges. A lack of consistent and standardized communication between the two departments and assumptions about what kind of instruction is the purview of the Department of Literacies and Composition (presumably, a focus on "the basics") continue to cause inter-departmental difficulties.

The theoretical framework that best reflects the primary goals and preferred pedagogies of the UVU Department of Literacies and Composition are rooted in and have evolved from social constructionism. We teach our first year composition course to help students function more effectively as members of the academic society and society in general by understanding the socially dependent and socially influenced nature of writing. Specifically, we use a rhetorical approach (awareness of audience and context) to writing by teaching that writing (and literacy) is a social act affected not only by a consideration of audience and context but by circulating/conventional social discourses, historical events, and the material realities of the context in which a text is created. We also stress that the impact of and intent of writing goes beyond personal education and professional goals to goals of community and (local and global) citizenship. In line with the social constructivist philosophy, the preferred curriculum and pedagogy underscores writing as assemblage; the writing space is defined as a complex dialectical space of overlap and intersection, a gathering into one context, of not merely words, sentences, and paragraphs, but more important, histories, acquired literacies, experiences, events, people, and visions of the future, recycled, revised, and repurposed, to meet the needs of a new rhetorical context.

Despite its focus on the social nature of writing and the treatment of the writing space as a collective assemblage, this philosophy and theory of the writing space does not preclude pedagogies and approaches to writing that foster personal empowerment or personal expression. Nor does it preclude the teaching of those language and essayist conventions privileged by the academy. However, it may mean that teachers take a *critical* approach (rather than a conservative or current-traditional one) to the teaching of these conventions and that these conventions are viewed rhetorically, as a particular register within a particular discourse context.

The department also faces the challenge of continually educating legislators, administrators, and faculty across campus regarding the mission of our program and the actual reasons students might find themselves in pre-core writing classes. The lack of understanding on campus regarding the non-remedial nature of our curricula and the socio-economic reasons that disadvantage students in our classes has led to difficulties in securing credit for our classes and resources for our students.

In the spring of 2014, for the fourth time in twelve years, the Department of Literacies and Composition petitioned the university's Faculty Senate Curriculum Committee to allow us to change the numbering of our English 0990 course to 1000 so that students taking that course would receive elective credit. The English and Literature Department had successfully opposed our earlier petitions, fearing that a numbering change would confuse students or, perhaps, suggest to some that their English 1010 course, considered a basic writing course at some other Utah universities, should be housed in the Department of Literacies and Composition. Using appeals to ethics and current rhetoric and composition research in the fall of 2014 the Department of Literacies and Composition successfully won a numbering change and credit-bearing status for its English 0990 course, albeit, in the face of serious opposition from the English and Literature Department and the State Office of Education. That change went into effect in fall 2015.

POPULATION SERVED

The Department of Literacies and Composition serves all students who are identified by the institution as "underprepared" for college-level reading and writing, based on the results of standardized testing. Upon admission to the university, students submit their ACT scores (or, if ACT scores are unavailable or expired, Accuplacer Reading Comprehension and Sentence Skills Test scores). Students with scores below those required by the English and Literature Department for entrance into English 1010 (FYC) (approximately 29% of entering freshmen) are placed in Literacies and Composition courses. Consistent with educational findings from the last five decades, students enrolled in our classes are significantly more likely than those enrolled in first-year writing to fit into one or more of the following classifications: students of color, older students returning to study, recent immigrants, former ESL students, international students, and/or students from rural communities throughout the state. Over 50 percent of students in our classes self-identify as first-generation college students, non-traditional college students and "working-class" or even "lower-class students." According to this same survey, nearly 70 percent of students in Literacies and Composition classes work more than twenty hours per week while maintaining a twelve- to fifteen-hour course load. Qualitative data also show that our students are also more likely than "mainstream" students to be members of a minority group or non-native English speakers. The department serves approximately one thousand students per school year.

FUNDING

Like all academic units at UVU, the Department of Literacies and Composition is funded by the university through state and tuition monies. For the 2014–2015 school year, the department's total operating costs, including all faculty and staff salaries and benefits (including a recent 12% increase of adjunct faculty salaries), travel and research costs, and operating costs, was $1,040,883.58. (This number does not include grants and special funding received from our Dean's Office.) Because our enrollments have decreased over the last few years, our budget continues to be adequate to cover all operating costs. In addition, our new dean has been able to secure additional much-needed funds for full-time faculty travel and research.

The salaries of all faculty members and all operating costs of the Department of Literacies and Composition are hard funded by the institution through state allocations. Additional funding for faculty development and scholarly activities may be obtained through competitive applications made to the University College Dean's Office, the Office of Teaching and Learning (OTL) and the institution's Grants for Engaged Teaching and Learning (GEL). Our dean is extremely generous in his support of faculty travel and research, but his resources are also limited. OTL grants are given on a first-come, first-serve basis and cover no more than 50 percent of travel expenses. GEL grants are highly competitive and only include travel funding if that travel is directly related to a larger research project.

At the current time, UVU departments receive no hard funding for the support or professional development of adjunct faculty (in addition to compensation for teaching). Based on the Basic Composition Department's unique commitment to part-time faculty, we use funds reserved for full-time faculty travel and research to pay adjunct faculty for Faculty Seminar attendance and to support the annual Adjunct Faculty Travel Grant, which pays for one adjunct professor to travel each year to the Conference on College Composition and Communication. In addition, the three department faculty members who have written department textbooks have volunteered to contribute any future textbook royalties specifically to support adjunct faculty professional development.

OPERATIONS

Along with teaching a five-credit course every semester, Deb has all those roles and responsibilities associated with being a department chair: managing budgets, including those related to lab and course fees; section scheduling; hiring and staffing; strategic planning; curriculum review and revision; faculty and staff assessment; tenure and rank advancement review; and representing the department faculty and students in college-wide and institution-wide contexts.

In addition to maintaining a 2–3 teaching load, as Faculty InService coordinator, Jacque works closely with the chair in providing consistent and ongoing support to both full-time and part-time faculty. This includes coordinating a monthly Faculty Seminar, maintaining the programs online InService site, developing model syllabi, collaborating with distance education to develop online and hybrid courses, ongoing mentoring, and piloting new instructional models, such as a recently piloted stretch model that extends English 1000 to English 1010.

The full-time faculty in the department currently consists of five tenured, three tenure-track faculty members, and one lecturer. Depending upon semester and enrollment trends, we employ approximately fifteen to twenty adjunct faculty members per semester who teach one or two sections of English 0890 and 1000. We share an academic advisor with our ESL Department and have one administrative assistant who assists with staff scheduling, securing classrooms, textbook ordering, budgeting, scheduling meetings, advising students, coordinating computer classrooms, and generally supporting up to twenty adjunct faculty members and nine full-time faculty members.

Another benefit of having a small department of faculty focused only on pre-core is that all faculty members can and do participate in the running of the department. In addition to the department chair and InService coordinator, the department has a webmaster and technical support coordinator, a faculty mentor coordinator, an assessment coordinator, and a faculty member who serves as the faculty director of our campus-wide Writing Center. Our full-time administrative assistant is instrumental in the day-to-day running of the program, particularly in serving the needs of our adjunct faculty members. In addition to our monthly Faculty Seminars, described below under "Innovation," which include all faculty members, the full-time faculty meets as often as necessary to review and revise curriculum, set goals, and plan projects.

ASSESSMENT

UVU requires all departments to aggressively assess its programs and students. The Department of Literacies and Composition currently uses a triangulation of both quantitative and qualitative measures to assess whether the program is meeting its stated mission and objectives. Our Institutional Research and Information (IRI) Office provides us with data regarding retention and success of students within our classes throughout the Literacies and Composition sequence and throughout the entire English sequence (including UVU's two-semester freshman English courses, 1010 and 2010). These data show that nearly 80 percent of students pass our classes with a C- or better and a similar percentage go on to pass English 1010. IRI data also show a 75 percent correlation between the grades students earn in English 1000 and the grades they go on to earn in English 1010.

In addition to using IRI data to track student success, each semester the department also collects teacher assessments of specific student outcomes. Teachers are asked to assess whether students in their classes have "passing" skills and/or knowledge (a C- or better) in the five primary Student Learning Outcomes for the course: rhetorical knowledge;

critical thinking, reading and writing; knowledge of reading, writing and digital literacy conventions; composing in electronic environments; understanding of key processes in reading, writing, and digital literacy. Finally, for many years we have also administered a separate survey to students at the end of each semester to collect data on student attitudes toward certain assignments and how often they use resources such as the Writing Center. Some of the most interesting information to come from this student survey has been data about whether students plan to take the next class in the English sequence and, if not, why. These data indicate that the primary reasons our students drop- or stop-out of college are financial. The department is currently revising the student survey to reduce overlap between that survey and the institutional Student Rating of Instructor (SRI) survey and to gain additional information on students' "Habits of Mind" as defined by the National Council of Teachers of English (NCTE).

MARKETING/PR

Although UVU is an open admission university, students must meet prerequisite requirements in literacy and numeracy before taking English and math general education courses. Students may meet these requirements either through testing (ACT/Accuplacer) or by taking additional classes. Approximately 29 percent of entering freshman at UVU are placed into Literacies and Compositions courses. Thus, the reality is that the required nature of our courses doesn't necessitate extensive marketing and PR. However, classes in the department are often misunderstood by both students and other faculty on campus; therefore, we rely heavily on academic advisors, the yearly course catalog, and other university and department documents to help us educate others regarding the aims and content of the Literacies and Composition courses.

   In our efforts to better educate not only students but also part-time faculty, administrators, and external reviewers, the department has worked closely with the university's Web Development to redesign the department website to include video profiles of the instructors, and not only general overviews of the courses but also detailed descriptions from each of the faculty regarding their unique approach to these first-year writing classes. In addition to providing what we hope will be a useful resource for completing these courses successfully, we have taken concerted care to use language reflecting our mission statement—that is, specifically avoiding language that would support outdated notions that students enrolled in these courses are either underprepared or underserved, and instead situating students as individuals who arrive in our classrooms bringing with them rich histories, valuable experience, and acquired literacies, all of which are recognized as assets versus deficits in students' desire to write across multiple contexts and for a variety of purposes and audiences.

TECHNOLOGY

The department, thanks largely to the legacy of Dr. Forrest Williams (now dean of University College), leads our campus in the use of technology as pedagogy *and* technology (digital literacy) as instructional content. Ninety percent of all sections of 0890 and 1000 are hybrid classes that meet once a week in a designated computer classroom and once a week online. In addition to these sections, we also offer "multi-day hybrid" sections that employ a "flipped" classroom approach: using our online course curriculum for three-day per week and using the two face-to-face classroom days as true writing workshops. All sections of 0890 and 1000 are committed to helping students master the various tasks of the university's learning management system, *Canvas*, and composing in a variety of electronic environments and mediums. In addition, many instructors use social networking sites to increase communication and course relevance. Currently, one of our adjunct professors, Marie Knowlton-Davis, is investigating the impact of student electronic devices in the writing classroom, measuring the benefits (and possible distractions) when devices are welcomed and integrated into our pedagogy.

In 2012, our basic writing program partnered with the university's Distance Education division and worked closely with an instructional design team to turn the successful project-based, face-to-face English 1000 course and English 0890 into vibrant, multi-section online courses. This project was the culmination of the department chair's consideration and ultimate rejection of copyrighted course-packs for online delivery, which include slick, developed materials but also a neutered and market-driven voice. The team, including the professors assigned to the project, an online instructional designer, IT personnel, a videographer, and a graphic designer, used instructional design principles and multimedia resources to create an online course that had the same potential for success as its face-to-face counterpart. The online component included a multitude of interactives, discussion boards, multimedia tutorials, podcasts, and videos aimed at replicating students' experience of project-based learning in the online environment. What resulted was a resource that serves both students enrolled in hybrid and online courses but also students enrolled in face-to-face courses. Soon after the online course was piloted and final revisions were made, at the department's request, Distance Education produced a shell, which could be used by instructors in face-to-face and hybrid courses.

ROLE OF RESEARCH

As teachers of writing in a basic writing program, we recognize that writing includes representation; this faculty is equally committed to understanding the role that writing plays within the development, perpetuation, and circulation of culture. This broad research agenda is the foundation upon which we continue to build this distinctive program. Scholarship that examines language, literacy, and writing outside the classroom, including rhetorical ethnography examining how language functions in communities to bring about social change, workplace writing, and memory insists that we look beyond writing as primarily as representation, and it is this commitment to writing theory writ large that insists we rethink what it means to teach basic writing in the twenty-first century.

Recent work relevant to basic writing completed by department faculty includes *The Bedford Bibliography for Teachers of Basic Writing*, co-edited by Dr. Chitra Duttagupta and Robert Miller (Duttagupta and Miller 2015), numerous publications by Dr. Sheri Rysdam, including "The Economy of Expressivism and Its Legacy of Low/No-Stakes Writing," forthcoming in *Critical Expressivist Practices in the College Writing Classroom* (Rysdam 2015) and "From Cruel to Collegial: Developing a Professional Ethic in Peer Response to Student Writing," co-authored with Lisa Johnson-Shull, in *Peer Pressure, Peer Power: Collaborative Peer Review and Response in the Writing Classroom* (Rysdam and Johnson-Shull 2014).

Perhaps the most directly relevant and effectual scholarship, that which informed radical changes in the department, was research published by Deborah in 2008 on the program itself. Her study *Defining Literacy: How Basic Writers Define and Are Defined by Literacy* (Marrott 2008) ignited what would ultimately amount to radical changes for the Department of Literacies and Composition. Responding to the call for more student-present research in basic writing scholarship, her study examined the ways in which thirty-three pre-core students at UVU defined literacy and how those definitions, in turn, defined them. Findings of the study suggest that the students' definitions of literacy are overwhelmingly consistent with autonomous models of literacy and that this reliance both constrains and makes possible particular subject positions in relation to literacy. The data also shows that students' recollections of teachers' oral and written assessments of their literacy—particularly negative assessments, if not disrupted—contribute to a "thickening" of deficit literacy and educational subjectivities in ways that have dramatic and potentially life-altering consequences. The findings of this study suggest that providing opportunities (through particular kinds of curriculum and interviewing techniques) for students to disrupt some of this thickening process by not only representing but enacting alternate positions may allow them to challenge deficit-ridden descriptions of their own literacies.

Deborah's work provided the necessary stimulus for the radical evolution that has taken place within the program over the last twelve years. As a result of the research, the department sought out an approach to teaching writing that could begin to circumvent the deficit models that characterize so many first-year writing programs. Ultimately, the program adopted the project-model for both courses.

Shortly after this approach to teaching writing was implemented, a small team of researchers including Jacque, Deborah, and Jamie Littlefield, with the support of four undergraduate research assistants, designed and carried out a grounded theory study examining the experiences of students enrolled in these courses. At the heart of this study were three guiding questions:

- What does a project-based approach have to offer students in critical transitions?
- What criterion emerges through this approach, relevant to evaluating student progress in a first-year composition program?
- How does a project-based method improve or enhance student's educational experience in a variety of instructional modes, face-to-face, hybrid, and online?

This work was presented at the 2014 Conference on College Composition and Communication at a panel session titled, "Transformational Ownership: Creating and Navigating Ownership in the Design of a Departmental Online Composition Course" (Preston 2014).

In addition to numerous conference presentations, local, regional, and national, this research on writing space is featured in Jacque's article, "(Project)ing Literacy: Writing to Assemble in a Postcomposition FYW [First-Year Writing] Classroom" (Preston 2015). Jacque's work on "writing as assemblage," posits an approach to writing that moves beyond process and post-process theories of writing to situate writing as a gathering and an integration of multiple literacies, ideas, events, histories, and experiences into one context. For students placed in "basic writing" courses, this approach situates students' acquired literacies, experiences, and histories as assets versus deficits—necessary components in their development as writers. In an effort to promote such pedagogies, Jacque co-sponsored, along with Nancy Mack, a half-day workshop, "Active Support for Radical Pedagogies: The Post-Pedagogical Movement, Project-Based, Multigenre, and Multimodal Approaches" at the Conference on College Composition and Communication in Houston in March 2015. In addition to this work, Jacque's essay, "Disrupting the Pedagogical Imperative to Prepare the 'Underprepared': Reassembling Literacy, Language, and Writing in the FYW Classroom" (Preston 2017) is forthcoming in *Class in the Composition Classroom: Pedagogy and the Working Class*, edited by William Thelin and Genesea Carter.

Finally, Dr. Elena Garcia, an assistant professor in the Department of Literacies and Composition, is currently developing a study to examine how students respond to the program's emphasis on encouraging students to take risks in their writing. Her preliminary research indicates that many students hesitate to take risks in their writing and routinely write within their existing comfort zones. Dr. Garcia's research examines students' fears of failure in the project-based model writing classrooms in the basic writing program, with a particular focus on how methods of assessment contribute to students' reluctance to take risks. In the fall of 2014, Dr. Elena Garcia, Ben Goodwin, Dr. Joshua C. Hilst, and Jacque, presented their work on some of the issues related to "risk taking" in the project-model writing classroom taught in the Department of Literacies and Composition at UVU in a session titled, "Risky Business: Crisis and Consequence in Project-Based Pedagogy," at the *Western States Rhetoric and Literacy Conference* (Garcia et al. 2014)

PEDAGOGICAL AND/OR ADMINISTRATIVE HIGHLIGHTS

There are several highlights in our program:

Philosophy, Theory, and Curriculum

We reject a perspective on "basic writers" that would situate students as culturally deficient and "underprepared." We believe that the most effective way to shift attitudes about who these students are and how first-year writing programs, including basic writing, serve students is to adopt curriculum and pedagogy that rejects any philosophy or theory that regards students' rich and diverse histories, knowledge, skills, and acquired literacies as deficits to learning rather than assets. What is unique about this department and its faculty is expressed in our mission statement—that is, our commitment to "providing opportunities for students to recognize their own oral, written, and visual literacies as relevant to the academic setting and to helping them develop these literacies for the work they will do in the academy, in the workplace, and in their personal lives" (Utah Valley University 2017).

As the number of department faculty who privileged the works of post-process theorists grew, a desire to build curriculum that underscores "language in use" has come to the fore. Increasingly primed by the belief that FYW when treated solely as a service course to the humanities is restrictive and works to the detriment of students, the program seized an opportunity to give students a chance to practice writing outside the traditional pedagogical imperatives to teach essayist literacy. Therefore, in 2012, the program adopted the project-model for our Basic Writing II model syllabus, affording ample opportunity for faculty to take on more concretely, a constructivist approach in developing assignments and daily lessons for the classroom. The syllabi highlighted elements of context that inform writing: author, audience, purpose, genre, and medium. The new syllabi for both courses, Composition and Literacies across the University and Composition and Literacies across Communities, provide opportunities for students to take up their histories, acquired literacies, and experiences and to recognize writing as relevant to the work they do in the workplace, in their personal lives, and across the university. A primary goal in implementing the project-based curriculum is to help students connect and carry forward acquired literacies as a method for negotiating the writing challenges encountered across the university and in the workplace.

This approach to teaching placed at the center of the curriculum a project, rather than the "underprepared student subject" or the traditional academic essay. This project would be researched, designed, and proposed by the individual student because we believe that the project itself is where writing happens. The project:

- asks students to focus on a topic of particular interest to them and establish and identify problems relevant to the topic
- requires initiative by the student and necessitates a variety of research and writing activities, which recursively build on and inform one another
- requires that the student draw on his or her experience and interests and build upon previously acquired knowledge and skill, transferring this knowledge to practice
- results in an end product or deliverable (e.g., formal proposals, videos, short theses, public service announcements, brochures, events, and models)

- includes the possibility for work that often goes on for a considerable length of time, sometimes extending beyond the length of the course and the purview of the current instructor

While the project-model lends itself to any number of curricular designs, at the core is the belief that writing's significance is not its capacity to assess and establish a peculiar kind of proficiency but rather its capacity to make writing relevant to the literacy moments that mark students' lives.

Full- and Part-Time Faculty Support

In addition to an emphasis on supporting students, we are committed to supporting the ongoing professional development of our part-time faculty. In the face of financial and federally mandated constraints regarding part-time employment, we are committed to improving the quality of education our students receive by ensuring that our adjunct faculty receive appropriate professional development training and access to resources.

The Faculty Seminar, brings together full- and part-time faculty once a month for two-hour seminars. These sessions are structured similarly to graduate seminars and conference workshops in that the faculty member appointed to run the seminar chooses readings and designs the course work for the session. While the seminars consist of full- and part-time faculty, members of the part-time faculty are paid for their time. The seminars are largely theoretical or praxis based: focusing on the application of theory to practice. Our aim is to make clear the connections between the philosophical and theoretical underpinnings and the curriculum, department authored textbooks, and model syllabi provided to new and part-time faculty. These seminars provide opportunities for all members of faculty to sit in conversation with one another, flesh out concerns and questions about prescribed outcomes, recommended pedagogy, and assessment. Seminars include visits from guest speakers, discussion, and a variety of activities relevant to the session's focus.

In addition to face-to-face seminars, the program sponsors *Faculty InService Online*, which is an extension of the faculty's monthly InService meeting. This resource is designed to serve instructors at every level, from seasoned writing program administrators to full-time and part-time faculty. This online venue provides faculty opportunity and incentive to infuse their current teaching practices with new assignments, readings, and multimodal methods. Here faculty, both full- and part-time have an opportunity not only to review materials presented at our monthly meetings, to access important documents needed for teaching their courses, and enhance their professional development, but also to access and share lesson plans, assignments, in-class and out-of-class activities as well as a variety of multimodal resources that can be used either online or to supplement face-to-face teaching.

Program Sponsored Textbooks

Recently the department contracted with publishers to develop two textbooks, each tailored to its respective course. Because so much of the material supporting these courses is housed online, and because there is strong emphasis on production and not merely analysis of others' writing, the faculty concurred that the traditional costly textbook did not meet the specific needs of our students and reflected only in part the assemblage/project-based approach that the department has adopted. Therefore, two rhetorics, *Literacies across the University* and *The Write Project: A Concise Rhetoric for the Writing Classroom*, supplement online content and multimedia resources available to faculty (Preston and Hilst 2014).

Rhetorics and Literacies across the University, used in English 0890, walks students through a variety of reading and writing activities, encouraging them to experiment with a range of genres familiar to the university (Garcia 2015). The text is based on students' educational experiences and goals. Students use writing to explore the university they attend. The ultimate goal of this text is to help students develop confidence in their writing and their ability to successfully navigate their university. In an attempt to break away from traditional FYC textbook structures, this text uses student writing as examples and highlights student advice on making it through the course successfully. The text is written with students in mind. It includes diagrams, bold colors, and links to a support and resources website.

The Write Project: A Concise Rhetoric for the Writing Classroom, used in English 1000, introduces students to the concept of "writing as an assemblage" and promotes the notion that students bring to the writing space the necessary equipment for writing—a rich history, acquired literacies, and experience. This text lays the foundation for shifting students' orientation to writing as relevant to the literacy learning moments that occupy their everyday lives and treats writing as contextual, a cultural artifact poised for redistribution and circulation (Preston 2015).

PRIMARY DOCUMENTS (at writingprogramarchitecture.com)

We have provided two primary documents in the online companion, our curriculum document and a video. One way that Literacies and Composition makes accessible and transparent the philosophy and shared curriculum practices supported by the department is to make available to all faculty what we refer to as the "Department Curriculum Document." This document includes the department mission, the philosophy driving curriculum decisions, and a position statement regarding faculty responsibilities to students. The curriculum document was initially authored by the chair, Deborah Marrott, and is updated annually, reflecting changes in philosophy, curriculum practice, assessment procedures as needed based on administrative policy and input from faculty. The document is unique in that it articulates clearly the philosophical disposition that supports pedagogy, policy, and procedure in the Department of Literacies and Composition.

In the Department of Literacies and Composition, instructors take a project-based approach to the teaching and learning of composition. For many students, this approach is entirely new. We've found that most of our students enroll in their composition courses assuming that they will be writing traditional research papers, perhaps taking an argumentative stance on a controversial topic, and with little thought to audience and purpose beyond the immediate course. For this reason, in collaboration with the UVU Office and Teaching and Learning, we've created a video to help students better understand how this course might be different from other English courses they've taken. The video, "A Different Kind of Course," provides students an opportunity to hear from other students what it's like to take the course, how they've grown to see writing as an art, and what it's like to write a well-researched proposal for a real audience in place of a traditional research paper written for their instructor.

WPAS' VOICES

The strength of our program, the innovations and capacity to make decisions directly in service to our students, can in part be attributed to the institutional autonomy and support from our college that we, a small group of writing scholars, routinely experience. We recognize that this autonomy, stemming largely from the origins of the department as part of a technical college devoted to student access, in itself is unique and that it allows us to make decisions outside the political constraints that often accompany programs housed in departments whose faculty's interest and expertise lie elsewhere.

WPAs seeking to build and improve strong programs are reliant on the administration to support innovations. We have found, however, that key to moving a program forward is a willingness to do the hard work to develop working programs and to propose innovations based on the most recent developments and scholarship in the field of basic writing and the larger field of rhetoric and composition. Higher education is data driven; if we want administrators to support changes, we must base our proposals on persuasive data. In addition, the program continues to finds favor with upper level administration and curriculum committees and increasingly garners support, largely, we believe, because we remain committed to the students. The full-time faculty members that make up this program are eight tenure or tenure line instructors who hold doctoral degrees in one of three areas of scholarship: literacy studies, composition theory and pedagogy, and rhetorical theory. Though our research interests vary, all faculty members share a similar commitment to social justice in education and to the students enrolled in these courses.

There is no question that the strength of our program is due in large part to the structure of the program, the opportunities to draw on the expertise and strengths of faculty, opportunities for faculty to engage in creative projects relevant to their research interests and career aspirations, ample compensation for contributions at every turn, and strong support by administration to address the individual needs of faculty members.

Finally, department administrators want to stress the absolute importance of hiring well. UVU puts significant resources and time into careful nation-wide faculty searches. Our salary offers, while not exorbitant, are competitive, and our faculty is welcoming and collegial. Our commitment to social justice in education and autonomy for our students extends to our full-time and adjunct faculty members: we seek to build careers and foster professional growth.

References

Duttagupta, Chitralekha, and Robert J. Miller. 2015. *The Bedford Bibliography for Teachers of Basic Writing*. 4th ed. Boston, MA: Bedford/St. Martins.

Garcia, Elena. 2015. *Rhetorics and Literacies across the University*. New York: Person Education.

Garcia, Elena, Ben Goodwin, Joshua C. Hilst, and Jacque Preson. 2014. "Risky Business: Crisis and Consequence in Project-Based Pedagogy." Presented at the Western States Rhetoric and Literacy Conference, Reno, NV, November.

Marrott, Deborah. 2008. "Defining Literacy: How Basic Writers Define and Are Defined by Literacy." PhD diss., University of Utah Press, Salt Lake City.

Preston, Jacqueline. 2014. "Transformational Ownership: Creating and Navigating Ownership in the Design of a Departmental Online Composition Course." Presented at the Annual Convention of the Conference on College Composition and Communication. Indianapolis, IN, March.

Preston, Jacqueline. 2015. "Project(ing) Literacy: Writing to Assemble in a Postcomposition FYW Classroom." *College Composition and Communication* 67 (1): 35–63.

Preston, Jacqueline. 2017. "Disrupting the Pedagogical Imperative to Prepare the 'Underprepared': Reassembling Literacy, Language, and Writing in the FYW Classroom." In *Class in the Composition Classroom: Pedagogy and the Working Class*, ed. William Thelin and Genesea Carter. Chicago: Chicago Press.

Preston, Jacqueline, and Joshua C. Hilst. 2014. *The Write Project: A Concise Rhetoric for the Writing Classroom*. Southlake, TX: Fountain Head Press.

Rysdam, Sheri. 2015. "The Economy of Expressivism and Its Legacy of Low/No-Stakes Writing." In *Critical Expressivist Practices in the College Writing Classroom*, ed. Roseanne Gatto and Tara Roeder, n.p. Anderson, SC: Parlor Press.

Rysdam, Sheri, and Lisa Johnson-Shull. 2014. "From Cruel to Collegial: Developing a Professional Ethic in Peer Response to Student Writing." In *Peer Pressure, Peer Power: Collaborative Peer Review and Response in the Writing Classroom*, ed. Steven J. Corbett, Michelle LaFrance, and Teagan E. Decker, 159–70. Southlake, TX: Fountainhead Press.

Utah Valley University. 2017. "What Is the Department of Literacies and Composition All About?" http://www.uvu.edu/litcomp/.

PART 4

Writing Centers and Writing Support

20

DUQUESNE UNIVERSITY WRITING CENTER

James P. Purdy

Institution type: Catholic Research University
Location: Pittsburgh, Pennsylvania
Enrollment: 10,000 (approximate)
Year program was founded: 1990 as documented
WPA reports to: Provost
Program funded by: Provost's Office, English Department, and Student Employment Program Federal Work Study
Description of students: Largely from Pennsylvania, West Virginia, and Ohio, but we also enroll students from around the country and internationally.

PROGRAM SNAPSHOT

The University Writing Center at Duquesne provides writing instruction and support for undergraduates, graduate students, staff, and faculty. Consultants help with writing from all disciplines and all stages of students' writing processes. The center also offers workshops, class visits, and instructional support for anyone interested in writing, including instructors wanting to incorporate effective writing pedagogy into their classes. The center's mission is to serve as a space for dialogue about writing and to help make not only better writing projects but also better writers. In short, the center aims to serve and benefit the entire campus community. It has four locations: a main face-to-face location in the McAnulty College and Graduate School of Liberal Arts building, a satellite face-to-face location in the library, a satellite face-to-face location at Duquesne's Italian campus,[1] and an Online Writing Center (WCOnline) that serves distance students.

DOI: 10.7330/9781607326274.c020

WPA'S PROFILE

I became interested in writing center work as an undergraduate English major at Pennsylvania State University (Penn State). I enrolled in English 250: Peer Tutoring in Writing, the training course for peer tutors, which served as my introduction to writing center work and the discipline of writing studies. It was there that I found my disciplinary calling and met Dr. Jon Olson, Penn State's writing center director, whom I was enormously fortunate to have as a mentor. I continued writing center work in graduate school at the University of Illinois at Urbana–Champaign, where I worked as a writing consultant and, eventually, as assistant director at the Writer's Workshop (Illinois' name for its writing center).

After I earned my PhD (in English with a specialization in writing studies), I worked as an assistant professor of English and the University Writing Center director at Bloomsburg University of Pennsylvania, where I'm proud to have expanded that center's services to satellite locations in the library and residence halls as well as to lay the groundwork for converting the writing consultants to paid rather than volunteer positions. In 2008, I started as an assistant professor of English and the University Writing Center director at Duquesne, where I'm pleased to have expanded the center's role in supporting faculty and teaching assistants, particularly those teaching writing-intensive courses; developed additional training opportunities for staff members, including a mentoring program; argued to get the center a standing non-labor budget; and redesigned aspects of the physical and online environments of the center. I also hosted the Pittsburgh Area Regional Writing Centers Conference at Duquesne in 2009.

I continue to be drawn to writing center work because it models not only a pedagogical practice but also a way of being in the world where teaching, writing, and knowledge construction are collaborative; where authority is shared; where peer expertise is respected; and where active, attentive conversation, and listening are valued. Given insightful critiques of theories of social constructionism and collaborative learning (e.g., Myers 1986, Romberger 2007; Trimbur 1989), I find compelling applications of these theories to writing instruction, authorship, and meaning making more generally (e.g., Bruffee 1984; Ede and Lunsford 1990; Harris 1992; Kennedy and Howard 2014; Lunsford 1991). Writing center work remains, I think, their truest manifestation in postsecondary education.

PROGRAM CONCEPTION

The University Writing Center was originally housed in the English Department with the goal of meeting the needs of the students in the university's core curriculum classes, particularly the first-year writing two-course sequence. Since then the Writing Center has expanded its scope to assist with writing from across campus and with the writing needs of the entire campus community, including teachers as well as students and distance as well as on-campus students. Between 1995 and 2005, the Writing Center was directed by advanced graduate students from the English Department who each served a one- or two-year term. A full-time non-tenure track administrator directed the center from fall 2006 to spring 2008. I was hired in fall 2008 as the first tenure-track director of the center (and was tenured in 2014). At the time of my hiring, the Writing Center came under the purview of the Provost's Office rather than the English Department.

The decision to hire a tenure-track director was made, in part, to bring some continuity to the center's administration. It also reflected a desire for the center to expand its mission to support instructors teaching writing-intensive courses across campus—that is, to make it a resource for teachers as well as students—and a faculty member with a background in writing studies seemed well suited to this work. I am a member of the English Department faculty and teach courses within the English Department, though I report directly to the provost in my capacity as writing center director. This transition to a full-time tenure-track director has given the center stable leadership and afforded the pursuit and development of long-term relationships and initiatives. It has also arguably helped to substantiate the university's commitment to writing instruction and belief in the role and value of writing in supporting learning.

POPULATION SERVED

As expressed in our mission statement, the University Writing Center at Duquesne provides writing instruction and support for undergraduates, graduate students, staff, and faculty. The center's trained staff of graduate and undergraduate writing consultants provides one-on-one assistance for writers working on academic papers, professional applications, websites, presentations, and other projects. Consultants, who come largely from the English Department but also other majors across campus, including education (elementary and secondary), history, philosophy, law, and others, help with writing from all disciplines and all stages of students' writing processes. The center serves approximately 1,100 writers, including undergraduate and graduate students, staff, and faculty, through individual consulting sessions each academic year (including summer session), with roughly 90 percent meeting for face-to-face sessions and 10 percent meeting for online sessions. (In 2014–2015, consultants conducted 2,366 one-on-one consulting sessions with 1,061 writers.)

The center also offers workshops, class visits, and instructional support for anyone interested in writing, including instructors wanting to incorporate effective writing pedagogy into their classes. Each year I offer approximately four to five workshops for teachers (faculty, teaching assistants, and instructors) and the assistant director and I (assisted occasionally by senior members of the consultant staff) give roughly twenty-five to thirty-five workshops for students, often to individual classes. In 2014–2015, center staff, including me, gave class presentations and workshops to 1,079 students, faculty, and staff. Example topics for workshops for teachers include Designing Effective Writing Projects, Planning a Writing-Intensive Course, and Responding to Five Common Student Writing Struggles. Example topics for workshops for students include APA Citation and Source Use for Nursing, Writing an Annotated Bibliography for Professional Communication, and Writing Medical School Personal Statements.

FUNDING

As of fiscal year 2014, the Writing Center has a standing non-labor budget of $10,000 annually. Prior to this budget, non-labor funding was ad hoc. This standing budget allows me to know how much money is available for non-labor expenditures, which has proved particularly beneficial in permitting me to replace and purchase computer hardware and software and to improve the physical space of the main location of the center (e.g., to purchase new carpet).

The Writing Center's labor funding is complex and has evolved. The sources of funding as of this writing are presented in table 20.1.

The Provost's Office as of the time of this writing provides funding as outlined in table 20.2. Every fiscal year I submit a proposal to request this labor funding from the Provost's Office.

The complexity of this funding structure is a challenge. For instance, funded first-year MA and PhD students in the English Department work in the center as part of their fellowship, and this number of students can vary slightly each year. So, while I know a sizable cohort of the staff will come from and be funded by the English Department, I am uncertain exactly

Table 20.1. Labor Funding Sources for the University Writing Center

English Department	Salaries for seven to ten graduate student teaching fellows to work at the Writing Center part-time during the academic year
Student Employment Program Federal Work Study	Base pay for five undergraduate consultants (minimum wage, currently $7.25 per hour) to work at the Writing Center part-time during the academic year
Provost's Office	Remaining labor funding

Table 20.2. Labor Funding from the Provost's Office for the University Writing Center

Part-time salaries	Funding for a sixth undergraduate writing consultant to work during the academic year
	Pay increases for the six undergraduate writing consultants (currently $2.00/hour, so the undergraduate consultants earn $9.25/hour)
	Funding for three graduate consultants (with specialties in ESL writing, business writing, and science writing) to provide face-to-face consulting and two graduate consultants (for the Online Writing Center) to provide online consulting during the academic year
	Funding for two students to provide face-to-face consulting, one or two students to provide online consulting, and one student to manage the Writing Modules during the summer
Stipend	Funding for the assistant director to work during the academic year

how many students that will be, and these students work in the center for only one year (unless they start as funded MA students and continue as PhD students, in which case they would work two years non-continuously).

The variability of funding also creates problems with consistency. When I started as director, for instance, the hourly specialty and online graduate consultants all earned different hourly wages, which created undesirable tension on the staff. (Indeed, when I interviewed for the position, this was the concern most shared by the students.) To create parity among positions and to recognize that all positions are valued equally, I argued for the graduate specialty consultants all to earn the same hourly wage. The consultants for the Online Writing Center still earn more as they must be trained in the technology used for consultations and maintain and update that site. But this increased equality has helped staff cohesion.

OPERATIONS

The Writing Center conducts over two thousand consulting sessions annually and operates daily through the cooperation of me (the director),

Table 20.3. Administrative Responsibilities of Writing Center Director Position

Hiring	Hire approximately ten to twelve graduate and undergraduate writing consultants each year (the remaining staff is appointed by the English Department): answer applicant queries, review submitted applications, contact references, and interview position finalists.
Managing	Supervise all staff members, answer questions, provide guidance and mentoring, and observe sessions as needed.
	Manage the center's physical locations and virtual locations: order necessary instructional supplies and reference materials, prepare annual reports, and network with faculty and staff across campus
	Manage the Writing Center's budget: complete monthly expenditure reports and submit annual budget proposals
Advertising	Advertise the Writing Center's services and initiatives through print and digital media
Scheduling	Establish the consulting schedule: coordinate the schedules of all staff members to ensure double coverage of shifts
	Adjust shift coverage as necessary to accommodate consultant absences
	Input schedule and staff information into WCOnline, the center's online scheduling and recording-keeping system
Communicating	Create, implement, and communicate the Writing Center's policies and procedures
	Advise and answer questions of faculty, staff, and TAs regarding writing pedagogy and assignments
	Advise and answer questions of students, both on-campus and distance, regarding the Writing Center's services and policies
Record keeping	Keep statistics on the Writing Center's patronage and session evaluations using Microsoft Excel and WCOnline
Troubleshooting	Troubleshoot technology problems with the center's six desktop and three laptop computers and two Blackboard sites (one for the Writing Center staff and one for the Online Writing Center): fix the technology myself when possible, submit help tickets to Duquesne's Center for Technology Services, and/or WCOnline and follow up with them as necessary, and respond to student and faculty queries by phone and email

the assistant director, and the consulting staff. As University Writing Center director, I oversee an educational entity that serves and supports the entire university community: faculty, staff, graduate students, and undergraduates. Though this is titularly an administrative position, I see and describe my job primarily as teaching.[2] For the administrative component of my work as writing center director, I have the responsibilities outlined in table 20.3.

Approximately twenty undergraduate and graduate students work as writing consultants each semester and four to five work over the summer. In addition to me, staff is comprised as outlined in table 20.4.

Table 20.4. Writing Center Staff Composition

Fall and spring semester	6 undergraduate consultants
	7–10 graduate student consultants (teaching fellows from the English Department)
	5 graduate student "specialty" consultants:
	• Business writing consultant
	• Science writing consultant
	• ESL writing consultant
	• 2 writing consultants for the Online Writing Center (which serves students in distance education programs, primarily nursing and leadership)
	1 assistant director (an advanced graduate student from the English Department)
Summer	2 consultants for face-to-face sessions
	1 consultants for the Online Writing Center
	1 writing modules administrator for the School of Nursing3

The assistant director position, open to advanced PhD students in the English Department, provides valuable pedagogical and administrative experience that helps graduate students become better writers and writing teachers and prepares them for the academic or professional job market. Responsibilities of the assistant director include tutoring writing; assisting with class presentations, workshops, and orientation; managing staff payroll; coordinating print media distribution; and updating the center's online schedule and Blackboard site. The assistant director is encouraged to bring her or his own initiatives, and these have ranged from creation of an assistant director handbook to implementation of a new shift coverage request system to development of a presentation for a national conference.

Undergraduate and graduate specialty consultants come from disciplines across campus to help the center achieve its mission of working with writing from all disciplines. In recent years' applications for these positions have been increasingly competitive, so I have been in the difficult and wonderful position of being able to hire from a pool of strong student writers.

All consultants participate in an orientation prior to working and attend one-hour biweekly professional development meetings for ongoing support and training. Topics for these meetings, for which consultants usually read one to three relevant texts, include the role of the

Writing Center in the university, working with non-native speakers of English, teaching revision, working with writing from unfamiliar disciplines, working with graded writing, directive and nondirective tutoring approaches, working with reluctant writers, and other related topics. Scheduling these meetings is a challenge as there is no class associated with writing center training, so I offer two or three options each week that meetings are held. Regrettably, this arrangement means that the staff is never all together in the same room at the same time, though this arrangement does allow me to hire very capable busy students who would be unable to fit another class into their schedule.

I schedule shifts to have at least double coverage so consultants always have a colleague to consult for assistance and of whom to ask questions. The assistant director has a cubicle in the main location of the Writing Center and is available there during her or his scheduled hours. I have an office on an upper floor of this same building so am readily accessible. Staff members also have my contact information, including office and cell phone, so they can contact me, if necessary. Consultants and I are in frequent email contact.

Duquesne's Gumberg Library also provides the center with space to use for a satellite location, and the School of Nursing actively advertise the center's services as part of its distance education programs.

ASSESSMENT

I assess the center's performance by soliciting feedback from the writers who visit and from the consulting staff. At the conclusion of a session, students complete an evaluation form rating the session on a scale of 1 to 5 (with 5 being the highest) for how effectively it helped them improve their writing. They also indicate which areas of their writing process they worked on, circling from available options, and answer two free response questions: "In what particular ways was the session valuable in improving your writing?" and "What suggestions do you have for improving the services the Writing Center provides?" (This form is adapted for the Online Writing Center and also asks students about the convenience of the session time and ease of use of the technology.) I tabulate these numerical statistics each day and, with the data I describe below, report them in my annual report to the Provost's Office. Workshop participants also complete evaluations at the conclusion of workshops they attend, answering a similar set of questions.

Longitudinal assessment remains a challenge. For instance, the consulting staff and I only know what grades students receive on their academic papers, the effectiveness of their extracurricular documents (e.g., if they received an internship they applied for, if they were invited to an interview), and their success in applying strategies learned in a session, if they report back to us. Anecdotal evidence, however, is positive. Moreover, in 2013–2014, nearly 40 percent of all writers, a percentage consistent with 2012–2013, returned to the center for multiple visits, substantiating the value they found in the assistance they received.

Because the director position involves so much teaching, I also initiated an assessment protocol where the consulting staff completes an evaluation of me each semester. It includes four Likert-scale and several free response questions and is modeled on the evaluation forms students complete for classes. Because writing consultant training, orientation, and professional development meetings do not constitute an official class, however, standard class evaluation forms are unavailable to me to distribute to the staff.

MARKETING/PR

To increase student and faculty awareness of the center, I advertise the Writing Center's services in multiple ways. Print media include bookmarks, brochures, and flyers. Digital media include website announcements and emails, which I send to all students and all faculty at the beginning and end of each semester. I also advertise with slides broadcasted on TVs in the student union and the academic building where the center is physically located as well as on the Facebook page I created for the center, which the assistant director and I update. This past year, I worked with Duquesne Public Affairs to create a brief video explaining the center. This video is now available on the center's website and on YouTube. Finally, the staff and I visit classes to give brief presentations introducing students to the Writing Center and answering their questions about the center. I consider these face-to-face interactions crucial components of the Center's marketing efforts.

Students and faculty, as a result, are able to learn about the Writing Center in a variety of ways. However, I still struggle to reach all the constituencies the center serves. Students and faculty still sometimes have misconceptions about the Writing Center.

TECHNOLOGY

Digital and print technologies play an integral role in the Writing Center. In terms of day-to-day operations, the center uses an online record-keeping and scheduling system, WCOnline. This service allows for managing the daily tutoring schedule, compiling session statistics, and generating reports. The center has a website, which hyperlinks to WCOnline for students to schedule appointments and authenticates through the university's larger portal. The website also advertises the center's hours, describes the center's services, provides links to PDF and online instructional resources, offers instructions for applying for position vacancies, and provides brief bios of the current staff. The center's main location has six desktop computers and three laptops for use during sessions. Students and consultants often bring their own laptops to the center. The center, of course, also relies substantially on print technology. It has a library of instructional texts, including reference books and citation manuals, and handouts.

As of this writing, the Online Writing Center uses Blackboard Collaborate[4] to replicate desired aspects of face-to-face sessions (e.g., synchronous dialogue, simultaneous document viewing) and to capitalize on digital affordances (e.g., text chat, session recording, virtual sessions). I also have a Blackboard site for the Writing Center's staff through which I make announcements and post the professional development meeting schedule, topics, and links to readings.

More broadly, I take seriously calls for writing centers to be equipped to assist students with writing in all of its multimodal and multimedia forms. David Sheridan (2006), for instance, individually, with James Inman (Sheridan and Inman 2010), and with Valerie Balester et al. (2012) argues persuasively that digital technologies play an important role in positioning writing centers as "multiliteracy centers," and Rusty Carpenter (2009) advocates for the use of digital technologies for multimodal consultations (see also Lee and Carpenter 2014). I agree.

Creating and providing feedback on multimodal, multimedia, and hybrid texts in writing centers requires the technologies that support them. Writing centers without up-to-date computers, therefore, position themselves as offering assistance with exclusively print texts, thereby assuming a (limited) print-based identity. Print texts continue to comprise a crucial component of the writing brought to writing centers, including Duquesne's Writing Center, but they are not—and should not be—the only kinds of texts for which writing centers can provide assistance. A key to establishing the relevance of writing centers for the future—particularly in an era of significant budget cuts—is establishing that writing centers work with multiple kinds of texts, writers, and writing tasks, that they, in other words, accommodate and respond to students' writing practices, teachers' pedagogies, and scholars' research.

To work to accomplish these goals at Duquesne, in the last several years, I purchased additional laptops and specialized software for the center. In particular, the center currently has a subscription to Adobe Creative Cloud to accommodate students working on multimedia and multimodal texts and has ZoomText and Dragon Naturally Speaking to accommodate students with different learning needs.

ROLE OF RESEARCH

Research has served as an important part of the center's administration. My research on digital writing and research practices[5] impacts and has relevance for the work I do as director, though, prior to this chapter, I have not published explicitly about Duquesne's Writing Center. Ann N. Amicucci, the previous director, published about Duquesne's Online Writing Center for Nursing in the book chapter "Writing across the Web: Connecting the Writing Center to Nursing Distance Learners" in *Before and After the Tutorial: Writing Centers and Institutional Relationships* (Amicucci 2011). To pursue her interest in writing center work and scholarship, former assistant director Lee Ann Glowzenski became associate development editor of *The Writing Lab Newsletter*, where she works on social media initiatives.

The consulting staff also conducts research. Over the years, consultants have presented on their writing center work at writing center conferences, including the International Writing Centers Association, National Conference on Peer Tutoring in Writing, and East Central Writing Centers Association. Two undergraduate consultants, Melissa Unger and Jacqueline Weaver, published in *Southern Discourse* their research, "The Role of the Undergraduate Writing Center Consultant: Creating the 'Third Space'" (Unger and Weaver 2013), which they developed from a presentation at the Pittsburgh Area Regional Writing Center Conference. More recently, undergraduate consultant Emily Lamielle (2014) conducted an IRB-approved study, "An Examination of First-Year Students' Procrastination and the Role of the Writing Center," which I advised. She presented the results of her research at Duquesne's undergraduate research fair in 2014. I also advised graduate consultant Allison Keene on her IRB-approved study "The Absent Instructor: Translating Instructor Language in the Writing Center Session" (Keene 2015), which she presented at the International Writing Centers Association Conference in 2015.

Taken together, these publications, presentations, and accomplishments show center administration and staff to be invested in pursuing and sharing writing center research.

PEDAGOGICAL AND/OR ADMINISTRATIVE HIGHLIGHTS

Highlights of the Writing Center's work encompass assessment feedback and realized initiatives. In regards to assessment feedback, I am pleased that the Writing Center's patronage has increased five of the last six years. This steady growth shows increasing numbers of writers are finding value in visiting the Writing Center. I am also proud that in 2013–2014 approximately 99 percent of consulting sessions earned a satisfaction rating of 5 or 4 (on a 5-point scale), and workshop presentations earned an average rating of 4.70 (on a 5-point scale). This data evidences a consistent standard of excellence in writing instruction provided by the Writing Center.

Initiatives realized include enhanced staff training, instructor support, and community outreach. In the last two years, with the support and at the suggestion of the consultants, I implemented a mentoring initiative where experienced consultants observe and are observed by new consultants. This approach applies to staff training the peer tutoring model that guides consulting sessions. I also now provide ongoing support for writing across the curriculum/writing in the disciplines by hosting syllabus-planning workshops each semester for instructors of writing-intensive courses. These workshops provide teachers the opportunity to get hands-on assistance in developing their syllabus and course materials. Faculty and graduate students leave with an outline of the schedule of writing projects and tasks for their "W" course.

In terms of community outreach, this past semester the center hosted writing "coaches" from a local middle school writing center. Duquesne consultants conducted mini-consultations with the coaches—using writable glass table tops in one of Duquesne's new "FlexTech" classrooms—and answering their questions about approaching challenging sessions and working at a college-level writing center.

Future initiatives include further work in the areas of instructor support and community outreach and continued attention to the center's physical space:

—Increasing community engagement through piloting a community-based satellite location and working with local secondary schools

—Pursuing funding for a "digital and multimedia writing" specialist consultant to assist students with digital and multimedia writing tasks

—Providing focused writing support for writing-intensive classes, for example, by having "writing fellows" from the Writing Center connected to particular courses

—Incorporating more writeable spaces into the center (e.g., through glass table tops and whiteboards).

PRIMARY DOCUMENT (at **writingprogramarchitecture.com**)

A document that has been important to our program is the evaluation form I developed so that tutors could evaluate my performance as the director. Prior to my becoming director of the University Writing Center at Duquesne, the director was not formally evaluated by the staff members. To get feedback from consultants—as well as to explicitly frame my work as director as teaching—I instituted an evaluation that consultants complete each semester. Standard course evaluations were not available to me because consultants are not required to take a class. However, gathering assessment data to document the teaching that happens internally with the staff (not just externally to writers who visit the center) as well as to solicit consultants' feedback and ideas was critical.

WPA'S VOICE

Being a writing center director has been particularly rewarding for me in providing opportunities to work with students in a non-graded context. This situation allows for a different kind of relationship with students, where they are focused on performing job responsibilities well (rather than earning a grade) and are more willing to take risks (e.g., with teaching strategies, writing center projects). I am often surprised by the amount of work consultants willingly put into their non-graded work. The chance to work with students in such a context can be rare for higher education professionals, which makes writing center work special.

Writing centers likewise offer a unique opportunity for students to receive individualized writing instruction from a peer. They play a crucial role in supporting writing instruction across the university and in retaining students. Writing center work matters. A writing center director is therefore in a position to remind (or evangelize to) administrators about these reasons why writing centers deserve and require funding. Administrators must make difficult decisions about funding priorities, and it is important to help them realize why writing centers merit support rather than assume that these reasons are evident. For instance, I provide in my annual report summaries of students' evaluations of consulting sessions, teachers' and students' evaluations of workshops, and staff members' evaluations of their writing center positions. This data helps to illustrate what these constituencies learn about writing and how to teach it and how these skills are transferable to their current and future professional pursuits. I also make explicit the center's role in supporting students taking first-year writing courses and other required core classes.

In addition, I also reinforce the range of students, across discipline and year, who visit the center. I have found benefit, in other words, in making clear that the Writing Center supports students in meeting a university-wide requirement and assists students, from first-year students to graduate students, from across campus throughout their educational careers. I have been in the fortunate position of having a supportive administration, so I have not faced the difficult situations of some of my colleagues (e.g., Hamel-Brown et al. 2016), but I believe reiterating with data the educational purpose and benefits of a writing center helps maintain administrative support.

In addition to these rewarding aspects of writing center work, there are logistical aspects for writing center directors to consider regarding their own professional situations. First, a split reporting structure (e.g., reporting to the department chair for some duties and the provost or dean for others) is not unusual, so clarity in terms of performance reviews is important. Similarly, for tenure and promotion, it is important to emphasize the teaching components of writing center director work, which can include staff training, workshops, and professional development. Otherwise, this administrative position may not "count" toward tenure and promotion. Christina Murphy and Byron L. Stay's excellent *The Writing Center Director's Resource Book* provides helpful examples of writing center directors articulating the intellectual and pedagogical work of their positions (Murphy and Stay 2006).

Notes

1. This face-to-face location at the Italian campus was temporary, made possible by a staff member studying there. If a staff member studies abroad there again in the future, I may be able to revisit this face-to-face location. Otherwise, plans are to support this campus with the Online Writing Center.

2. In addition to teaching the Writing Center's staff through orientation and professional development meetings and conducting faculty and student workshops, I teach in the English Department. As a research-active faculty member with administrative course release, I teach one course each semester. My writing center work would take as much time as I give it, so I have to be conscious of balancing all of my responsibilities, allotting time to my research and departmental teaching activities. The beginning and end of the semester are when I am busiest with writing center work, so I take care to plan ahead accordingly. Both as writing center director and as a classroom instructor, I see myself doing the same kind of teaching: I instruct consultants, students, and other faculty members with the goal of fostering better writing at the university—and beyond. The training I provide the consulting staff carries over into the writing instruction the center's student clientele receives. I also instruct teachers in disciplines across campus in how to teach process-based writing, integrate digital technologies into their courses as instructional tools, and use writing as a means to help students learn material rather than just to demonstrate knowledge.

3.   The writing modules are a Blackboard site with writing lessons, activities, and tests that graduate nursing students are required to take and pass. Modules address topics such as avoiding plagiarism, using the library and choosing sources, using APA style, writing a literature review, and writing an article abstract. Each module includes several steps with videos of narrated PowerPoint presentations. The administrator sets up and, if necessary, revises the modules; responds to student inquiries about the modules; provides students feedback on the writing they complete for the modules; and communicates nursing students' completion of the modules with the faculty members teaching the summer courses for the Master of Science in Nursing (MSN), Doctor of Nursing Practice (DNP), and PhD programs.

4.   The university has now replaced Blackboard Collaborate with GoToMeeting.

5.   To stay current, I also do research regarding consulting best practices and the operations of local and peer writing centers and regularly update the center's library of reference materials to reflect this research. Readings for professional development meetings, moreover, are drawn from writing center scholarship.

References

Amicucci, Ann N. 2011. "Writing across the Web: Connecting the Writing Center to Nursing Distance Learners." In *Before and after the Tutorial: Writing Centers and Institutional Relationships*, ed. Nicholas Mauriello, William. J. Macauley Jr., and Robert T. Koch Jr., 65–74. Cresskill, NJ: Hampton Press.

Balester, Valerie, Nancy Grimm, Jackie Grutsch McKinney, Sohui Lee, David M. Sheridan, and Naomi Silver. 2012. "The Idea of a Multiliteracy Center: Six Responses. *Praxis: A Writing Center Journal* 9 (2): 1–10.

Bruffee, Kenneth A. 1984. "Collaborative Learning and 'The Conversation of Mankind.'" *College English* 46 (7): 635–652. http://dx.doi.org/10.2307/376924.

Carpenter, Rusty. 2009. "Writing Center Dynamics: Coordinating Multimodal Consultations: The UWC's Multimodal Consultations." *Writing Lab Newsletter* 33 (6): 11–15.

Ede, Lisa, and Andrea Lunsford. 1990. *Singular Texts/Plural Authors: Perspectives on Collaborative Writing*. Carbondale: Southern Illinois University Press.

Hamel-Brown, Christine, Amanda Fields, Celeste Del Russo, and Marisa Sandoval. 2016. "Activist Mapping: (Re)framing Narratives about Writing Center Space." Chap. 9 in *Making Space: Writing Instruction, Infrastructure and Multiliteracies*, ed. James P. Purdy and Dànielle Nicole DeVoss. Ann Arbor: University of Michigan Press.

Harris, Muriel, and the Peer-Response Groups. 1992. "Collaboration Is Not Collaboration Is Not Collaboration: Writing Center Tutorials vs. Peer-Response Groups." *College Composition and Communication* 43 (3): 369–383. http://dx.doi.org/10.2307/358228.

Keene, Allison. 2015. "The Absent Instructor: Translating Instructor Language in the Writing Center Session." Presented at the *International Writing Centers Association Conference*, Pittsburgh, PA, October 8.

Kennedy, Krista, and Rebecca Moore Howard. 2014. "Collaborative Writing: Print to Digital." In *A Guide to Composition Pedagogies*, 2nd ed., ed. Gary Tate, Amy Rupiper Taggart, Kurt Schick, and H. Brooke Hessler, 37–54. New York: Oxford University Press.

Lamielle, Emily. 2014. "An Examination of First-Year Students' Procrastination and the Role of the Writing Center." Presented at *the Duquesne University Undergraduate Research Fair*, Pittsburgh, PA, April 9.

Lee, Sohui, and Russell Carpenter, eds. 2014. *The Routledge Reader on Writing Centers and New Media*. New York: Routledge.

Lunsford, Andrea. 1991. "Collaboration, Control, and the Idea of a Writing Center." *Writing Center Journal* 12 (1): 3–10.

Murphy, Christina, and Byron L. Stay, eds. 2006. *The Writing Center Director's Resource Book.* Mahwah, NJ: Lawrence Erlbaum.

Myers, Greg. 1986. "Reality, Consensus, and Reform in the Rhetoric of Composition Teaching." *College English* 48 (2): 154–171. http://dx.doi.org/10.2307/377298.

Romberger, Julia E. 2007. "An Ecofeminist Methodology." In *Digital Writing Research: Technologies, Methodologies, and Ethical Issues,* ed. Heidi McKee and Dànielle Nicole DeVoss, 249–267. Cresskill, NJ: Hampton Press.

Sheridan, David. 2006. "Words, Images, Sounds: Writing Centers as Multiliteracy Centers." In *The Writing Center Director's Resource Book,* ed. Christina Murphy and Byron Stay, 339–350. Mahwah, NJ: Erlbaum.

Sheridan, David, and James Inman, eds. 2010. *Multiliteracy Centers: Writing Center Work, New Media, and Multimodal Rhetoric.* Cresskill, NJ: Hampton Press.

Trimbur, John. 1989. "Consensus and Difference in Collaborative Learning." *College English* 51 (6): 602–616. http://dx.doi.org/10.2307/377955.

Unger, Melissa, and Jacqueline Weaver. 2013. "The Role of the Undergraduate Writing Center Consultant: Creating the 'Third Space'." *Southern Discourse* 17 (2): 8–9.

21

INDIANA UNIVERSITY OF PENNSYLVANIA KATHLEEN JONES WHITE WRITING CENTER

Leigh Ann Dunning and Ben Rafoth

Wendy Bishop earned her PhD at Indiana University of Pennsylvania (IUP). She embraced her colleagues like family. Before her death in 2003, Bishop would become the Kellogg W. Hunt distinguished professor of English at Florida State University, chair the Conference on College Composition and Communication, and publish twenty-two books and numerous articles. We dedicate this chapter to Wendy's memory.

Institution type: Public Research University

Location: Indiana, Pennsylvania

Enrollment: 14,000+

Year program was founded: mid-1970s

WPA reports to: Dean of College of Humanities and Social Sciences

Program funded by: College of Humanities and Social Sciences, Jones White Endowment

Description of students: The students who attend IUP come mostly from small towns and rural communities in western Pennsylvania or from the urban areas of Pittsburgh, Harrisburg, and Erie. Many of these students are the first of their families to attend college, but many students also come to IUP from across the state; about 7 percent of the university's student body are international students.

PROGRAM SNAPSHOT

The Kathleen Jones White Writing Center is under the College of Humanities and Social Sciences and is available to undergraduate and graduate students, faculty, and staff university-wide. Many of our writing workshops are aimed at students in required writing courses, while our tutoring sessions span all levels and disciplines.

DOI: 10.7330/9781607326274.c021

WPAS' PROFILES

Ben

After earning my master's in linguistics and doctorate in language education, my first job out of graduate school was in the Department of Speech
Communication at the University of Illinois Urbana–Champaign. I took
over the coordination of Verbal Communication, a required two-course
sequence that focused on speaking in the first semester and writing in
the second. I was an adjunct professor and younger than many of the
teaching assistants and temporary faculty who taught the course. Three
years later, I was at IUP in a tenure-track job in the English Department
and co-directing the writing center. I intended to stay in the writing center for a year and then find someone else to take over the position. That
was twenty-eight years ago.

It was not always clear to me how I could make a career and earn tenure by focusing on writing center work. I had worked hard on my dissertation topic (audience and writing), and I felt I should focus on that
instead of diving into a new subfield. And when I attended my first writing center conference, everyone seemed to know one another while I
knew hardly anyone except my own tutors. By the second year, though, a
colleague at IUP, Lea Masiello, and at Pennsylvania State University, Jon
Olson, reached out to me, and I became more involved in regional and
national writing center organizations. Attending the conferences, especially the business meetings, helped me to see how others were developing their professional identities, and they helped me to figure one out
for myself. I saw that writing center directors were publishing and presenting with their tutors, hosting conferences, and building professional
networks. Today, as one of IUP's awarded Distinguished University
Professors and a teacher in the graduate program in Composition and
TESOL (C&T), I have the opportunity to advise and mentor undergraduate and graduate students, including my assistant director and members of our staff of twenty-five to thirty peer tutors.

Leigh Ann

I enrolled in the tutor preparation course at Elon University during my
undergraduate coursework mostly because it fulfilled a requirement for
both my journalism and English majors. However, as the semester pro-
gressed, I realized that this class would end up being one of the most
rewarding of my undergraduate career. I spent time volunteering in
the writing center and facilitating the relationship between students
and their papers while, simultaneously, I learned more about my own

writing. As a writing center consultant, I felt like I had a greater involvement in my academic community because I wasn't just thinking about the writing I had to turn in for class, I was responsible for supporting my peers with their writing. Many consultants at the writing center worked overtime because we felt like we were useful and we were making an impact on our university. I ended up spending the next couple of years tutoring and heading up the writing center marketing campaign, which nicely tied my two majors together.

This experience helped me to earn a graduate assistantship as the assistant director of the Jones White Writing Center my first year as a doctoral student in the C&T program. My hands-on experience as the assistant director re-inspired my love for writing centers. During my C&T coursework and, now, as I work on my dissertation, I keep returning to the writing center to study and do research. One of my favorite aspects of the writing center field is the opportunity for undergraduate tutors to participate in and add to the larger writing center conversation. During my second year as the assistant director of the Jones White Writing Center, I mentored twelve tutors through the process of writing proposals and presenting at regional, national, and international conferences. For most of them, this was their first time presenting at an academic conference and the experience provided them many opportunities for personal, professional, and academic growth. As I sat in the audience watching them give their presentations, I realized that I wanted to anchor my career in writing centers studies.

In fall 2015, I began a full-time position as the Writing Center director and assistant director of the Writing Program at Stetson University.

PROGRAM CONCEPTION

The Jones White Writing Center began in the mid-1970s and was co-directed by two faculty members; Ben took over in 1988. The university's first public computer lab had just been installed in the writing center. Co-director Lea Masiello was a mentor to Ben, and together Ben and Lea co-hosted the National Conference on Peer Tutoring in Writing in 1992. Wendy Bishop delivered the keynote address on the conference theme, "All About Talk." At the time, she was the writing center director at the University of Alaska and spoke passionately about the transformative effects of conversations among peers. She energized everyone in the auditorium, but for Ben, her keynote had a particular impact. It helped him to frame many questions and possibilities surrounding tutoring that he could explore as a writing center director, researcher, and teacher.

The university's writing center has long been a busy place that benefits from an influx of new ideas and talent from the graduate programs. In the 1990s, tutors taking courses and doing research in conversational interaction, language and gender, second language writing, and think-aloud protocols gave the center a laboratory feel, something that persists to the present. Having a large computer lab meant that the center was a good place to bring classes, teach workshops, and experiment with ways to collect contact data, use dot matrix printers, make banners, and explore a cutting-edge technology called "email attachments." When the center began using email attachments for online tutoring, several of us worried the trend would catch on so quickly that we would be overwhelmed with work. Jennifer Ritter, a doctoral student at the time, paved the way for a grant, and within the next twelve months, tutors conducted over nine hundred online sessions and could work as many hours as they wanted, for minimum wage. The grant ran out and the online writing center waned, but never completely disappeared. A decade and a half later, two other graduate students, Brian Fallon and Lindsay Sabatino, redesigned the online platform using Google Docs and Google Calendar. In the last few years, Emily Weber, an undergraduate tutor, and Leigh Ann took the online writing center to a new level with an improved, real-time platform using Cisco's WebEx, an appointment program named Setmore, and a report-generator called JotForm.

The university's graduate programs have also been a draw for multilingual teachers and tutors from around the globe who have shared their culture, education, and language experiences with the center. Most recently, for example, one of our graduate tutors from Japan developed and taught a unit about second language writers' writing anxieties. Another tutor shared her unique insights and experiences working with Ghanaian students. Currently, one of our tutors is studying our writing center so he can start his own in Afghanistan.

The writing center has benefitted from relationships with various undergraduate programs too, including English, English education, and journalism, in which many of our tutors major. Tutors can pursue their passions at the writing center. For example, we have formed a communications team that creates a distinctive profile for the writing center in social media, campus news, and print media.

POPULATION SERVED

The Jones White Writing Center serves the university writing community, working with writers on diverse assignments and personal writing, at all levels, throughout the composing process. For example, a tutor might help a first-year student focus their thesis for an argumentative essay during one session and then work with a graduate student to organize their thesis proposal during the next session. Although in most cases graduate students request graduate tutors, because of availability and other logistical restraints we often see graduate students engage in successful sessions with undergraduate tutors and vice versa.

Our tutors must also be prepared to work with multilingual writers. Approximately one-third of our clients are international students; they often visit on a daily basis. The Office of International Education provides significant funding each year to help us hire tutors to work with international students. Many of these students choose IUP because the writing center is highlighted in the university's admissions information as a resource where students can receive one-on-one support with their writing. The American Language Institute, which provides intensive English instruction for international students and visitors, is located next to the writing center, and its close proximity fosters frequent contact between their students and our tutors. Writing center tutors work with students who use multiple Englishes and whose proficiency ranges from limited to very advanced.

Because of the blend of composition, TESOL, and applied linguistics within our graduate programs, many of our faculty and students' research interests emerge from or intersect with experiences in the writing center. International students and visiting scholars who come to the center can be an inspiration for tutors who wish to teach or study overseas. For example, this year our tutors have taught or tutored in South Korea, Taiwan, Japan, and Thailand.

FUNDING

The budget for the center is approximately $40,000 per year, nearly all of it designated for tutor wages. These funds come from the College of Humanities and Social Sciences. The director's 50 percent teaching load reduction, the assistant director's graduate assistantship, computer upgrades, and IT services are funded by the university's Academic Division. As a public university, IUP must follow strict guidelines for expenditures: buying food is generally not allowed, for example, although support for travel is generally approved. The director's annual contribution to the university's foundation, along with donations from other contributors, helps to fund snacks for staff meetings, some travel, and other incidental expenses. A large gift created a generous endowment for the center, providing funds for a variety of purposes, including research, staff development, travel, and writing awards. A dedication ceremony to rename the center and celebrate the legacy of our new namesake was held in the fall of 2015.

How did we manage to obtain an endowment? Reputation and luck helped. Our writing center enjoys a relatively high profile on campus—something we work hard to maintain. When a donor expressed an interested in writing, staff in the Advancement Office thought of the writing center. In addition, when the donor visited the writing center prior to making a commitment, a small group of tutors gave a very impressive presentation about their work and research. Luck played a role, too. Before the donor became interested in supporting writing, he visited campus and was shown various naming options, like a garden, auditorium, and building, but there was no spark. In an off-hand remark, he referred to his late wife as a writer, and he soon warmed to the idea of helping students become better writers. Then he visited the writing center, and eventually decided to fund an endowment to support tutor education and travel, writing awards, and other writing-center based efforts.

OPERATIONS

Our staff comprises of a diverse group of twenty-nine undergraduate and graduate tutors from disciplines across the university. We are also fortunate to have retired English professors, graduate students, and individuals from the Indiana community who volunteer in the center. In 2013, we hired a secretary to create schedules, maintain usage reports, and provide support to the director and assistant director. Our two most recent secretaries have been former tutors. Ben has a dual appointment in the writing center and the English Department. He teaches one class each semester for the C&T doctoral program. As a team, the director and assistant director work together to educate the tutors, develop programs, and manage resources.

Each year the writing center provides over four thousand one-on-one tutoring sessions in the main center, and several hundred more online and at our satellite center in the library. Much of the work in the IUP writing center is done collaboratively with tutors, like staff education, workshops, publicity, and outreach. With so much tutoring occurring every day, it is a challenge to keep up, stay organized, and remain open to new possibilities.

Tutors arrive at 9:00 AM, when the center opens. Tutees arrive soon and are sometimes waiting at the door before we open. Except for the

Online Writing Center, we do not offer appointments and all sessions are handled first come, first serve. When a tutee arrives, he or she signs in at the reception station and may wait for a tutor on one of our chairs or couches. We have magazines and the university newspaper for students to read, as well as an interactive bulletin board to have fun with while they wait. For example, one spring semester we featured a community Scrabble board where tutors and tutees could show off their word making skills by picking letters, creating words, and posting them on the wall. We also have forty-seven networked computers for students to use, as well as color and laser printers and a scanner. Our paper handling station has a paper cutter, hole punch, stapler, correction tape, and a stuffed animal, for when nothing's going your way.

During each session, the tutor asks the tutee if he or she would like a faculty report emailed to their professor (and a copy for themselves). This JotForm electronic document is written by the tutor and tutee. It tells the professor what they worked on in the session. At the end of the session, the tutee completes an evaluation of the session and a copy is saved with our internal records.

In theory, the director handles hiring, budgets, payroll, and some operations, while the assistant director coordinates workshops, faculty reports, and special projects, and the secretary provides support to both directors. Typically, however, these responsibilities merge, overlap, and cross over. We collaborate well together, but we also keep tabs on one another. To facilitate this, our secretary puts our tasks and projects on an app called Trello, an electronic to-do list, and we use Slack to communicate among the directors and secretary.

Together, we respond to the day-to-day concerns, questions, and victories of our tutors. One major task is helping students deal with their emotional responses to tutoring as well as establishing a rapport with tutees who may be resistant or struggling. We have found that it is important to provide a space for tutors to talk with us about their daily challenges and because of this we have an open-door policy with our tutors. In addition to working openly, we also tutor and spend time in the center with our tutors so that they are comfortable coming to us with challenges, academic or personal, that they may be experiencing. Leigh Ann introduced an electronic tutoring journal where tutors can contribute their thoughts and read about the experiences of other tutors. We invite tutors to talk to each other about what seems to work in sessions and to help each other with their writing. It is encouraging to see tutors engage in a tutoring session with another tutor.

ASSESSMENT

In 2011, the Center for Educational and Program Evaluation (CEPE) at IUP looked at students using the writing center, the tutors employed here, and faculty members who referred students to the center for help. Their report confirmed that students who used the writing center perceived it to be effective in improving their writing. An encouraging 81 percent of professors believed that students do better on their papers when they visit the writing center. However, the evaluators did find that tutors were not consistent about following up at the end of the session to plan the tutee's next steps. This is something Ben had repeatedly asked tutors to do, and the report found it wasn't happening nearly as much as it should. About 48 percent of tutors reported that they did not plan the next step of the paper with the student at the end of the session. As a result of this report, recent staff-training sessions have focused on this important step in every tutoring session.

We also conduct in-house assessments. For every session, tutees use JotForm to record intake data, collect the writer's evaluation of the session, and provide a report to the instructor. JotForm has allowed us to go paperless. The information is easily routed to instructors and students, and it is downloadable to Excel for our internal recordkeeping. For example, we sort sessions by department so that we can determine where our students are coming from within the university. This tells us who is, and is not, making use of the writing center across campus. For example, although we promote the writing center to students in all disciplines, a large percentage (about 89% of tutorials in a recent spring semester) of all visits were related to required general education writing courses. Most general education writing courses are offered by the English Department, but they are taken by all students in the university.

Before Bryna Siegel Finer came to IUP and created a writing across the curriculum (WAC) program, the writing center was the go-to place for a wide variety of concerns faculty had about writing assignments, assessments, pedagogies, and plagiarism. For example, Leigh Ann visited a senior seminar class in the Food and Nutrition department to discuss how to write personal statements when applying for internships and graduate school. We also assisted with writing in a political science class. It was difficult to respond to the many faculty requests for one-on-one meetings and presentations for their classes. With the new WAC director, however, we are able to refer faculty to her office and focus more on students' writing concerns. Our relationship with the WAC program continues to become stronger as we find ways of supporting each other. The WAC director performs an annual survey of graduating seniors on their writing experiences across their time at IUP, which includes questions about using the writing center. She also surveys faculty on how they teach writing. This type of data is helpful to us in the writing center to assess our success across the university.

MARKETING/PR

Two years ago we decided that in order to sustain a consistent marketing plan for the writing center, we needed to create a communications manager position. At this time we had a tutor on staff who, as an undergraduate double major in journalism and English, was especially interested in marketing and social media. In her new position, she worked ten hours a week on the marketing campaign. She also tutored a couple of hours each week. Since creating this position, we have increased the number of tutoring sessions and attendance at our events by 10–15 percent.

Our tutors introduced a Lunch and Learn series that takes place on the second Friday of each month in the writing center's computer lab. Leigh Ann and the communications manager reached out to the IUP community to find interesting topics related to writing. For example, one semester our series included:

- a presentation on how to market oneself for internships, graduate school and jobs
- a discussion about using comic books and graphic novels in education
- a workshop on how improvisation comedy can generate ideas for writing
- a workshop on creating resumes and curriculum vitas

We promote these events to all departments through flyers, our Facebook page, Twitter, our website, and the university's online daily news bulletin that is emailed to all students, faculty, and staff. A major problem with this, as it is a new endeavor, is finding a diverse range of community members to lead presentations. One reason for this difficulty may be that other departments do not always see how these topics connect to writing. As the Lunch and Learn presentations become more widely recognized around campus it may become easier, through word of mouth, to find people interested in leading discussions. In the spring 2013, we organized focus groups and began collecting data on how we could attract more students to our events. We received helpful feedback from students who suggested that we target specific departments and organizations on campus that incorporate genres of writing other than creative writing and research writing, such as writing for business, natural sciences, and health and human services programs. This helpful feedback was implemented over the next couple of semesters.

The writing center website can be a helpful resource for students and faculty. The center's communication manager keeps the site fresh with frequent updates. On the website there is also a link to schedule appointments for synchronous Online Writing Center tutorials. Recently we created and uploaded a video via YouTube that gives step-by-step instructions for how to schedule and join an Online Writing Center tutorial. The video has proven to be a great way to raise awareness of the Online Writing Center and show how easy it is to use WebEx, our platform for online tutoring.

Our center's presence on Facebook and Twitter is updated every couple of days to reflect what is going on in the center. On our Facebook page we also "spotlight" tutees who visit regularly. For this, a tutor chooses a tutee they feel has benefited from tutoring, and after obtaining the tutee's permission, interviews them briefly about their experiences and takes their picture. This is a great way to connect students to the Facebook page because many students like to see their pictures on Facebook and it serves to demonstrate our mission and services to others linked to our page. The trick is keeping the Facebook page interactive with students. We continue to explore new ways to get students to comment, like, or share our posts.

TECHNOLOGY

In addition to the technologies related to marketing (discussed above), the Jones White Writing Center is a large space that is home to forty-seven networked computers arranged in two rooms, one of which also houses a multimedia station. This section may be closed or opened to the rest of the writing center depending on our needs. Often, for example, we sponsor workshops and we welcome professors to use our technology for their classes. Professors can sign up on our website for any of our eleven workshops; during their class period a tutor will lead the workshop. These workshops center on writing strategies directly and indirectly, including advanced applications of Microsoft Word and Publisher, Prezi, and Google Scholar. Our "Wednesday Workshops" cover popular topics like documentation, proofreading, and resumes; they are offered weekly at 7:00 PM and are open to anyone who shows up. When the computer room is not being used for workshops, it is a quiet space for students to work with a tutor or individually on their writing.

WebEx, our web conferencing tool, helps students and their tutors connect online for a real-time tutoring session. WebEx allows a student to share their desktop with their tutor so that they can view and edit the paper simultaneously. They can discuss the paper using their computers' microphones and Internet audio. Although WebEx allows for video when both users have computer cameras, we have found audio to be sufficient. To set up an appointment, the student logs in to our website and selects "schedule an appointment on our calendar." This link brings them to another application, Setmore, where they can select available days and times on the calendar menu. Setmore then sends an email to our online writing center coordinator, who then sets up the appointment in WebEx. Our online writing center coordinator oversees the daily operations of the online writing center and keeps things running smoothly. WebEx, Setmore, and our website are almost glitch-free, but whenever students or tutors do have a problem, someone on the staff is available to help.

ROLE OF RESEARCH

Many research studies have taken place in the IUP writing center. Some begin when undergraduates conduct studies, which they then present at regional and national conferences. Graduate students from the C&T program also use the center for their thesis and dissertation research. They often make writing center work their careers. It is encouraging for an assistant director to see the research published by the current IUP alumni in the field. At a recent International Writing Centers Association meeting at CCCC, there were many familiar names and faces of published scholars, many of whom had graduated from our program. As a PhD student working as a graduate assistant, it is often difficult to think past writing a dissertation. However, the writing center assistantship provides its recipients with invaluable professional experience and research opportunities in addition to coursework. In fact, one of the many pieces Ben and graduate assistants have coauthored includes a chapter with Kevin Dvorak, a former assistant director of the university's writing center and past president of the International Writing Centers Association, entitled, "Examining Writing Center Director-Assistant Director Relationships" (Dvorak and Rafoth 2006) in *The Writing Center Director's Resource Book*. The professor-mentor relationship inherent in the writing center assistantship position has historically provided the foundation for successful writing center careers and research.

The directors try to get tutors involved in research and participate in professional organizations. In 2003, several tutors became interested in a new computer program that some institutions, including IUP, had begun using to check student papers for plagiarism. They became concerned when a student came to the writing center holding a paper their professor had submitted to Turnitin. The writer said, "This says I plagiarized my paper and my professor told me to bring it here." The tutors were energized. They researched Turnitin and the company behind it, presented at local and national conferences, and eventually published an article in the *Writing Center Journal* (Brown, Fallon, Lott, Matthews, and Mintie 2007). The article eventually won the IWCA Best Article Award for 2007 and was anthologized.

PEDAGOGICAL AND/OR ADMINISTRATIVE HIGHLIGHTS

Over the years, three principles have been our guiding lights: (1) we work as a team; (2) each person uses his or her best judgment; and (3) we welcome feedback. The first and second principles speak to the necessary tension in every writing center between working collaboratively and individually, and the third offers a check on the first two. In other words, being open to receiving and giving feedback is necessary when individual judgment and collaboration falter. If there is a theoretical perspective that informs these principles, it would probably be collaborative learning (Bruffee 1984) and the emphasis on conversation, although we resist allegiance to any single body of work or perspective. Instead, we find ourselves drawn to theory and research that speaks to our needs and aspirations, and to look beyond our walls to see what we might be missing. This orientation leads us to books that resonate with our experiences and creates discussions among our tutors. A few of the most recent include Rebecca Day Babcock and Terese Thonus's *Researching the Writing Center* (Babcock and Thonus 2012), Chris Thaiss et al.'s (2012) *Writing Programs Worldwide*, and Ilona Leki's (2007) *Undergraduates in a Second Language*.

A lot of our productivity and innovation originates from ideas spurred by tutors. A diverse staff is key for propelling any writing center forward. We hire tutors from a variety of disciplines who come to us with different experiences with, and beliefs about, writing and learning language. The range of expertise and interests that they bring to staff meetings, tutor education, and the day-to-day operations encourages new and better ways of doing things. For example, a couple of years ago, a group of tutors requested that we email professors their faculty report forms instead of mailing hard copy forms in campus mail. The tutors felt that going paperless would allow for quicker response time, neater forms, and a streamlined process for everyone. We decided to try it. One tutor took the lead in training the rest of the staff on the new protocol and provided one-to-one assistance when needed. But as the weeks went on, we found we were misplacing and losing forms outright. Professors called and emailed to say they had not received a report form. After some digging, we realized that the saved report forms were getting deleted or saved over with new forms before being sent out. At the end of the semester we went back to paper forms. But, the tutors continued to push for paperless forms. A year and a half later, we began using JotForm (mentioned earlier). This program creates a form that can be easily accessed and saved. So far, it has been extremely helpful. From this experience and others like it, we have learned two things: (1) let new ideas spring forth, and (2) keep trying. The writing center benefits from the stream of new ideas and energy our staff brings to tutoring, staff meetings, and everyday discussions.

Openness to new ideas not only promotes innovation, but also allows the tutors to cultivate their individual talents. The combination of experience in the center, along with their degrees from IUP, have helped many of our graduates become teachers, writing center directors, writing program administrators, journal editors, authors, and leaders in their field. We encourage tutors to think about their time in the writing center as a way to prepare for their future careers. For example, a tutor studying English education sometimes wants more practice creating lesson plans and teaching in front of a classroom of students. We encourage him or her to create new writing workshops. To do this, the tutor is asked to do research and create a proposal to share with the directors. After their plan is in place, they create a PowerPoint, practice giving the workshop, and finally, present the workshop to classes who visit the center. We also encourage tutors to watch each other's presentations and provide constructive feedback. These presentations infuse new material and incorporate the pedagogical theories and practices our tutors learn about in their classes, continually feeding the cycle of innovation.

PRIMARY DOCUMENT (at writingprogramarchitecture.com)

Safety is a concern at universities worldwide. We have contributed two documents to the online companion that demonstrate our commitment to safety in the writing center. One is a flyer for an event we held on our campus. Staff development reaches a new level when it involves tutors from other schools. One cold February weekend, more than thirty tutors from three nearby universities gathered for the day to discuss the topic, "Writing Centers: How Safe a Space?" College and campus life are often in the news lately, with reports and opinions related to campus safety and security, including debates over trigger warnings, political correctness, microaggressions, tolerance of hate speech, and so forth. Many of these issues relate to writing centers as safe spaces. What do tutors think about these issues? Our emergency procedure bulletin for peer tutors and writing center staff is also important to the security and sustainability of our center. It helps guide our discussions about questions such as, do writing center staff know what to do if there is a tornado warning? If someone in the center suddenly collapses and stops breathing? If there is a report of an active shooter? What should a tutor do if they witness a crime? We go over it in staff meetings and post it where everyone can see it.

WPA'S VOICE

Ben

As I look back at my career in writing centers, I would say that one of the most important pieces of advice for a new WPA or writing center director is to think beyond the writing center or program and become involved in university-wide programs, committees, and activities. Serving in this way for me has meant opportunities to meet and network with administrators, professors, trustees, job candidates, foundation officials, and other people who hold a variety of leadership positions. It has also given me a chance to learn how the university works and discover new avenues to promote the writing center and to connect its mission with the university's. Many of the ways I reach out are familiar to writing center directors—new faculty orientations, assessment projects, and so on. Others are important more for who they involve than for the committee or project itself. When the graduate school was considering reallocating the pool of graduate assistantships across the university, I volunteered to serve on the committee and was able to protect the center's assistantship from being cut. Similarly, when a donor contacted University Advancement about making a gift, a fund-raising officer contacted me and we worked together to enlist the donor's support for the writing center.

This kind of openness extends to our tutors. We encourage tutors to extend a friendly welcome to everyone who visits. Because we operate on a walk-in basis, we ask tutors to greet students at the door and be prepared to explain what we do. We remind our tutors that the writing center is a place staffed by students for students, and students are more likely to thrive and learn when they feel supported and encouraged. We advise our tutors to be especially conscious of the experiences of international students in the writing center.

By keeping the Jones White Writing Center in the spotlight across the IUP community, we have encouraged many faculty and students to reach out for help. There is always a steady demand for teaching students to write well, and I try never to say no. Leigh Ann and I have taught a class for education majors struggling to pass the Praxis test. We've also helped faculty create writing assignments and incorporate peer-review and other collaborative strategies into their classes. Now that IUP has a WAC director, though, we are able to direct faculty to the WAC director, which allows us to focus on helping students directly. This work has helped to give the writing center a positive reputation across campus.

References

Babcock, Rebecca Day, and Terese Thonus. 2012. *Researching the Writing Center.* New York: Peter Lang. http://dx.doi.org/10.3726/978-1-4539-0869-3.

Brown, Renee, Brian Fallon, Jessica Lott, Elizabeth Matthews, and Elizabeth Mintie. 2007. "Taking on Turnitin: Tutors Advocating Change." *Writing Center Journal* 27 (1): 7–29.

Bruffee, Kenneth. 1984. *Collaborative Learning.* 2nd ed. Baltimore: Johns Hopkins.

Dvorak, Kevin, and Ben Rafoth. 2006. "Examining Writing Center Director–Assistant Director Relationships." In *The Writing Center Director's Resource Book,* ed. Christina Murphy and Byron Stay, 179–186. Mahwah, NJ: Lawrence Erlbaum.

Leki, Ilona. 2007. *Undergraduates in a Second Language.* Mahwah, NJ: Erlbaum.

Thaiss, Christopher, Gerd Bräuer, Paula Carlino, Lisa Ganobcsik-Williams, and Aparna Sinhaet, eds. 2012. *Writing Programs Worldwide: Profiles of Academic Writing in Many Places.* Fort Collins, CO: WAC Clearinghouse.

22

UNIVERSITY OF CONNECTICUT WRITING CENTER

Thomas Deans and Kathleen Tonry

Institution type: Public Research University
Location: Storrs, Connecticut
Enrollment: 25,000
Year program was founded: 2005
WPA reporting: Both the director and associate director have dual appointments, reporting to the director of the Center for Excellence in Teaching and Learning for writing center matters, and to the head of the English Department for faculty matters.
Program funding: Center for Excellence in Teaching and Learning, a division of the Provost's Office
Description of students: University of Connecticut's (UConn) main research campus is in Storrs, and serves 18,800 undergraduates and an additional 6,500 graduate students. The acceptance rate is currently 47 percent; half of the most recent freshman class were ranked in the top 10 percent of their high schools. Minority students comprise 30 percent of undergraduates. Nearly 11,000 undergraduates live in on-campus or university-affiliated housing, and most students at Storrs are enrolled full-time. A majority (79%) are from Connecticut, and 4 percent come from abroad (representing 113 countries). Storrs also runs a large and selective Honors Program with over 2,000 students. While this profile is about the University Writing Center at Storrs, UConn also has four regional campuses across the state, which together serve an additional 4,500 undergraduates; each of these also has a writing center under the direction of a faculty writing coordinator, and we share best practices across our campuses.

PROGRAM SNAPSHOT

The University Writing Center sponsors a large tutoring operation, faculty development for teaching writing in the disciplines, a writing fellows program, graduate writing support, research, community outreach, and a variety of campus partnerships.

DOI: 10.7330/9781607326274.c022

WPAS' PROFILES

Tom

Throughout my career, I have balanced teaching, research, and writing program administration. After completing my PhD at the University of Massachusetts, I joined the English Department at Kansas State University and served as associate director of the Expository Writing Program. Later, as director of College Writing at Haverford College, I launched a freestanding, interdisciplinary writing program. I came to UConn in 2005 as associate professor of English and founding director of a new tutoring/writing-across-the-disciplines hybrid center intended to support a revitalized university-wide WI (writing-intensive) curriculum. At UConn I also teach, mentor graduate students, lead assessment of writing in the disciplines, run writing pedagogy workshops for faculty and teaching assistants, and serve on many committees. I have published three books on university/community partnerships, plus a range of articles on composition, rhetoric, and representations of literacy in literary and sacred texts. I am also series co-editor for the *Oxford Brief Guides to Writing in the Disciplines*.

Kathleen

I completed my PhD at the University of Notre Dame in 2005 and came to UConn as assistant professor of English and associate director of the Writing Center. My graduate training focused on medieval literature, and my dissertation addressed the transition between manuscript and print in England. I also held a position as graduate assistant director at Notre Dame's Writing Center, and in that role I had mentored tutors and founded a community partnership with a local newspaper and two area high schools. At UConn I continue to split my investments between writing center administration and research/teaching/service in the English Department as a medievalist. I have published a monograph, edited collection, and articles on topics in late-medieval literature.

Since arriving at UConn, we have both been promoted to professor and associate professor, respectively. We collaborate on all aspects of University Writing Center work, although Tom does more of the faculty development and community outreach and Kathleen does more of the tutor recruitment and training.

CONCEPTION

Two exigencies prompted the founding and funding of the University Writing Center in 2005: one early, a 1990 CWPA Consultant-Evaluator external review that sharply criticized the university for neglecting its writing-intensive courses; and one immediate, a 2004 revamping of general education requirements. The 1990 external review by Edward White and Linda Peterson (requested by Lynn Bloom, then Aetna Chair of Writing) praised UConn for some programs but took it to task for many others, particularly poor oversight of WI courses, absent faculty development, and an underfunded writing center, which at that point consisted of one graduate student, one computer, and one small room. The Writing Resource Center was expanded to two graduate student co-directors and a small staff of undergraduate tutors, but when the university revisited its general education requirements more than a decade later, it realized that a renewed emphasis on WI (writing-intensive) and Q (quantitative) courses would require a much more ambitious response. The W Center (as it was initially named) was envisioned as a locus of support for WI course instructors and students. Two tenure lines in English were created—one for an associate professor/director and one for an assistant professor/associate director (along with parallel positions in mathematics to lead the Quantitative Learning Center [Q Center]). It is rare for a university to create two new tenure lines specifically for a writing center, and that UConn did so signaled a notable institutional commitment to writing across the curriculum and student writers. Funding for several graduate assistantships was also built into the budget.

In 2006 we renamed ourselves the University Writing Center and embraced a broader range of responsibilities: tutoring, workshops on personal statement and L2 writing, a writing fellows program to support first-generation college students, administration of awards for excellent undergraduate writing in the disciplines, programs to support graduate students and international students, partnerships with a wide range of campus constituencies (library, First-Year Writing, First-Year Programs, regional campuses, athletics, etc.), faculty development workshops on teaching writing in one's discipline, WI teaching orientations for graduate teaching assistants, advocacy for writing on key academic committees, leadership of writing assessment, sponsorship of research (especially undergraduate and graduate research on writing centers), mentorship of graduate student writing program administrators, and community outreach to secondary schools statewide.

POPULATIONS SERVED

Like most writing centers, our bread and butter is individual tutorials for student writers. We currently deliver more than four thousand per year. In various other capacities, we work with UConn faculty, graduate instructors, and departments, as well as high schools across the state.

Writers come to us from across the full range of UConn's academic programs—freshman negotiating their first college-level essays, sophomores writing for general education courses, juniors and seniors writing papers and lab reports for WI courses. Students also bring in self-sponsored writing, especially personal statements for graduate school applications. We have developed a partnership with First-Year Experience (which is distinct from First-Year Writing) that brings in 1000+ first-year students (the only classes for which we allow a required tutorial); we accommodate most of these through group tutorials of three or more so they don't overwhelm us. Following the national trend among public universities, we are also seeing more international, multilingual writers. We are designed for undergraduates, who comprise 90 percent of our traffic, but we have always welcomed graduate student writers. In recent years we have formalized and expanded graduate support.

For faculty and teaching assistants we offer curricular support and pedagogy workshops that focus on strategies for writing to learn and writing in the disciplines. Each year about fifty faculty participate in lunchtime workshops (on topics like implementing successful peer review, integrating informal writing into courses, responding effectively to student writing, etc.); each year more than one hundred teaching assistants participate in an August or January day-long WI Teaching Orientation that is required for any graduate student involved in WI course or lab instruction. We also do individual consultations with faculty on course design and teaching. Since our founding, more than one thousand instructors have participated in some form of faculty development.

As part of an innovative outreach program, we also work with middle and high school teachers across Connecticut to found peer writing centers in public schools.

OPERATIONS

Having a director/associate director faculty leadership team is pivotal to the versatility and vitality of our many partnerships across campus; it is also essential to program continuity when one or the other of the directors goes on research, family, or sabbatical leave. Tom has primary responsibility for leading faculty development in writing across the disciplines; Kathleen has primary responsibility for recruiting, educating, and mentoring a diverse staff of peer tutors. We receive course releases for our writing center duties (normal teaching load at UConn is 2–2; we each teach 1–1).

Originally there was no program assistant to handle daily administrative tasks (payroll, scheduling, record-keeping, reimbursements, website development, etc.), and this proved a serious sinkhole of time for the faculty directors, who meanwhile had a wide range of responsibilities in the Writing Center and across campus, not to mention the very high research expectations at a doctoral institution. We negotiated for a part-time unionized staff position by trading some funding that had originally been budgeted for graduate assistantships.

Two doctoral students (each on twenty hour/week assistantships, usually doctoral students in rhetoric and composition, but sometimes from other disciplines) serve as assistant directors of the Writing Center. They assist the faculty directors in training the staff and managing programs, delivering workshops, tutoring, and conducting research; meanwhile they receive an apprenticeship in writing program administration (several have moved on to writing center directorships elsewhere). One additional graduate student coordinates graduate student support programs (this assistantship is funded by the Graduate School). Our six-person administrative leadership team meets weekly and works collaboratively.

Our tutoring staff includes twenty-five undergraduates hired from across the disciplines to reflect the UConn curriculum, plus five graduate students, with at least two of them from the sciences (our graduate student assistant directors are hired on twenty hour/week assistantships, but the five additional graduate tutors are hired on an hourly basis and typically work five to eight hours per week). We work hard to recruit a diverse staff—through faculty nominations, outreach to cultural centers, networking within our Writing Center and fellows program—and now typically receive ninety-plus competitive applications for ten or so openings per year. All staff must attend a two-day August orientation and monthly staff meetings, which involve ongoing professional development. All new tutors must take a semester-long, one-credit practicum on writing center theory and practice.

In all, we have a robust, sustainable staffing model that features faculty directors, graduate WPAs apprentices, peer tutors, and administrative support.

We offer about two hundred one-hour tutoring slots available each week, scheduled Monday–Thursday 10:00 AM–10:00 PM, Fridays 10:00

AM–4:00 PM, and Sundays 2:00–10:00 PM. We invest a great deal in training our tutors but then trust them to handle their shifts without regular supervision. Still, we try to schedule a mix of veterans and newcomers on each shift so that the newcomers have support.

In 2011 we received a CCCC *Writing Program Certificate of Excellence* and the selection committee recognized us as "an exemplar for a large public university." It went on to remark that UConn is "running a rich, complex, and ambitious program touching multiple aspects of students' writing lives. The program is embedded in multidisciplinary writing tutoring, WAC, FYE and FYC courses, and local high schools. Writing center tutors are well trained and given multiple opportunities for professional development . . . The Center is very busy, very diverse, very proactive" (Deans and Tonry 2011).

FUNDING

Our budget comes from UConn's Center for Teaching and Learning (CETL) and nearly all of it goes into supporting people: salaries for the director, associate director (half of whose salary is covered by the College of Liberal Arts and Sciences), and program assistant (who has recently moved to 70% time); stipends for graduate assistants, which at UConn cost departments about $36,000/year each (CETL pays for two and a half assistantships, the Graduate School for one, and the English Department for one); and hourly tutoring wages for undergraduates at $12/hour, along with a few graduate tutors at $25/hour (in 2015–16, the total hourly tutoring budget was $60,000). When we take on projects for other departments, we often charge our going rates for student labor. For example, we supply UConn's Athletics Department with tutors in writing, and they reimburse us for those tutor wages; likewise, when our tutors work as writing fellows for courses enrolled with students in a bridge program sponsored by the Center for Academic Programs (CAP), that department covers about half of the costs.

PEDAGOGICAL AND ADMINISTRATIVE HIGHLIGHTS

Our most notable innovation is the range of our programs and partnerships—each distinct but all contributing to our vision of academic writing as a collaborative, campus-wide enterprise. We have never limited ourselves to tutoring, in part because that could create the impression that our mission is fixing individual student deficits. From the start we have resisted a deficit-driven ideology and instead have adopted a social and entrepreneurial approach to forging partnerships with both academic departments and other units across campus—the library, the Q Center, the University Senate, the Office of First-Year Programs, and Aetna Chair of Writing, Athletics, the CAP (an office that houses several programs for first-generation and minority students), and the Graduate School. Brief sketches of our most robust partnerships follow.

Library and Quantitative Learning Center

Quantitative Learning Center was founded at the same time as the University Writing Center—we share a common origin story, having both been created to support a new general education reform. We teamed with the main library on campus to form the core of learning commons that includes the Writing Center, the Q Center, hardware and software tech support, world languages tutoring, the library reference desk, and study space.

Office of First-Year Programs

UConn, like many universities, invites first-year students to take a First-Year Experience (FYE) course that helps the newcomers navigate a big institution; it also orients them to college life and tries to instill academic values, especially inquiry. UConn's FYE courses have proven popular (80+% of first-years elect to take one) and quite effective in improving retention rates. In 2007 we began discussions with FYE administrators about how writing might be woven into the FYE curriculum, and shortly after began a pilot program encouraging FYE instructors to include one significant writing assignment (and revision) in their courses. As part of the assignment students bring a draft of their essay to the University Writing Center. We supported this pilot program with instructor workshops and online resources; we continue to offer those and to train our own tutors for the special challenges of FYE papers. The initial pilot program involved 10 percent of sections; in 2008–09 participation grew to 30 percent; and as of 2015 participation was about 70 percent.

Center for Academic Programs/Writing Fellows

One of our most ambitious and successful partnerships is focused on diversity and access. For the last six years we have worked with the CAP, which oversees a cluster of programs for first-generation and minority students. CAP has long run successful summer programs for incoming at-risk students, but it struggled to continue academic support for those same students once the academic year began. The Writing Center developed a specialized writing fellows program though which selected First-Year Writing sections populated with CAP students are linked with an experienced writing tutor. The undergraduate fellow attached to each section meets weekly with students in small lab sections to support critical reading and writing. We have developed a handbook and hosted a half-day orientation for instructors and fellows. CAP has tracked the progress of students who take sections with fellows versus those who take a typical section, and reports improved retention. Our tutors have also reflected on their roles as fellows in conference presentations and publications (Bugdal and Holtz 2014). A similar fellows program for First-Year Writing sections populated with international students was piloted in 2016.

University Senate/General Education Oversight Committee

The University Writing Center was founded through the advocacy of members of the University Senate, and it has maintained that relationship, mainly through Tom and Kathleen's participation on key Senate committees, especially the General Education Oversight Committee (GEOC). That oversees new course proposals, including WI course proposals, and sets policies for general education. That committee has also funded a multi-year WID (writing in the disciplines) assessment project led by Tom. Several reports on WI course outcomes are now available for download from the assessment section of UConn's GEOC website.

Aetna Chair of Writing/Aetna Writing across the Disciplines Awards

The Aetna Endowed Chair of Writing has long been a source of advocacy for writing at UConn. The writing center has partnered with the Aetna Chair to create the Aetna Writing across the Disciplines Awards. The University Writing Center proposed this award program to fill a gap: freshman writing already had awards, as did creative writing, but there were no awards to recognize excellent undergraduate writing across the curriculum. We now typically receive 100+ submissions in three award categories: humanities, sciences, and social sciences.

Athletics

The director of academic support for UConn's athletics program approached us in 2012 about supporting that unit's writing tutoring.

She had heard good reports from the athletes who use our tutoring centers; she also knew that we offered extensive tutor training. Over the past two years we have incorporated tutoring into mandatory study halls; we have also supported their summer writing courses for athletes.

The Graduate School

While we have always welcomed graduate students for individual tutorials—and hundreds come each year—in recent years we have developed a systematic portfolio of graduate writing support. Starting in 2012, when the Graduate School agreed to fund a full graduate assistantship, we created a new graduate writing coordinator position and launched several programs to serve graduate writers. These include offering five-week, non-credit academic writing seminars, three dissertation boot camps per year, monthly writing retreats, and individualized tutoring (for a detailed account of our approach, see Reardon, Deans, and Maykel 2016).

Connecticut Middle and High Schools

In partnership with the Connecticut Writing Project, we work to launch and sustain peer writing centers at secondary schools in our region. We work intensively with one school per year. The outreach coordinator (an experienced undergraduate or graduate student on staff, usually one aspiring to teach high school) meets with prospective partners to plan and set the groundwork; then during the academic year, graduate and undergraduate students from UConn's Writing Center visit the partner school weekly to mentor high school students in how to conduct peer tutoring. When the high school students are ready to tutor on their own, the UConn weekly visits end, but we invite our partner schools to stay involved with us (and each other) through participation in our annual High School Writing Centers Conference, which since 2007 has been bringing together 100+ students and teachers to recharge and share strategies. Now that our outreach model is maturing, we are seeing our former outreach coordinators become high school English teachers, in turn founding new centers at their schools and coming to our annual conference; we are also seeing their high school tutors come to UConn and join our staff.

MARKETING/PR

Early on we worked with UConn's art students to develop an identifying mark and color—a jaunty "W" in a bright blue that riffs on UConn's more official deep blue—which has served us well in maintaining a brand across campus. In those first years, we also developed an explanatory brochure and published a newsletter each semester. Promoting ourselves was a priority during our first five years but is no longer because now most on campus understand who we are and what we do. We still do "tutor talks" (quick presentations by our tutoring staff to courses around campus, given at the invitation of the instructors) and distribute bookmarks, but otherwise we rely on our website, digital outlets, social media, and word of mouth to promote our activities. Students continually learn about us through required tutorials in First-Year Experience courses, by seeing us on a busy floor of the main library, by way of faculty referrals, and by talking to their friends. Over time, good programs speak for themselves, and self-promotion becomes less and less necessary.

We now focus on sustaining the quality of our programs rather than on promoting our services. Most weeks our tutorial schedule is full to overflowing (especially in the fall semester); our workshops draw plenty of students; faculty seek us out with their questions (and occasionally their unrealistic expectations); we have several partnerships and research projects afoot at any one time. Because we are stretched to capacity, more and more we find ourselves needing to say "no" to constituencies around campus who seek us out. At the same time, we do not have ambitions to grow larger because we fear that if our staff roster expands beyond thirty, we will lose the tight sense of community and shared purpose that we value. Our most consuming priority is sustaining ongoing partnerships and, because one-third of our staff graduates each year, constantly recruiting, training, and mentoring new peer tutors and new graduate assistant directors.

TECHNOLOGY

We rely heavily on our website and on WCOnline's scheduling and record-keeping software. Students find us through our website: more than 85 percent of our traffic comes via appointments scheduled online (which means that now, unlike in our early years, we have little capacity for walk-in traffic during busy weeks of the semester). We record and deliver our tutor notes/session summary reports through WCOnline's integrated system.

Perhaps because our campus is residential (75% of students live on campus) and because our main tutorial location is in a busy central library, students consistently tell us that they prefer in-person to online tutorials. Still, we have experimented with online tutorials, using media-rich, synchronous sessions via Google Hangouts. When we piloted this initiative in 2013–14—promoted it, trained staff, offered regular appointments, assessed performance—student demand proved very weak, so we now offer online tutorials by request only.

We maintain modest Twitter and Facebook activity, use free EventBrite web-based software for student workshop registrations, rely on WordPress to create and update our website, and collect workshop registrations, writing award submissions, and tutor application submissions using online forms embedded in our WordPress website.

ROLE OF RESEARCH

We have a robust tradition of encouraging research across all levels of our staff, from faculty directors to graduate assistant directors to undergraduate tutors. Research maintains our intellectual vitality, keeps us connected to ongoing national conversations and best practices, pays dividends in the prestige economy of the research university, and contributes to the professional and career development of our tutors. One of the most important reasons to have research-active faculty in charge of a writing center is because they can mentor tutors in research and scholarly writing.

Each year, several UConn tutors—usually undergraduates and graduate students—present papers at conferences, primarily the Northeast Writing Center Association Conference. Most of our research questions emerge from everyday tutoring challenges, discussions in our monthly staff meetings, and topics covered in our tutor practicum. But it takes faculty mentoring for questions to develop into conference papers or publications. For instance, two graduate students, one in anthropology and one in English, teamed up to explore the topic of bias and racism in writing as it was raised during a staff meeting. After presenting their initial ideas and data at conferences, they continued to work with Tom to refine their methodology and collect more data, which allowed them to craft a journal article, "Addressing the Everyday Language of Everyday Oppression in the Writing Center," which was published in *The Writing Center Journal* and won the Council of Writing Program Administrators 2012 Award for Graduate Writing in WPA Studies (see Suhr-Sytsma and Brown 2016; for a more recent research project, see Bugdal, Reardon, and Deans in press). Undergraduate research (often done collaboratively and occasionally done as a senior thesis) usually results in conference presentations rather than publications, but those presentations mark real accomplishments—both for individual tutors and for the collective intellectual ethos of our center. A full list of conference presentations and publications by our tutors is available on our website.

ASSESSMENT

We do regular program assessment. Using the WCOnline scheduler, we tally total users and parse them into categories. Using a separate online survey at the end of each semester, we solicit feedback from all students who come to our center, asking them to report how they discovered us and why they came, to rate how our tutors are performing, and to reveal how much post-tutorial time they devoted to revising and whether they plan to return (we gave up on immediate post-tutorial paper reviews long ago, finding them of little value). The survey data was most helpful during our initial years as we were experiencing rapid growth and refining our policies and practices; now it typically confirms that our mature organization is sustaining its performance. Each year's data is funneled into an annual report.

All our tutors undergo a mid-year review that focuses on formative feedback. Each tutor composes a self-assessment; the leadership team meanwhile compiles notes on each tutor's performance. The director, associate director, and assistant directors divide up the staff and schedule individual meetings with tutors to review past performance and set future goals. We also invite their feedback for how to improve our program practices.

In 2010, five years after our founding, we requested an external program review, opening our records, staff, and doors to a three-day review visit by Joan Mullin. Her report affirmed the scope and quality of our programs and bolstered our *CCCC Writing Program of Excellence* application; it also helped us defend against several rounds of university budget cuts.

PRIMARY DOCUMENT (at writingprogramarchitecture.com)

We never had to campaign to create our center. Instead, before either of us were hired, committees of faculty and administrators had already articulated a need for a substantial, faculty-led writing center within the context of a larger general education reform. We were then hired as an integral part of the writing component of that curricular reform. We included an excerpt from UConn's 2003 General Education Guidelines. This document frames the University Writing Center as part of larger general education effort. We have not been entirely faithful to the letter of this document—for example, we do not maintain an archive of all WI syllabi and our tutors are predominantly undergraduates rather than graduate students—but we have been faithful to its spirit. This origin story led us to one of the conclusions in our program profile: that a particularly opportune time to found a large writing center/WAC hybrid like ours is when a curriculum overhaul is afoot.

WPAS' VOICES

In light of our program's origin story, a fundamental take-away is this: *the most opportune time to found a large writing center/WAC hybrid like ours is when a curriculum overhaul is afoot.* Only such major curricular reform—typically carried out through a faculty senate or interdisciplinary faculty committee, preferably including at least one member in writing studies—presents the exigency and *kairos* to create new tenure and budget lines.

Another important lesson from our experience is this: *keep the center's reporting lines and budget outside of the English Department.* We certainly value that our home for tenure, teaching, research, and service is in English, but we equally value that our center is distinct from the department. The history of writing programs in English is too vexed, and the interests of any single department rarely align with the larger writing needs of the university, particularly over the long term (see David Russell's [2002] *Writing in the Academic Disciplines* for confirmation of that).

Too often writing programs are championed by one person on campus ("the writing person") and then put in the hands of that same person to run, often for decades. *Our model of two faculty directors is much more sustainable.* Our tandem model has made us more ambitious and entrepreneurial; more important, it guarantees continuity over the long term. Sabbaticals, family leaves, medical leaves—managerial structures should anticipate these rather than respond to them one at a time with improvised work-arounds. When we're both here, we build and innovate. When one of us goes on leave, the other fills the gap and holds the program steady. We also build in continuity by mentoring graduate assistant directors, who typically stay with us for two years.

One thing we underestimated when we started was the need for everyday administrative and clerical support: getting the weekly payroll done, the schedules set, the reimbursement paperwork in, the phones answered, the website updated, the rooms reserved, and other such tasks. The cumulative demands of these tasks cannot be covered by faculty without doing damage to their teaching and research productivity. Nor are students (undergrad or grad) fitting for this work, as learning bureaucratic university systems anew each year is ineffective. *A staff program assistant is essential to the smooth daily functioning and institutional memory of a good writing program.* Having such administrative support is particularly important to the tenure prospects of junior faculty writing program administrators. Once we hired our part-time program assistant, everything got better, and better still in years that followed.

References

Bugdal, Melissa, and Ricky Holtz. 2014. ""When Writing Fellows Become Reading Fellows: Creative Strategies for Critical Reading and Writing in a Course-Based Tutoring Program." Praxis*: A Writing Center Journal* 12 (1). http://www.praxisuwc.com/bugdal-holtz-121.

Bugdal, Melissa, Kristina Reardon, and Thomas Deans. in press. "Summing Up the Session: A Study of Student, Faculty, and Tutor Attitudes Toward Tutor Notes." *Writing Center Journal.*

Deans, Thomas, and Kathleen Tonry. 2011. Application for the Writing Program Certificate of Excellence Award.

Reardon, Kristina, Thomas Deans, and Cheryl Maykel. 2016. "Finding a Room of Their Own: Programming Time and Space for Graduate Student Writing." *WLN: A Journal of Writing Center Scholarship* 40(5–6): 10–17.

Russell, David. 2002. *Writing in the Academic Disciplines: A Curricular History.* 2nd ed. Carbondale: Southern Illinois University Press.

Suhr-Sytsma, Mandy, and Shan-Estelle Brown. 2016 (2011). "Theory in/to Practice: Addressing the Everyday Language of Oppression in the Writing Center." In *The Oxford Guide for Writing Tutors*, 508–32. New York: Oxford University Press. Originally published in *Writing Center Journal* 31(2): 13–49.

23

SHEPHERD UNIVERSITY ACADEMIC SUPPORT CENTER

Christy I. Wenger

Institution type: Liberal Arts College
Location: Shepherdstown, West Virginia
Enrollment: Over 4,000 students
Year program was founded: 1998
WPA reports to: English Department Chair
Program funded by: Student activity fees
Description of students: a majority of local West Virginian, first-generation college students with a large population of commuter students

PROGRAM SNAPSHOT

Shepherd University offers learning support to its undergraduates through a variety of programs housed under the umbrella of the Academic Support Center (ASC). While faculty and students both colloquially refer to a "writing center" on campus, officially there is instead an ASC staffed with writing tutors as well as tutors for the additional subjects undergraduates typically encounter as they complete their general education requirements. The central learning commons structure of the ASC, removed as it is from academic departments on campus, is meant to convey the message to students and faculty that its services are open to all. The ASC also offers a FYC Stretch course.

WPA'S PROFILE

I graduated from Lehigh University with my PhD in English, rhetoric, and composition and assumed WPA responsibilities with my tenure-track position at Shepherd University upon graduation. Prior to my hire, the university managed the writing program in a more ad hoc manner from within the English Department, typically asking faculty with PhDs

DOI: 10.7330/9781607326274.c023

in literature to take charge of the first-year writing courses and to lead the writing instructors, who were primarily employed as adjuncts. At that time, the writing program itself was quite different, vested more in a writing about literature model. In 2011, however, with pressure from national trends to have on staff a WPA with a writing studies background and with a growing writing program offering at least thirty sections of FYC each semester, I was hired as the first faculty member with officially-documented WPA duties as part of my contract.

Prior to my position at Shepherd and as a doctoral student, I had worked for both the writing program and writing center at Lehigh as a graduate WPA. While the early professionalization of graduate students is a contentious subject in our field, and many warn against the political and personal dangers of assuming administrative positions prior to being tenured, I found that most jobs on the market asked for WPA responsibilities in conjunction with assistant professor positions. Even if we are ideologically opposed to the idea of a "genadmin," or the rise of a generation of writing studies professionals who identify as administrators early in their careers (Charlton et al. 2011), graduate training and hiring trends currently reward this identification. While there are real risks incurred by pre-professionalization (in addition to those of carrying administrative duties as a tenure-track professor who must also prove teaching effectiveness and demonstrate scholarly ability), my hire at Shepherd was due in large part to the experience I had as a graduate WPA. My beginning success as a WPA has been just as dependent on this valuable graduate training. My on-the-job experience suggests that graduate WPA training can help new WPAs navigate the complexities of running a university writing program—and this is especially true on my campus where I am the only faculty member with a writing studies background, and, therefore, the sole writing resource for the entire university. That's a huge responsibility for anyone, especially someone completely inexperienced with higher education administration.

Along with my administrative experience as a graduate student, I would cite my decade of experience as a writing tutor through my graduate and undergraduate programs as a primary reason why I pursued my doctorate in writing studies and why I found myself drawn to writing administration.

PROGRAM CONCEPTION

Because the Academic Support Center was established in 1998 (before my hire in 2011) and because I am the first WPA at my university, it was assumed that my position would run the writing program as removed from writing tutoring. Of course, it's been impossible and undesirable for me to lead the writing program without getting involved in the ASC since I certify and train the writing tutors and create the writing curriculum that governs the FYC Stretch courses housed in the ASC.

While my position as WPA has been well received by the campus as a whole, I'm still developing the kind of "referent power" Irene Ward (2008) talks about as earned through relationship-building and time (64). Challenges I've faced with collaborations between the writing program and the ASC have been largely structural and monetary in nature. I am in chiefly uncharted waters as a WPA on my campus, and it has sometimes been challenging to lend my expertise and services to the ASC without disturbing its chain of command. Because the ASC and writing program are separate by design, they have two different sources of funding, and neither of these sources is plentiful. Both the director of the ASC and the "writing specialist," who organizes writing tutoring there, are in staff positions so they face a different set of political constraints than I do as a faculty member, which dictates the ways we can spend our budgets.

My department, in particular, has questioned the arbitrary divisions between writing faculty employed through the ASC and those employed through the writing program and has been supportive of my desire to collaborate with the director of the ASC to improve the campus' writing culture at large. In my four years on campus, I have successfully attempted to build bridges between the ASC and the writing program in order to strengthen both. For instance, I began inviting the Stretch writing instructors and the ASC's writing specialist to the writing program workshops and writing roundtables I hold throughout the academic year. However, because of the separate budgets I outline above, I typically cannot offer stipends for contingent faculty who teach Stretch to attend these writing events.

POPULATION SERVED

As the ASC runs on a peer-to-peer tutoring model, only undergraduate students benefit from our services, particularly first- and second-year students who are completing their general education credits. By administrative policy, graduate students are not permitted to use ASC services because they do not pay the student activities fees that provide funding for the center. The ASC offers tutoring in many subject matters, and the majority of students who visit do not currently make an appointment with a writing tutor. In 2014, approximately 5,052 total tutoring appointments were executed by tutors of all subjects in the ASC. Of these, about 15 percent of total tutoring appointments were scheduled with a writing tutor; the remaining appointments were scattered among the other core curriculum subjects also tutored in the center. Students who schedule writing tutoring appointments are typically those from the population taking first-year writing, either as sequenced entirely through the writing program, or as a combination of Stretch writing coupled with the required second-semester course offered through the writing program.

Writing tutors also serve the Stretch writing students as attached tutors in these courses. We attempt to provide an attached tutor for as many Stretch classes as possible, or at least as university funding and student scheduling will allow. Writing tutors working in this capacity regularly attend their assigned class and help instructors by working one-on-one with students both inside and outside of class time. Possible duties attached tutors can take on in these classes include: teaching mini writing lessons; leading discussions and/or small groups; working with students during peer review and writing conferences; and fulfilling additional course- and instructor-based needs.

FUNDING

The ASC has an annual budget of $20,000 as allocated by the university itself. Our operating costs—specifically paying for the tutors themselves—tend to be higher than this budget allowance every year, however, meaning that we are often running a couple thousand dollars over budget by the middle of the spring semester and more so by the end of the academic year. The Budget Officer for Academic Affairs approves overages as needed. Beyond basic office supplies and photocopying costs, the majority of our budget is spent paying for our student tutors and staff. The center largely goes over budget because more funds are needed to pay our tutors than are allocated for our use.

OPERATIONS

As an assistant professor of English at a teaching-focused school, I teach a part-time appointment, which reduces my teaching load to 2–2. Effectively, then, my time is supposed to be equally split between teaching and administration. My role as WPA is to administer the writing program, hire and provide professional development and training to writing instructors, and to teach and train the writing tutors who work in our ASC. As a member of the English Department, I also teach in our first-year writing program and offer upper-level writing and rhetoric seminars for our majors on topics largely of my choosing.

Officially, as a WPA, my leadership does not extend to the ASC, since this office has separate administrative system in place; unofficially, I serve as a consultant for the ASC since it employs no full-time, tenure-track faculty and no one with a background or advanced degree in writing studies. Further, I am required to train our writing tutors through a theories and methods of composition studies course I teach within the English Department. It is mandatory for students to pass this course and complete a sixteen-hour practicum in the ASC before they may even apply for a position as a writing tutor. Because of my early involvement with potential tutors, I work with the staff of the ASC to make hiring decisions for writing tutor positions.

The ASC has a central director who provides leadership to a writing staff that includes a writing specialist, who supervises the writing tutors and serves a part-time appointment as clinical (teaching) faculty of Stretch writing; a small and variable number of adjunct and/or clinical instructors who teach our Stretch writing courses; and the student tutors themselves. The center currently employs ten writing tutors and one administrative assistant.

The administrative hierarchy in place in the ASC is such that the director reports to the dean of Teaching and Learning on campus. The writing specialist, who organizes the writing tutors, reports to the director, as do the several Stretch writing instructors employed through the ASC each academic year. All student tutors report to their subject specialists or to the director herself; they also work with both to create their tutoring schedules each semester and to troubleshoot any problems as they arise. The tutors themselves fill out tutor reports after each session to keep a record of student visits and concerns. Of course, the administrative assistant in the ASC does the payroll and the countless other duties that help the center run on a daily basis.

In addition to my involvement with the writing tutors' training, the director and the writing specialist also use me as a professional resource. These two individuals regularly meet with me to determine the writing curriculum of the FYC Stretch courses under their jurisdiction and to evaluate policies for writing tutoring. Because our Stretch courses must teach the same curriculum as the mainstream FYC courses, any changes I make to those mainstream courses determines the curriculum of the Stretch courses by default—an instance of why my separation from the ASC can become logically problematic. To help alleviate the communication problems that could otherwise result, I offer professional development opportunities and workshops to the contingent faculty staffing those courses and share resources with the ASC whenever possible.

The writing tutors in the ASC pride themselves on their continuous model of learning and training; as part of this model, the writing specialist offers bi-weekly meetings for the writing tutors. These writing meetings include time spent on various business aspects of keeping the center running smoothly, including the communicating of policies to student tutors, but are primarily devoted to troubleshooting pedagogical scenarios and providing additional training to tutors. Often, various authorities from across campus will lead these meetings to provide instruction. For instance, the director of Career Services visits each year to discuss how to write successful cover letters and resumes. Writing tutors must attend these special trainings if they wish to work with students on related projects, such as providing feedback on job materials.

ASSESSMENT

A comprehensive university assessment of the ASC is currently underway. Because the ASC supervises Stretch math and writing courses, assessments of the center include pass rates for those classes as well as data collected from tutoring. Particularly, we are currently collecting online surveys from our student clients during the last three tutoring weeks of each semester for the 2015–16 academic year. Those surveys ask students to rank their tutors on how knowledgeable they were and how helpful they were in improving the student's understanding of the writing process. Because we're currently mid-way into our assessment cycle, we do not yet have final data on these survey results. In addition to these client-based assessments, either the director or the writing specialist observes each writing tutor twice over the course of the academic year to provide support and feedback. In-house assessments of tutor performance provide valuable qualitative feedback and also serve as another means of tutor professional development.

MARKETING/PR

Marketing to both students and fellow faculty could be much improved. Since budgets have been cut recently due to the same low enrollments that universities nationwide have faced, marketing the center has been removed from the budgeting allowance; this obviously limits efforts to advertise the ASC's services. Currently, we tend to use email most frequently to advertise. At the beginning of every semester, the director sends out a list of student tutors, indicating which subjects are represented by which tutors. These emails do not adequately address the process of tutoring or the reasons why faculty might encourage their students to seek it out, however. They also place the responsibility of sharing this information with students on the faculty themselves.

There are other free means of marketing we take advantage of on campus. For instance, the common syllabus template adopted by courses across the disciplines, which outlines basic university policies about university-wide learning goals, financial aid, and the like, includes a recommended section outlining the ASC and encouraging students to take advantage of this resource. How many faculty (aside from those teaching first-year writing) who actually include this information on their syllabi is unknown: as WPA, I mandate that all writing faculty include this information in their syllabi, and I review syllabi before the start of each semester to make sure crucial information like this is present. The ASC tutors themselves are asked to market and advertise among their friends, campus groups, and classes. In particular, they are asked to be ambassadors in all of their classes: to request from their professors a moment to explain the ASC and the process behind tutoring writing as a means of grassroots marketing.

As WPA, I've taken on the job of marketing the writing tutors within the writing program in several additional ways. First, I added a description of the ASC, what students can expect from a tutoring session and a detailed description of how to sign up for a session, in a Writing Program Handbook I created a year ago, which is now a required resource for all students enrolled in FYC. Second, I've asked the writing tutors I train to add their own essays to this Handbook, detailing various aspects of the writing process as well as specifics about the tutoring process from an insider's perspective. Even when tutors' contributions to the Handbook don't explicitly address the tutoring process, these essays serve as an advertisement for tutoring by humanizing the tutors and creating a culture where writing is shared and discussed among teachers and students. Third, I've worked with the director and the writing specialist of the ASC to offer writing tutor "roadshows" in all FYC classes. Roadshows are required features of FYC classes and feature writing tutors who visit each class within the first month of a new semester to talk with students about the tutoring process. Fourth, I've used my tutor training class as a means of marketing the work our tutors do. While in training, tutors taking my required theories and methods course can earn practicum hours not only by working in the ASC but also by embedding themselves into existing courses where professors have expressed interest in using them to support student writing. By bringing tutors to the faculty, it is my hope to align the faculty's perception of writing with our own and to illustrate the value of the writing tutoring process through example. Often, after these experiences with an embedded tutor, faculty express greater interest in tutoring and will encourage their students to make appointments at the ASC.

Even so, writing tutor lore suggests that many students find their way to the ASC because they failed a writing assignment in a course and were directly instructed by a teacher to get their writing "fixed" by a tutor. Stephen North (1984) may have written "The Idea of a Writing Center" almost thirty years ago to counter the idea of a writing center as a "fix-it" shop, an idea easily dismissed now by scholars in writing studies, but this infamous notion of writing tutoring is still prevalent on campuses like mine today despite our efforts to educate faculty and students otherwise.

TECHNOLOGY

The ASC maintains a fairly basic website that details its mission and provides contact information for the staff as well as an overview of services offered. From this website, students can also navigate to "MyWCOnline" to schedule an in-person appointment with a tutor. The ASC also offers a separate ShepOWL feature, its Online Writing Lab (OWL), through which students can send an email to a designated account with a paper attached and receive feedback electronically from a writing tutor. We currently do not have a social media presence on Facebook or other such networks. We recognize the need for such a presence but haven't been able to resolve the logistics of who would take charge of these accounts and how their online work would be remunerated.

ROLE OF RESEARCH

While there are certainly strengths to having an ASC set up as ours is and run by those outside writing studies occupying staff and not faculty positions, there is a tradeoff as well. Scholarship on our program is lacking because, while I am perhaps the best poised of all to complete such scholarship, my placement outside the ASC makes it difficult for me to engage in such research. Because the director and the writing specialist are in staff positions that do not expect nor reward research agendas or publications, there is little incentive for them to conduct scholarly work.

Center-based research on writing tutoring has primarily consisted of tracking the number of appointments scheduled and executed each semester. Such tracking began in 2013 and continues. From this research, we have learned that our total writing tutoring appointments have decreased from approximately 20 percent of total appointments in 2013 to 15 percent in 2014. In response, we have attempted to use free marketing by advertising the center better in our first-year writing classes in the ways outlined in the section above. As part of a larger move toward university-wide assessment, efforts are also currently underway to survey students who are tutored, asking them to rate their satisfaction with their tutors and the tutors' ability to improve their understanding of the writing process. These surveys will be used to improve tutor training and to help us increase the likelihood of recurrent visits.

A professional research activity that our writing tutors and the writing specialist engage in regularly is attending the Mid-Atlantic Writing Centers Association Conference. While we have never presented research at this conference, it has been a way for staff to learn new methods and to stay in touch with field scholarship. In addition, as mentioned above, all writing tutors conduct a research project as part of their training in the theories and methods of composition and peer tutoring that I teach. These projects are driven by original research and have resulted in the improvement of the ASC website, the creation of "how-to" guides for tutors and multiple contributions to the Writing Program Handbook (a required document for all first-year writing students I mention above) covering various writing topics and essays that demystify the tutoring experience for new students.

PEDAGOGICAL AND/OR ADMINISTRATIVE HIGHLIGHTS

What defines our program is its independence from other programs on campus. Before I was a WPA, I was a writing tutor for approximately ten years. And as a graduate WPA, I also served as an assistant director of the writing center at my doctoral institution. What I can say from those experiences is that it is very challenging to get students across all majors and fields on campus to make writing tutoring appointments when the center is housed within a particular academic department, like English. Location means a great deal not only because of visibility but also because of the perceptions of faculty and students, who may associate writing tutoring with students enrolled only in English classes, if that happens to be the building in which that tutoring occurs. With writing across the curriculum (WAC) and writing in the disciplines (WID) gaining strides every year on campuses nationwide, it makes sense that universities would adopt learning commons models such as ours for their tutoring centers.

What makes our program interesting is the level of training received by our writing tutors. All of our writing tutors have a Level 1 College Reading and Learning Association certification because of their preparation in a field and methods course prior to their employment and because they must first complete a practicum in the center before they are able to be hired as tutors. We continue to offer our writing tutors training throughout their entire employment period in the theories and practices of writing studies and writing tutoring. Our writing tutors take great pride in their training and continual support. Though we do have a minimum GPA required by all tutors, no matter their subject specialties, and before hire, each tutor must pass a rigorous interview and recommendation process, we would like to use writing tutoring as a model example to begin to offer additional training to all our tutors in the center.

As WPA, I'd like to see our writing tutoring numbers double from their current level of about 15 percent of appointments made in the next few years. To achieve this, I believe it will take me working with both the director and writing specialist in the ASC to better advertise tutoring in our first-year classes and other writing-intensive classes across campus as a first step. We also need to keep brainstorming ways to build more synergy between the writing program and the ASC, bridges we must intentionally build up and around our standing administrative structures since our programs are separate and could, therefore, communicate very little if we desired. As my own writing pedagogy has made the "digital turn," and I've guided my writing instructors to navigate this turn as well, I'd also like to see our writing tutors become more conversant in the strategies of a "multiliteracy" center.

PRIMARY DOCUMENT (at **writingprogramarchitecture.com**)

Of significance to our tutoring platform is the instructor handout that overviews the possible roles that attached tutors in the learning center can perform in Stretch English classes. This handout is given to all new writing instructors to provide guidelines for the use of attached tutors in their classes.

WPA'S VOICE

Before I took my current position, I assumed that as a director of writing I'd be working with other campus WPAs to create a healthy writing culture on my campus. Because I'd always thought about a healthy writing culture in terms of the three legs of a stool—the writing center, the writing program, and writing across campus (WAC and WID)—as director of writing, I expected I'd be part of an integrated team of writing studies professionals at my university to deliver a program that helped the other two "legs" stand up and complement my own. That hasn't been my experience.

Instead, I ended up on a campus where I am the only writing administrator and the only "composition expert," as my university likes to call me. Now, instead of working on the single leg of a stool, I feel more like a spider weaving a web between a bunch of writing nodes (people, programs, courses) on campus. What this means it that I am not only called upon as a de-facto expert for all writing-related matters across campus, but that I must also work with a diverse body of faculty and staff for the sake of promoting a healthy writing culture. Even if my job duties don't entail directing the writing tutors in the ASC or supporting the Stretch faculty, for instance, I must involve myself in these processes if I hope to have a functional writing program. Of course, because there are others officially in charge of such duties, I can't simply take them over myself, nor, quite frankly, would time allow it.

Instead, I have to work on creating co-mentoring relationships across campus so that I can both teach and learn from other faculty and staff who also have a responsibility to the writing culture by virtue of their campus positionality. As a leader of this movement, I'm still working on developing a culture-appropriate method of co-mentoring on my campus, but I am making strides. That leads me to another piece of advice: it takes time and much patience to generate lasting and successful change on small campuses. It's taken me a few years of on-the-job experiences to fully realize that I must track change over years and not months. Sustainable writing and tutoring programs change slowly from both the top-down through administrative developments and bottom-up through instructor and tutor buy-in, which takes time but hopefully produces lasting results.

References

Charlton, Colin, Jonika Charlton, Tarez Samra Graben, Kathleen J. Ryan, and Amy Ferdinandt Stolley, eds. 2011. *GenAdmin: Theorizing WPA Identities in the 21st Century*. South Carolina: Parlor Press.

North, Stephen M. 1984. "The Idea of a Writing Center." *College English* 46 (5): 433–446. http://dx.doi.org/10.2307/377047.

Ward, Irene. 2008. "Developing Healthy Management and Leadership Styles: Surviving the WPA's 'Inside Game'." In *The Longman Sourcebook for Writing Program Administrators*, ed. Irene Ward and William J. Carpenter, 49–67. New York: Pearson/ Longman.

24
WALLACE COMMUNITY COLLEGE CENTER FOR WRITING AND WRITING INSTRUCTION

Emily W. Cosgrove

Institution type: Two-year college
Location: Dothan, Alabama
Enrollment: 5,000 (Wallace Campus in Dothan); 800 (Sparks Campus in Eufaula)
Year program was founded: 2013
WPA reports to: Associate Dean of Instruction and Department of Education
Program funded by: Department of Education Title III-A Strengthening Institutions Grant
Description of students: The college strives to bridge the divides between the differing demographics of students on each of our two campuses, whether traditional or nontraditional, single, single parents, or family providers, or unemployed, full-time, or part-time employees.

PROGRAM SNAPSHOT

The Center for Writing and Writing Instruction (CWWI) is a department that oversees a writing center and a writing lab on each of two campuses, Wallace and Sparks, each with its own site coordinator; the director oversees both coordinators. The entire operation is typically referred to as the Writing Center. The Writing Center offers free tutoring to all students with an "all students, all writing" approach, a variety of writing-related activities for students, such as workshops, word game days, and writing groups, a lab space for developmental English student lab sessions, as well as other course or individual students use, and faculty support in writing across the disciplines

WPA'S PROFILE

I would say that I came to work as a WPA through a non-traditional route. Yes, I was an English major as an undergrad and worked as one

DOI: 10.7330/9781607326274.c024

of the first peer tutors in my college's writing center during my senior year, but I turned down a writing center tutoring assistantship in graduate school in favor of a residence director position. So, while I was working to earn an MA in English with a focus on community college teaching, I opened myself up to consider other things that I loved—and that included working with college students within the mindsets and realm of Student Affairs. As such, after finishing my master's program I accepted a position as a learning support specialist, and several weeks later accepted an additional role as the assistant director of the college's new writing center. I worked in these two positions for several months, and then accepted a promotion of sorts to fill the position of career center director. I served in this role for almost two years while keeping the prior teaching opportunity that my previous position provided to teach an academic support and college acclimation class for struggling students; through these two opportunities, I once again realized the passion and strengths I had for working with college students to help them further develop holistically. Because of this, I enrolled in a PhD program in higher education administration at Auburn University with the fuzzy end goal of perhaps serving in a dean of students role one day so that I could put my skills in administration and experiences in residence life, student leadership, community service, and career services to good use.

While at Auburn I worked in Student Affairs for a year, then transitioned to a new program assistant position within the university's writing center. This decision quite literally changed the course of my next several years. This position afforded me so many opportunities to gain new skills, spend time with engaging and inspired professionals in the field (both in the office, at meetings across campus, and at conferences), work with the student tutors and front desk staff to plan and orchestrate center-related tasks (hiring and training committees, conference presentation panels, etc.), and really put my student development skills, passions, and experiences to good work while meshing my love for reading, writing, and sharing ideas.

As I was wrapping up my PhD, an incredible opportunity came my way. As luck would have it, a community college (Wallace) several hours away was looking for a writing center director with skills in administration and student retention. So, even though I had passed up a past opportunity to teach composition courses in graduate school, the deep learning and work experiences that I had gained through my assistantship, as well as my past experiences and coursework related to higher education administration and student development, turned out to be a great fit for this institution and for me. While I was hired as a WPA, this position also includes serving as the director of the Writing Center and the Title III-A grant that funds the center, as well as facilitating faculty development in writing, among other responsibilities. Because of this, I am able to both pull from my wheelhouse and have the opportunity to constantly learn new things, as well as collaborate with others to build and better these new programs. This is a wonderful position, and I am thankful for the opportunity to serve this institution and work alongside so many amazing educators along the way—it really is a great job!

PROGRAM CONCEPTION

The initial idea and framework for the Writing Center were developed through a Title III-A Strengthening Institutions grant proposal that the college submitted to the Department of Education (DOE) in 2013. The college was awarded a little over $1.5 million in order to increase student retention through the creation of a writing center, an Enhanced English 101 course that the Writing Center would support through course-required engagement with students through a list of options named the portfolio program, a lab space in which our developmental English students would receive extra support one hour a week through the leadership of their instructor and assistance of one of our tutors, and faculty support in writing with the aim of developing a writing in the disciplines program on both campuses from 2013 to 2018. This grant proposal has been an important guiding document used in the creation and development of each of these objectives, as it outlines the staffing structures, initial conceptual frameworks, and proposed budgeting allocations to accomplish these tasks.

When I began my job (a few months after the grant had been awarded, but before any of these programs began serving students or faculty) in late February 2014, my initial reaction to the grant was that we needed to get approval to hire more tutors. Essentially, there were not nearly enough tutors allocated to work the number of hours that the Writing Center and Writing Lab were supposed to be open, as well as for the number of students that these tutors and coordinators were expected to serve. I also quickly learned that serving as the director of this grant and our Writing Center initiatives made me the servant of two masters as I needed to find ways to meet both college and DOE expectations and requirements in order to be successful and work to ensure the sustainability and longevity of this program. For example, even though the grant stipulated that certain objectives would be met, we still needed to gain formal college approval to do each of the things listed (e.g., requesting approval to attend a particular conference, order something mentioned in the grant, etc.). Further, we also had to ensure that everything that we did was in accord with Title III-A policies and procedures. For instance, since no grant funds can be spent on publicity, we had to be creative in finding ways to advertise the Writing Center to students, faculty, and staff through either free means (creating website content, leading class visits, and including information about the Writing Center into scheduled workshops, etc.), or as an addition to information that advertised open tutoring positions. Regardless of these challenges, both the English Department, the faculty who would be most immediately and directly affected by the grant's goals, and the rest of the college were welcoming, supportive, and collaborative as we all worked together to create structures and frameworks that would help make these programs come to life.

POPULATION SERVED

While the focus of our grant is to assist with at-risk student retention, and therefore provides a lot of support to our developmental writers, the Writing Center has an "all students, all writing" approach in order to give us the opportunity to assist more students and cast a wider net of impact and engagement on our campuses. Aside from professional tutors with backgrounds in teaching, tutoring, and English-related disciplines, we also hire qualified peer tutors from all disciplines, and help all writers at any stage of any sort of writing, from brainstorming and drafting to working through patterns of error and foundational grammar rules. Since we're a community college that also provides technical education, our students range from those in criminal justice to biology, music to mathematics, so we need to be prepared to assist with everything from nursing reports to resume writing and essays. Since we officially opened our doors in March 2014, we have held over 3,100 appointments, as well as close to 1,000 other contacts through workshops, instructional video engagement, and our weekly word Game Days by the end of the fall 2015 semester. Further, we are showing progress in our aims to assist with success rates in our English 092, 093, and 101 courses, which produce our cohorts for grant tracking purposes. The 092 and 093 courses attend a weekly one hour help session as a class with their instructor and one of our tutors, and our 101 students participate in activities listed within a portfolio program that we facilitate with the collaboration of the English Department. Prior to fall 2014, the success rate of a student who scored lower than a 77 on the COMPASS Writing Skills test was 63.56 percent. The chart below outlines our progress thus far.

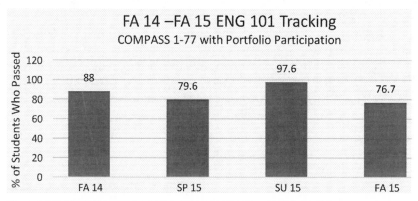

Figure 24.1. *FA14–FA15 ENG 101 Tracking, COMPASS 1-77 with Portfolio Participation*

In addition, our data shows increases in the fall-2014-to-fall-2015 retention of our ENG 092, 093, and 101 cohort at 50.44 percent, whereas the baseline was originally 45.57 percent prior to the availability of these Writing Center services. We will continue to brainstorm creative ways to engage and support our student population, as well as collaborate with other stakeholders on campus whenever possible.

FUNDING

All aspects of our writing centers were fully funded by our Title III-A grant for the first two years of our five-year grant period. However, after year two, our college then began to take on certain aspects of the budget, such as 20 percent of professional tutor and staff's salaries in year three, 30 percent in year four, and 40 percent in year five, as well as faculty professional development funding for years four and five. However, all of our peer tutors' salaries will be paid through the grant for the entire five-year period.

The question of cost in regard to running our program on a yearly basis is an interesting one, because in our case we stepped into a pre-set budget with the expectation that all grant funding be spent by the end of our five-year grant period. So, even though certain monies have been allocated for specific purposes, we still hold the responsibility of spending this money in ways that both college and DOE guidelines and policies. For just the Writing Center aspect of the CWWI (not including the Writing Lab, the purchase or maintenance of our computer and center equipment, professional development for faculty, our English 101 program, our external evaluator fees for the grant, or our other endeavors),

I would estimate that we could run the Writing Center for approximately $245,000 each year. This projection includes three full-time staff salaries, two professional tutor salaries, eight to twelve peer and professional tutor salaries, travel to the international and regional writing center association conferences each year for the director and coordinators, writing center association memberships, supplies, our WCOnline subscription, and our external evaluator fees.

OPERATIONS

I believe very strongly in teamwork, and have done my best to set up an empowered leadership structure in which my two coordinators and I keep our program running on a day-to-day basis. Running the CWWI takes quite a bit of brainstorming, troubleshooting, problem-solving, and planning (you should see my to-do lists and the white board in my office), so I have set up a system where each coordinator serves as the leader of the day-to-day operations of the Writing Center location on his or her campus. I assist in this process by helping with hiring processes, semester schedules, discussing issues and providing professional development opportunities, and spend the other 75 percent of my day working on other grant-directed projects and initiatives, which range from day-to-day to months in advance.

To provide a more in-depth view of our daily tasks, the job description charts for the director, coordinator, professional, and peer tutor positions are included below.

ASSESSMENT

As of this writing, we have completed the fall 2015 semester, which was our first full year of complete program implementation with all aspects of our grant requirements to the fullest capacity. We are seeing great results in our student success and retention goals. Further, our data also reveals that are efforts to support writing in all disciplines across campus is showing great progress as well. Regarding our cohorts of students, all incoming students take a COMPASS Writing Skills Test, and their scores on this test lead to their placement in either developmental English courses (ENG 092 and 093 with a score of less than 62) or English 101 at 62–100. For us, we are tracking students who are considered at-risk, or who score lower than a 77 out of 100 on this exam. Therefore, our grant requires the implementations that we've made to provide additional support for these at-risk students, while also creating these centers

Table 24.1. Title III Coordinator/CWWI Director

Position: Title Project Coordinator/CWWI Director	
Duties & Responsibilities	• Monitor and assist with all implementation strategies
	• Monitor project budget and ensure appropriate use of funds
	• Prepare project reports for submission the US Department of Education and other interested stakeholders
	• Ensure compliance with applicable policies, grant terms, and conditions
	• Oversee project evaluation activities
	• Provide oversight for setting up writing center spaces on both campuses
	• Interview, hire, and train CWWI staff
	• Develop CWWI policies
	• Conduct outreach to faculty and campuses
	• Meet regularly with administrators and faculty to discuss issues pertinent to the writing requirements
	• Ability to work effectively and professional with faculty, staff, and students

Table 24.2. The Writing Center Coordinators

Position: The Writing Center Coordinator (1 Dothan Campus and 1 Sparks Campus)	
Duties & Responsibilities	• Coordinate all writing center activities
	• Recruit, supervise, and train writing center tutors
	• Conduct training sessions and workshops
	• Network with appropriate college groups and departments
	• Assist the project coordinator/CWWI director with data and report preparation

and spaces to serve the whole campus. So, we are tracking students with certain test scores but are not considering other factors such as race, ethnicity, class, academic background, and so on.

After this fall 2014 semester ended, and once all students registered for their spring classes, we were able to see immediate connections and improvements between participating in programs within the CWWI and student persistence. To assess this information, we compare a list of our targeted students with those who attended CWWI programs, and then track the academic progress of these students with enrollment and grade data from our Instructional Effectiveness Office. If these students pass their courses and either graduate or enroll the next semester, then

Table 24.3. The Writing Center Professional Tutors

Position: The Writing Center Professional Tutor	
Duties & Responsibilities	• Tutor and encourage students on their writing on an appointment or drop-in basis
	• Supervise and serve as a resource for peer tutors
	• Address tutoring or general questions from students and other members of the college community or refer those questions they cannot answer to the Writing Center coordinator
	• Present classroom workshops
	• Complete a survey after every tutoring session
	• Relate to and work with students individually and/or in small groups
	• Exercise good judgment and communicate effectively both orally and in writing
	• Exercise strong organizational skills
	• Promote positive student, faculty, and staff relations
	• Use basic computer software programs

Table 24.4. The Writing Center Peer Tutors

Position: The Writing Center Peer Tutors	
Duties & Responsibilities	• Be familiar with all resources (e.g., handouts, reference books, computer software and manuals) located in the Writing Center
	• Answer grammar questions
	• Attend tutor training meetings
	• Write articles for the newsletter/website
	• Be aware of and able to use a variety of strategies to work with a diverse clientele whose writing skills cover a wide range of ability
	• Work no more than nineteen hours per week

we will meet our grant's qualifications for our success regarding course completion and persistence.

Ultimately, this data is presented to the DOE in varying forms every year after an initial six-month report, and we meet with our External Evaluator once a year to help ensure that we're on track to meet goals and are following our procedures appropriately within the guidelines set by the DOE. I also report to an on-campus advisory board to help share our progress, as well as send information up our supervisorial chain to help keep our stakeholders in the loop regarding our efforts, challenges, and successes.

MARKETING/PR

Since our centers are funded through a Title III-A program, we are not permitted to use grant funds for publicity purposes, such as giving away t-shirts, food, or buying banners to advertise our services. Therefore, we have been creative in devising as many free means of publicity as possible through word of mouth activities that we would be doing anyway, such as class visits and encouraging instructors to talk about the Writing Center. One example of creative thinking was devised by one of our peer tutors, who created our center's first logo so that we could install it as the desktop background on the computers in the Writing Center, Writing Lab, and other publicity materials. Since that time, a professional tutor has updated this logo, as well as designed a staff t-shirt for us to wear on our college's Wallace Wednesdays and campus presentations. We also participate in speaking at new student orientation events, have held a come-and-see open house at both campuses for the community and media, and are engaging with our students in nonacademic settings, such as hosting an ultimate Frisbee game and holding weekly word board game sessions. We are also in the early stages of creating our own instructional videos, voice recordings, and other media content, which we will highlight on our center's new Facebook and YouTube pages, as well as in other forms as our social media presence expands over the next few years.

The one caveat to using grant funds for publicity is that they can only be used to advertise available tutoring positions, and thus far we've created promotional bookmarks and flyers that advertise both the Writing Center services and our open positions. So, basically, we have no marketing budget. However, we do have budget lines for materials and supplies that we need, so we're working within those perimeters to help get the word out about our services and open positions.

One of the ways in which we, over the next five years, are ensuring that our targeted population (developmental writers) uses our services is through enacting the structure for new programs laid out within the grant, such as hosting hour-long, weekly sessions with certain classes, creating a writing support program for students who are required under the grant to receive writing center support, and building relationships with faculty in order to better our professional development options for their specific needs and disciplines. However, there are some challenges that might arise as we begin each of these objectives this fall, such as the fact that the vast majority of our students do not use, or even know, their college email address. Therefore, our advertising options are limited to what they see or can pick up around campus, things that they see on our college webpage, YouTube, or Facebook accounts, and what they happen to hear from another student, instructor, or staff member. Therefore, we must continue to be vigilant in the consistency and accuracy of our message in all of our print, published, or verbal publicity in order to help ensure that correct information reaches our students.

TECHNOLOGY

The use of technology for publicity purposes has recently expanded at our institution over the past semester, and we were thrilled to be selected as a pilot program for the college that gave us the ability to work with our Publicity Office to create our own Facebook page and YouTube channels thus far. Prior to this time, we were approved to set up a private and hidden staff-only Facebook page in which staff from both campuses can dialogue with one another, share resources, and form an online community as long as the PR director of our school can access the page to check it occasionally. Since our accessibility to social media is expanding, we are in the process of hiring an additional member to our team who will continue to create instructional videos, as well as oversee the further development of these social media sites and our college webpage. We also make use of Google Docs, Google Chat, and our institution's Outlook email for staff collaboration on projects, idea-sharing, etc.

We have a webpage on the college's website that matches the same template, fonts, color styles, and formatting of the rest of the college's website. This site contains the basics of the Writing Center—who we are, where we're located, what a writing center is and does (and doesn't do), and our hours each semester, as well as information about open tutoring positions and links to our social media sites. We've also been working to expand this site to contain the faculty writing resources that we have created and shared over the past year. Furthermore, our webpage also contains a link to WCOnline, which we use as our appointment-scheduling and session assessment platform. I, along with the two coordinators, have full administrative access to WCOnline, and the tutors have basic administrator access so that they have the ability to create clients, update appointments, and complete client report forms. Overall, we are thrilled to have the opportunity to expand our media presence and will continue to seek out ways to engage and encourage our students in as many mediums as possible.

Further, we have access to technology as it relates to instruction. Our Sparks Writing Center and Lab host almost thirty computers and an instructor podium with projector and speaker access, and our Wallace spaces host close to 110. These spaces also contain printers for student use (students purchase print cards and pay for their own printing on campus). This access to computers is important for our students since many of them do not own or bring personal computers to campus, so they benefit from both computer access and a place to work and print. All of these computers are set up with Microsoft Office and the Internet so that students have access to Blackboard. Our developmental English classes also work with My Writing Lab, but this program is not funded or controlled through the grant in any way.

ROLE OF RESEARCH

No research agenda is expected of us other than the in-house tracking that we collect regarding the students targeted through the grant. A good barometer of our "success" in this grant is being able to show whether or not course completion, persistence, and retention of certain student populations increase over the next several years. Therefore, while traditional research in itself will not assist with the continuation of our grant since this is not listed as one of our grant objectives, we believe in working to better both ourselves and our institution, so we will continue to learn new things and work to share that with others through conference and publication opportunities. Ultimately, our hope is that our research work helps us gain better understandings of ourselves, our students, and our programs, while also spreading the word about the great work being done at Wallace.

One early research project underway in 2014 was the work of one our coordinators who presented at IWCA that year; she conducted a mixed methods study relating to the persistence of students who have attended writing center appointments and the other coordinator and I helped fill in the rest of the presentation. Since then, all three of us had proposals accepted at regional writing center association meetings, as well as another IWCA and statewide community college conference, and our hope is to continue research of this kind, since it will both publicize our program and add to academic dialogue relating to developmental student persistence at community colleges, but also to legitimize our efforts since this research matches the mission of our grant.

PEDAGOGICAL AND/OR ADMINISTRATIVE HIGHLIGHTS

We in the CWWI believe in creating a culture of writing on campus, and we are doing our best to create sustainable programs where students feel welcomed, encouraged, and empowered by their writing and opportunities to engage in writing with others. By culture of writing, I mean that we're helping to promote writing on campus in a positive way by showing its relevancy to all educational programs, as well as academic and work-related pursuits. Prior to our arrival, our instructors were mandated to include three writing assignments in each of their courses—but without much support and guidance in doing that. Therefore, one of our goals is to provide this sort of assistance to instructors and to empower them to develop writing assignments that are both purposeful as they relate to course material and engaging as they teach students about writing in their respective disciplines.

We're also using our Writing Center spaces to make connections between writing and whatever else students might be interested in—reading, board games, creative writing, current events. We believe that bringing options, opportunities, and support for bettering student writing on campus will work to enhance a culture that we want to create where students feel that writing isn't a scary, boring, or awful thing to avoid but rather a chance to try something new and realize potential that they have to communicate in different arenas through academic, professional, and social writing support. From what I've learned about community college writing centers thus far, I would venture to say that ours is special because its creation has been incorporated into other new writing programs and initiatives at our college, all of which fall under my umbrella as the director of the CWWI.

While we do have a Writing Center location on each campus that serves all students and any type of writing at any stage, we also have a computer lab on each campus that is used by our developmental writing classes once a week, as well as by other courses and students throughout the week. During these hours in the Writing Lab, a writing center tutor assists the instructor with that day's class activities, whether working on writing, learning a new concept, meeting with individual students to discuss their work, etc.

Furthermore, all students in the college's English 101 classes participate in a portfolio program in which they self-select twelve options from a list that the CWWI staff developed with the English Department, which range from attending a weekly writing group session or monthly workshop, engage in a Writing Center appointment, and participating in a plethora of other options that vary each semester, such as submitting a piece of writing to a literary journal that one of our tutors created and oversaw during the fall 2014 and spring 2015 semesters. These activities count as a part of an instructor's daily grade assignments; our hope was, and still is, to implement purposeful assignments that engage and educate students without putting additional burdens on our stretched faculty, so we were pleased to collaborate on the creation of these assignments together.

PRIMARY DOCUMENT (at **writingprogramarchitecture.com**)

Our Writing Center began as a Title III-A grant proposal entitled, "Improving Student Retention and Success through the Center for Writing and Writing Instruction," which was awarded to Wallace Community College in 2013. The document included in the online companion serves as the foundational structure that helped establish our center's framework, gain an understanding of our student population and the specific needs that we were tasked with addressing, and provided timelines that enabled us to forecast our program's growth and expansion campus-wide. Kay Whaley, the college's director of grant development, composed this grant proposal with assistance from campus stakeholders and the educational consulting firm, JCCI Resource Development Services.

WPA'S VOICE

If you feel that you have an interest in a WPA role, or even think that you might be remotely interested one day, I would recommend meeting with the WPA at your current institution if you have one to discuss aspects similar to what we've covered in this book. While there, or through an online search to find a nearby WPA, take the time to ask this person about aspects of any job that are either deal-breakers or deal-makers for you, because whether you're interested in the work or not matters very little if the environment or culture doesn't align with your personal beliefs or desires. (However, regardless of what they tell you, also remember that each institution carries with it its own culture and environmental variables.)

My other piece of advice is to shadow or volunteer there, get a job as a tutor if possible, and consider attending a writing center conference or two. If nothing else, start reading past issues of *Writing Lab Newsletter, Writing Center Journal,* and others that you can access online. I don't believe that anything could have prepared me better for this current position than having the opportunity to work directly under two different WPAs for a few years because through these experiences I was given exposure to the ins, outs, and rationales behind all of our administrative functions, tutoring approaches, and plans for the future. Truly learning about writing centers gave me the tools that I needed to come to a new environment and build a writing center that fits this campus' culture and needs, rather than just trying to replicate something that I had seen, read about, or studied at some point along the way.

In addition, my own doctoral program in higher education administration provided a wonderful curriculum related to institutional management, legal issues, history, and trends that can align seamlessly with any specific department or division within a university setting. Because of this, I would also recommend taking a course in college student development, higher education management, and administrative leadership if you have these options available.

Regarding translating our array of experiences and proficiencies into this sort of work, I recommend assimilating into campus life as quickly as possible at your new institution. Even if it is not in your nature to do so, take time to meet and interact with different types of people on campus—students, faculty, staff, administrators, maintenance workers, etc. It's important to learn the campus and its population before trying to make changes to things that might be a certain way for a particular reason, or to learn that no one has considered doing X, Y, or Z.

Our grant certainly helped provide initial credibility for my coordinators and I because we were the ones hired to fulfill this prestigious project for our institution, and its stipulations for what work needed to be accomplished over the next several years laid out a map for us. Further, the professional development requirements within our grant provide opportunities for exposure and education in areas that might not be as familiar to us as others; for instance, I attended my first writing across the curriculum conference during the summer of 2014, which was foundationally helpful in beginning our Writing in the Disciplines (WID) journey here.

25

WESTMINSTER COLLEGE WRITING CENTER

Christopher LeCluyse

Institution type: Liberal Arts College
Location: Salt Lake City, Utah
Enrollment: 3,000
Year program was founded: 2004
WPA reports to: Dean of Arts and Sciences
Program funded by: School of Arts and Sciences
Description of students: The Westminster student body consists of about 2,200 undergraduates and 700 graduate students. While 60 percent of the student body comes from Utah, the other 40 percent come from at least thirty-three other states, and 4 percent of our students come from other countries. About two-thirds of our students are commuters. While the majority of our undergraduates are of traditional college age and are not the first people in their family to go to college, significant numbers of first-generation, non-traditional, and transfer students attend Westminster. The college continues to diversify its student body, a challenge in a state whose population has been predominantly white but is rapidly growing and changing. Currently, 17 percent of our students are of color.

PROGRAM SNAPSHOT

The Westminster College Writing Center serves undergraduate and graduate students, alumni, faculty, and staff across the entire college. In addition to one-on-one writing consultations, the center offers in-class writing workshops. We also operate Write Here, a community writing center in the City of South Salt Lake.

WPA'S PROFILE

I completed a PhD in English language and linguistics at the University of Texas (UT) at Austin, studying multilingualism in medieval English verse, but discovered writing centers through working in UT's Undergraduate

DOI: 10.7330/9781607326274.c025

Writing Center (UWC). As a graduate student, I was able to work as an assistant director in the UWC and then went on to coordinate training for our staff of about a hundred in a part-time postdoctoral position. On the side I taught as an adjunct at St. Edward's University and as a lecturer at the University of Texas. While such positions didn't afford me the opportunity to be promoted or take on greater responsibilities, I was able to gain additional writing center experience as interim coordinator of the UWC while our regular coordinator was away on a six-month writing fellowship and by serving as a sabbatical replacement for the writing center director at Southwestern University. Every step of the way I benefitted greatly from the support and mentoring of previous UWC administrators.

Writing centers opened up to me a collaborative, affirming environment that I found much more attractive than the more isolating and competitive world of English medieval studies. When I went on the job market for the second time after a limited foray during graduate school, I applied for both WPA positions and medievalist jobs. The market spoke, and all of my on-campus visits were for writing center directorships. I accepted the position at Westminster and have since led an "amphibious" existence, combining teaching, writing center administration, and now program administration as chair of English. In my various capacities I am the only program administrator serving the general student population and supporting faculty who assign writing. In addition to the privilege of working with our peer consultants, I am also involved with national writing center organizations and publications, having served as president of the Rocky Mountain Writing Center Association, regional representative to the International Writing Centers Association, and submission reviewer for *The Writing Center Journal,* the *Writing Lab Newsletter,* and *Praxis: A Writing Center Journal.*

PROGRAM CONCEPTION

In 2004, the Westminster College Writing Center opened in the Giovale Library as part of a larger initiative to enhance support for students and co-curricular programs. From the beginning, the director of the writing center has been an English faculty member, while the center's staff and operations budgets have been housed separately within the School of Arts and Sciences. When I became director in 2006, the center had been operating on a limited scope, working primarily by appointment and with students required to visit for developmental writing courses. The center had been without regular leadership, requiring undergraduate assistant directors to manage day-to-day operations.

My first efforts, therefore, involved reorienting the center's focus, building trust with the staff, and reaching out to academic programs. I shifted the center to working primarily with walk-ins so that more students would be encouraged to visit. To enhance student agency and investment, I also eliminated the required visits for developmental writing courses and in general discouraged faculty from requiring writers to come to the writing center. Since I did not inherit many materials, I set about developing handouts and other resources and created an Access database to record consultations.

To build trust with staff, I offered continuing employment for all consultants who had previously worked at the center, interviewing and training new consultants as needed. We treated staff training as a place where consultants could gather to share best practices and invent new ones (see LeCluyse and Mendelsohn 2008). Transferring this model to Westminster, I involved consultants in leading regular continuing training meetings and sharing their experiences in the writing center. As much as possible, I encouraged consultants to take ownership of the space and to offer suggestions for developing our policies and practices.

I also enhanced staff training by requiring future consultants to take ENGL 310: Theory and Teaching of Writing, the spring before they went on the job as paid consultants. This undergraduate course grounds students in composition theory and situates writing center praxis within the larger world of college writing pedagogy. Students complete a thirty-hour internship in the writing center so they can go on the job with at least some experience under their belts and conduct a series of observations to encourage reflective practice. This requirement is not without its drawbacks, however. So, we recruit students from all majors by soliciting recommendations from faculty.

To build bridges with academic programs, I met individually with deans of the various schools and asked how the center could best support their efforts. These meetings led to my developing a workshop for Arts and Sciences faculty on evaluating writing. I also became involved in a writing curriculum initiative in the School of Business, and somehow I ended up teaching a science writing course and sharing the load for an MEd thesis class! In effect, in the absence of anyone else responsible for supporting writing instruction, these efforts established me as a one-person Writing across the Curriculum program—a situation that Jill Gladstein and Dara Rossman Regaignon found was common to two thirds of the small liberal arts colleges that they surveyed (Gladstein and Regaignon 2012).

Eight years later, I can say with some confidence that the writing center has become a regular part of faculty's and students' experience on campus. A majority of graduating seniors report having visited the center (56% on the 2015 survey), and we conduct about two thousand consultations per year for a student body of about three thousand. We of course must face misconceptions and continually educate students and faculty about what we do—a situation every writing center director is familiar with. A large majority of visitors are satisfied with our services, however, and report that their visits to the writing center not only help them develop the particular assignment they are working on but their writing in general.

A new phase of our center's development began when I was approached in 2013 to open a community writing center in South Salt Lake City as part of a partnership between Westminster and the Promise South Salt Lake initiative. The center, called Write Here, is located at the Historic Scott School Art and Community Center, one of a network of community centers that serve the citizens of South Salt Lake, a number of whom are refugees and non-native speakers of English. Consultants from the campus writing center staff Write Here for sixteen hours per week, conducting individual consultations with adult community members and K–12 students as well as conducting workshops in area schools and other neighborhood centers.

POPULATION SERVED

The Westminster College Writing Center is open to Westminster students, alumni, faculty, and staff, as well as occasional community members who happen to stop by. The majority of the writers we work with, however, are students. Comparing the representation of various student groups among our clientele with their representation across the college gives a sense of how much they have integrated us into their writing practices. First-year students make up about one-fourth of the writers we see, for example, even though they make up about one-fifth of the entire student body. Graduate students comprise about 15 percent of the writers we see, though much more opportunity exists to work with them since they make up about a quarter of our student body. About a fifth of the students we see are non-native speakers, who visit the center twice as frequently as their native-speaking classmates. Our writers represent a wide variety of academic programs: the top majors served included psychology, nursing, English, the MBA program, economics, neuroscience, and accounting. While academic writing is the focus of most consultations, around 10 percent of our sessions focus on non-academic writing such as resumes and cover letters, application essays, and personal creative writing.

About half of the consultations we conduct at Write Here are with non-native speakers, including students in the Venture Course, a free college-level humanities sequence for low-income community members offered by the Utah Humanities Council and Westminster College. In general, native-speaking adult community members visit to work on personal and creative writing, while non-native adults and youth visit to work on academic writing.

FUNDING

The center is funded through the School of Arts and Sciences and receives about $33,000 per year for student worker positions and $1,200 for operations (our WCOnline subscription is thankfully paid for by Information Services, and regular office supplies and photocopies are covered by the School of Arts and Sciences). My one-third teaching load reduction is handled as part of my contract through the Provost's Office. Student travel to writing center conferences is generally funded through student-faculty research grants made available by the provost. Although the City of South Salt Lake provides the space for Write Here, the Westminster Center for Civic Engagement pays consultants while the outreach coordinator is paid by the School of Arts and Sciences. The community writing center currently has no designated operations budget.

OPERATIONS

My position involves directing both the campus writing center and Write Here and typically teaching two courses per semester when I do not receive an additional course release for serving as English chair. In addition to spending time in the center, I regularly give in-class workshops and attend meetings for efforts tied to writing and curriculum. I am also responsible for hiring and scheduling as well as budgeting and payroll. This combination makes for a busy but varied work life—enough to keep me constantly moving but not so much that I feel exploited or burned out. It does mean, however, that I am often away from the center and do not have as much time as I would like to observe and visit with consultants.

Two consultants also serve as assistant directors. Since I can be in the writing center only twelve or thirteen hours a week, I rely on assistant directors to help coordinate communications and presentations and act as "go-to" people when consultants have questions. The assistant directors coordinate communications and presentations and meet with me weekly to plan and direct our operations. I see the assistant directors as a source of "creative content" for our policies and initiatives; new ideas for what we can do differently or better often come from them. Assistant directors also help choose and facilitate topics for our annual start-up meeting and continuing training meetings.

The core of our staff consists of about twenty writing consultants, most of whom are undergraduates. While the majority of consultants are English majors, our current staff includes majors in communication, philosophy, sociology, neuroscience, and economics/finance as well as two Master of Arts in teaching students. Consultants' primary responsibility is conducting individual writing consultations, but consultants also volunteer to publicize the center, lead in-class writing workshops, and develop resources such as handouts.

Our consultants conduct about two thousand consultations per year. Typically two or three consultants are on staff at any given time; a decent staff budget allows us to be open sixty hours per week, including weekends. The entire staff meets for continuing training at the start of the year and about every three weeks thereafter. Topics for training come from consultant surveys for the prior year and input from the assistant directors. I often have asked various consultants to take responsibility for leading particular training topics based on their interests and areas of expertise.

While many writers make appointments before coming to the center—a process much facilitated by WCOnline—we regularly take walk-ins. The online appointment form indicates what writers would like to work on going into the consultation. We observe no strict time limit but try to keep consultations around thirty to forty-five minutes. Afterwards, consultants fill out a report form to record everything they discussed with the writer. If the writer would like his or her instructor to know about the visit, consultants send a copy of this form to the instructor. Otherwise, we keep writers' visits confidential to encourage and respect their agency.

Write Here operates with much more modest resources. On-site operations are supervised by an outreach coordinator who is paid by the Westminster School of Arts and Sciences as an adjunct instructor and also networks with area schools and other centers to arrange off-site workshops. One or two consultants who have already worked in the campus writing center are on staff for four-hour shifts four days per week. These positions are funded separately by the Center for Civic Engagement as work study appointments—a way of involving students in community service while giving them paid professional experience. A few volunteers also work one shift per week. In addition to conducting about a hundred consultations per year at Write Here, paid and volunteer staff conduct off-site workshops and presentations. In 2014–2015, we reached at least 150 community members through these workshops. This "flipping" of the usual work of a campus writing center to focus more on group instruction than one-on-one consultations is borne out by the experience of our pioneering neighbor, the Salt Lake Community College Community Writing Center (CWC). As the CWC's founder, Tiffany Rousculp (2003), noted early in its history, "much of our work is in collaboration with organizations . . . in writing workshops for the general public or targeted groups" (12).

Each year I compile an annual report both to characterize the writing center's business for that year and to assess our effectiveness. Tallying who visits the writing center by status (undergraduate, graduate, alumni, staff, faculty, or community member), class year, major, and first language helps us see who makes use of our services and identify areas for growth. Satisfaction surveys completed soon after consultations and by graduating seniors gauge how students regard our services. I undertake this kind of data-driven assessment not so much to satisfy an institutional mandate—though Westminster has beat the steady drum of assessment for some time now—but to provide concrete ways of demonstrating the impact and reach of the writing center.

A common challenge to writing center assessment is moving beyond "bean-counting" and satisfaction to more direct measurements of our effectiveness (e.g., see Schmidt and Alexander 2012). Our post-consultation survey asks writers to indicate how the consultation addressed or supplemented their concerns, whether similar kinds of assignments will be easier for them in the future, and how the experience affected their writing in general. With the switch to WCOnline in 2013, I added a question asking students to score their self-efficacy in writing to measure how students regard their own ability to complete a writing task. Comparing pre- and post-consultation self-efficacy scores provides a sense of our impact on student learning, as does comparing the kinds of concerns students identify when making appointments with those the consultant indicates they addressed.

Besides determining how the writing center affects writers, our assessment efforts also focus on how working in the writing center affects consultants. At the beginning and end of the academic year, staff members complete a survey that asks them to rate their comfort with various aspects of the consultation, from greeting the writer and establishing rapport to addressing issues of grammar, usage, and mechanics. Tracing the trajectory of consultant responses over the course of the year allows us to show what students gain by working in the writing center and helps us identify topics for future training.

While these various survey responses contribute to our annual summative assessment, day by day consultants reflect on their practice and support each other through informal assessment. Simply completing database records, which include a prose summary, requires consultants to reflect on their practice, and consultants' many interactions during their shifts provide opportunities to share strategies and debrief on recent consultations.

MARKETING/PR

We promote the writing center through brochures distributed at undergraduate and graduate orientations, announcements in weekly campus information flyers, and class visits. Campus tours regularly stop by the writing center, and we have worked to ensure that messaging from campus tour guides is consistent with our own by meeting periodically with campus tour coordinators. We also maintain a website, which includes electronic copies of our handouts, and a Facebook page, which one of the assistant directors routinely updates. Most recently, we have designed an ad to feature on the various information screens on campus.

I feel that the primary challenge to students' using the writing center is attitudinal. If they—or the faculty who tell them about the writing center—conceive of it primarily as a place for people "with problems," they may not realize how we can help even the most confident writers. I have been approached by colleagues who think they are being supportive by saying, "I always send my worst writers to the writing center." To correct this misconception, I have become more proactive at reminding faculty that we really are there for everyone.

Promoting Write Here has proven to be a continual challenge. Considering that traditional college students still need to be educated regarding what a writing center is and does, it is no surprise that community members from other cultures are new to the concept. Operating within Promise South Salt Lake creates the opportunity to serve people involved with other neighborhood centers, but we find that drawing people to Write Here requires constant outreach on our part.

TECHNOLOGY

Our writing center primarily uses technology to promote our services and record data on consultations. Because the college has a campus-wide laptop initiative, both consultants and writers have ready access to computers. Our current location in the Giovale Library's Information Commons also puts us close to public-access computer carrels where students often do their work, making it easy for them to pop into the writing center when they need feedback on their writing. All classrooms feature LCD projectors and computer consoles, so the in-class publicity presentations and writing workshops that my staff and I conduct can easily be facilitated by technology.

ROLE OF RESEARCH

Students in ENGL 310: Theory and Teaching of Writing regularly conduct quantitative and qualitative research in our writing center. Past topics have included a discourse analysis of consultations, investigations of how various majors use the writing center, and a time study to determine when we are busiest. In 2012, four undergraduate consultants studied how gendered expectations play out in consultations, motivated in part by the fact that our staff at the time was made up entirely of women. They analyzed over three thousand writing consultation records to determine whether men were more likely to focus on lower-order concerns than women (they weren't) and whether they visited the center closer to when an assignment was due (they did to an amazingly high degree of statistical significance). This group and other student researchers have presented their work at the Rocky Mountain Peer Tutoring Conference and the International Writing Centers Association Conference.

Some of my own scholarly work has fed back into our daily operations. For my article "The Categories We Keep: Writing Center Forms and the *Topoi* of Writing" (LeCluyse 2013), I identified the ten most common writing concerns included on record-keeping forms from a broad range of writing centers. When we replaced my less-than-adequate Access database with WCOnline, I used this top-ten list to define boxes that writers check to identify what they would like to work on and consultants use to indicate what they discussed with writers.

PEDAGOGICAL AND/OR ADMINISTRATIVE HIGHLIGHTS

Key to my approach to writing center administration is extending to consultants the same cooperative, inclusive, and nonhierarchical ethos that drives our work with writers (see LeCluyse 2004). I work to include consultants as fellow collaborators and in fact rely on them to suggest innovations to our practice. I also try to promote the center as a place of learning. We are never merely a student service, never simply "getting it done." Instead, we continually strive to make informed choices that will be of greatest benefit to writers, understanding that teaching well is a constant challenge, that we will often make mistakes, and that sharing those moments is important and healthy.

My conversations with consultants suggest that this collaborative, supportive ethos is coming across. One of our assistant directors commented, "We're collaborating with the students [writers], but we're also collaborating with each other." She and another assistant director observed that the staff gets along well and openly collaborates. They saw this cohesion facilitated by our training model; group dynamics start to evolve in Theory and Teaching of Writing before consultants even go on the job. The open layout of the center also makes it easier for consultants to seek feedback and assistance from each other.

Our move into a larger, even more open location has continued to facilitate such interaction. Originally occupying about two hundred square feet in the library, we now share space with the college's Eportfolio Studio, an open room with plenty of tables and computers where students can work on electronic portfolios and other multimedia projects. In this new space, writers have room to work and consult us as needed. We are also able to physically fit the entire staff in the space for continuing training and have a back room where consultants can socialize and relax.

Those campus consultants who also work at Write Here have had to develop their practice as they work with writers from a broader range of ages and English language proficiency. The collaborative, non-directive methods that we privilege with traditional college students do not always communicate clearly to older community members used to more directive teaching. Some of our Write Here visitors are just learning to read and write English, requiring consultants to focus more on basic literacy and language skills rather than the advanced academic writing they are used to. Together we have negotiated new ways of working in the center, for example, by patiently reading one sentence at a time with an Afghan refugee required to read George Orwell for the Venture Course or comparing consultations with a frequent visitor completing a memoir on raising her severely disabled daughter.

PRIMARY DOCUMENT (at writingprogramarchitecture.com)

Consultants complete a pre- and post-survey each year to measure what they gain by working in the center. These surveys have been important to our center in a variety of ways, and so I have included the post-survey with the online companion of primary documents. Consultants' evaluations of their comfort with various aspects of the consultation and the effect of writing consultation on their own writing help determine topics for future training.

WPA'S VOICE

Writing program administration can be a fruitful and satisfying career precisely because there are many entry points to the work and many ways to apply it. Alongside those who from day one knew they wanted to teach in and administer academic writing programs, there are "late converts" like myself (e.g., Peter Elbow and Lester Faigley also went into graduate school as medievalists). What's more, compositionists actually get jobs, and those who can develop an administrative skill set while still in graduate school are even more attractive candidates. I would encourage graduate students to take advantage of whatever opportunities exist for them to gain such administrative experience.

The main hitch is that however important WPA work is in practice, however many credit hours of composition classes are taught, or however many students visit the writing center, we must constantly push against larger cultural narratives that undervalue our work both among the general public and within academia. The key for me is to find and connect with other like-minded individuals, even if that means going outside a smaller institution and connecting with WPAs elsewhere—some of my closest fellow "comp-friendlies" are in other programs or teach at Salt Lake Community College. The meaningful relationships we develop with our colleagues and with the students we teach and serve greatly compensate for the lack of understanding we may experience from administrators or faculty who simply need to be educated about what we do.

References

Gladstein, Jill M., and Dara Rossman Regaignon. 2012. *Writing Program Administration at Small Liberal Arts Colleges.* Anderson, SC: Parlor Press.

LeCluyse, Christopher. 2004. ""Lost in Theory: Avoiding the Pitfalls of Using Theory in Training." *Praxis: A Writing Center Journal* 1 (2). http://www.praxisuwc.com/lost-in-theory-12/.

LeCluyse, Christopher. 2013. ""The Categories We Keep: Writing Center Forms and the *Topoi* of Writing." *Praxis: Writing Center Journal* 10 (2). http://www.praxisuwc.com/lecluyse-102.

LeCluyse, Christopher, and Sue Mendelsohn. 2008. "Training as Invention: *Topoi* for Graduate Writing Consultants." In *E)merging Identities: Graduate Students in the Writing Center*, ed. Melissa Nicolas, 103–117. Southlake, TX: Fountainhead.

Rousculp, Tiffany. 2003. "Into the City We Go: Establishing the SLCC Community Writing Center." *Writing Lab Newsletter* 27 (6): 11–13.

Schmidt, Katherine M., and Joel E. Alexander. 2012. "The Empirical Development of an Instrument to Measure Writerly Self-Efficacy in Writing Centers." *Journal of Writing Assessment* 5.

PART 5

Integrated Programs

26

ARIZONA STATE UNIVERSITY WRITING PROGRAMS IN THE DEPARTMENT OF ENGLISH

Shirley K. Rose, Susan Naomi Bernstein, and Brent Chappelow

Institution type: Public research university

Location: Phoenix, Arizona

Enrollment: 83,301 all campuses; 67,446 Tempe campus (fall 2014);

Year program was founded: as early as the university's founding in 1885

WPA reports to: English Department Chair

Program funded by: English Department, College of Liberal Arts and Sciences; this Writing Programs serves students in all academic programs on the Tempe campus.

Description of students: In fall 2014, 49,940 (60%) of Arizona State University (ASU) students were residents of Arizona and 8851 were graduate or undergraduate students from countries other than the United States. These numbers reflect a trajectory that has seen the university enrollment grow from 58,156 students in the last ten years. Arizona State University is an "open access" institution, which means that all students who are qualified are admitted.[1]

PROGRAM SNAPSHOT

In 2014–2015, ASU's Writing Programs offered 949 sections of writing courses to 22,536 students, taught by a faculty consisting of one hundred graduate teaching assistants, sixty full-time instructors, thirteen full-time lecturers, thirty-eight part-time faculty associates, two postdoctoral scholars, and nine tenured/tenure-track faculty. The curriculum consists of:

- A two-semester first-year composition sequence that is required for graduation in all academic programs. We offer an accelerated one-semester course as an alternative to students who meet advanced placement criteria and a "Stretch" program for students enrolled in basic writing that "stretches" the first semester of first-year composition (FYC) across two semesters. In addition, we offer sections of FYC designed for multilingual students.

DOI: 10.7330/9781607326274.c026

- A series of 200-level writing courses that meet a "literacy" requirement in general studies, which are popular with several majors across the university. These courses typically enroll more than four hundred students every year. Included in our 200-level offerings are courses that focus on writing for public audiences, analysis of academic writing practices, and reflective writing.
- Two professional writing service courses that are offered in the upper division to serve students who are majoring in programs offered by the W. P. Carey School of Business and other majors.
- An undergraduate Professional Writing Certificate consisting of nineteen credit hours of advanced writing courses. This coursework includes a professional writing internship and culminates in a digital writing portfolio.

WPAS' PROFILES

Each of the three of us will briefly tell our WPA story, since we represent three different kinds of WPAs.

Shirley

I am Writing Programs director, which is my fourth WPA position and my sixth administrative position over the course of my thirty-year career since completing my PhD at the University of Southern California, where I studied under W. Ross Winterowd, Louise Wetherbee Phelps, and Marilyn Cooper. I have held WPA positions more years than I have held regular faculty or other administrative positions. My first administrative position was focused on writing teacher preparation at Eastern Michigan University (EMU), and work on TA pedagogy has been an enduring teaching and research interest for me for my entire career. When I went from EMU to San Diego State University (SDSU), my responsibilities were mainly in writing faculty development. I was a primary author of a successful proposal to establish an independent Department of Rhetoric and Writing Studies at SDSU, and I was the first director of Graduate Studies for the new department. I went to Purdue in 1994, where I was director of Composition for two terms and also served as assistant department head for three years before moving to Arizona State University in 2009. In all of these positions, I have been fortunate to be supported by local departmental colleagues who recognized my research and scholarship on writing program administration as legitimate intellectual work on par with, if not similar to, their own. In addition to work on pedagogies of writing teacher preparation, I have published work on graduate education for writing program administration, writing program administration as intellectual work, writing programs as sites of research, and archival work in writing program administration. Being able to pursue an active scholarly research agenda grounded in writing program administrative practice has made it possible to sustain a long-term interest in WPA work. My WPA work has also been sustained by colleagues around the country whom I've met and worked with through the Council of Writing Program Administrators. I've been active in that organization since 1988, when I first attended the WPA Summer Workshop. I served on the Executive Board for a term and was president of the organization for two years, and a few years ago, I had the privilege of being a WPA Workshop leader. In the last decade, I have been active in writing program evaluation and consulting. I've served as an academic program reviewer on department review teams and as a member of the WPA Consultant-Evaluator Service, for which I became director in 2014. I am also a frequent peer reviewer for the Higher Learning Commission of the North Central Association of Schools and Colleges, the largest regional accreditation association in the United States.

Susan

I am a lecturer in Writing Programs in the English Department and co-coordinator of the Stretch Program for students enrolled in basic writing. I came to ASU from College of New Rochelle-Coop City, Bronx, New York, in 2013, and also have taught in Ohio, Pennsylvania, Texas, and Queens, New York, in both urban and rural settings. I have been recognized nationally as a leader in developing basic writing pedagogy through my book *Teaching Developmental Writing: Background Readings* (Bernstein 2013) for Bedford Books and regularly author "Beyond the Basics," a blog for teachers of developmental writing. My graduate training at Ohio University and Pennsylvania State University offered significant exposure to pedagogy and practice in basic writing. My first job after graduate school at an urban community college offered my first experience with WPA work as a coordinator of the first-year writing course. I also have served as co-chair of the Council of Basic Writing (CBW) and now sit on the CBW Executive Board. This service included co-editing CBW's *Basic Writing e-Journal*, for which I am currently an associate editor.

Brent

I am a PhD candidate in writing, rhetorics, and literacies as well as a graduate teaching associate in the English Department at ASU. I first encountered WPA work in my master's program at Northwest Missouri State University, where I was tasked with compiling information regarding end-of-sequence writing assessment practices to help the department consider possibilities for revamping its second semester FYC assessment. I worked with the writing center director and composition coordinator to gather resources on large-scale assessment, to summarize scholarship on the topic, and to suggest assessment possibilities for a new assessment program. It was after I submitted this project that I realized how much I enjoyed this type of work, and I began exploring WPA scholarship in greater depth. When I applied to the PhD program at Arizona State University, I wanted to work with Shirley Rose and learn about the administrative work involved in a large university. Because of the size of ASU's Writing Programs, I have been able to serve as the assistant director of Writing Programs for two separate academic years, during which time I worked on programmatic initiatives, visibility work for the programs, and developing a praxis of administration. As a PhD candidate, my research has shifted to an inquiry regarding visuality and audience in ancient Greek rhetoric, but I maintain a strong interest in the ways in which classical rhetorical theory can inform writing program administration as a field of inquiry and the ways in which the visibility work of WPA scholarship reflects many concerns of ancient teachers of rhetoric attempting to validate rhetorical study. My journey as a WPA has been one of exploring the field in greater depth and identifying those areas where I can best contribute to its continued development.

PROGRAM CONCEPTION

As Ryan Skinnell's (2011) dissertation showed, the history of ASU's Writing Programs can be traced as far back as the university's origins as Normal School for the region. Skinnell's dissertation describes the first one hundred years of writing instruction at ASU, and he concludes, "Rhetorical theory and writing instruction have enjoyed a relatively prominent place in the institution's curriculum and structure throughout its existence" (220). ASU's Writing Programs has a venerable history of being led by directors who have been recognized for their contributions to WPA scholarship since 1971 when Frank D'Angelo was the de facto director, although he served without official title. David Schwalm, while by no means the first WPA for the program, was one of the longest serving. Others have included Duane Roen, Maureen Goggin, Keith Miller, Greg Glau, who initiated the Stretch Writing Program with David Schwalm and John Ramage, and Paul Matsuda, who expanded Stretch with a new course for students identified as second-language writers. When Shirley took over the director role in 2009, the program was strong in most aspects. She was given the charge of developing the program's visibility on campus. Articulating and communicating a coherent message about the substance and value of the Writing Programs' teachers' and students' work has been a chief goal of program leadership efforts under her direction.

POPULATION SERVED

The total enrollment for the Arizona State University system in fall 2014 was 83,301 students, approximately 81 percent of whom were enrolled at the Tempe campus. Approximately 11,000 students were first-time freshmen, and more than half of those students were from Arizona high schools. ASU also admitted more than 9,000 transfer students, more than 40 percent of whom transferred from colleges in the Maricopa Community College district. The university reported a total racial/ethnic minority population of 24,731 (37%), with 20 percent of all undergraduate students identifying as Hispanic/Latino. In addition, approximately 11 percent of enrolled students are international students.

The Writing Programs at the Tempe campus serve a large percentage of these students. Roughly 98 percent of Writing Programs' courses could be considered "service courses," as they are offered for students in multiple majors in multiple colleges at ASU. First-year composition is required in all undergraduate majors, and many students who transfer in with all lower division general education requirements completed will enroll in one of our 300-level professional writing courses, which are recommended courses in many majors and qualify as upper-division "literacy" general education credit hours. In the fall 2014 semester, Writing Programs offered 523 classes, 53 percent of which were for ENG 101/102/105 first-year composition students. Fifteen percent of our classes were for students enrolled in the Stretch program including sections of Stretch dedicated for second language (L2) students. Twelve percent of courses offered were in the ENG 107/108 sequence for L2 students. Finally, 20 percent of our classes were for students in our 200-level course offerings, professional and business writing classes, or upper division courses for English majors and students enrolled in our Writing Certificate program.

FUNDING

The Writing Programs, like other programs under the umbrella of the English Department, has no budget independent of the English

Department and, at this time, no department funds designated specifically for Writing Programs. The cost of instruction for Writing Programs' classes is built into the department budget, which is reviewed and adjusted every year. Requests for support for items such as a $100 or so for refreshments for an all-faculty meeting at the beginning of the year or for more substantial support such as $10,000 or so to support our pilot of ePortfolio software are made on a case-by-case basis. Under current department leadership, a memo estimating funding needs for the upcoming academic year, based on funding received in the previous year, is forwarded to the chair and the department business operations manager. Although this funding request is not formally approved, it is used as a guideline for budgeting and it informs the chair's decisions in response to specific follow-up memos of request for specific items. When new one-time or recurring needs are identified, a memo detailing the costs precisely as possible and providing a rationale is prepared and sent to the department chair for review. The rationale is usually grounded in identifying the direct or indirect benefit to writing students. Typically, this begins a round of negotiations before the request is approved. Requests that involve additional compensation for any employee must be approved by the College of Liberal Arts and Sciences as well.

As Writing Programs accounts for roughly 70 percent of the department course offerings, staffing these classes is a major financial commitment for the department, costing roughly $6 million per year for teaching staff alone. The university budget allocations for instruction are, ostensibly, based on enrollments, and Writing Programs consistently meets or exceeds enrollment targets. Writing Programs has its own full-time program manager as well as two part-time student workers, and is served by department-level Business Office and Human Resources staff.

OPERATIONS

Shirley is one of thirteen tenured and tenure-track faculty members in the rhetoric and composition "area" of the English Department, which altogether has sixty-seven tenured and tenure-track faculty in seven areas. As a tenured faculty member serving in the Writing Programs director role, her time is officially assigned as follows: 40 percent research, 20 percent teaching, and 40 percent institutional and professional service. Half of that 40 percent service assignment, or the equivalent of one course per semester, is considered to be dedicated to her work as Writing Programs director. Most tenured and tenure-track faculty in the department have a 40 percent research, 40 percent teaching, 20 percent service assignment, and thus teach two courses per semester. Shirley's teaching assignment is usually related to her WPA work, as she teaches a graduate seminar in writing program administration once a year and also frequently assists with or leads the Seminar and Practicum in Teaching College Writing for the First-Year Graduate Teaching Assistants and Associates. Likewise, a large portion of her research agenda for most of her post-graduate professional career has been dedicated to scholarship on issues in writing program administration. This integration of the three main areas of faculty work into a shared focus on writing program administration has made it possible for her to remain engaged with WPA work throughout her career.

Susan shares her duties regarding Stretch courses with co-coordinator and senior lecturer Dr. Karen Dwyer, who troubleshoots issues of registration and placement not handled by the university registrar's office. In a university as large as ASU, Karen adds a crucial face-to-face component that contributes to Stretch's significance in building retention for first-year students enrolled in the program. Karen and Susan collectively run Stretch breakout meetings at Writing Programs Convocation in the fall, offer meetings and workshops throughout the year for Stretch Writing faculty, and engage in faculty mentoring. Susan focuses on faculty training, curriculum development, and outreach to local and national communities in basic writing. Beginning in fall 2014, we offered a practicum in Teaching Basic Writing. Assignment to teach a Stretch course for the first time is contingent upon participation in the practicum, either for credit or as official or unofficial auditors, and experienced Stretch teachers are encouraged to participate.

She designs and teaches the practicum, works on revising Stretch as a blended curriculum that includes online innovations and multimedia writing, responds to queries regarding Stretch history, curricula, and administration from faculty across the country, and writes and speaks about Stretch to national audiences. Her work with outreach includes developing and teaching Stretch onsite at an American Indian community in Central Arizona. The tribe provides funding for tuition and fees for students to enroll at ASU in an Indian Education cohort designed to train local tribal educators and support them in completing undergraduate work, and beginning the first year of a master's degree.

Brent served as an assistant director of Writing Programs for the 2011–2012 and 2013–2014 academic years. PhD students in the rhetoric and composition program who have a strong interest in WPA work can apply to serve a one-year term as assistant director of Writing Programs. Beginning with the 2011–2012 academic year, Writing Programs began appointing two graduate students each year to serve as assistant directors. Graduate students in this position do a variety of tasks for the program, including work with the Visualizing Teaching in Action (ViTA) classroom research project (discussed below) and organizing Writing Programs visibility efforts such as participation in the National Day on Writing or ASU's Night of the Open Door program. In addition, assistant directors have helped communicate with Writing Programs faculty through email and serving as editors for the program's newsletter, *Writing Notes*. In this position, assistant directors learn more about administrative work with the program and are encouraged to explore research related to their work with the program.

Several other tenured and tenure-track faculty contribute significantly to Writing Programs leadership, including Professor Paul Matsuda, who has been director of Second Language Writing for the last five years, and Elenore Long, who has served as faculty leader for the Seminar and Practicum for First-Year TAs for the past five years. Other tenure-track English Department faculty in rhetoric and composition frequently teach Writing Programs' courses. In fall 2014, seven of them taught Writing Programs' classes.

Writing Programs has thirteen lecturers, who are full-time contract faculty. They typically teach four courses per semester, are expected to do departmental and university-level service, and engage in an active agenda for professional development. Lecturers provide critical leadership for the Writing Programs with course releases from their standard four-courses-per-semester load for fulfilling leadership roles. In fall 2014, Lecturers taught 9 percent of the courses in Writing Programs. The associate director of Writing Programs visits the classes of new teachers in the program, arbitrates student and faculty conflicts, and assists with planning faculty development. Other lecturers serve in a variety of leadership roles related primary to faculty professional development, such as preparation for teaching online and hybrid sections or developing teaching portfolios.

Writing Programs faculty also includes sixty full-time instructors on renewable annual contracts. Instructors usually teach four classes each semester and also serve on committees that organize Writing Programs activities and event such as our Writers' Place awards for student writing, our annual Composition Conference, and our Celebration of the National Day on Writing. Instructors are expected to maintain active programs of professional development through participation in faculty development activities sponsored by the Writing Programs as well as pursuing other opportunities across the campus or in the area, such as attending workshops and lectures or participating in regional conferences. In fall 2014, our sixty instructors taught 50 percent of the Writing Programs' classes.

Approximately one hundred graduate teaching assistants and associates teach in Writing Programs. TAs study in a variety of areas in the department, with roughly one half of the TA appointments being held by MFA in creative writing students and the other half held by PhD students in literature, rhetoric and composition, or linguistics. Most of these TAs have an opportunity to teach a lower division, 200-level course in their areas of study before they finish their graduate studies, but their primary assignments are in Writing Programs. TAs taught 28 percent of Writing Programs' classes in fall 2014.

In fall 2014, we had twenty-six faculty associates, who teach one or two courses each semester in Writing Programs on a part-time basis and are hired on a semester basis. In fall 2014 faculty associates taught 13 percent of our Writing Programs' courses.

Our program manager is responsible for most of the tasks that keep the program running, such as scheduling and staffing classes and ensuring that program policies are followed. She oversees Writing Programs office operations such as copying and printing and mail delivery and also determines office assignments for teaching staff. The program manager also systematically collects and reports data on enrollment that the director uses for strategic planning for the program.

ASSESSMENT

Although Writing Programs in the English Department has conducted periodic assessment projects to measure student learning outcomes for writing in our courses, we have not had a sustained program-wide assessment design in place for a decade or more due to lack of essential resources for supporting the effort. Since the summer of 2013, however, we have received support for a pilot of Digication ePortfolio software, which has several features that support critical elements of portfolio-based writing assessment, including random sampling for any given criteria, systematic circulation of work to be reviewed to participating evaluators, long-term recordkeeping, and basic descriptive statistical data analysis. The Digication ePortfolio software we are currently piloting will allow us to conduct a variety of program assessment projects. An example of an assessment project we are currently conducting is a comparison of the performance of students in ENG 301 Professional Writing with performance of students in ENG 302 Business Writing in meeting the student learning outcome "Exhibit effective visual presentation skills," which is shared across the two courses. For a project such as this one, the ePortfolio software allows us to develop a rubric specific to our research question, select a random sample of student work from among more than 3,000 students enrolled in the course during an academic year, circulate the sample course portfolios and rubric to a group of program teachers who have been trained to read and evaluate for the project, and collect and analyze the resulting scores accurately and efficiently. In addition to supporting standard portfolio-based writing assessment, Digication has features that support showcasing student work as well as features that allow us to maintain a long-term archive of student writing for which students have given their consent for research.

MARKETING/PR

Given that our Writing Programs offers primarily service courses that meet graduation requirements for a variety of majors, we have little trouble filling our classes, typically enrolling slightly over 100 percent of the official enrollment capacity. Our "marketing" efforts are directed more to the "visibility" projects discussed below, which are designed to help us communicate our goals, explain our practices, and clarify our policies for the wider campus community.

TECHNOLOGY

Our program has a well-developed website, where we make basic information about our courses, policies, and activities available. We also have a Blackboard shell dedicated to internal communications and collecting important documents such as course syllabi from program teachers. We have an active Facebook page where we publicize activities and a Twitter account that we use to promote participation in special events. Development and maintenance of these digital spaces is a primary responsibility of the program's assistant directors. As mentioned above, we are developing our use of Digication ePortfolio software and anticipate extensive use of our own program ePortfolio as a way to publically share the work of our students and teachers.

ROLE OF RESEARCH

Serving as a site of inquiry is a major aspiration for ASU's Writing Programs. Our size, the credentials of our teachers, and our situation in a department with a large and nationally prominent PhD program in rhetoric and composition makes research a centrally important activity. We maintain a frequently updated list of published research for which Writing Programs served as a site, which can be viewed on our website. Our two most recent program research initiatives are the ViTA visual ethnography project and development of our Archive of Student Writing.

The ViTA project was designed to open up conversations about work within writing classrooms and provide visible evidence of the pedagogical practices of writing teachers. The project invites teachers, students, administrators, and the public to explore what happens in Writing Programs' courses. Through cooperation among teachers, students, and ViTA researchers, classroom activities are documented through combinations of photography, video, and audio as outlined in Institutional Review Board protocols. Participants in the project are invited to comment on the evidence presented on the ViTA blog. In addition, participating teachers are encouraged to discuss other "outcomes" of ViTA participation, including the development of pedagogical tools, conference presentations, or publications using ViTA data. Further developments, including the creation of a taggable photo archive, have been proposed and are under investigation. The ViTA project blog can be viewed online.

Our Archive of Student Writing is a collection of digital portfolios of students' projects from all of our writing courses for the past three years. In fall 2014, fifty of our teachers piloted assessment features of the Digication ePortfolio software, which will allow us to further develop our Archive of Student Writing and make the work collected there, all deposited with consent by student writers, more accessible to researchers at ASU and elsewhere. The Digication software allows for students and teachers to develop ePortfolios of their work that have varying levels of privacy options such as private to the individual, only visible to ASU accounts, or publicly visible. Digication also allows for course management and archival uses. One key challenge to developing and implementing the Archive of Student Writing has been the sheer number of students who enroll in our courses each semester. Our current use of the Digication ePortfolio software allows us to accommodate those numbers.

PEDAGOGICAL AND/OR ADMINISTRATIVE HIGHLIGHTS

Operating as "the largest writing program in the country," a title for which we appear to have no contenders, brings with it a number of size-related features that are suggested throughout this profile. We have a huge faculty of highly qualified teachers, thanks to our location in a major metropolitan area. Our situation in a very large research university also gives us access to an abundance and variety of intellectual resources, including but not limited to the ASU Institute for Humanities Research, Center for Games and Impact, Center for Science and the Imagination, the Origins Project, and Project Humanities. These programs and institutes offer featured lectures for faculty and students, grant funds for research projects, and opportunities to converse with scholars and community members because of their public engagement efforts.

We support a robust program of curriculum initiatives, in which one or more Writing Programs teachers pilot new curricula for Writing Programs' courses. Teachers who wish to design and develop a curriculum initiative present a detailed proposal to the Writing Programs Committee, describing their curricular design, assessment design, and plans for sharing outcomes with other teachers in the program.

Due to its size, our student body is very diverse, which adds immeasurably to the richness of classroom experience. Size also brings challenges, especially challenges to effective communication within the program. Our faculty are housed in numerous locations across campus, and casual meetings in passing are too infrequent to suffice for building community and shared sense of purpose. Faculty strongly desire to stay informed about all aspects of the program, but at the same time are overwhelmed by the number of daily emails required to simply keep the program running smoothly to maintain the status quo. Building community is challenging in the face of these conditions. Our beginning of the year convocation involves Writing Programs teachers in a day of activities designed to foster conversation about ways we demonstrate that we value student writing. Since spring 2014, we have shifted our major community-developing event from a convocation at the beginning of the semester to a Celebration of Writing showcase of student work at the end of the term. Historically, we have offered additional opportunities for community involvement, such as an annual conference focused on writing studies pedagogy, and meetings and workshops offered by Writing Programs staff.

PRIMARY DOCUMENT (at writingprogramarchitecture.com)

In 2010, we underwent a six-month process of collective reflection involving all teachers in ASU's Writing Programs in the English Department in the College of Liberal Arts and Sciences in preparation for a visit from the WPA Consultant-Evaluator Service. The 2010 program self-study included in the primary documents companion, as well as the recommendations prepared by the WPA consultant-evaluators after their visit, helped us to establish a solid grounding for our work to develop the program over the next five years. Some of that development will be evident in a comparison of data in the initial self-study with data in this profile.

WPAS' VOICES

Shirley

At the end of my first year as director of ASU's Writing Programs, we hosted a visit by a team from the WPA Consultant-Evaluator Service. We spent most of that first year preparing the self-study that informed the visit. The research that we collectively engaged in as a writing program in order to respond to the heuristic questions from the Self-Study Guidelines was a critically important reflective process, one that gave me an opportunity for extended conversations with program participants as well as with stakeholders outside the program. We have continued to collect much of the same program data on an annual basis, which informs our planning processes, as it gives us a chance to identify ways in which our students and teachers are changing and to make strategic decisions about the directions we need to take as a program in response.

The report and recommendations the consultant-valuators wrote at the end of their site visit has also served as an invaluable guide for directing our planning. I encourage all WPAs, novices and experienced, new to their particular position or having held it for many years, to arrange for a visit by a team for the WPA Consultant-Evaluator Service. As the current director of the service and an experienced consultant-evaluator, I obviously believe in the value of its work; but I am speaking here as the WPA of a program that has benefited immeasurably from a visit when I offer it as my best advice for new WPAs.

Susan

In the years I have worked as a basic writing teacher/scholar, there have been many changes across the discipline, including a new national focus on acceleration, as well the elimination of many programs at large urban universities that were foundational to our discipline, such as open admissions access courses at City College at the City University of New York, and General College at the University of Minnesota. Yet the Stretch Writing Program has, to paraphrase novelist William Faulkner, not only survived, but prevailed. This resilience is due in part to the wide-ranging vision of Stretch's founders, as well as the ability of Stretch to adapt and grow with the needs of changing times.

My interest in basic writing predates the beginning of the Stretch Program by several years. In the mid-1980s, as a new MA student in Betty V. Pytlik's composition theory course at Ohio University, I read an excerpt from Mina Shaughnessy's (1977) *Errors and Expectations*. In reading Shaughnessy, I felt intrigued by the possibilities of the basic writing course as a social justice imperative that offered students experiences with writing that had been unavailable to them in their previous education. The next year, as a second-year MA student, I taught my first basic writing course at Ohio University. The course included commuting students from the local Appalachian community, students from Ohio's economically underserved inner cities, and students from suburban and exurban areas in Ohio and elsewhere. Two critical details stand out from this first experience with teaching basic writing. First, the demographics of this course were much more diverse than the rest of the university. Indeed, the state of Ohio often is cited for the prevalence of segregated education, and the basic writing course proved an opportunity for students to interact for the first time with students from communities other than their own. Second, the students enrolled in the basic writing course seemed more attuned to the intellectual possibilities of engaging with the processes and products of writing. These two attributes of the basic writing course have remained constant throughout my career, which has included such diverse teaching locations as rural Pennsylvania and the Bronx, New York City. Both of these attributes are present in ASU's Stretch course. Both semesters of Stretch offer students credit toward graduation, which signifies that Stretch is not "remediation" and does not focus on accelerated acquisition of "basic skills." Instead, Stretch emphasizes the importance of academic writing as intellectual work that takes time and energy to develop through a variety of writing processes and products, over the course of two semesters.

We have added courses for multilingual writers and are building connections with a local tribal community. We are adding curricular changes to prepare students to learn and work with technology in blended and online environments, and we have added a practicum for new and interested returning Stretch faculty that focuses on best practices in basic writing pedagogy. This last development adds a strong sense of purpose to my work as Stretch co-coordinator. In working with Stretch teachers on faculty development, we not only address the present needs of our program, but we also work to ensure a promising future for basic writing as a discipline and the diverse needs of our students enrolled in basic writing courses. The opportunity to become co-coordinator of Stretch required the difficult decision of leaving New York City for Central Arizona. Yet the work of participating in Stretch's present, and helping to shape its futures, is well worth the journey.

Brent

I came into WPA work at the beginning of my graduate study not knowing exactly what it was, but my journey of reading the history of WPA issues, researching topics of interest, and conversing with practicing WPAs has led me to appreciate the complexity of connecting theory, research, pedagogy, and administrative concerns. It has led me to a much deeper appreciation of the field as a whole. What has been most useful to me as a graduate student interested in WPA work has been seeking opportunities to work with program administrators and participating in local and national conversations regarding WPA work. I highly advocate that graduate students interested in WPA work explore opportunities to work with administrators, including suggesting work that they might contribute to their programs. Furthermore, involvement in the WPA-Graduate Organization through the CWPA allows for students to engage in WPA work and develop strong national networks of engaged scholars.

Note

1. "Open access" differs from "open admissions." Open admissions institutions have no admissions criteria except the most minimal, such as completion of high school diploma. At the other end of the admissions spectrum are institutions that selectively admit students from among all of the applicants who have met their admissions criteria.

References

Bernstein, Susan Naomi. 2013. *Teaching Developmental Writing: Background Readings*. 4th ed. Boston: Bedford/St Martin's.

Shaughnessy, Mina P. 1977. *Errors and Expectations: A Guide for the Teacher of Basic Writing*. New York: Oxford University Press.

Skinnell, Ryan. "Writing, Programs, and Administration at Arizona State University: The First Hundred Years." Diss., Arizona State University, Tempe, 2011.

27

COLBY COLLEGE WRITING PROGRAM AND FARNHAM WRITERS' CENTER

Stacey Sheriff and Paula Harrington

Institution type: Selective liberal arts college

Location: Waterville, a small town in central Maine

Enrollment: 1,900

Year program was founded: The Farnham Writers' Center opened in 1984. The Colby Writing Program began as a pilot "Colby Writing Initiative" in 2009.

WPA reports to: Provost

Program funded by: Provost's Office. The Farnham Writers' Center operates as an ongoing budget center of the college, supported partly by an endowment from an alumni family. The Writing Program was started with external seed-grant funding from the Davis Family Foundation (three years) is now also an independent budget center under the academic affairs as well.

Description of students: Colby's admissions process is very competitive, so students are typically in the top 10 percent of their high school graduating class with high SAT (the average score was 1998 in 2014) and ACT scores (average composite score of 30). Colby's student body is predominantly white (59.4%), and it has slowly become more ethnically, internationally, socioeconomically, and regionally diverse. In 2014, 23 percent were students of color and 16.5 percent international[1] from sixty countries. About 15 percent of Colby students self-identify as the first in their families to attend college, and 47 percent of students receive financial aid. Forty-three percent of US resident students are from New England states, and 42 percent are from other states nation-wide. About 10 percent of students are from Maine.

PROGRAM SNAPSHOT

The Colby Writing Program (CWP) is an independent academic unit reporting to the provost. It oversees the first-year writing program, upper-level writing course development, faculty development around writing pedagogy, and the Farnham Writers' Center (FWC) for peer-to-peer tutoring. Five faculty—including Stacey and Paula plus three

DOI: 10.7330/9781607326274.c027

part-time faculty—teach first-year writing and varied upper-level courses in the Writing Program and English Department.

WPAS' PROFILES

Stacey

During my PhD studies in English, specializing in rhetoric and composition, at the Pennsylvania State University, I taught a variety of writing-intensive courses and gained the kind of WAC and program management experience that introduced me to inter-disciplinary writing projects and paved the way for my transition to WPA work. At Penn State, for instance, I had the invaluable opportunity to direct the Graduate Writing Center, which meant that I coordinated office logistics, worked as a writing consultant for doctoral students in departments from Meteorology to Religion, and taught writing workshops for graduate student instructors across disciplines. Later, as an assistant professor of English at Bridgewater State University, I joined a department that coordinated the university's multi-part writing requirement and included a strong cohort of rhetoric and composition faculty, and a generous WAC director, from whom I learned a great deal. Though I had training in composition theory, there was no graduate-level coursework on WAC/ WID or WPA work during my doctoral study. So, I developed my knowledge in this area through the literature in sources like the *WPA: Writing Program Administration, Writing Lab Newsletter,* and the *WAC Clearinghouse,* and by working directly with colleagues in a wide variety of disciplines. Eventually, I began to move into WPA work as chair of the Writing Committee and through faculty development work. For instance, a colleague in mathematics and I created a three-day summer professional development workshop on writing and quantitative reasoning. Based on strong faculty interest, we started an interdisciplinary Quantitative Reasoning across the Curriculum Initiative for the university.

In 2012, I joined Colby as the inaugural WPA to help the college move from a small, grant-funded "writing initiative" to a more sustainable and formally organized writing program. My position is a permanent, non-tenure track, staff-faculty hybrid position, and I have dual administrative and academic titles. In this capacity, I do a little of everything: coordinate and oversee the first-year WAC writing program, create faculty development around writing pedagogy, teach writing-intensive classes, lead all writing assessment, and chair the college's Writing Committee, which vets new proposals for writing-intensive courses, develops curriculum guidelines, and provides curriculum development grants.

Paula

I became director of the FWC after teaching literature and composition part-time in the Colby English Department. Before that, I had been
director of the writing center and director of composition at Marymount
College of Fordham University in Tarrytown, New York, where I was also
a member of the English Department. While the Marymount/Fordham
program, especially the writing center component, was quite small—only
about ten tutors and no formal tutor-training course—it did provide
initial experience that allowed me to transition successfully to my position at Colby. More important, it sparked my interest in writing center
administration over teaching exclusively. Looking back, that interest had
begun in graduate school, when, as a teaching assistant in the English
Department at the University of California, Davis (UC Davis), I took a
series of pedagogical training courses in order to teach undergraduate
composition classes there. At UC Davis, I taught composition at the beginning, intermediate, and advanced levels for four years as a graduate student instructor. I was also a peer teaching consultant, a mentor teacher,
and a Chancellor's Teaching Fellow. These experiences combined to
make me realize that my core interests involved administration (for its
creative potential in building and running programs), writing studies (for
its pedagogical and collaborative aspects), and mentoring (for learning
relationships outside of the classroom and the grading system).

PROGRAM CONCEPTION

The longest-running part of the CWP, the FWC for peer-to-peer tutoring in writing, was started in 1984 by English Professor Jean Sanborn. In
2009, Paula, who had been teaching as a visiting professor of English,
began as director of the FWC. The FWC had established traditions
and the important elements of a strong peer-to-peer tutoring center:
appointment-based tutoring; English 214, the tutorial pedagogy course;
and outreach programs in local schools. Institutionally, the FWC was
housed within with English Department, and the director both taught
in the department and ran the FWC with a course release of two classes
a year. Yet, while the FWC was certainly a known and familiar entity, it
had, over the years, developed some reputation for being a place of
last resort for "students who can't write." As director, Paula developed
a Writing Fellows program, an imbedded writing assistant program,
that paired individual tutors as the designated writing assistants for
with specific courses. She also increased outreach to individual faculty
and at all-faculty meetings. The FWC has grown steadily through these

initiatives, and now employs fifty tutors (normally, about forty-five tutors each semester accounting for those studying abroad). It is well known to faculty on campus, and typically serves about a third of the Colby student population each year. The growth of the Writing Fellows program is especially notable: from an initial faculty participation of only five the first semester it was offered, it now typically has twenty faculty participating every semester. While the program supports courses in all subjects and at all levels, it has developed its strongest collaborations with W1 (first-year writing) faculty, where fellows serve as an important link between first-students and W1 faculty, offering feedback to students on writing and to faculty on assignments.

The genesis of the CWP began almost a decade ago with the efforts of faculty in the English Department and the Communication Skills Working Group. The latter was one of three curricular working groups created in response to self-studies conducted for Colby's 2007 reaccreditation and tasked with making recommendations for curricular change. This working group ultimately advocated for the creation of an independent writing program. In 2009–10, the dean of faculty responded to this recommendation, which was based on lingering dissatisfaction and staffing issues with the first-year composition course, English 115; faculty feelings that too many students were placing out of this course; and exit survey evidence that students reported feeling less well-prepared in writing than their peers. The dean convened a task force to create a WAC initiative, in which first-year and subsequent writing courses would be developed and taught in a range of disciplines, and he applied successfully for a three-year grant to start the initiative from the Davis Family Foundation. Paula served on this task force from its inception.

In 2012, Colby created the position of writing program administrator to oversee and direct this new WAC/WID program. The college hired Stacey Sheriff as the first WPA; she has worked successfully with faculty since to develop more than forty first-year, writing-intensive courses (called W1s) and some thirty-five upper-level WID courses (W2s/W3s) taught by faculty in departments across the college, create W1 student learning outcomes and faculty guidelines, start an assessment program, and begin a successful faculty development program around writing and WAC/WID pedagogy. Her most current initiative is a Writing Enriched Curriculum (WEC) initiative to create departmental writing plans with two pilot departments, in collaboration with Pamela Flash and the University of Minnesota's WEC Program. Paula's position as director of the FWC was moved from the English Department to the CWP that Stacey heads; Paula is now an administrator who teaches. The open, collaborative working relationship between us has been crucial to building the program on both the faculty and tutoring ends. In addition, being able to collaborate has been crucial in thinking about strategies for teaching faculty about writing studies pedagogy, the WPA role, and opportunities for program research. The Writing Program now provides pedagogical services that focus the faculty on writing, which in turn creates greater investment in the teaching of writing and the value of peer tutoring, also allowing the FWC to serve faculty and students better.

POPULATION SERVED

We aim to serve the entire college community by creating a "culture of writing" at Colby that supports the spirit and principles of Writing across the Curriculum. More specifically, the Writing Program and FWC serves about five hundred first-year students through the W1 courses. At least one-third of the faculty, from all four academic divisions, have participated in Writing Program faculty development events, and some seventy teach writing-intensive courses. The FWC is open to any Colby student who would like to receive one-on-one peer tutoring in writing. It conducts 1,200 tutoring appointments annually and approximately another 1,000 through appointments with writing fellows. In addition, about 350 appointments occur through a one-on-one, one-credit tutoring course we offer (WP112) in which a student meets with the same tutor for one hour a week throughout the semester. The majority of 112 courses are taken by first-year, international students at Colby, and the course plays an important role in their transition to academic writing in English. We are currently conducting program research to identify which of our resources provide best support to second language (L2) students and to improve and expand services.

FUNDING

The FWC operates with a budget of about $63,000 a year, up from $49,000 in 2009–10, composed primarily of hourly student wages. It is a cost center (a numbered component of the budget) funded by the college. Stacey and Paula are paid out of the Provost Office's compensation budget (not the English Department). Neither of us have any formal partition of the staff and faculty sides of our positions; teaching two courses annually equals 40 percent of the standard five-course load, which is a good proxy for the proportion of the faculty component of our positions. As of 2014, the CWP has an independent budget of $15,000 for faculty development, refreshments, travel, materials, three to four hours/week for a student RA, one annual honorarium for a guest speaker, and curriculum development grants. In addition, the Provost's Office contributed $5,000 toward the WEC initiative, and Stacey is currently developing a grant proposal to seek startup funding to continue this project.

OPERATIONS

The CWP has two full-time staff, Stacey and Paula. We have hybrid staff-faculty, primarily administrative roles. We each teach one course per semester, in the Writing Program and the English Department, serve as instructors of record for two courses, and conduct independent studies. We manage all logistics from ordering food and booking rooms to photocopying, travel, and budget management. Stacey meets frequently with faculty across campus to consult on course development, student writing concerns, and grant funding. She develops and leads four to five writing pedagogy lunch workshops each semester, often developed in collaboration with Academic ITS or research librarians, and teaches an annual full-day WID workshop in December and May. She conducts the W1 assessment cycle and late-August reading day and chairs the Writing Advisory Committee that approves writing-intensive courses, establishes policy, and reviews grant proposals. As coordinator of the first-year writing program, most weeks Stacey also talks or meets with people in the Registrar, Provost's Office, and deans of Students about course enrollments, writing waiver requests, and struggling students. The first-year writing requirement is staffed almost entirely by full-time faculty, and we typically have two or three part-time instructors who teach seven to eight W1 sections each year.

The FWC director teaches the tutor-training course that includes theory and practice, as well as first-year writing classes, including one for international students entering at the pre-W1 level (formerly identified as those with an "ESL" requirement). Paula's duties also extend to working in collaboration with the WPA, the multilingual specialist, the dean of admissions, and the international dean to guide incoming international students into the most appropriate writing classes, and to following the progress of these students during their first year and beyond. In addition, the FWC director serves on the Writing Committee. The FWC also employs three head tutors, each of whom is responsible for helping with a given area of operational logistics, and about forty-five peer writing tutors each semester (depending on the number studying abroad any given semester). Until 2014, the FWC operated with a coordinator, a one- to two-year paid internship position, but the position was discontinued by the Dean's Office soon after the formal organization of the Writing Program.

Stacey and Paula hold a standing weekly meeting that has proven invaluable in setting joint priorities and doing weekly and semester-long planning. Paula also holds weekly meetings with the head tutors, and the FWC has a weekly staff meeting for all tutors, at which they discuss issues related to sessions and participate in in-service sessions on topics such as learning difference, sexual harassment, citation forms, and writing in specific fields.

ASSESSMENT

As a private college, Colby had not, until recent years, experienced the same pressures to assess the academic program as have public colleges and universities. As part of its initial work in the summer of 2010 and 2011, the Writing Steering Committee gave a diagnostic essay-writing exercise to all incoming students. The data from internal scoring of these essays by faculty was compared to SAT verbal and AP English scores, and it was determined that standardized tests did not reliably predict who did well on the assessment essays. This finding helped support the development of the first-year W1 requirement, with students not being able to "place out" based on SAT scores.

Shortly after arriving, Stacey began requesting faculty help with collecting writing for first-year W1 courses to build an archive for annual readings and for professional development purposes. Initially, many faculty were reluctant to participate, in part because they were concerned that this writing might be used to evaluate *them*. Stacey has emphasized that readings are anonymous (all essays are all blinded before reading) and for improving students' outcomes, which has helped to increase participation and faculty comfort. This past year, faculty beyond those who teach first-year writing courses were invited to help evaluate a large sample of first-year student writing as part of an assessment workshop for faculty who received WID curriculum development grants. Stacey used this first, formal W1 assessment reading as the springboard to create, collaboratively with participating faculty, a detailed list of student learning outcomes for W1 courses. Selected outcomes from the list were then used in the August 2015 W1 assessment readings. Based this reading, the twenty-two participating faculty made small revisions to the student learning outcomes to parse and clarify them. Lastly, as part of the WEC initiative, faculty in the two pilot departments have created evaluation criteria that they will use in a summer assessment reading of majors' writing.

The FWC also has two kinds of formative assessment: exit evaluations, which students complete at the end of a tutoring session, and writing fellow evaluations, which faculty complete at the end of a course. While the latter has provided some useful feedback, the former tend toward broad praise that has been of little use. Paula would like to collect better feedback from these exit evaluations and is in the process of exploring how best to do so. Overall, the FWC tracks its success through its usage, which has risen year-to-year and expanded through the Writing Fellows program. The FWC has seen some reduction in traditional sessions as tutoring has been shifting to writing fellows and to Writing Program 112.

MARKETING/PR

Because the FWC is so longstanding at Colby, it is generally well known. Even so, Paula promotes its services and events on the website, on e-announcements on various college-wide lists, and through targeted lunchtime writing workshops for students. Paula also sends tutors to make class visits. The FWC is on Facebook and Twitter. While Facebook has increased the FWC's profile, we also find that word-of-mouth and the website remain successful in maintaining a presence on campus. Stacey and Paula meet at the end of each semester to review the FWC student usage figures and the courses for which students most frequently seeking writing-related help. These conversations help us in reaching out to associated faculty and, at times, requesting modest budget increases. Our arguments for hiring a professional multilingual tutor for additional hourly support were also bolstered by such information.

The CWP has built awareness among faculty by offering small, competitive writing course development grants (from $1,500-$3,000), which are promoted by email, all-faculty meeting announcements, and individual encouragement from members of the Writing Committee. In addition, Stacey's regular faculty development writing lunches and full-day WAC/WID workshops during the December or May reading periods have acquainted many new faculty with writing scholarship and the goals of the program. The Writing Program also now has a website colby.edu/writingprogram (as opposed to the internal wiki we had before), and faculty report using this site for things like the guidelines for writing-intensive courses and the resources posted from writing pedagogy workshops.

TECHNOLOGY

The CWP and the FWC have websites. We work hard to keep both sites up to date, and the FWC also connects their Facebook and Twitter social media presence to their site. The Writing Program site is used regularly by faculty for things like writing workshop materials, grant applications, and writing lunch/special event registrations. All tutoring appointments are made online through the FWC website using WCOnline. Students from Kennebec Valley Community College (KVCC), the local community college, can also submit papers electronically for asynchronous tutoring feedback (using track changes) within a forty-eight-hour window. The FWC tried using Skype in the past for KVCC students and for Colby students during the Maine winter but found that students preferred to come into the FWC or (for KVCC students) sending their papers electronically.

Stacey has also worked with Academic ITS to create workshops on teaching writing with technology. Sessions on teaching writing in the wireless collaboration classroom, organizing student peer review feedback cycles in Google Docs, and using WordPress for collaborative writing projects in upper-level writing classes have been a popular and low-stakes way of encouraging faculty to integrate technology into their pedagogy intentionally.

ROLE OF RESEARCH

Developing a programmatic research agenda is important to both of us. In recent years, the work of program building and significant new curriculum development limited the time available for such research and meant that many of our research investigations are still new. We are in the process of documenting our successful collaboration in building the CWP; we think our work has been unusual in creating a "virtuous cycle" among the Writing Program, FWC, faculty, tutors, and students.

In 2013, Paula was a Fulbright scholar in France researching Mark Twain's stereotypes against the French in ways that have since allowed her to focus on global identities of the Colby writing community. On one hand, she is able to employ her experience of living abroad and functioning in a second language to build strong bridges with international students, especially first-year students. On the other, she continually uses that experience to inform and reinforce her training work with NES students on their approaches to tutoring L2 students.

Stacey recently worked with a writing tutor, Andrew Finn, to research the literature on teaching and tutoring multilingual students, which resulted in the creation of an annotated bibliography and resource archive for faculty. To continue this work, Paula and Finn presented at NCPTW in the fall of 2014, and Paula and Stacey created a confidential survey and focus group project about international students' experiences, self-perception, and writing resources at Colby, which they discussed at CCCCs in March 2015. Stacey also worked with the former writing coordinator, Alexander Champoux, and a faculty member at the University of Maine Orono to develop an IRB-approved study of the development of international students' writing abilities and their preferred teaching strategies for his master's degree program. As part of the new Colby Writing Enriched Curriculum pilot with the Computer Science and the Art Department, Stacey worked with Pamela Flash from the University of Minnesota to adapt Minnesota's IRB-approved writing surveys, which she has administered to students, faculty, and outside professional affiliates in both departments. They are also documenting the portability and adaptation of a holistic, faculty-driven model from a large research university to a small, liberal arts college.

PEDAGOGICAL AND/OR ADMINISTRATIVE HIGHLIGHTS

One element of the CWP that has been particularly successful is the Faculty Writing Pedagogy Lunch series that Stacey started in 2013. Colby had held special writing workshops a few times a year as part of the development of the W1 courses, and they were well-regarded and attended. As the number of faculty teaching writing-intensive courses expanded, Stacey and Paula recognized that a more organized and regular form of faculty development was needed. But scheduling proved to be a major challenge because there were no regular time slots that faculty across disciplines had in common, and 4:00 PM, the hour after classes, was already crammed with meetings and special events. Offering lunchtime workshops with sandwiches from 12:00–1:00 on alternating weekdays has proved to be the best solution. Stacey runs four to five workshops a semester, often in collaboration with Academic ITS and the library, and she has so far reached about a third of the faculty from across the curriculum. Colby's Writing Enriched Curriculum project is also a highlight. Colby is the first liberal arts college in the United States to adapt the full WEC model and to create a research partnership with Minnesota.

Another thing that makes the program special is the close working relationship that we have—one that facilitates tight connections between student-facing and faculty-facing programs. We have found, at conferences and when talking to other WPAs, that the extent to which we work together surprises others. It's not uncommon for the director of the writing center and the WPA to have very little to do with each other, which we think is a shame. It took us time to build this relationship, but it helps us to continually consider the holistic implications of program changes and the importance of "closing the loop" between academic initiatives and faculty development/tutor training. For instance, we found that faculty are more receptive to participating in W1 assessment efforts since we began explaining how the results are useful to future writing workshops.

Similarly, FWC's staff meetings have been enriched by their talking to tutors about local tutoring and curricular issues—for example, indirect tutoring and ELL students, faculty concerns about "coverage versus content"—and how these resonate with national research. On this campus, some faculty tend to align themselves with the FWC and what tutoring can do for students and others with the program's curricular and faculty-focused initiatives. Having a close working relationship means that Stacey and Paula can keep each other apprised of faculty feedback and concerns across such campus divides. This is especially important given the small size and intimacy of Colby's faculty; the liberal arts curriculum requires students to circulate widely and talk travels quickly among faculty and students—often across disciplinary lines and through diverse interpersonal relationships.

PRIMARY DOCUMENTS (at writingprogramarchitecture.com)

We have made three documents available in the online companion of primary documents. Each semester, we distribute our five-page "Writing Fellow Program" document electronically and by paper to all faculty members who have writing fellows; it sets clear guidelines for both faculty and fellows. In addition to outlining roles and responsibilities for writing fellows, it suggests specific ways that fellows might assist with writing-related tasks. It also provides faculty with suggestions on how to work best with their fellows and informs them about what fellows can and cannot do.

We've also included two flyers that illustrate one year's worth of offerings in the Writing Pedagogy Lunch series that I (Stacey) started at Colby College. Each semester, I offer four to five sixty-minute workshops on a variety of topics related to writing pedagogy. As part of this program, I collaborate with faculty colleagues across disciplines and with colleagues in Academic ITS and research librarians. Each year, I try to balance offering workshops on both important, recurring topics (e.g., responding to students' writing, assignment design, and inclusive writing pedagogies) and new subjects that respond to faculty needs and interests (e.g., group writing, blogging in advanced majors' courses).

WPAS' VOICES

In a small college setting, relationships are everything and programs are intimate. New WPAs at small colleges—especially if they are located outside a specific academic department—should work to be identified with faculty and with academic affairs rather than with "administrators" to build credibility. We have both found that teaching and using stories from our own classroom experience has been especially important to this process. The good news is that if you are successful in building trust with other faculty, and you respond promptly to problems and concerns, broad curricular change can happen quite quickly. The small scale also means that individuals can loom large and be incredibly helpful in facilitating change or create roadblocks and raise doubts with a few well-placed public comments. The small liberal arts college (SLAC) network has a very useful listserv and an annual convention, which have been very helpful to Stacey in negotiating the many differences between WPA work at a large university vs. a residential college.

Stacey

When I first started at Colby, I was surprised that there was very little campus conversation about general education. As a private institution without mandates or funding from the state, the college has little shared curricula and, for most faculty, the idea of working from a common syllabus was foreign and highly unpopular. The discourse of "sections" and "placement" was an unfamiliar one that did not fit well with the independent ethos on campus. There are also important implications for this setting when it comes to writing assessment. You can't assume much anonymity (of students or of faculty) when collecting a writing sample for assessment, and, of course, you won't get large bodies of writing data for research or to assess for trends by working across a given year or two. This means that program research must balance quantitative and qualitative data carefully, and take care not to discuss findings in a way that might seem to point at particular faculty or departments.

Paula

I came to writing center administration in a way that has become less common—moving over mid-career from American literature. My background teaching English and American studies courses at Marymount/ Fordham and UC Davis has proven key in her pedagogical outreach to faculty. When I first became director of the writing center, for example,

I found that faculty members voiced two main concerns about teaching WAC courses: not "sacrificing content to writing" and having the "training" to do direct instruction in writing. Having taught "a subject" lent her credibility with faculty in talking about teaching writing in disciplines beyond composition and rhetoric. Even if a new WPA doesn't have a broad teaching background, I recommend responding from one's classroom experience in discussing WAC and tutoring programs. It may seem obvious, but validating faculty concerns about "covering" content and teaching writing goes a long way to opening a broader dialogue. Sharing specific ideas and models about how you have approached these problems helps make you a collaborative colleague rather than an administrator.

In terms of the FWC, I see its strength in the dedication of its tutors, which in turns derives from having a small, personal program that allows tutors, faculty, and administrators to know each other well and work together closely. Even so, the purpose and pleasure of writing center work is to engage on an individual level with writers, and to do so takes a commitment to close, respectful listening. The FWC strives to be a place of true collaboration, where all learn about writing and communication from listening to each other.

In keeping with that philosophy, I have sought to build a truly diverse community in the FWC, one that models inclusion for the entire campus. I have made special efforts not only to serve but also to recruit as tutors LGBT, ALANA,[2] first-generation, and international students, and these efforts are proving successful across the board. I have found that students and faculty alike appreciate her personal outreach in this area, and I emphasize a focus on diversity as an important priority in serving today's college population.

In reflecting on our programs, we want to highlight three themes. The first is thorough-going outreach, whether to faculty, students, or other administrators. We have been most successful when we have worked with partners across campus: with the international dean on guiding new L2 students into courses, with faculty in developing new writing-intensive courses, with research librarians in supporting those courses, with the Admissions Office for summer writing sample readings, or with students in improving tutoring programs and services. While it was daunting at first to reach across institutional boundaries, doing so has proved one of our most successful strategies for building a coordinated and successful writing program and writing center. The second theme is the importance of creating an internal research-to-practice loop that has allowed us to identify strengths and weaknesses and apply that knowledge to courses and services. We regularly survey faculty (online and in year-end gatherings), and our survey of international students, for instance, will inform how we refine and revise our programs. Finally, we recognize the theme of patience and persistence. Some valuable programs, such as Writing Fellows, simply take a while to get off the ground; others, such as the development of required first-year WAC courses, need time for institutional memory to adjust. Having the opportunity to work closely with many different stakeholders over time has made creative program development and improvement possible.

Note

1. This includes resident and non-resident aliens only. An additional 5.6 percent are dual citizens, bringing the total proportion of "international students" to 22.1 percent.
2. ALANA stands for African, Latino, Asian, and Native American.

28

DREW UNIVERSITY VERTICAL WRITING PROGRAM

Sandra Jamieson

Institution type: Liberal Arts College
Location: Madison, New Jersey
Enrollment: 2,200
Year program was founded: 1970s
WPA reports to: English Department Chair
Program funded by: English Department / College of Liberal Arts Dean's Office
Description of students: A mix of middle- and upper-class mostly traditional-age students, 25 percent of whom are first generation college students and 32 percent Pell Grant recipients. Students come from almost every state in the United States; 5 percent are international, and 20 percent identify as African American or Hispanic. Drew University is SAT optional, but the average submitted SAT-verbal score is 560. Drew has an 85 percent retention rate.

PROGRAM SNAPSHOT

Drew's vertical writing program begins with a topics-based writing-intensive seminar taught by master teachers from throughout the college, and focusing on reading, writing, critical thinking, and information literacy skills. After the first year, students take two or more writing-intensive courses from across the curriculum and a discipline-specific writing in the major course or course sequence. All Drew Seminars (DSEMs) and many writing-intensive courses are assigned course-embedded undergraduate writing fellows, trained by the Center for Writing Excellence (CWE) and the WAC director to work with students in and outside of class and to share best practices with faculty.

WPA'S PROFILE

My journey to higher education was not a carefully planned progression but a series of context-based decisions, yet looking back I can't imagine

DOI: 10.7330/9781607326274.c028

being able to plan it any better. By always making the decision to do what I love in the place I want to be, I have ended up in a field and an institution that work very well for me. Unending curiosity is a kind of ambition, and I think it is the better kind for WPAs because we are called on to shape our field much more than members of any other discipline. I was very lucky, too. I did my undergraduate work in English and American studies in the United Kingdom (where I was born and grew up) at a time when higher education was still fully funded for those who could not afford to pay. After a few years in the corporate world, I came to the United States with the intention of earning an MA in American literature. Because my real objective was to get a few years away from Margaret Thatcher's England, I simply selected the university where I already knew some undergraduates, the State University of New York at Binghamton (now known as Binghamton University).

Yet as it turned out, my TA assignment to the Writing Center in my first semester and as assistant to a developmental writing course my second totally changed the trajectory of my career. Instead of returning to the United Kingdom with my MA I remained at Binghamton in the PhD program, teaching composition and writing a dissertation on the ideological grounding of composition textbooks. I was steeped in literary and critical theory but was mostly self-taught with regards to composition theory. I took several rhetoric and linguistics courses and a course providing an excellent overview of the field taught by Pamela Gay, who arrived after I had officially completed coursework, but aside from that I worked entirely with critical and literary theorists. Most notable among my mentors was William Spanos, who one day after a long conversation about ideology and education challenged me to describe the ideal first-year writing program based on the analysis in my dissertation. I described the interdisciplinary writing program at Colgate without knowing it even existed, but three years later I was hired there. I was lucky enough to work with Rebecca Moore Howard to develop that program into a major and also begin a writing partnership that has already spanned a quarter century.

Most of my grounding in theory and practice of WAC and WPA work was learned on the job at Colgate; however, my position was not tenure-track, so four years later I moved to Drew University where I still teach. I began as director of Composition, became director of College Writing, and am now director of Writing across the Curriculum and first director of the New York Semester on Communications and Media. I was hired at Drew at least in part because of my training and publications in American literature, and although my tenure and subsequent promotions were based on my writing studies scholarship, the fact that I could (and did) teach literature courses and creative nonfiction from the introductory to the graduate-level was important in a smaller English Department where we all pitch in as needed. As the only compositionist for almost two decades, it was essential that I had a generalist writing background. In addition to first-year writing and creative nonfiction, my courses range from electives to first-year courses to graduate seminars and international programs. There has always been plenty for me to teach, and I think a more narrowly focused WPA would not have been such a good fit.

PROGRAM CONCEPTION

I took over an existing FYW program at Drew in 1993; one in which 60 percent of the incoming class was placed into a section of FYW based on a placement test during orientation. The student abilities varied widely, and most sections of the course were taught by literature graduate students, not all of whom followed the prescribed modes structure. It was, in short, a typical 1990s course, and one my new colleagues did not believe needed to be changed. Today, Drew has a radically revised writing-enriched first-year program, a flourishing WAC program supported by course-embedded undergraduate writing fellows, and a proposal in place for a discrete track in writing and communication studies in the English major. The journey from that one course to this place was not smooth as presidents and deans changed, budgets shrunk, and lines were added and then lost, but it was always grounded in research and relevant theory. Although retired from the college, my predecessor and the program founder, Jacqueline Burke, author of the very early composition textbook *Twenty Questions for Writers* (Burke 1975), still taught the graduate course in the teaching of writing for my first few years at Drew. She and several faculty had regularly attended the CCCC in the 1960s and 1970s, and the design of the program reflected what she had learned there. It also reflected the work in social justice, civil rights, and early feminism of one of the full professors who taught in it every semester, Joan Steiner, who in the 1970s also developed courses in African American literature and co-founded our University Writing Center with Megan Simpson, the center's first director. Although the program has changed, I share the founding philosophy and strive to honor it.

My first task was to introduce shared outcomes and expectations in a spirit of equity and transparency, and within three years we had program-wide mid-term and final portfolios that represented 60 percent of the course grade, and were assessed holistically by the writing faculty.

The next year we began ability-level placement, with a two-semester stretch course capped at twelve students; standard semester-long first-year writing for most students, capped at fourteen; and a half-semester, research writing course for students with advanced writing skills. Four years later we had adopted guided self-placement, with students selecting their own writing courses and then writing an extended, source-based justification for that placement. Working with Les Perelman and his MIT-based online placement platform iMOAT, we developed a system that allowed long-term assessment and comparative research (see Irvin Peckham's [2009] description of how iMOAT was used at Louisiana State University). But at the same time, retirements and departures left the staffing of FYW entirely part-time aside from me. In retrospect I realize that the hiring of a trained WPA allowed the department to slip into the model of composition instruction familiar to us all from graduate school where full-time faculty teach literature and doctoral students in literature and adjunct faculty teach writing. Gladstein and Ragainon's (2012) research reveals how unusual that is for a small liberal-arts college (SLAC), and it is something we are finally changing.

In 2009, a general education revision moved us from one FYW course required of all students in their first year to the vertical writing curriculum we have today. That revision also resulted in two additional tenure-track hires and three postdoctoral fellowships. A second general education revision in 2015 combined a two-credit First-Year Seminar and a two-credit College Writing course into a four-credit writing-intensive Drew Seminar supported by course-embedded undergraduate writing fellows and a linked writing studio for those in need of additional support. In the economic downturn we lost both tenure-track lines and the postdoctoral fellowships, but nevertheless today we have a vertical writing program that incorporates the WAC-based writing seminars that are common at SLACs, a robust WAC program that is part of our general education program and all majors and minors, and undergraduate course-embedded writing fellows at all levels of the program. The first-semester topics-based writing-intensive Drew Seminar is taught by carefully selected faculty from across the curriculum and focuses on reading, writing, critical thinking, and information literacy skills. As such, it prepares students for the intellectual expectations of college and creates a foundation on which later writing-enriched courses build. After the first year, students take two or more writing-intensive courses that may count as general education breadth courses and/or toward the student's major or minor. Finally, one of the requirements for each major is a writing in the major course or in some cases course sequence. More than half of our students also do some kind of internship work in which most of them are required to write, and about which they write a paper in order to earn academic credit. In each case, writing is not presented as an isolated skill but as an integral part of the academic endeavor and the broader professional world. More significantly, these different locations for writing help students understand that each writing situation occurs within a discourse community that has different expectations and purposes. The revised first-year class introduces students to these principles as soon as they arrive at Drew, and thereby sets a firm foundation on which the vertical curriculum can build.

What makes it possible for students to learn and articulate this degree of meta-cognition about the writing they are asked to complete is the existence of undergraduate course-embedded writing fellows. In addition to the peer mentors, already assigned to Drew Seminars, each professor selects a trained course-embedded writing fellow to help students make the transition to college-level writing, but also to introduce them to and help them understand the writing process and the role of feedback and peer review in that process. In later semesters, students will encounter some of those same writing fellows embedded in writing-intensive courses within their majors, and this continuity helps to reinforce both the attitudes and the skills introduced in the first year. Perhaps more important, by working with fellows in different courses who use the same language to talk about writing, students are immersed in the concepts and language they need to scaffold their movement from one disciplinary discourse community to another. As they create and revise the four-year ePortfolio used to assess the program, students work with tutors in the CWE who have also been trained as fellows, which further emphasizes the connection and coherency of the program. That coherency is also very apparent to the fellows themselves, fueling student-designed majors and minors in writing studies. The English Department recently proposed a writing and communication studies track within the English major, and we also have a new Semester on Communications and Media located in New York City directed by writing and communication studies faculty. Over my two decades at Drew writing has moved from an underfunded service course to a core part of Drew's mission, evolving as our field evolved and incorporating research in teaching, learning, and program design.

POPULATION SERVED

Drew enrolls a population of students fairly typical of private liberal arts colleges: they are reasonably well-prepared (with an average SAT-verbal score of 560 but significantly higher scores in our honors program) and predominantly middle to upper-middle class although a third receive Pell Grants and a quarter are first generation college students. We have a four decades old summer bridge program for students from educationally and economically disadvantaged New Jersey school districts, funded by a State-level Equal Opportunities Scholar's Program, and I have taught writing-intensive courses within that program linked to various other courses, most recently a grant-funded STEM program. In 2014, Drew entered into a partnership with an international pathways program (INTO), which we hope will significantly increase our enrollment of international students but also ensure that they receive whatever necessary second language instruction and cultural immersion they will need to succeed at an American college.

These changes reflect our educational goals and commitment to mentoring and to diversity of background, experience, and knowledge, and revisions to the writing program also reflect these changes, especially the development of a more robust and intentional first-year experience and a linked and scaffolded writing curriculum. The most recent decision to incorporate the University Writing Center into a Center for Academic Excellence that also includes general course-based subject tutoring, disability services, and a new STEM tutoring program in the same space, will undoubtedly serve our changing population of students more efficiently; however, it may also reinforce a skills-based deficit model of writing support. The grant-funded WAC Writing Fellows program is designed to balance that and help students and faculty continue to perceive writing as a mode of learning and a structure for making meaning. These fellows serve the students but also WAC faculty as they seek to more effectively teach and respond to writing (see Gladstein 2008; Holly-Wells, Jamieson, and Sanyal 2014; Ottery et al. 2005; Spigelman and Grobman 2005) and they themselves become stronger and more reflective writers as a result of serving as fellows. Finally, the new writing and communication studies track in the English major is designed for students who already perceive themselves as writers and wish to move into writing-related careers along with those who are pursuing other majors but want to develop their writing and rhetorical skills.

FUNDING

While the Writing Center has always had a budget, and still does as the CWE, the Writing Program does not. Staffing of courses and any related costs come from the English Department budget, which is controlled by the chair of the department (a position that rotates every three years based on seniority). Budget cuts and staffing cuts have taken their toll, although each chair has recognized the department's responsibility to support first-year writing and the model put into place by my predecessor worked for over two decades even as collective responsibility for *teaching* the course declined. The dean I reported to for fourteen years provided funds for faculty development, assessment activities, and guided self-placement (and our membership in the iMOAT consortium), and worked with the deans of the two other schools to persuade the president to create a new tenure-track line for a director of the University Writing Center.

Everything changed with the arrival of a new president in 2005 and the dean of the college he hired in 2008, just as we finalized the general education revision that created the vertical writing curriculum along with the tenure-track coordinator of Writing across the Curriculum and three postdoctoral fellowships that supported it. The president, trained in English literature, was on record as opposing the teaching of writing, and faced with the need to make radical budget cuts his dean saw the writing program as, in his words, "low hanging fruit." Everything that used to be supported directly from the Dean's Office was cut, and when the two tenure-track writing faculty left, their lines were lost, along with the three postdoctoral fellowships. We are now back to one tenured writing position (the WAC director), and a director of First-Year Writing in a renewable two-year, non-tenure track position.

With the new Drew Seminar program, the cost of initial and ongoing faculty development, assessment, and stipends for the Drew Seminar writing fellows is now bourn by the Dean's Office, allowing five full days of faculty development in May with a stipend (and food), and a further stipend for faculty participating in portfolio assessment. Resource and duplicating costs for ongoing training of faculty and writing fellows also comes from the Dean's Office. WAC, on the other hand, remains entirely unfunded beyond my position and duplicating/print costs covered by the English Department. My predecessor in the position secured a renewable grant from the Edward W. and Stella C. Van Houten Memorial Fund to begin an undergraduate embedded Writing Fellows program, and when she left I implemented and expanded it into the current WAC Fellows program, described below. It is a one-year renewable grant and as long as it continues to be awarded, the program will continue. As with all writing work at Drew, my colleagues support it and can articulate the necessity for it, but do not believe it should be supported at the expense of departmental budgets.

OPERATIONS

Initially my role at Drew was the "go to girl for writing" as a colleague once put it. I primarily oversaw the teaching of first-year writing from placement to plagiarism hearings. I interviewed and recommended part-time faculty for hire and trained them; taught a graduate course on teaching composition, and mentored graduate students as they developed the teaching skills; developed and revised student learning outcomes with the writing faculty, oversaw the portfolio assessment process, and handled grade disputes; and was responsible for scheduling, faculty and program assessment, textbooks, and course-related technology and course management programs. I also worked with the Writing Center director (at times also overseeing the center). Finally, I work with faculty across the curriculum on writing-related issues from feedback, grading strategies, and plagiarism-avoidance to course assignment design and course structure. I called this a "stealth WAC" approach and it laid the foundations for the current program. Since my arrival at Drew I have taught two four-credit courses each semester, which represented a one-credit course release for administration. The nature of that administration has changed over the last two decades, but what remains constant is that it is always much more than one-course worth of work.

Now, although we have lost two of the three tenure-track faculty in writing and the three postdocs, administratively I am responsible mostly for WAC (including the grant that pays for it) and the undergraduate writing fellows, and for ensuring that we scaffold the vertical writing program from first-year through the majors, including adequate training and assessment using an ePortfolio. To this end, I work closely with the director of First-Year Writing but do not oversee her work. I also work with the director of the CWE, and co-teach the course for writing tutors and fellows with her. The more Writing Center tutors and WAC writing fellows are cross-trained, the better I believe our programs will be (see Holly-Wells, Jamieson, and Sanyal 2014), especially now that the writing-intensive seminars are all assigned an embedded writing fellow.

Tutors in the CWE and embedded Drew Seminar and WAC writing fellows are undergraduates, the latter funded by renewable grant money (for which I have to apply, write reports on, and manage). We do not have any administrative support in the writing program, although the English Department secretary is at least theoretically available to work with us as needed. She does not work in the summer, so placement, hiring, and initial training are done without administrative assistance. Now that the renamed Center for Writing Excellence has become part of a Center for Academic Excellence, it has a different administrative support structure, budget, and website and is no longer operationally connected with the Writing Program.

ASSESSMENT

When they were worth four-credits, all first-year writing courses included a mid-term and a final portfolio (constituting 60% of the final grade) each with a metacognitive reflective introduction, and, in addition to assessment of the students themselves, our process of holistically reading and scoring them functioned as our only direct assessment of the program. In 2009 when the course was reduced to two-credits, we moved to one end-of-semester portfolio, but it was still a major part of our assessment. Guided self-placement gave us a sample of high-stakes writing produced before the students had taken any Drew courses, allowing us to measure the progress by the end of the writing course or course sequence. Over the years, small and larger changes to the structure, outcomes, and pedagogy of the course came as a result of the portfolio sessions and the conversations that accompanied them (e.g., see Hausmann 2006; Holly-Wells 2006; McCoy-Pieper and Inskeep 2006).

What we did not know directly was how well—if at all—the skills we taught in the first year transferred beyond it. Anecdotally we could speak about students who did better than expected in subsequent classes went on to write honors theses and attend graduate school, but we could not assess the direct impact of first-year writing. Called on to do so more systematically as part of the general education revision, we designed an electronic portfolio to accompany students as they moved through the writing-intensive and writing-in-the-majors courses. The plan was to collect the placement essays, selected work from FYW, a paper from each writing-intensive course, and another text of the students' choosing, along with a metacognitive reflection—a fairly standard model. I created the portfolio shell (in Moodle), but because of various administrative changes it was never populated beyond the first year, or assessed beyond the program. As with pretty much everything described here, our lack of program budget or sanctioned advisory committee left assessment and faculty development work dependent on support from the Dean's Office. In 2015, that support became part of the revised first year along with significant faculty development, and the ePortfolio was implemented as designed in 2009. Holistic assessment by seminar faculty provide assessment of the writing and value added resulting from the first-year Drew Seminars. Separate but similar assessment will trace the longitudinal development over four years.

I also participated in a Council of Writing Program Administrators (CWPA) and National Survey of Student Engagement (NSSE) initiative to explore the relationship between writing and deep learning, which began with a group of CWPA members devising twenty-seven new NSSE questions based on "effective writing practices," which were then tested at eighty institutions including Drew (Anderson et al. 2015, 206). We used that Drew data for assessment in 2008, making modifications to assignments and the way we talked about writing as a result. Although Drew joined the NSSE Consortium for the Study of Writing in College in 2011, the data was not available to me. With the publication of the longitudinal study (Anderson et al. 2015) and a new institutional research (IR) director I hope we can incorporate new data as part of our assessment of both students' first-year and the four-year experience.

MARKETING/PR

Work at a SLAC includes a lot of service and face-to-face interactions, and this understanding might have been the most important element I took from my time at Colgate. Those interactions make it easier to garner support for change and marketing for existing programs happens all by itself because everybody knows about them and makes use of them—or so goes the theory. But there are two problems with this. The first is that negative attitudes and criticisms may not be shared because to do so could harm general collegiality. The second is that as programs change, old understandings frequently do not, and the challenge of rebranding them is probably harder. When I launched the WAC Writing Fellows program, I sent an email to faculty and received so many requests for fellows that I did not need to send a second email. There were not enough undergraduates trained as Writing Center tutors who could serve as writing fellows, and that coupled with what I learned was a stereotype of the Writing Center as a resource for weaker students, led many of them to ask if they could be assigned a specific student who was a major in their field, so I began on-the-job training in weekly meetings and now a one-credit independent study in addition to College Reading and Learning Association (CLRA) certification through the Center for Academic Excellence. The faculty knew and trusted the students they had recommended as fellows, so they were comfortable working with them and recommending students to them although they admitted not recommending that stronger students visit what was then the University Writing Center. This experience and the fellows themselves, helped me to see that at Drew, writing support of all kinds still tended to be perceived as remedial; indeed writing fellows and tutors admitted that they didn't even ask each other for help on papers—something that has been an essential part of the tutoring community everywhere I have worked. Suddenly a PR problem I had been unaware of needed to be addressed if WAC was to succeed.

The close work of writing fellows and faculty in the Drew Seminars is beginning to turn that around, as faculty see the value of fellows for all students and the word starts to get out that it is the better students who benefit most from working with writing fellows, especially those who can never seem to break out of the B range although their ideas are always identified as "good." Cultural change is slow, but the same realization has now pervaded the Biology Department where a WAC writing fellow was assigned to the intermediate "Writing in the Major" labs. Initially one fellow served all five labs, now we need at least three fellows to meet demand and students who worked with fellows as sophomores are applying to be fellows as juniors. Some of those fellows also work in the CWE, thus further breaking down the stereotypes, aided further by increased cross-training and programming and social media resources.

Our web page now includes profiles of writing fellows and writing experiences, an ongoing "Best Practices for WAC Faculty" guide written by the fellows, and short videos targeting individual aspects of writing from grammar to honors theses and graduate school applications (see "Technology"). The Drew website also includes profiles of successful graduates and students, many of whom, coincidentally, also writing fellows. Both the writing fellows and the CWE Tutors have started Facebook pages and Twitter accounts and plan to share resources and support each other's outreach through social media and the Drew website. Drew has a community site which sends out a daily email listing events and news, and the writing fellows post weekly "mid-week writing tips" for students and, less frequently, "WAC Tips" writing advice for faculty. A mix of strategies and humor, the idea is to keep writing and the availability of writing resources in the forefront in addition to advertising those resources. Together, we hope these things will showcase the work of writing fellows and tutors and thereby also educate faculty and students.

Related to this are high profile events like the SLAC International Writing-In started by Jill Gladstein at Swarthmore, which has provided the best opportunity for writing-related publicity at Drew. At the end of each semester over a period of about ten days the contributing schools (over a hundred now) hold a day of writing, shaped to suit local circumstances, but publicized collectively through social media, a shared hashtag (#IntlWriteIn), and a tagboard. At Drew, the writing fellows take over the ground floor of the library for twelve hours wearing superhero themed tee-shirts (a different hero each year, but the same message—see @DrewU_WF). A huge glass bowl of candy attracts students to a central table, which also includes a "guess the candy in the jar" contest, a collection of stress relievers and toys, and a huge poster board covered with descriptions of what people are writing that day. At that table students share their projects on post-it notes and learn about relevant resources via the writing fellows and the Center for Academic Excellence. The fellows sign up to work shifts, but tend to stay in the library afterward working on and sharing their own work, providing writing help but also modeling what it means to take writing seriously. This has generated ideas for smaller-scale projects like DSEM Sundays with a similar large group of writing fellows available in the library the day before Drew Seminar papers are due. Smaller-scale projects like providing fellows for workshops to help students applying for scholarship programs and to assist students as they revise their work for a Drew publication of best essays also publicize the existence of writing fellows and the fact that they work with all students. I have learned that PR needs to be ongoing and that I can't always trust positive face-to-face interactions to mean there are no negative assumptions and attitudes that need to be addressed.

TECHNOLOGY

After a brief experiment with Blackboard, Drew was an early adopter of the free course management software Moodle. When we shifted from iMOAT for guided self-placement, we collected the essays and placement questionnaire through Moodle, and I built our ePortfolio in it as well. Most faculty use it for their courses, at least to share the syllabus, readings and resources, and collect assignments, although some are now using various Google programs to supplement it. As WPA in our old writing program, Moodle allowed me to make course templates with already embedded resources, policies, outcomes, and other basic information into which the teachers of first-year writing could add their own syllabi and resources. This provided a program-wide consistency while giving instructors the freedom to make the course their own. At the same time, I could access the work for program-wide assessment. The revived ePortfolio is still in Moodle, with each incoming class enrolled in a four-year long "course" with groups for each seminar and the option of (manually) creating additional groups by major, minor, or other cohort. This allows us to assess the program in different ways and collect writing from a number of different cohorts over the student's journey through the vertical curriculum (see "Assessment").

Until 2015, each of the three parts of the writing program (the Writing Center, First-Year-Writing, and WAC) had a separate website linked from the main writing studies page. Each site included information and resources and the Writing Center site included a link to an online appointment scheduling program (WCOnline). The CWE now has a site connected to the Center for Academic Excellence with a link from writing studies. Writing program websites are important places for students, faculty, alumni, family, and others outside of the college to know what we are doing and learn about our program. They create a greater sense of transparency and provide one central place for resources and links to other related sites. In an ongoing project, writing fellows are developing short video guides (using Camtasia) accessible to the Drew community through the website so that faculty may embed links to them in their syllabi as appropriate, along with written guides already available. The fellows select the topics for the videos based on issues identified as important by the faculty with whom they work and so far have created entertaining and informative three to five minute videos on topics such as developing ideas, getting started, organizing your paper, developing a paragraph, creating smooth transitions, structuring a lab report, citing sources, and grappling with commas. Currently underway are others on structure and using secondary sources in specific disciplines and courses.

Social media is clearly the future, though, and as I noted above, the writing fellows and the CWE tutors are using social media and community forums to reach out to other students and increase faculty awareness of the work they do. They have set up Facebook pages and Twitter accounts to this end and are exploring how to use Instagram or Tumblr for resources. Drew also has community pages that send out daily emails to faculty and students listing group-specific events and news, and the writing fellows post relevant tips, strategies, advice, and occasional humor on the student and the faculty pages.

ROLE OF RESEARCH

I learned a decade into my time at Drew that one's program is a rich site for research and deeper comprehension of the field in general. I described an early version of our scaffolded writing program in a WPA paper in 2003 (Jamieson 2003), described a small study of WAC faculty attitudes at CCCC (Jamieson 2004), and published a version of our current WAC program in "The Vertical Writing Curriculum: The Forgotten Core of Liberal Arts Education" (Jamieson 2010a; written in

2007). I can't imagine designing a program not grounded in theory and research, so each time I consider changing our program in response to developments in the field it is an opportunity to expand our understanding of that topic and I at least present my ideas at conferences. Before we moved to our version of directed self-placement I read about how it worked elsewhere and met with those who had already adopted it. Once it was in place (we called our process "guided self-placement" because that title more accurately reflected Drew's culture and the process of advising we used), I conducted research on how the self-placement differed from where the students would have been placed if we had used SAT scores and presented it at the Conference on Computers and Writing (Jamieson 2009), and on how the students used sources in the placement essays we assigned, presented at the CCCC (Jamieson 2010b).

I have always also encouraged those teaching in Drew's writing program to research and write about it. After an overhaul of our portfolio process in 2004, four advanced graduate students who served as teacher-mentors presented papers at the New Jersey College English Association (NJCEA) Conference describing the process and the assessment feedback loop they had developed as part of it (Hausmann 2006; Holly-Wells 2006; McCoy-Pieper and Inskeep 2006). More recently, in 2012, Drew's first WAC coordinator, Melissa Nicolas, described her experience teaching reading along with writing in our newly designed first-year writing program in her first year at Drew in an article in the journal *Reader* (Nicolas 2012). She also collaborated with one of our first postdoctoral fellows, Michelle LaFrance, on two articles exploring issues related to the Writing Center and the WAC program, one published in *College Composition and Communication* in 2012 and the other in *Writing Lab Newsletter in* 2013 (LaFrance and Nicolas 2012, 2013). Finally, in 2014 one of our last postdoctoral fellows, Jennifer Holly-Wells, teamed up with the acting director of the University Writing Center, Maya Sanyal, and me to write an article for the Writing Center journal *Praxis* on the undergraduate embedded writing fellows (Holly-Wells, Jamieson, and Sanyal 2014). I am working with five former writing fellows on an article about the advice writing fellows can give WAC faculty, a version of which I presented on everyone's behalf at the 2014 IWAC Conference.

In recent years, my own research has taken a turn toward what Richard Haswell describes as "RAD: replicable, aggregable, and data supported" research (Haswell 2005, 198), and since 2008 I have been a principal investigator in the Citation Project, a multi-institutional study of source use practices, beginning with those of first-year college writers. Drew was one of the three institutions in the first study and also participated in the sixteen institution study that followed, and in addition to publishing our findings (Howard and Jamieson 2015), I have used them to inform pedagogy and program revision at Drew. As a result of this research, we removed the extended research paper from the first-year writing course, which my coauthor and I describe in "Researched Writing," in *A Guide to Composition Pedagogies* (Howard and Jamieson 2013), focusing on creating academic conversations between a few texts and developing deeper information literacy. Based on the findings of that research, we also revised our plagiarism policy to reflect a greater focus on pedagogy and a reclassification of cited patchwriting as poor writing rather than a breach of ethics.

PEDAGOGICAL AND/OR ADMINISTRATIVE HIGHLIGHTS

The broad-based faculty support for a WAC program as part of both general education revisions (2008 and 2015) and the awarding of tenure-track lines for the director of the Writing Center in 2005, the director of Writing across the Curriculum in 2008, and the three postdoctoral fellowships in writing also in 2008 were certainly administrative highlights for me at Drew. They emphasized the support of my colleagues for writing and their understanding of the importance of developing and staffing writing programs with trained faculty. The development of the postdoctoral fellowships in writing allowed me both to move beyond underpaid contingent faculty and also to help prepare faculty of the future for work at small colleges and liberal arts colleges—something that few graduate programs at large research institutions can do. While that program did not last long, it was a privilege to work with those who came through it, all of whom are now successful faculty and program directors. I am also gratified to be a part of our graduate concentration "Teaching in the Two-Year College," team-teaching the gateway course with a colleague—and former student—from Morris County College. One thing that has been reinforced for me over the years is that program directing in particular, and the teaching of writing in general are context-specific and I believe we serve the field if we can develop programs drawing on contextual knowledge and research that deepens our understanding of how it works.

My greatest pleasure, though, comes from the success of Drew graduate students who learned to teach writing in my program and have gone on to make careers as teachers of writing and directors of programs across the country. More recently, I am delighted to see the enthusiasm of the undergraduate writing fellows as they work to strengthen the writing skills of their peers and seek ways to deepen their own understanding of the writing process—and as they apply to graduate school, some of them in writing studies.

PRIMARY DOCUMENTS (at writingprogramarchitecture.com)

Two documents were essential to the development of our current program, and I offer them as models for others. The first is a position description and rationale for the postdoctoral fellows in writing, which I posted to WPA Listserv when they were approved in 2008. Although Drew no longer funds our program, I consider post-docs to be more ethical than non–tenure track (NTT) lines, staffing key positions while providing WPA experience and mentoring in return. The second is an extract from the most recent application for the grant that funds the undergraduate course-embedded WAC writing fellows, on which our DSEM writing fellows are modeled.

WPA'S VOICE

As a WPA for over two decades, the major advice I would give to those just starting out is to think long-term, but remain flexible and open to new opportunities and changing contexts; to move slowly, intentionally building and tending connections, alliances, and personal relationships across the campus among faculty, staff, and administrators; and to always consider program sustainability as you make changes. But the most important thing that I believe determines success in these others is to not make things personal. I was lucky enough to have been part of an evolving interdisciplinary writing program at Colgate before I came to Drew, so I had some sense of what might work and what to avoid.

The first thing I learned *not* to do is take things personally. This is hard, as can be seen in the many conversations, listserv postings, Facebook status updates, and even articles on the subject by composition faculty and WPAs. I have had to relearn it on many levels. There will always be faculty who have issues with writing. Perhaps they struggle with their own writing, perhaps they believe good writing demonstrates intelligence, or perhaps they don't feel confident teaching it. In any case, when this manifests as aggression toward the WPA, it is generally about them not you. Many faculty enjoy finding errors in emails and announcements for example, and I hate the power dynamics of grammar shaming, but if I am caught in an error I reply right back with "Good catch!" and sometimes a threat to send them drafts of my articles to proofread. While I admit I do double-proofread emails before I send them, refusing to see reactions as mean-spirited reinforces the idea that nobody turns out perfect prose all the time.

Not taking it personally also means not "owning" your program. That one has been harder for me. Taking an "I built that" approach suggests that the only way to change a program is by changing the director—even if that is actually very far from the truth. Linking a program too closely to a person also increases the likelihood of that program not continuing when the person leaves that institution. Shared ownership is difficult, especially when those who might share it don't necessarily want to share the work, yet the more people who feel proprietary about a program (especially if it can be tied to the mission of the institution), the safer it is and the easier it is to build broad support for incremental change. Program sustainability might be built through an advisory committee or rotating directors, but documentation and transparency are also important because nobody can take over a program if they don't know how it works or what it does. When I came to Drew, I sought advice from other program directors, and Katherine Gottschalk who directed the John S. Knight Institute for Writing in the Disciplines at Cornell told me to find someone to endow my program because then I could develop, run, and sustain it as I wished. That's the best advice I wish I had taken.

References

Anderson, Paul, Chris M. Anson, Robert M. Gonyea, and Charles Paine. 2015. "The Contributions of Writing to Learning and Development: Results from a Large-Scale Multi-Institutional Study." *Research in the Teaching of English* 50 (2): 199–235.

Burke, Jacqueline. 1975. *Twenty Questions for Writers*. San Diego, CA: Harcourt Brace.

Gladstein, Jill. 2008. "Conducting Research in the Gray Space: How Writing Associates Negotiate between WAC and WID in an Introductory Biology Course." *Across the Disciplines* 5.

Gladstein, Jill M., and Dara Rossman Ragainon. 2012. *Writing Program Administration at Small Colleges*. Anderson, SC: Parlor Press.

Haswell, Richard H. 2005. "NCTE/CCCC's Recent War on Scholarship." *Written Communication* 22 (2): 198–223. http://dx.doi.org/10.1177/0741088305275367.

Hausmann, Jessica. 2006. "Portfolios and Parity: Engaging an Adjunct Faculty with Structured Flexibility." Presented at the New Jersey College English Association Conference, Seton Hall University, South Orange, NJ, March.

Holly-Wells, Jennifer. 2006. "From Collaborating to Piloting: Making Ideas Work." Presented at the New Jersey College English Association Conference, Seton Hall University, South Orange, NJ, March.

Holly-Wells, Jennifer, Sandra Jamieson, and Maya Sanyal. 2014. *"From Silos to Synergies: Institutional Contexts for Writing Fellows."* *Praxis: A Writing Center Journal.* Special Double Issue on Course-Embedded Writing Support Programs in Writing Centers.

Howard, Rebecca Moore, and Sandra Jamieson. 2013. "Researched Writing." In *A Guide to Composition Pedagogies*, 2nd ed., ed. Amy Rupiper Taggart Taggart, Brooke Hessler, and Kurt Schick, 231–247. New York: Oxford University Press.

Howard, Rebecca Moore, and Sandra Jamieson. 2015. "What Is the Citation Project?" The Citation Project. Accessed December 20, 2015. http://citationproject.net/.

Jamieson, Sandra. 2003. "When the Bridges Don't Need to Be Built: The WPA and the Vertical Curriculum at a Small College." Presented at the Annual Convention of the National Council of Writing Program Administrators. Grand Rapids, MI, July 10–13.

Jamieson, Sandra. 2004. "Listening to and Learning from WAC Faculty Representations of Student Writers." Presented at the Annual Convention of the Conference on College Composition and Communication, San Antonio, March 25.

Jamieson, Sandra. 2009. "Using Online Essays for Ubiquitous and Sustainable Assessment and More." Presented at the Conference on Computers and Writing, UC Davis, June 18.

Jamieson, Sandra. 2010a. "The Vertical Writing Curriculum: The Forgotten Core of Liberal Arts Education." In *Composition(s) in the New Liberal Arts*, ed. Joanna Castner Post and James A. Inman, 159–184. Cresskill, NJ: Hampton Press.

Jamieson, Sandra. 2010b. "The Use of Source-Based Writing and Source-Use Analysis to Guide Student Placement Decisions in a Guided Self-Placement Program." Presented at the Annual Convention of the Conference on College Composition and Communication, Louisville, KY, March 20.

LaFrance, Michelle, and Melissa Nicolas. 2012. "Institutional Ethnography as Materialist Framework for Writing Program Research and the Faculty-Staff Perceptions of Work Project." *College Composition and Communication* 64 (1): 139–150.

LaFrance, Michelle, and Melissa Nicolas. 2013. "What's Your Frequency?: Preliminary Results of a Survey on Faculty and Staff Perspectives on their Work in Writing Centers." *Writing Lab Newsletter* 37 (5): 10–13.

McCoy Pieper, Terrie, and Kathryn Inskeep. 2006. "Mutiny and Group Portfolio Review." Presented at the New Jersey College English Association Conference, Seton Hall University, South Orange, NJ, March.

Nicolas, Melissa. 2012. "I Should Have Known: Teaching Reading and Writing." *Reader* 67 (2): 79–97.

Ottery, Jim, Jean Petrolle, Derek John Boczkowski, and Steve Mogge. 2005. "Writing and Reading Community Learning: Collaborative Learning among Writing Center Consultants, Students, and Teachers." In *On Location: Theory and Practice in Classroom-Based Writing Tutoring*, ed. Candace Spigelman and Laurie Grobman, 112–125. Logan: Utah State University Press.

Peckham, Irvin. 2009. "Online Placement in First-Year Writing." *College Composition and Communication* 60 (3): 517–540.

Spigelman, Candace, and Laurie Grobman, eds. 2005. *On Location: Theory and Practice in Classroom-Based Writing Tutoring*. Logan: Utah State University Press.

29
NEW MEXICO TECH WRITING PROGRAM AND WRITING CENTER

Maggie Griffin Taylor, Julianne Newmark, and Steve Simpson

Institution type: Science and engineering research university
Location: Socorro, New Mexico
Enrollment: 1,633 undergraduates, 494 graduate students
Year program was founded: ~1995
WPA reports to: The Department Chair, who reports to the Dean of Arts and Sciences and the Vice President of Academic Affairs
Program funded by: Communication, Liberal Arts, and Social Sciences Department and the Academic Affairs Division. Some funding for writing tutors comes from the Center for Graduate Studies.
Description of students: New Mexico Tech (NMT) students tend to be high-performing, driven students aiming for careers in STEM fields. Most self-identify as "geeky." As a Hispanic Serving Institution, we have an undergraduate Latina/o population of 33 percent. We also have a growing international student population (mostly from China) as a result of several international agreements.

PROGRAM SNAPSHOT

NMT's Communication, Liberal Arts, and Social Sciences (CLASS) Department offers courses in humanities, has a technical communication major, and is home to the Writing and Oral Presentation Center. The writing program is housed along with the Writing and Oral Presentation Center in the CLASS Department. The writing program offers a three-course required writing sequence, consisting of two first-year academic writing courses (ENGL 111, College Writing: Exposition; and ENGL 112, College Writing: Argument and Analysis) and one junior- and senior-level course (ENGL 341, Technical Writing). Recently, our department has added writing courses for ESL students and even for graduate students, which expands our program's reach to nearly every student on campus. A supplemental one-credit English studio course

DOI: 10.7330/9781607326274.c029

(ENGL 189) is recommended but not required for incoming students whose placement scores in English fall below the admission standard.

WPAS' PROFILES

The three authors of this article represent various stages of service to NMT's writing program.

Maggie

I am the current writing program coordinator (WPC) at NMT and the 2011 recipient of NMT's Distinguished Professor Award. I received my PhD in rhetoric and composition from Texas Tech University. While not formally trained in writing program administration, I have served as director of academics and coordinator for technology training. I have taught a variety of writing courses, including developmental courses, ESL, and first year academic writing courses. In spring 2012, I became associate coordinator of the writing program, working under the chair of the CLASS Department. In 2013, I became the WPC, bringing my research expertise in ethics and the rhetoric of health and medicine to bear on my leadership of the writing program. In addition to teaching in the writing program, I teach courses in the technical communication major and in the philosophy program.

Julianne

Until 2015, I was an associate professor of English at NMT, and I served as writing program coordinator from 2008 to 2013. Now, I am a faculty member at the University of New Mexico (UNM). Though my PhD from Wayne State University is in American literature, my training as a teacher of writing and my years at NMT teaching courses in the writing program enabled me to take over as writing program coordinator in 2008 when the previous coordinator left NMT. I inherited the previous WPC's "files," but serving as WPC came to be an odd hybrid of "hitting the ground running" and "learning as you go" for me. I was committed to serving as a WPC who devised new approaches for curriculum design and assessment based on consensus-derived objectives voiced by the faculty as a collective. After collecting input from all writing program instructors in twice-per-semester meetings, I would present to CLASS chairs programmatic writing program changes (such as textbook selections or measures to adjust assessment areas) only if endorsed by all writing program instructors. My goals as WPC were to clarify the articulation and design of courses across the writing program, to create a usable website for the writing program that would provide concise information and resources for students and faculty, and to coordinate department-wide assessment approaches with those suited specifically to the program's focuses and realities. Today, in addition to teaching in the writing program, I teach American, multi-ethnic, and environmental literature courses, and courses in the technical communication major. I am founder and editor of the ejournal *Xchanges*.

Steve

I am an associate professor of communication at NMT; I direct the Writing and Oral Presentation Center and serve as chair of the CLASS Department. I joined the CLASS Department in 2010 after receiving my PhD from University of New Hampshire in composition studies. My interest in writing center work and graduate program development began during my graduate school days, as I found myself often in the position of having to create writing resources for graduate students where none had existed previously. I brought this interest in program development to NMT, where I came to develop programs in support of a five-year, $2.8 million Department of Education grant for graduate students (Title V: Promoting Postbaccalaureate Opportunities for Hispanic Americans [PPOHA]). Through my work on this grant and with the writing center, I have developed numerous partnerships with departments, services, and administrators campus-wide. Now, as chair, I have moved into a position where I must utilize these networks to benefit the entire department, which means finding ways not only to publicize the writing center, but also to support other programs within the CLASS Department, such as the writing program and the music program. Thus, in a very short period of time, I have had to develop a campus-wide view of how all the interlocking pieces within my home department fit with the school's strategic mission.

PROGRAM CONCEPTION

Our department has delivered writing courses for as long as anyone can remember. An excerpt from the 1908–1909 course catalog humorously describes the importance of these early writing courses:

> Especial stress is placed on work in English writing. It is being recognized
> that a most necessary part of a technical graduate's equipment is an ability

to express himself in concise, consecutive, idiomatic English. Slovenly, inconsequential, ambiguous English in a report, a letter, an application, can readily lose a desirable position to an otherwise valuable technical man." (New Mexico School of Mines Course Catalog n.d., 13)

However, our department did not begin thinking in terms of a *writing program* until the early- to mid-1990s. Many mark 1995 as the official conception of the writing program, as that was the year we hired our first dedicated rhetoric and composition specialist.

In its earliest stages, the NMT writing program was loosely articulated through casual conversations within the department, which at the time was the Humanities Department. These early writing courses often emphasized literature with writing instruction in the background, and instructors had autonomy in their curriculum and pedagogy. The Humanities Department also experienced autonomy on campus due to fairly rigid divisions between academic units common to universities prior to the mid-1990s. While autonomy had its advantages, it also exacerbated the "two cultures" division between humanities and sciences on our campus. With the emerging interest in business writing in technical communication circles and Writing across the Curriculum (WAC) and Writing in the Disciplines (WID) in composition studies, the Humanities Department took steps to bridge this cultural divide. Our department's technical communication (TC) major emerged as a result of new faculty and expanding interests of current Humanities Department faculty. For many years, the technical writing class that developed was tacitly tied to the nascent writing program. Developing the TC major created traction for cogent discussions of writing theory and helped clarify the boundaries between what would materialize as a writing program and a separate TC major. These discussions crystalized in 1995 with the hiring of a writing specialist, who not only engaged the NMT community in dialogue on the importance of writing in STEM fields but also established the first writing center at NMT. Emily Nye's (1998) article in *The Writing Lab Newsletter* describes these developments well.

By 2003, the Humanities Department had hired two additional technical communication faculty, one of whom assumed the responsibility of WPC. This coordinator oversaw the sequence of courses in the program, articulated expectations for each course, observed faculty in the classroom, and collaborated on writing projects with faculty from other disciplines. This coordinator also continued the tradition of giving writing program instructors freedom to design courses around their interests.

Over the last decade, the department has experienced many changes, starting with the relocation to a new building (a renovated dormitory) with no classroom space and a few years later a name-change to "CLASS" (Communication, Liberal Arts, and Social Sciences) to better reflect the breadth of courses that the department offered. There have been five different department chairs in the last ten years. While each of these chairs made valuable contributions, the department has felt the effect of the changeover in this position. In this same time period, we have had three WPCs (including the chair of the CLASS Department who served as interim coordinator), and the writing center has been moved and restructured three times. For a short period, the writing center was folded into the general campus science and math tutoring center, though it was brought back to the CLASS Department in spring 2010. Numerous faculty members within the writing program left the department; some, but not all, of those positions were filled with new faculty hires, leaving the writing program stretched thin. The program was fortunate to have Julianne in a stable WPC role for seven years, to have Steve's additional capacity upon entering the department to stabilize and expand the writing center, and established faculty members like Maggie.

These many changes to the writing program's leadership and identity, and to the identity of its home department, have created numerous challenges. One challenge that coordinators face is balancing the autonomy and the quality of the writing instruction with economic realities of the university, such as hardline budget cuts. Adjunct faculty may feel these budget cuts most immediately, but tenured and tenure-track faculty are also affected as they are reassigned to cover core courses. The role of WPC often involves advocating for faculty members regarding course loads, equitable pay, and benefits, schedules, and course requests. Economic constraints also endanger certain courses that university administrators deem unnecessary, such as basic writing classes, which become more necessary each passing year as the university seeks to increase admissions and retain at-risk students.

In addition, at a science and engineering university, WPCs and program faculty often find themselves having to demonstrate the importance of the required writing classes and negotiate with other departments who want more discipline-specific content in the writing program's required technical writing course. Arguably, these conversations have become easier in recent years as professional organizations in many STEM disciplines and accrediting agencies such as the Accreditation Board for Engineering and Technology (ABET) have stressed the need for scientists and engineers to communicate outside of their disciplines. Thus, numerous opportunities have emerged on campus to connect our program with innovative STEM research initiatives. For example, we have connected several of our ENGL 111 and 112 courses with the Living Learning Communities (LLC) initiative started through another Department of Education grant (Title V: Student Engagement and Success [SES]). These initiatives do ease the perceived gap between the "two worlds." Nonetheless, our attempts to build these relationships with other departments are complicated, and we find that successes (e.g., one of our department faculty assuming a position teaching in the Mechanical Engineering Department) often create new problems to address (e.g., an unfilled tenure-track position, and more pressure from other engineering departments for department-specific instruction).

POPULATION SERVED

NMT's student body has grown increasingly diverse. As a Hispanic-Serving Institution, NMT has a 33 percent Hispanic undergraduate population with an additional 18 percent reporting a race or ethnicity other than white. While NMT has traditionally enrolled more men than women, the overall male–female student ratio has improved in recent years to 2:1. Also, while our graduate programs have always attracted international students, we have recently experienced a sharp increase in the international undergraduate population through several international agreements with overseas universities. For example, a Memorandum of Understanding (MOU) between the Petroleum Engineering Department and Yangtze University has brought close to sixty Chinese undergraduates to our school on a 2+2 agreement (i.e., students complete their first two years at Yangtze University and their last two years at NMT). In the following section, we describe some of the diverse student needs our program encounters.

Advanced Student Writers

As a nationally-ranked engineering school, we see numerous students in our classes who enter college with strong academic backgrounds. Many of these students are children of researchers at one of New Mexico's many national labs or students who have attended elite private or preparatory schools and have received strong prior writing instruction. While NMT students can place out of the first-semester composition course (ENGL 111) with AP English scores or strong ACT or SAT scores,[1] they still generally take ENGL 112 with students who might be far less confident or proficient writers.

"Underprepared" Student Writers

At a STEM school, the majority of students identify English as a difficult subject. However, with increased efforts to recruit from rural parts of New Mexico and to attract and retain students from historically underrepresented groups, we have seen a rise in students with less preparation in academic writing. Some come from rural or "underperforming" schools and might have had fewer opportunities for sustained writing. Others might come from language minority communities within New Mexico and might feel less confident with English communication (e.g., some of our Spanish-speaking and Navajo-speaking students). For reasons explained later in this chapter, we do not have a "basic writing" program, though we have been working to provide more options for students. The challenge is to provide additional assistance for "underprepared" students without marginalizing them in classes that also include stronger writers.

ESL/International Students

Due to our recent international agreements, we have had increased undergraduate international student enrollment, particularly from China. These students very often come to NMT with relatively low English proficiency but enter at the junior-level. Thus, the learning curve for these students is very steep. We have had to create a separate (but parallel) English sequence that more quickly prepares these students for the linguistic demands of upper-level science and engineering classes.

Graduate Writers

As part of our participation in a Department of Education grant, our department developed a graduate-level communication program aimed to support students in STEM disciplines writing their theses and dissertations. NMT has a large international graduate student population (at least 25%) and has been working to improve its Hispanic graduate population (currently at 12%). See Simpson (2012) for more on these programs.

FUNDING

Writing professionals taking jobs at smaller schools need to be prepared for the fact that the funding and budgeting process is often much different from what one might encounter in a larger school or program. Our writing program does not have a separate budget; in fact, there is not even a specific line item for the writing program. We have just one budget for the entire CLASS Department, and everything must come from there. So, for example, our department is given a base of $9,000 for student workers for an entire fiscal year, though we have successfully negotiated with Academic Affairs for $12,000. This amount not only funds undergraduate writing center tutors and graders for first-year composition classes (approximately five to six writing tutors/graders), but it funds other department student worker needs, as well (e.g., IT support for department computer labs). Thus, one must strategize these costs as much as possible (e.g., hiring students via work study, hiring students who assume multiple roles, etc.). Further, one must take advantage of opportunities for outside funding when possible. For instance, our graduate student writing tutors are currently funded through a quarter-time fellowship offered through the Center for Graduate Studies. (We have three graduate fellows for each year).

Funding for writing instructors operates differently at our institution, as well. More than half our general education writing classes are taught by tenure-track faculty or permanent non-tenure-track faculty. In any given semester, we might still need anywhere from five to seven writing classes to be taught by term adjuncts. Our department does not have an adjunct budget. Rather, there is one pool of adjunct money managed through the Academic Affairs division. Each semester, every department on campus submits adjunct needs for the following semester, and adjunct contracts are doled out based on need and availability. For this reason, increased adjunct need in the Math Department—or even elsewhere in our own department—might affect the amount available for additional writing instruction.

WPAs working in this type of context must come to expect that they might not have as much control over a budget as they might have elsewhere. In our context, the writing program coordinator must communicate often with the department chair about program needs and allow the chair ample time to plan for how she or he might cover a writing program cost (which might come at the expense of other needs in the department). Also, WPAs in such contexts are wise to establish connections outside of the department that might be a source of funding. At a STEM school, for instance, there are opportunities to collaborate with colleagues across campus on proposals to agencies such as the National Science Foundation or the Department of Education, which helps with expenses considerably.

OPERATIONS

The writing program is staffed by eleven faculty members, most of whom teach additional classes for the CLASS Department, including courses in literature, philosophy, communication, and technical communication. Instructors who are permanent non-tenure-track faculty, tenured faculty, tenure-track faculty, and adjunct faculty teach the (roughly) twenty-two sections of writing classes (ENGL 111, 112, and 341) in the fall and spring terms. Occasionally a faculty member teaches English 189, the one-hour one-credit studio class that focuses on grammar and basic skills.

All administrative jobs tied to the coordinator role are seen as service to the department and are evaluated as such, yet the WPC has histori-cally received no course release for the coordinator position and has no dedicated staff to aid in completing tasks associated with the position. Typically, the WPC role is filled by a tenure-line faculty member. Maggie is the first non-tenure-track faculty member to serve in this role. Since she teaches a 4–4 load, she was the first coordinator to receive a release for the WPC position. Each WPC is allowed to construct her or his own agenda and priorities, though the position consists of several regular duties. Each coordinator must collect syllabi from writing faculty at the beginning of the semester, field questions from students about place-ment and transfer credits in collaboration with the CLASS Department chair, plan regular meetings of all program faculty (at least twice a semester), and create end-of-semester assessment forms in collaboration with the department chair and representatives from Academic Affairs to maintain course articulation standards for transferability across state institutions. The coordinator is the "face" of the writing program, and students with questions or concerns about individual instructors, assign-ments, grades, or policies seek out the coordinator to receive answers to their questions.

After an agreement was made between the department chairperson and the WPC in 2009, undergraduate writing program student workers were hired, two per semester, to work roughly ten hours per week each. Writing program faculty nominated students who had excelled in writing program classes, and the students were hired by the consensus of faculty. Eligibility for work-study employment was an additional consideration. The purpose of these student workers was to assist all writing faculty with tasks associated with teaching and to help the coordinator with any work with which an undergraduate student might be able to assist. Since the reconfiguration and relaunching of the writing center in 2010, depart-ment funds previously used exclusively for these student workers were also needed for funding writing center tutors. After a particularly busy fall 2011 semester in the writing center, Steve and the department chair had the numbers to approach the vice president of Academic Affairs and request more money for student workers, a request that was whole-heartedly approved. As a result, the CLASS Department has at least a little more money to staff both the needs of the writing center and of the writing program. In some cases, many writing program student workers double as writing center tutors.

Even with this increase to the department's student worker budget, staffing the writing center has taken a bit of creativity. Steve has received funding from both the PPOHA and the SES grants, often in exchange for allowing his tutors to help with other initiatives on campus, such as the Student Research Symposium or general tutoring hours in the dormitories. Since the PPOHA grant with which Steve has worked closed in September 2014, he has received a commitment from the Center for Graduate Studies to continue supporting graduate tutors in the writing center by attaching this service to a minority scholarship program. (For more on this graduate tutoring program—known at NMT as the STEM communication fellows program—see Simpson, Clemens, Killingsworth, and Ford 2015).

ASSESSMENT

In New Mexico, state-funded colleges and universities are strongly encouraged—if not required—to align to a set of state-wide standards to encourage articulation of general education courses across state institutions. Currently, our writing program assessment is folded into our general assessment procedures for all courses offered in our department. Our three-course writing sequence (ENGL 111, ENGL 112, ENGL 341) falls under Area 1 (Communication) of these New Mexico state standards. Our program assessments seek to determine the effectiveness of these courses against six student learning outcomes identified by the state (in consultation with writing specialists throughout New Mexico):

1. Analyzing and evaluating oral and written communication in terms of situation, audience, purpose, aesthetics, and adverse points of view

2. Expressing a primary purpose in a compelling statement and ordering supporting points logically and convincingly

3. Using effective rhetorical strategies to persuade, inform, and engage

4. Employing writing and/or speaking processes such as planning, collaborating, organizing, composing, revising, and editing to create presentations using correct diction, syntax, grammar, and mechanics

5. Integrating research correctly and ethically from credible sources to support the primary purpose of communication

6. Engaging in reasoned civil discourse while recognizing the distinctions among opinions, facts, and inferences

At the end of each semester, program faculty rate each student's performance on each of these measures. Each faculty member uses a 1-to-3-point rubric (1 = inadequate; 3 = adequate) to measure students' final writing project in each on the six learning outcomes. For ENGL 111, instructors assess a final essay. In ENGL 112, instructors assess the final ten-page research paper. In ENGL 341, instructors assess the fifteen-page technical report. While each instructor writes his or her own material for each of these assignments, all instructors must ensure that their assignment meets common requirements for all courses under a designated number (e.g., ENGL 112 final essays for all course sections must include a certain number of pages, a thesis-driven argument, and a certain number of scholarly sources). After assessing students' final projects on the 1-to-3 scale, instructors submit their tallies (anonymously) to our department's assessment coordinator, who tallies the assessments for the entire department and submits the aggregate data to the school administration.

Granted, this process is not flawless, and program faculty share concerns that the current assessment procedure relies heavily on instructors' self-assessment and reflects outcomes developed outside our program. Nonetheless, we find some solace in the fact that the state standards—while problematic in many ways—are not bad outcomes to pursue in a process-based writing course, and the assessment reports do give our department an overall sense of trends in student performance from year to year. We have as a department discussed alternate assessments that we would like to conduct, all of which need to be weighed against the amount of time and energy such additional procedures would place on faculty who are already extremely overwhelmed with course loads.

MARKETING/PR

Our writing program is improving its marketing and PR strategies. Historically, the "promotion" of the writing program's offerings has been implicit, in that all students enrolled at NMT must take the three-course sequence to fulfill their general degree requirements. As more students on campus have expressed interest in taking courses in our technical communication program as electives, and as we have developed new programs such as graduate communication courses and our new graduate certificate in scientific and professional communication, we have had to broaden our publicity efforts. We have promoted these classes via email distribution of information and flyers to faculty and advisors throughout the STEM departments. Social media, such as the TC and CLASS Facebook pages, help promote the program and its offerings. Also, the Graduate Student Association has promoted these classes. Students in the technical editing course give presentations to various classes on campus and raise awareness for the writing program and the technical communication program. At a small campus such as NMT, however, the best form of advertisement is word-of-mouth and one-on-one discussions with faculty, advisors, and students in other departments. In the early stages of the revamped writing center, Steve would generally make regular announcements at faculty senate meetings or visit main department offices with his graduate tutors to discuss departmental needs. He also set up an informational booth in the student union and had writing tutors talk one-on-one with students during lunchtime about the writing center services.

Also important to our marketing efforts has been involvement with campus initiatives and community events. Though not directly related to the writing program, the work our department has done in support of the university's Department of Education grants has helped raise the writing program's institutional profile. The graduate communication efforts—the graduate-level communication in the sciences courses, the thesis and dissertation boot camp, and the graduate writing center hours—have helped create more of a discussion around writing on campus. Writing program instructors periodically attend courses outside of CLASS, when invited by a faculty member, to address specific writing scenarios; non-CLASS faculty have also asked writing program instructors to lead workshops for students in their majors. Steve, for example, led a report-writing workshop for an upper-level Earth sciences course and worked with the course TAs on responding to student writing and articulating course expectations. Maggie also teaches a community education yoga class on campus, a venue that has led to interesting dialogues about the writing program with many campus-wide faculty members. The writing center has also partnered with the community literacy center to provide ESL instruction for community members and students and has partnered with the local farmer's market on numerous events for NMT students, such as the annual green chile roast. These examples demonstrate the creativity that those associated with our writing program must utilize to inform others on our campus of the importance of the writing program and the importance of on-campus and community visibility.

TECHNOLOGY

Our program has a website designed by Julianne in 2010. The website could use renovation and hiring a student worker, likely a technical communication major, to take on this project as a program goal. The website lists our classes, each class's outcomes, the requirements for moving from one class in the sequence to the next, and provides answers to students' (and parents') frequently asked questions. Our writing program does not have its own Facebook presence, though information related to the program is shared on the CLASS Department's Facebook page. The CLASS Department also maintains two computer labs that can be used both by writing program faculty and writing center staff. The larger computer lab is equipped with all-in-one touchscreen computers, a Smart Sympodium, and distance education technology that can be used to record student presentations or to host live videoconference sessions. We also have a web and video design lab equipped with brand-new iMacs, Adobe Creative Suite, and Final Cut Pro video-editing software, the last of which was used by technical communication students to create a video advertisement for the school's tutoring center and the writing center.

ROLE OF RESEARCH

A primary focus of internal programmatic research has been the need for better developmental English courses. We have a three-credit developmental writing course in the catalog (ENGL 103), though it is not formally part of the writing program required sequence and has received inconsistent support from both administration and the department. In its current form, English 103 is not credit-bearing and can be perceived as an obstacle to progress. With statewide changes in scholarships, students, advisors, and administrators have voiced concerns about courses that do not contribute to students' direct advancement toward graduation. Thus some advisors have discouraged students from enrolling in ENGL 103, since it is not a "required" course and seems to some advisors to just take up space in a student's schedule. (For this reason, we have not offered this course for a while). Yet, our data concerning this optional-but-encouraged course show that many students with low ACT scores did score a passing grade (72.5%, or a C, and above; courses in the writing sequence require a C to pass) in English 111 without taking ENGL 103 first. The data sample was small and the data results did not factor in the amount of time and effort that writing program faculty spend outside the classroom helping students or the time the students spent in the writing center. Thus, while some evidence suggested students could advance with a passing grade of a C or higher without a three-credit remedial course, many faculty both inside and outside the CLASS Department feel some entry-level work is still needed. To address some of these concerns about English 103, a one-hour English 189 studio course was developed and piloted in spring 2013 and has been offered as an add-on to ENGL 111 in the fall semesters ever since. Enrollment is voluntary and the one-hour course will count as an elective toward degree requirements. The writing program has communicated with the advisors of the twenty-seven entering students who have scores below the admission standard, but at the time of this writing, this course still suffers from under enrollment.

Aside from the current institutional research and ongoing conversations about developmental and ESL writing-course needs, faculty members in our program have historically conducted research on our program as well as on individual courses within the writing sequence and have presented their findings at national conferences and in published articles. Such research has been of value to the individual faculty members, for reasons of promotion and tenure, but there has not been significant departmental or institution attention paid to research on the program, in that internal consumption of this research at the administrative level has not occurred, and thus programmatic changes and budget adjustments have not been made as a result of research findings.

Some specific research highlights of our faculty include studies that have indicated points of contact between NMT's writing program and WAC pedagogies and between the writing program and NMT's TC program. Julianne's presentations at the 2012 Council of Writing Program Administrators (CWPA) annual meeting investigated the ways in which attention to southwestern American writing can enhance students' sense of placement within their community and region and thereby foster the application of experiential knowledge to their writing coursework. Her presentation at the 2008 International WAC conference discussed methods of enhancing modes of cross-disciplinary skill transfer in first-year writing classrooms at NMT, a subject of unique importance at an institution such as NMT where STEM faculty members regularly indicate their desire for first-year writing instructors to design courses to suit the needs of specific disciplinary standards. Steve has published on the graduate-level writing initiatives in journals such as *WPA: Writing Program Administration* and *Praxis: A Writing Center Journal*. He also discussed his experiences negotiating ESL writing support for Chinese students in NMT's 2 + 2 program at an invited pre-conference institute at the 2015

CWPA conference in Boise, Idaho. Further, Steve and Elisabeth Kramer-Simpson, the technical communication program director, have started work on research related to a proposal-writing service learning project that has so far brought in $12,000 for a rural homeless shelter in Socorro, New Mexico. They presented their initial findings at the 2015 Conference on College Composition and Communication in Tampa, Florida.

PEDAGOGICAL AND/OR ADMINISTRATIVE HIGHLIGHTS

While many from humanities backgrounds might feel initially over-whelmed by NMT's dominant STEM culture, the science and technology emphasis actually offers new WPAs and writing faculty numerous opportunities for innovation. Recent first-year and at-risk student retention efforts on our campus have put many students in cutting-edge research projects during their first year, and many faculty in our writing program have taken the opportunity to become involved. The LLC program (run by a former writing center graduate tutor) has students working on everything from designing apps for Samsung Galaxy phones, to collecting and analyzing radio telescope data, to designing robots that can disarm explosives. Many of these LLCs are linked to ENGL 111 or ENGL 112 courses. One writing program instructor, who specializes in environmental literature and policy, worked with a LLC group collecting lichen samples from areas of New Mexico ravaged by forest fires.

In addition to reading and analyzing secondary materials on environmental issues, students in this class worked on reports conveying their primary research and prepared research posters that they delivered at the school's annual Student Research Symposium. Julianne participated in a LLC concerning "engineering disasters" and had students read both technical and popular accounts of engineering failures—such as the Challenger disaster—and then complete writing assignments that satisfied commonly held ENGL 111 requirements, such as that students develop skills in summarizing, identifying arguments, and locating supporting research in the documents they read and via their own database searching. Maggie has also lead the way in the department in embracing NMT's STEM culture and working ethical and philosophical issues related to science and technology into her writing classes.

PRIMARY DOCUMENT (at writingprogramarchitecture.com)

One document that has been most important to our program is a memo that was written to the vice president of Academic Affairs in spring semester 2012. In it, we requested more money for writing tutors in the writing center. This request was made in writing and in person and was granted with very little opposition, which enabled our departmental to fund student workers to serve both the writing program and the writing center. Historically, our department's student workers were employed to support writing faculty specifically; eventually, these student workers became the trained tutors in the writing center. Because of the success of the writing center and its significant growth, as detailed in this memo, we needed to secure additional resources to employ more tutors and to ensure that these tutors were trained, that the center was staffed adequately at peak hours, and that certain tutors were trained specifically for graduate students and L2 learners. This memo succeeded in securing that funding.

WPAS' VOICES

Our experiences with writing program administration should highlight several critical points for new WPAs or for graduate students who have not yet entered the job market.

First, none of the authors of this profile had any idea as graduate students that we would eventually assume the type of administrative duties that we have. Both Julianne and Steve, in fact, were asked to take on numerous administrative duties very early in their careers, which not only required them to learn the logistics of program administration very quickly but also to take positions of authority over faculty—part-time and full-time—who had been at NMT for a very long time. Many current graduate students might have received advice when applying for jobs to avoid entry-level positions with administrative duties. While this advice is sound, it can still be very difficult to predict the type of administrative duties one might be asked to assume as a composition professional. (We are very often expected to be jacks-of-all-trades!) And indeed, the realities of the highly competitive job market often require faculty fresh out of graduate school to take on many responsibilities beyond those of teaching and research.

With this reality in mind, we strongly encourage graduate students to seek out small opportunities to learn the logistics of program administration. Certainly, one should take a course on program administration if offered by your program, though one might also consider assisting a WPA on placement-oriented tasks or talking to a writing center administrator about her or his budget, among other things. These bits of real-world experience can be valuable. We also agree with Micciche (2002) and Strickland (2011) that rhetoric and composition graduate programs should provide more explicit training in writing program administration.

Second, we would like to emphasize again the importance of visibility at a small campus. New WPAs, or junior faculty who foresee themselves assuming administrative duties early in their careers, should look for opportunities to step outside their department bubbles and network with faculty and colleagues from other departments or campus offices (even in a yoga class). Such networks can yield critical allies or cross-campus partnerships that can benefit your program in countless ways.

Third, and most important, we would encourage graduate students to see writing program work as a tremendous opportunity for professional (and personal) growth and, in many cases, a concrete opportunity to expand one's research agenda. The role of the WPC is a challenging one at a small STEM institution such as ours, but it is a rewarding and dynamic role as well. We hope new PhDs who are looking to teach writing and perhaps serve as administrators of writing programs will consider institutions such as ours that might not initially seem like the perfect fit for someone from a humanities background. While one experiences a little initial culture shock, one soon finds that writing program work at a STEM school offers bright and energetic new faculty members incredibly rich opportunities for innovation, growth, and cross-disciplinary collaboration.

Note

1. Out of 300–400 entering freshmen, approximately 25 percent place into ENGL 112 based on SAT/ACT scores, and 15 percent place into 112 based on their AP scores. Naturally, placing out of ENGL 111 does not necessarily mean a student is an advanced writer.

References

Micciche, Laura M. 2002. "More Than a Feeling: Disappointment and WPA Work." *College English* 64 (4): 432–458. http://dx.doi.org/10.2307/3250746.

New Mexico School of Mines Course Catalog. 1908–1909 (n.d.). "New Mexico Tech, Socorro, NM." *Skeen Library Archives.* Accessed 1 January 2016.

Nye, Emily F. 1998. "The New Mexico Tech Writing Center: The First Year." *Writing Lab Newsletter* 22 (5): 1–3, 10.

Simpson, Steve. 2012. "The Problem of Graduate-Level Writing Support: Building a Cross-Campus Graduate Writing Initiative." *WPA. Writing Program Administration* 36 (1): 95–118.

Simpson, Steve, Rebecca Clemens, Drea Rae Killingsworth, and Julie Dyke Ford. 2015. "Creating a Culture of Communication: A Graduate-Level STEM Communication Fellows Program at a Science and Engineering University." *Across the Disciplines* 12(3).

Strickland, Donna. 2011. *The Managerial Unconscious in the History of Composition Studies.* Carbondale: Southern Illinois University Press.

30

POMONA COLLEGE WAC-BASED FIRST-YEAR WRITING SEMINAR AND WRITING CENTER

Dara Regaignon

Institution type: private liberal arts college
Location: Claremont, California
Enrollment: 1,500
Year program was founded: First-Year Writing Seminar (FYWS), 1986; Writing Center, 2005
WPA reports to: Dean/Vice President for Academic Affairs
Program funded by: Academic Affairs
Description of students: Pomona's student body is exclusively undergraduate. One of the wealthiest schools in the country (as measured by endowment dollars-per-student), Pomona has used its wealth to help defray the cost of attending; it has need-blind admissions and a strong financial aid program that offers students grants rather than loans.

PROGRAM SNAPSHOT

The writing program at Pomona consists of the interdisciplinary writing-intensive, first-year seminar program (FYWS), which is the first-year writing requirement, and the peer tutoring Writing Center. This is a WAC-based approach to writing program design and first-year writing instruction.

WPA'S PROFILE

I became a WPA both accidentally and by choice; there's no other way to characterize it. The accidental portion was probably crucial in giving me experiences that prepared me for the moments when I could choose WPA work, and in retrospect I think that it revealed to me that I had interests in that direction—and that those interests weren't simply about taking on leadership positions when they were offered. Initially, I was offered the

DOI: 10.7330/9781607326274.c030

position as assistant director of University Writing while a graduate student in the English Department at Brandeis University where I focused on nineteenth-century British literature and culture. This was a mentoring position, designed for an advanced graduate student. I took it not because I had a strong interest in WPA work or even composition as a field but because I cared a lot about teaching undergraduates and because I was honored to be offered a leadership role. (I also needed the money.) That said, I had been inspired by a composition pedagogy seminar taught by John Brereton in my first year in graduate school, and I already had a strong sense of the intellectual and scholarly nature of writing studies.

My identity, however, remained that of a Victorianist. That changed when, a couple of years after completing my PhD, I became one of the first set of postdoctoral lecturers hired by Kerry Walk for the Princeton Writing Program (PWP). Postdoctoral lecturers from all different fields represent the core of the PWP faculty, supplemented by graduate students, tenure-track faculty, and administrators. The program offers theme-based writing seminars that focus on academic writing. Although Kerry brought curriculum and pedagogy from Harvard's Expository Writing Program, those first years of PWP were a moment of tremendously exciting growth and learning for all of us. I switched fields from Victorian studies to writing studies, although I still work on Victorian texts part of the time. After three years as a lecturer, I applied for and became an assistant director there, with responsibilities both with the PWP faculty and Writing Center tutors. The following year, I applied for writing program faculty and leadership positions all over the country, and was hired as Pomona College's first-ever director of College Writing.

Decades ago, this path from a PhD in literary studies to WPA was a common one. As writing studies has grown as a field and developed more doctoral programs, this has shifted. My approach to teaching writing and to writing program administration are shaped by my early training and ongoing work as a historically-minded literary critic. Even more, however, my experience in the WAC-based approach to teaching writing represented by PWP has given me an orientation outward from the first-year course toward the rest of the institution and the subsequent years of undergraduate education. That orientation has been crucial to developing and fostering an explicit, college-wide culture of writing at Pomona.

PROGRAM CONCEPTION

The Writing Program at Pomona College has two key parts: the WAC-based first-year writing seminars (FYWS), required of all entering first-year students in their first semester and taught by a rotating group of tenure-track faculty from across the college; and a peer-tutoring Writing Center. I started the Writing Center and reinvigorated the FYWS program (which had been founded in 1986), when I arrived in 2005.

Part of my mandate was to launch a writing center, but the budget allocated was inadequate. I therefore wrote to a dozen writing center directors at peer institutions: how many hours are you open per week? How many peer tutors do you employ? What do you pay them? And so on. They were incredibly helpful. (Now, with the National Census of Writing, this will be easier to do without making direct appeals.) I used those data to make the successful case to the dean of the college that the Writing Center needed a larger budget. Our initial staff was twelve peer tutors who worked a total of thirty hours per week. To hire tutors, I wrote to both my colleagues in the English Department and to the previous year's FYWS faculty, asking for nominations of likely students. I developed flyers and had the newly hired Writing Center tutors to visit each of the sections of the FYWS in the first two weeks of classes. First-year students were the focus of our outreach for the first few years.

For the FYWS program, there was already a strong architecture in place. That program came into being in 1986, after a faculty com-mittee—having educated itself about writing instruction and WAC—became convinced that writing instruction at a liberal arts college should not be the province of a single department but the faculty as a whole. Sections are capped at fifteen; all departments contribute faculty, according to their size. Each section has its own topic designed by the professor but shares some common goals and workload standards. Every spring, the faculty who will teach the FYWS the following fall meet for two-and-a-half days of discussion of "curriculum and pedagogy" for the program. Until 2004, the program was coordinated by a tenured faculty member on a rotating basis.

Until 2004, entering students took a writing placement exam; those who failed were placed into a special composition course called "Elements of Composition" that was taught by adjuncts. In 2003, the Teaching and Learning Committee reviewed first-year writing instruction and made two significant recommendations: (1) abolish the placement exam and the associated basic writing course; and (2) create a director of College Writing position with the charge to emphasize writing instruc-tion in the FYWS and to build a WAC writing center that would serve the entire community. That was the position I was hired into.

My primary moves in the first year were (as I saw it) to bring the program into more direct conversation with the field. There were two program documents, for example, that focused on writing but seemed ignorant of the WPA Outcomes Statement for First-Year Composition. Working with a group of faculty who taught regularly in the FYWS, I revised our outcomes statement for student writing and our course evaluation forms. My other focus was on faculty development, creating a conversation about writing and writing instruction that hinged on the faculty development workshop every May and that offered a vocabulary for teaching writing that was in conversation with the field, but that was also fluid and flexible enough for these faculty to adopt and adapt it for themselves, both in their FYWS courses and (ideally) in their departmental courses.

Some of the initial challenges had to do with navigating the politics of age and experience; I was five years out of my PhD, leading a program staffed by faculty from across the college, some of whom were brand new to the institution and some of whom had been teaching there since well before I had attended college myself. I had to find ways to honor their extensive pedagogical experience, knowledge, and pride while also encouraging them to try new ways of teaching writing. In my first two years, I was told on more than one occasion by various senior colleagues that I "didn't really understand the place of the program at Pomona." There were times when I went to allies (in my department or in the Dean's Office) to ask how to navigate those strange emails and conversations; there were other moments when I learned to temporize, smile, and bide my time. Change is a process, and a slow one.

POPULATION SERVED

The FYWS program and the Writing Center at Pomona serve all the students who attend the college. The FYWS is required of all entering first-year students in their first semester. Through the Writing Center and our Writing Fellows program, we serve students from the other Claremont Colleges (Scripps, Pitzer, Harvey Mudd, and Claremont McKenna) when they are enrolled in Pomona classes. We also serve all faculty at Pomona College as a pedagogical resource. The primary vector for faculty development is the FYWS; as they cycle through the program they benefit from writing faculty development that they carry back with them to their departments. In addition, I consult with individual faculty and with departments on teaching with writing and writing enhanced curricular ideas. This reinforces the WAC-based approach to teaching writing that we take, since we hope to influence how writing is taught (and how major subjects are taught with writing) in every department and program.

FUNDING

There are several sources for our annual budget of roughly $90,000 (not including staff salaries). Much of it comes from the college's core operating budget; roughly $65,000 comes from a variety of endowed funds dedicated to either writing instruction or undergraduate teaching that the college has allocated to us. Most of these funds were alumni gifts to the English Department that, through the generosity of the college and that department, were reallocated. That budget covers operating costs, including events and so on; tutor wages; faculty stipends for attending the FYWS workshop; and some limited funds for course development or field trips for the FYWS. It does also include money to send the Writing Center tutors to the Southern California International Writing Centers Association (SoCal IWCA) peer tutoring conference every year and, alternate years, to the IWCA and National Conference on Peer Tutoring in Writing (NCPTW) conference.

OPERATIONS

As WPA, I teach two courses a year (that is 50% of the standard teaching load at Pomona). In the fall, my course alternates between a section of the FYWS and the writing pedagogy course required of all new peer tutors. In the spring semester, I teach a course for the English Department because that is my departmental home. In addition, I oversee and provide pedagogical and curricular leadership for the FYWS program, oversee the Writing Center, and work with faculty and departments across the college on writing in the disciplines. This last category is the most amorphous: there is no writing requirement beyond the first year, and while there is a strong culture of teaching writing in the disciplines, it is diffused and difficult to identify key delivery moments or sites. My position is a hybrid faculty-staff position: I am appointed in an administrative position as director of College Writing (staff) that carries coterminous faculty status (initially as assistant professor of English, now associate). I cannot be tenured, but I do have multi-year contracts and considerable security.

The same is true for the assistant director of College Writing (the Writing Center director position). This is also a coterminous position; Pam Bromley, the current assistant director, is an assistant professor of politics and international relations. She teaches a 1–1 load; the fall course alternates FYWS and peer-tutoring course with me and the spring course is a course in the Politics Department explicitly thematizing writing or writing studies methodologies.

Roughly thirty faculty teach in the FYWS program each year; they are full-time, tenure-track faculty from across the college and drawing from all ranks. In 2013, we had sixteen departments represented. From 2009 to 2013, we had at least one faculty member from each department at the college teach an FYWS.

The peer tutor staff is now at thirty. These are all undergraduates, sophomores through seniors, and represent the full range of majors. Four of them serve in leadership roles within the Writing Center (typically, all are seniors). We try to hire students in the spring of their first year to start the following fall, although we typically hire a couple of sophomores every year as well (who start their junior year). Most of the tutors work for the Writing Center their remaining time at Pomona, apart from a semester studying abroad, and most spend at least one semester working as a writing fellow (attached to a course). Students are invited to apply after being nominated by a faculty member; it is considered on honor and a desirable job on campus. There are three head writing fellows, each responsible for directly mentoring a group of (about three to four) new writing fellows and for supervising the tutoring work of an additional six to seven experienced writing fellows. In addition, each head fellow has a specific area of focus:

- *Training:* Working with the assistant director and small groups of writing fellows to plan and implement tutor development workshops)
- *Outreach:* Working both to build a sense of community among the staff and to coordinate supplement writing-related events and workshops for Pomona students)
- *Scheduling:* Working with the assistant director and administrative assistant to coordinate the Writing Center schedule and pair writing fellows with students who need regular bi-weekly appointments

In addition, there is a fourth leadership position of science writing coordinator. This student works with the faculty teaching the introductory biology sequence (Genetics, Cell Biology, and Ecology) to train the student mentors in writing pedagogy to support the extended science-writing assignments included in those courses.

We also have a part-time administrative assistant who supports the Writing Program as well as the Teaching and Learning Committee. We have roughly twenty hours per week of that position's time.

The collaborative efforts of the director, assistant director, administrative assistant, head writing fellows, and the faculty committee (particularly the assigned associate dean of the college) are all essential to maintaining the running of the program. That said, there are clear domains of influence and authority. The Dean's Office and associate dean are primarily responsible for faculty recruitment to teach the FYWS; the assistant director is primarily responsible for recruitment, hiring, and training of peer tutors. The director is primarily responsible for designing and delivering faculty development. The administrative assistant is primarily responsible for taking care of the Writing Center space. The core leadership team—director, assistant director, and administrative assistant—meet every other week throughout the semester. The faculty committee meets at roughly the same intervals (and includes both the associate dean and the director). The assistant director works closely with the peer tutor leadership team, meeting formally every other week.

ASSESSMENT

The culture of faculty autonomy at Pomona, combined with the fact that the FYWS program does not have a uniform faculty from year to year, have made assessment of that program a challenge. The primary ongoing approach to assessment is narrative. Every fall, I ask that the faculty teaching in the FYWS program write a brief (paragraph-long) narrative reflection on their students' progress as writers over the course of the semester. I collect and synthesize these, identifying trends across seminars. Those trends lead to shifts in the emphasis of the faculty development workshop the following May. Recent areas of focus have included: the ways in which students stage and enter scholarly conversations (a particular area of source-use); students' skills as peer reviewers; and the related issue of students' ability to assess their own works-in-progress. Typically, faculty are pleased with the progress students make as critical thinkers and also with the ways in which students move away from formulaic writing over the course of the semester.

In 2011, as part of a self-study, I undertook an assessment of student research papers in order to better understand how students were grappling with that sort of large, complex assignment. We also surveyed then sophomores and seniors about their FYWS experiences. In 2012, we launched a longitudinal study of student writing in which we are following seventeen members of the class of 2016. For this study, we have collected (or will collect) papers across their careers at Pomona: the first and last or longest paper from their FYWS; a paper of their choosing from their sophomore year in fall; and a paper from their major (excluding a senior thesis) from their senior year in fall. In addition, we are surveying this group annually in the spring semester, to learn more about their experiences and growth as writers. In examining the papers, we are using rubrics adapted from national studies: Andrea

A. Lunsford and Karen J. Lunsford's "'Mistakes Are a Fact of Life': A National Comparative Study" (Lunsford and Lunsford 2008) and the Citation Project (Moore Howard and Jamieson 2015). The error study findings are thus far encouraging: students make errors less frequently than the national average, and their error rates go down over the course of their first three semesters at Pomona. This confirms our expectations and hopes. The citation study is more concerning, and indicates that we have considerable work to do in helping students learn better habits and practices of source-use. This has become a sustained focus in faculty development, particularly around assignment design.

Writing Center assessment happens through two metrics: the exit survey described in Pam's articles; and annual reflections that the Writing Center tutors write, evaluating and reflecting on their own experience. The results of these lead to new emphasis in tutor development workshops.

MARKETING/PR

First-year students are required to take the FYWS in their first semester. Faculty are recruited to teach in the FYWS program by the Dean's Office by emails they send to the faculty listserv, by the efforts of the faculty Committee on Writing and Critical Inquiry (which oversees the FYWS), and by word of mouth. It is a small community, so everyone knows about it. In addition, there is the expectation that all departments will contribute faculty to the program regularly; the Dean's Office oversees a target formula whereby departments with eight-plus full-time equivalents (FTEs) are expected to contribute two courses to the program per year, departments with four to eight FTEs contribute one course per year, and departments with four or fewer FTEs contribute one course alternate years. Individual faculty are encouraged to teach in the program early in their time at Pomona—in part to benefit from the faculty development program.

We advertise the Writing Fellows (course-attached peer tutoring) program to faculty with emails to the faculty listserv and, some years, by offering brief workshops for faculty considering the possibility. In the fall semester, we provide a writing fellow for every section of the FYWS whose professor is interested. We talk about this with the individual faculty and work with both faculty and students to make appropriate matches. For the spring semester, we advertise the possibility of working with writing fellows to the faculty as a whole. We usually have more interest than we can support.

The Writing Center advertises its services to students much more extensively. Peer tutors visit all sections of the FYWS in the first two weeks of the fall semester to educate students about the Writing Center and to pass out basic half-sheet flyers with information about how we work with students and the URL for our online scheduling system. One of the head writing fellows is in charge of further outreach. The approach varies year to year, but typically includes offering and advertising workshops in the residence halls; advertising with leaflets or table tents in the dining halls; planning and advertising special events; and advertising on social media.

TECHNOLOGY

We have a website, but the main ways we use technology are: a locally-designed online writing center scheduler that allows us to track appointments, file reports, and the like; and a password-protected course management site of teaching resources for the FYWS program. At this time, there is no college-wide sense that technology is a central part of the mission of the FYWS. "Writing" at Pomona—in FYWS and beyond—is primarily focused on the traditional academic essay in the various forms it takes in different disciplines. While there is increasing interest on modes of oral presentation and the forms and presentation technologies that go along with speaking assignments, that is at this time an informal emphasis.

ROLE OF RESEARCH

I can't imagine undertaking leadership of a program without also undertaking research about it. To a certain extent, that comes from my original training as a historically-minded literary studies scholar: I always want to know the history of a program, and I believe that such histories leave traces that influence current practice in ways that are both fascinating and important. I also always want generalizations to be grounded in data, so I want to know what is actually happening for students or faculty in my program, and I also want to know what other similar programs look like. Finally, I think that intelligent program design requires gazing outward as well as inward, a balance that I think enacts the double perspective of research—learning the conversation(s) in the field and then contributing to them. That said, I think that program design, implementation, and assessment all require thoughtful, research-based work that is not necessarily publishable. And I think that the timing and rhythm of program research (how many semesters to study a curricular or pedagogical innovation before claiming its success, for example) should not be determined by tenure or other publication timetables but by the needs of the research and the program themselves.

When we piloted the Writing Fellows program at Pomona, Pam and I conducted a quasi-experimental study and published the results in *WAC Journal* (Regaignon and Bromley 2011). In addition, I have published a short piece describing a pedagogical strategy I developed in FYWS: "Traction: Transferring Analysis across the Curriculum" (Regaignon 2009). With collaborators at Kansas State University and the University of Denver, Pam has published about student experiences in the Writing Center (Bromley, Northway, and Schonberg 2013) and about mixed methods research in writing center studies (Bromley, Northway, and Schonberg 2010). She has also published a study of active learning strategies in her FYWS (Bromley 2013) Although it is a more oblique connection, I would also say that my coauthored book with Jill Gladstein, *Writing Program Administration at Small Liberal Arts Colleges* (Gladstein and Regaginon 2012)—an empirical study of the writing programs at one hundred private small liberal arts colleges—and our current research project, the WPA Census, both emerge from my work as Pomona College's WPA.

Pam and I have worked together to cultivate a culture of research among the Writing Center tutors, as well. This starts with the pedagogy course, which culminates in a writing studies research project. (Students can elect the half-credit version of the course if they have significant scheduling conflicts; in those cases, many elect to do a follow-up half-credit independent study so that they can undertake the research project.) These projects result in follow-up research with some regularity. In addition, Pam takes a group of tutors to the Southern California International Writing Centers Association peer tutoring conference every year and has taken current and recently-graduated tutors to the IWCA/NCPTW regularly.

PEDAGOGICAL AND/OR ADMINISTRATIVE HIGHLIGHTS

FYWS as an approach has come under fire recently, particularly as a contrast to the Writing-About-Writing approach to first-year writing instruction (see Adler-Kassner 2012; Wardle 2009; Friedman 2013). But it's also a valuable approach at certain types of institutions, and—as Jill Gladstein and I found in our research for *Writing Program Administration at Small Liberal Arts Colleges*—small liberal arts colleges are one of them.

At Pomona, faculty in all fields take undergraduate teaching seriously, and every department requires students to write in major courses at some point. (Usually, at several points.) This means that writing and writing instruction saturate students' educations here. The FYWS program sets that stage at the very outset of students' career; in addition, it provides a central and powerful vector through which writing faculty development—rooted in the knowledge and research of the field, and in many of its threshold concepts—are disseminated throughout the college.

PRIMARY DOCUMENT (at writingprogramarchitecture.com)

"Writing and ID1" serves as a programmatic statement of the writing goals for Pomona College's first-year writing seminar program, called "ID1" on campus after its registration code. The document itself was developed collaboratively over the course of roughly five years, from 2001 to 2006. Multiple groups of faculty from across the college were involved. Since it was finalized in 2006, it has served as part of the central nervous system of writing at Pomona, helping not only faculty who teach first-year writing seminars but also tutors in the Writing Center communicate in similar terms about writing as process as well as product.

WPA'S VOICE

A WPA is positioned both at the center and on the edge of a program. The job, as I've come to understand it, involves both positioning yourself at the center of things—demonstrating good pedagogies, overseeing the various pieces of the program to make sure that they remain coordinated—and at the edge, translating the field and your program to the institution as a whole. Depending on the size of the institution and the nature of the particular program, and depending on the particular day, which way you need to look more will vary. I'm increasingly convinced that the greatest challenge of many WPA positions is translating what we understand in the specialized language of the field into language that is both intelligible and compelling to smart people who work in very different fields—and therefore have very different ways of understanding the world.

In that sense, you have to listen all the time. I don't mean that you shouldn't also speak (indeed, speaking calmly, responsively, and nondefensively is another essential WPA skill), but I do mean that you need to understand your audience(s) if you're going to achieve your purposes or understand your program. Every program has a history in an institution that has a history. You need to learn those in order to understand what constraints and affordances you operate under. What's the institution's historical mission? How does that mission (and the related institutional values) shape current practices and structures? How does your program fit into those, and how can you take advantage of them to make things happen? Listen, and listen genuinely. It is easy to interpret people's motivations in ways that serve our own egos; if you want to help change happen, you have to be genuine (and hence generous) in your desire to learn and understand. Be open.

And, finally, be patient. Change rarely happens overnight and when it does it may not be the kind of change that lasts. There may be some things that have to happen quickly, but try to always cultivate the long view. You need to see the whole ecosystem in order to understand the possibilities and impossibilities for your particular piece. I don't know that coursework can help with this, although I do think studying the histories and practices of writing programs (and writing program administration as a field) is essential. But I also think that the ways of paying attention I've sketched out in the previous two paragraphs are things that one can practice everywhere and all the time. I do think that seeking out smaller leadership opportunities of all kinds is essential, and learning about as many different kinds of programs is, too. There's no one right kind of program, and you never know what kind of program you might be asked to lead. You want to see the possibilities and promise clearly, even if it's very different from what you might have designed yourself with a blank page in front of you.

References

Adler-Kassner, Linda. 2012. "The Companies We Keep *or* The Companies We Would Like to Try to Keep: Strategies and Tactics in Challenging Times." *WPA: Writing Program Administration* 36 (1): 119–140.

Bromley, Pam. 2013. "Active Learning Strategies for Diverse Learning Styles: Simulations Are Only One Method." *PS: Political Science & Politics* 46 (4): 818–822. http://dx.doi.org/10.1017/S1049096513001145.

Bromley, Pam, Kara Northway, and Eliana Schonberg. 2010. "Bridging the Qualitative/Quantitative Divide in Research and Practice." *Praxis: A Writing Center Journal* 8 (1).

Bromley, Pam, Kara Northway, and Eliana Schonberg. 2013. "How Important is the Local, Really?: Cross-Institutional Quantitative Assessment of Typical Writing Center Exit Surveys." *Writing Center Journal* 33 (1): 13–37.

Friedman, Sandie. 2013. "This Way for Vampires: Teaching First-Year Composition in 'Challenging Times.'." *Currents in Teaching and Learning* 6 (1): 77–84.

Gladstein, Jill M., and Dara Rossman Regaignon. 2012. *Writing Program Administration at Small Liberal Arts Colleges.* Anderson, SC: Parlor Press.

Lunsford, Andrea A., and Karen J. Lunsford. 2008. "'Mistakes Are a Fact of Life': A National Comparative Study." *College Composition and Communication* 59 (4): 781–806.

Moore Howard, Rebecca, and Sandra Jamieson. 2015. "What Is the Citation Project?" The Citation Project. Accessed December 20, 2015. citationproject.net.

Regaignon, Dara Rossman. 2009. "Traction: Transferring Analysis across the Curriculum." *Pedagogy* 9 (1): 121–133. http://dx.doi.org/10.1215/15314200-2008 -020.

Regaignon, Dara Rossman, and Pamela Bromley. 2011. "What Difference Do Writing Fellow Programs Make?" *WAC Journal* 22:41–63.

Wardle, Elizabeth. 2009. "'Mutt Genres' and the Goal of FYC: Can We Help Students Write the Genres of the University?" *College Composition and Communication* 60 (4): 765–789.

ABOUT THE AUTHORS

Bryna Siegel Finer is an associate professor, director of Liberal Studies English, and the founding director of the Writing Across the Curriculum program at Indiana University of Pennsylvania, where she has also coordinated the first-year writing placement program. She teaches primarily basic writing, first-year writing, and researched writing. Her scholarship has been published in *Rhetoric Review*, the *Journal of Teaching Writing*, *Teaching English in the Two-Year College*, and *Praxis*, among others. With Jamie White-Farnham and Cathryn Molloy, she is currently preparing an edited collection on the rhetorics of women's health activism.

Jamie White-Farnham is an associate professor and writing coordinator in the Writing Program at the University of Wisconsin–Superior. She teaches first-year writing, business and professional writing, and courses in the major and minor. Her research is split between feminist rhetorical studies and the scholarship of teaching and learning with a focus on writing program administration. Her work has been published in *Community Literacy Journal*, *College English*, *Rhetoric Review*, and *Peitho*.

* * *

Susan Naomi Bernstein serves as Stretch Writing Program coordinator at Arizona State University–Tempe. In that capacity, she taught Stretch at an American Indian community in Central Arizona and participates in an ongoing Stretch Writing Redesign project in collaboration with Stretch Writing faculty at ASU–Downtown and ASU–Tempe. In 2014–15, this project won a CCCC Research Initiative grant. Susan's most recently published articles include: "Occupy Basic Writing" in Welch and Scott's edited collection *Composition in the Age of Austerity* (2016), and "Dr. King Did Not Negotiate" in *Community College Moment* (2015). Her book is *Teaching Developmental Writing* 4e (Bedford/St. Martin's 2013).

Remica L. Bingham-Risher is the director of Writing and Faculty Development and the QEP director at Old Dominion University (ODU). Currently, she works with faculty to improve student learning through writing by means of faculty workshops as well as oversees the implementation of various Action Projects supported by internal grants that help improve departmental disciplinary writing. In addition, she is an accomplished writer and teaches in the MFA program at ODU. Her first book, *Conversion* (Lotus Press, 2006), won the Naomi Long Madgett Poetry Award and her second book, *What We Ask of Flesh*, was published by Etruscan Press in 2013.

At the time of writing, **Brent Chappelow** was a graduate teaching associate and doctoral candidate in the writing, rhetorics, and literacies program in the Department of English at Arizona State University. He has since completed his doctoral degree, and he now works as a lecturer in the University of Southern California Writing Program. His primary area of research is classical Greek rhetorical theory and concepts of visuality and audience.

Malkiel Choseed is a professor of English and the Writing Program coordinator at Onondaga Community College in Syracuse, New York, where he has worked since 2005. His current research interests center on developmental education in its various forms and assessment of programmatic learning outcomes as a path toward professional and program development. He is a recipient of the SUNY Chancellor's Award for Scholarship and Creative Activities.

At the time of writing, **ANGELA CLARK-OATES** was the course manager for the Arizona State University Writers' Studio. She is now assistant professor of English at California State University, Sacramento, where she teaches undergraduate and graduate courses focused on research methods, composition pedagogy, and teaching writing in high schools. Her research is focused on high school-to-college transition, writing program administration, composition pedagogy and theory, and theories of literacy and teacher identity. She has published on a variety of topics including writing assessment, multimodal composition, and faculty writing groups.

PATRICK CLAUSS is the director of first-year writing and rhetoric at the University of Notre Dame. He studies the relationships among argumentation theory, rhetoric, and composition pedagogy. He is the author of *iclaim: visualizing argument*, and he teaches multimedia writing and rhetoric, public speaking and debate, and a graduate practicum on the teaching of writing. He has recently worked with the College Board, serving as a consultant regarding AP examinations and high school and college curricula. In the spring of 2014, he was named a recipient of the Rev. Edmund P. Joyce, C.S.C. Award for Excellence in Undergraduate Teaching.

EMILY W. COSGROVE is the director of the Center for Writing and Writing Instruction and the Title III-A Project, as well as an English instructor, at Wallace Community College in Dothan and Eufaula, Alabama. Prior to this position, she served as program assistant to the Miller Writing Center at Auburn University, where she completed her PhD. In addition to writing-center-related research, her conference presentation records on administrative structures and sustainable organizational change at IWCA, NCPTW, SWCA, and the Conference on Higher Education Pedagogy, among others, reflect her passion for creating sustainable higher education initiatives that assist and empower students.

THOMAS DEANS is the director of the University Writing Center and a professor of English at the University of Connecticut. He is the author of *Writing Partnerships: Service-Learning in Composition* and series co-editor for the *Oxford Brief Guides to Writing in the Disciplines*.

At the time of writing, **BRIDGET DRAXLER** was an assistant professor of English at Monmouth College. As director of Communication across the Curriculum, Bridget provided faculty support across disciplines, with a focus on innovative strategies in interdisciplinary writing and speaking, and special emphasis on collaborative practice and technology. She also directed the Monmouth College writing center, whose twenty peer tutors serve writers across campus while gaining personal and professional development opportunities. Bridget is currently the Writing and Speaking Specialist at St. Olaf College. Trained in eighteenth-century British literature, her current teaching and research focus on the digital humanities, public scholarship, and the scholarship of teaching and learning.

LEIGH ANN DUNNING is the director of the Writing Center and the assistant director of the Writing Program at Stetson University. At the time of writing this chapter, Leigh Ann served as assistant director of the Writing Center at Indiana University of Pennsylvania, where she is currently a PhD candidate in the Composition & TESOL program.

GREG A. GIBERSON is an associate professor in the Department of Writing and Rhetoric at Oakland University (OU) in Rochester, Michigan. He is co-editor of the collections *What We Are Becoming: Developments in Undergraduate Writing Majors; Writing Majors: Eighteen Program Profiles;* and *The Knowledge Economy Academic and the Commodification of Higher Education*. His work has appeared in *Composition Forum, Pedagogy, TETYC*, as well as other journals and collections. He teaches various courses in OU's first-year writing program and undergraduate writing major.

MAGGIE GRIFFIN TAYLOR's dissertation explored the philosophy of science and medicine. Maggie directs the New Mexico Tech (NMT) Writing Program. She also teaches for three programs at NMT: Writing, Philosophy, and Technical Communication. She was named the 2010/11 Tech Goddess and is the 2011 recipient of NMT's Distinguished Teaching Award.

PAULA HARRINGTON, PhD, is the director of the Farnham Writers' Center at Colby College, where she is also an assistant professor of writing. She directs a peer tutoring staff of some forty-five writing assistants, who work with students across disciplines. At Colby, she introduced a Writing Fellows program, which embeds writing assistants in courses across the curriculum, and she also teaches multilingual students. Previously, Paula taught composition and literature at Marymount College of Fordham University and the University of California, Davis. She was a Fulbright Scholar in Paris for her research into French and American stereotypes in the work of Mark Twain and has a book, *Mark Twain and France*, forthcoming from the University of Missouri Press.

SANDRA JAMIESON (sandrajamieson.net) is the director of Writing across the Curriculum at Drew University. She teaches writing and writing studies courses including media studies, writing center theory, travel writing, social media writing, authorship, and narrative. Her publications include a coauthored book, *The Bedford Guide to Writing in the Disciplines;* three co-edited collections, *Coming of Age: The Advanced Writing Curriculum* (Heinemann-Boynton/Cook), *Information Literacy: Research and Collaboration across Disciplines* (UP of Colorado); *Points of Departure: Rethinking RAD Methods for the Study of Student Writing* (Utah State UP), and articles on the vertical writing curriculum, the writing studies major, information literacy, plagiarism, WAC, and textbooks.

MARSHALL KITCHENS, an associate professor in the Department of Writing and Rhetoric at Oakland University, teaches creative nonfiction, digital media studies, and first-year composition. He received his PhD in rhetoric and composition from Wayne State University, where he was co-director of computers and composition, and served as the inaugural department chair for Writing and Rhetoric at Oakland University from 2008 to 2014. He is also the director of the Meadow Brook Writing Project.

MICHAEL KNIEVEL teaches undergraduate and graduate courses in composition and technical and professional communication in the Department of English at the University of Wyoming (UW). He currently coordinates UW's professional writing minor. His research focuses on professional writing programs and on the rhetoric of police use-of-force policy.

In 2011, **AMY LANNIN** became the director of the Campus Writing Program (CWP) at the University of Missouri (MU). Lannin is an assistant professor of English education in the College of Education and also directs the Missouri Writing Project. Directing the CWP is a year-round position, which includes research and some teaching. Her research interests include the impact of professional development on teacher practice and student achievement, program assessment, and WAC. Before coming to MU, she taught middle and secondary English language arts. She completed her PhD at the University of Missouri.

CHRISTOPHER LECLUYSE began his writing center career in 1999 while completing his PhD in English at the University of Texas at Austin. Since 2006 he has directed the writing center at Westminster College in Salt Lake City, where he is also an associate professor of English. He served as president of the Rocky Mountain Writing Centers Association and co-chaired the 2015 National Conference on Peer Tutoring in Writing. He continues to draw on his background as a medievalist by relating medieval literacy, ancient rhetoric, and religion to composition and writing center pedagogy and by singing early music.

At the time of writing, **SARAH LIGGETT** was the Donald & Norma Nash McClure alumni professor in the Department of English at Louisiana State University (LSU) where she was director of First-Year Writing, director of the Writing Center, and director of LSU's Communication across the Curriculum program during her thirty-two-year career there. With Betty Pytlik, she co-edited *Preparing College Teachers of Writing: Histories, Theories, Programs, Practices.* Her recent articles have appeared in the *Writing Center Journal* and *Across the Disciplines.* She served on the 2015 Task Force that wrote the "CCCC Statement on Preparing Teachers of College Writing." Now a professor emerita, she continues to advocate for quality writing instruction.

DEBORAH MARROTT is a professor and chair of the Department of Literacies and Composition at Utah Valley University. Her scholarship focuses on educational linguistic anthropology, social justice in education, and pre-core writing pedagogy. Her work appears in *Living, Learning, and Composing in College Cultures: An English 0890 Reader for Utah Valley University.* She is currently authoring an article for *The Journal of Basic Writing* entitled, "(More) Public Conversations about Writing and Literacy: Renewing the Call for More Student-Present Research in Basic Writing" and a book-length biography of Ellis Reynolds Shipp, pioneer doctor and polygamist.

MARK MCBETH, associate professor, teaches courses in composition and rhetoric, creative nonfiction, and queer theory at John Jay College of Criminal Justice and the English PhD program of the Graduate Center, CUNY. During the past two decades, he has coordinated the composition program at City College of New York as well as directed its writing center; at John Jay he has acted as deputy chair of Writing Programs, coordinated the WAC program, chaired multiple assessment teams, and initiated a variety of college-wide literacy programs; he currently acts as the deputy executive of the Office of Placement in the CUNY Graduate Center English PhD program. His book *Teacher Training at Cambridge: The Initiatives of Oscar Browning and Elizabeth Hughes* (coauthored with Pam Hirsch) explores the history of education in nineteenth-century England.; his work has also appeared in various journals and book collections.

TIM MCCORMACK, assistant professor, has directed the first-year writing program at John Jay College of Criminal Justice, CUNY, for six years. In his career, McCormack has worked extensively at all levels of writing program administration, including in high school-to-college bridge programs, writing centers, first-year writing, WAC programs and graduate-level writing programs. He has written about writing program administration for the *WPA: Writing Program Adminstration* and *Composition Forum.* McCormack is currently at work on an ethnographic study of first-year writing courses at the City College of New York and Bronx Community College, titled *The Dividing Line.* This research chronicles the impact of high stakes placement testing on student learning outcomes and retention rates in senior and community college writing programs.

JOHN MCCORMICK teaches developmental and first-year writing at the University of Wisconsin–Superior. He received his MA in creative writing—Poetry from Miami University. His research interests include developmental writing, rhetoric, blending genres, and writing about writing.

HEATHER MCGREW has been teaching writing in the Midwest for sixteen years, most recently at the University of Wisconsin–Superior. She holds a BA in professional writing from Bethel University (St. Paul, Minnesota) and an MA in writing with an emphasis in creative nonfiction from Illinois State University. In addition to specializing in teaching developmental writing, she also teaches argument, research writing, and business writing.

HEATHER MCKAY has been a teacher of English as a second/foreign language for more than thirty-five years teaching and training teachers in the United States and overseas. She taught ESL at St. Louis Community College for twenty years and also served as the ESL coordinator on the Meramec Campus. She holds an MA in applied linguistics and an EdD in T.E.F.L. She has also coauthored a number of books for ESL/EFL teachers, including *Teaching Adult Second Language Learners* published by Cambridge University Press.

HEIDI A. MCKEE is the Roger and Joyce L. Howe professor of written communication and the director of the Howe Writing Initiative in the Farmer School of Business at Miami University. She is an associate professor of English and from 2011 to 2014, she served as the founding director of Miami's professional writing major. She has coauthored and co-edited a number of books, including: *Digital Writing Research: Technologies, Methodologies, and Ethical Issues* (winner of the Computers and Composition Distinguished Book Award); *The Ethics of Internet Research: A Rhetorical, Case-Based Process* (2009); *Technological Ecologies and Sustainability* (2009); and *Digital Writing Assessment and Evaluation* (2013).

JULIANNE NEWMARK, assistant director of Core Writing at the University of New Mexico, was at the time of writing an associate professor of English at New Mexico Tech. She specializes in two areas: technical communication and American literary studies. As a technical communication scholar, she has published in *IEEE Transactions on Professional Communication, Kairos, Technical Communication* and *The Journal of Technical Writing and Communication*. In literary studies, she has published the book *The Pluralist Imagination from East to West in American Literature* (University of Nebraska Press, 2015) as well as many journal articles and book chapters. She is the founding and current editor of *Xchanges*, an undergraduate and graduate-student ejournal that publishes traditional and multimodal texts in writing studies fields.

LORI OSTERGAARD is an associate professor and chair of the Department of Writing and Rhetoric at Oakland University in Rochester, Michigan. She is a former member of the CCCC Executive Committee and served on the committee charged with revising the CCCC Statement on Preparing Teachers of College Writing. Her co-edited collections include *Transforming English Studies: New Voices in an Emerging Genre, Writing Majors: Eighteen Program Profiles;* and *In the Archives of Composition: Writing and Rhetoric in High Schools and Normal Schools.* Her work has also appeared in *Rhetoric Review, Composition Studies, Composition Forum, Studies in the Humanities,* and *Peitho.*

At the time of writing, **JOANNAH PORTMAN-DALEY** was the digital pedagogy specialist for the Department of Writing and Rhetoric at the University of Rhode Island (URI). She has since assumed the role of assistant director of Online Education in the Office for the Advancement of Teaching and Learning at URI where she oversees online pedagogy, curriculum design, and course approvals. She continues to teach in the Writing and Rhetoric Department.

JACQUELINE PRESTON is an assistant professor for the Department of Literacies and Composition at Utah Valley University. Her scholarship and research focus on new materialist rhetorics, post-pedagogy, and first-year composition, project-based/multi-genre and multimodal approaches to teaching writing. Her work has appeared in *Community Literacy Journal* and *College Composition and Communication.* She is a contributor to the forthcoming *Class in the Composition Classroom: Pedagogy and the Working Class.* Most recently, with Joshua C. Hilst, she has coauthored *The Write Project: A Concise Rhetoric for the Writing Classroom.*

JAMES P. PURDY is an associate professor of English and the director of the University Writing Center at Duquesne, where he won the 2016 McAnulty College and Graduate School of Liberal Arts Faculty Excellence in Teaching Award. He has published in *CCC, Pedagogy,* and *Profession,* among other journals and collections. He has edited two award-winning volumes with Randall McClure, *The Next Digital Scholar* and *The New Digital Scholar,* and has two more forthcoming. With coauthor Joyce R. Walker, he won the 2011 Ellen

Nold Award for the Best Article in Computers and Composition Studies and the 2008 *Kairos* Best Webtext Award.

BEN RAFOTH teaches at Indiana University of Pennsylvania, where he is a distinguished university professor and the director of the Kathleen Jones White Writing Center. He is the author of *Multilingual Writers in the Writing Center* and editor of *A Tutor's Guide: Helping Writers One to One*. He also published, with Shanti Bruce, *Tutoring Second Language Writers* and *ESL Writers: A Guide for Writing Center Tutors*. He served as an executive officer of the International Writing Centers Association and is a recipient of the Ron Maxwell Award from the National Conference on Peer Tutoring in Writing.

From 2005 to 2015, **DARA REGAIGNON** was the director of College Writing at Pomona College. She is now the director of the Expository Writing Program at New York University. She is the author with Jill M. Gladstein of the first national empirical study of writing programs at small liberal arts colleges, *Writing Program Administration at Small Liberal Arts Colleges* (2012), and is currently working on a book-length study of the rhetorical cultivation of material anxiety in Victorian Britain. Her articles have appeared in *College English*, *Pedagogy*, *WAC Journal*, and *WPA: Writing Program Administration*, among others.

While preparing this chapter, **NEDRA REYNOLDS** was the chair for the Department of Writing and Rhetoric at URI (2011–2015), where she also served as program director/ WPA (2002–2008). She teaches undergraduate courses in argument, rhetorical theory, and science writing and advises fifty-plus undergraduate majors; she is also currently directing three doctoral dissertations.

SHIRLEY K. ROSE is a professor of English and director of ASU Writing Programs. She regularly teaches graduate courses in writing program administration and archival research methods. Her publications include three collections on writing program administration research and theory, co-edited with Irwin Weiser, and numerous articles and chapters on writing teacher preparation and issues in the professionalization of graduate students in rhetoric and composition. She is director of the WPA Consultant-Evaluator Service.

BONNIE SELTING became a coordinator in the University of Missouri's (MU) Campus Writing Program (CWP) in 2007. Previously, she was one of five faculty at the University of Central Arkansas (UCA) to design and develop a free-standing, independent writing program. This department served writing students across the campus, allowing constant opportunities to see the importance of WAC theories and pedagogies. Selting holds bachelor's and master's degrees from the University of Colorado, and a PhD from Purdue University in English. At MU, she works closely with faculty from all disciplines by facilitating seminars, workshops, and retreats.

STACEY SHERIFF is the director of the Writing Program at Colby College in Waterville, Maine. She was the college's first WPA. Stacey is also assistant professor of Writing and teaches first-year writing and rhetoric courses. Previously, she taught technical writing, rhetoric and new media, and composition at Bridgewater State University. Her research interests include histories of rhetoric, rhetoric and social justice, and multilingual writing. She has published in *Rhetorica*, *Rhetoric Society Quarterly*, *Technical Communication Quarterly*, and *The Internationalization of US Writing Programs* (Rose and Weiser, 2016). Stacey is also the primary investigator for a multi-year grant, from the Davis Educational Foundation, to support multilingual writing pedagogy and a Writing-Enriched Curriculum initiative.

STEVE SIMPSON, associate professor of communication, came to New Mexico Tech to direct the writing center and develop graduate writing support through a Department of Education grant. He is now chair of the Communication, Liberal Arts, and Social Sciences (CLASS) Department. His book *Supporting Graduate Student Writers: Research, Curriculum,* *and Program Design* was published through the University of Michigan Press in 2016 (co-edited with Nigel A. Caplan, Michelle Cox, and Talinn Phillips). He has also published in *WPA: Writing Program Administration, RTE: Research in the Teaching of English,* and *ATD: Across the Disciplines.*

PATRICIA SULLIVAN teaches methodology, media, and theory in technical communication and also teaches rhetorical history at Purdue University where she is a professor of English. She also directs the graduate program in rhetoric and composition at Purdue and has published recently on research methods, mentoring, history, and usability.

KATHLEEN TONRY is an associate professor of English at the University of Connecticut and associate director of the University Writing Center. She is the author of *Agency and Intention in English Print, 1476–1526.*

At the time of writing, **SANFORD TWEEDIE** served as the chair of the Department of Writing Arts at Rowan University. At publication, he is the dean of Rowan's College of Communication and Creative Arts. Tweedie has also taught at the University of Erfurt in Germany while on a Fulbright and has received Rowan's Lindback Distinguished Teaching Award. He is the author of *In the Shadows of a Fallen Wall* from University of Nebraska Press. His writing has also appeared in *College Composition and Communication, English Journal, Liberal Education,* and *Writing on the Edge,* among others.

MEG VAN BAALEN-WOOD has taught professional/technical writing and communication at the University of Wyoming (UW) since fall 2002 and served as the first coordinator of UW's professional writing minor. In fall 2014, Meg moved into a faculty development position in UW's Ellbogen Center for Teaching and Learning. She continues to teach regularly in the professional writing minor.

SHEVAUN E. WATSON served as the director of the University Writing Program, known as the Blugold Seminar in Critical Reading and Writing, at UW–Eau Claire for six years. Currently, she is associate professor of English and director of composition at UW–Milwaukee. Shevaun's research and teaching spans writing program administration, information literacy, and historical and cultural rhetorics. She is writing a composition textbook focused on teaching research, as well as coauthoring a book on Southern tourism, public memory, and race in America.

CHRISTY I. WENGER is an assistant professor of rhetoric and composition and English at Shepherd University in Shepherdstown, West Virginia, where she serves as the director of writing and rhetoric. She is the author of *Yoga Minds, Writing Bodies: Contemplative Writing Pedagogy,* and her articles appear in *English Teaching: Practice and Critique, JAEPL,* and *WPA: Writing Program Administration.* She has also published several chapters in collections such as *Rethinking Ethos: A Feminist Ecological Approach to Rhetoric.* Christy serves as the treasurer and membership chair for the Assembly of Expanded Perspectives on Teaching and edits the organization's professional blog.

LISA WILKINSON is an associate professor and the ESL coordinator at St. Louis Community College–Meramec. She has a master's in TESOL and a graduate certificate in the teaching of writing. She has worked at St. Louis Community College since 1995. The St. Louis Community College ESL program was recognized by CCCC as a Writing Program of Excellence at the 2011 CCCC conference in St. Louis. Highlights of the program noted in the award included the program's use of literature, popular fiction and non-fiction, our individualized placement system, and our portfolio system for all reading and writing classes.

CANDACE ZEPEDA is the director of the QUEST First-Year Writing Program at Our Lady of the Lake University in the Westside of San Antonio, Texas. Her scholarship continues to center on how Hispanic Serving Institutions are "serving" their students by means of culturally relevant pedagogies, programs, and writing practices.

INDEX